Commercial Real Estate Transactions: A Project and Skills Oriented Approach

DOCUMENT BOOK

Debra Pogrund Stark
Associate Professor of Law
The John Marshall Law School

David L. Cameron
Professor of Law
Willamette University
College of Law

James Geoffrey Durham
Professor of Law
University of Dayton
School of Law

Thomas R. White, 3rd
John C. Stennis Professor of Law
University of Virginia
School of Law

2001

LEXIS Publishing™

LEXIS®-NEXIS® ■ MARTINDALE-HUBBELL®
MATTHEW BENDER® ■ MICHIE™ ■ SHEPARD'S®

ISBN: 0820550337

Editorial Offices
2 Park Avenue, New York, NY 10016-5675 (212) 448-2000
201 Mission St., San Francisco, CA 94105-1831 (415) 908-3200
701 East Water Street, Charlottesville, VA 22902-7587 (804) 972-7600
www.lexis.com

(Pub.3117)

FOX VALLEY AUTO CARE CENTER LIMITED PARTNERSHIP

ACQUISITION OF

PROPERTY IN THE CITY OF AURORA AND DUPAGE COUNTY, ILLINOIS

Buyer/Borrower: Fox Valley Auto Care Center Limited Partnership, an Illinois Limited Partnership

Sellers: Metropolitan Diversified Properties, Inc.
Alan W. Johnson and Barbara L. Johnson

Lender: First Mortgage Bank

Buyer/Borrower's
Representative: Donna Smith, Esq.
Kaplan & Miller
450 Wacker Drive
Chicago, IL 60606

TABLE OF CONTENTS

TITLE, SURVEY, AND RELATED MATTERS

LOAN DOCUMENTS

CONSTRUCTION DOCUMENTS

LEASING DOCUMENTS

AGREEMENT OF LIMITED PARTNERSHIP
OF FOX VALLEY AUTO CARE
CENTER LIMITED PARTNERSHIP,
AN ILLINOIS LIMITED PARTNERSHIP

AGREEMENT OF LIMITED PARTNERSHIP made and entered into as of the 31st day of July 1989, by and among REGENT REAL ESTATE DEVELOPMENT CORP., an Illinois corporation, as General Partner and WALTER SIMMONS, SAMUEL WILKINS and ACROSSTOWN PARTNERS LIMITED PARTNERSHIP as Limited Partners.

ARTICLE I

DEFINITIONS

"Act" means the Revised Uniform Limited Partnership Act of the State of Illinois as in effect from time to time.

"Affiliate" means a person or entity that directly or indirectly controls, is controlled by, or is under common control with the General Partner.

"Agreement" means this Agreement of Limited Partnership amended, modified, restated or supplemented from time to time.

"Capital Contributions" means the aggregate capital contributed to the Partnership by the Partners in connection with their acquisition of Partnership Interests together with all subsequent contributions, if any, by the Partners to the capital of the Partnership.

"Cash Flow" - See Net Cash Receipts.

"Cash Funds from Operations" means gross receipts, Sale Proceeds and other income derived from the development, ownership and operation of the Property (other than funds received as Capital Contributions or the proceeds of any loan or refinancing of the Property).

"Financing Proceeds" means the proceeds to the Partnership resulting from borrowing in connection with placing mortgages, liens or security interests on the Partnership Property (not including any mortgages, liens or security interests to which the Property is subject at the time of its acquisition by the Partnership or becomes subject in connection with such acquisition) less the sum of: (i) any expenses incurred in connection with such financing; (ii) any portion of such proceeds applied by the General Partner toward the payment of any indebtedness being refinanced; and (iii) any portion of such proceeds retained by the Partnership as reserves by decision of the General Partner.

"General Partner" means REGENT REAL ESTATE DEVELOPMENT CORP., an Illinois corporation ("REGENT").

1

"Johnson Parcel" means certain real estate adjacent to the Parcel which the General Partner is purchasing from Barbara L. and Alan W. Johnson.

"Limited Partners" means those individuals and entities who from time to time are admitted to the Partnership as Limited Partners.

"Net Cash Receipts" or "Net Cash Flows" with respect to any period means all Cash Funds from operations in such period, less the sum of the following (to the extent not paid from Capital Contributions or Financing Proceeds; the determination of the General Partner of the source of such payments being conclusive for all purposes): (i) all principal and interest payments on indebtedness of the Partnership and all other sums paid to lenders in such period; (ii) all cash expenditures (including expenditures for capital improvements, real estate taxes and insurance and amounts paid into a reserve account pursuant to the requirements of any lender made in such period incident to the operation of the Partnership business); and (iii) such operating expenses and cash reserves as the General Partner in its discretion deems reasonably necessary for proper operation of the Partnership business.

"Parcel" means that certain real estate which Regent has contracted to purchase from Metropolitan Diversified Properties, Inc. A copy of the purchase contract is attached as Exhibit F.

"Participating Percentage" means the percentage interest of a Partner in the Partnership as set forth in Section 6.1.

"Partners" means the General Partner and all Limited Partners, where no distinction is required by the context.

"Partnership" means the limited partnership hereby formed.

"Partnership Interest" means the interest in the Partnership held by a Partner.

"Property" means the real estate identified by outlining on the site plan attached as Exhibit A, together with all buildings, improvements and fixtures now located or hereafter constructed thereon and accessions thereto, and any other real estate obtained by the Partnership as a result of exchange, trade or sale, including all personal property and fixtures owned by the Partnership for the benefit and use of the Partnership. The Property represents a portion of the Parcel.

"Sale Proceeds" means the proceeds to the Partnership from the sale of any Partnership Property less the sum of the following: (i) brokerage commissions and other expenses incurred by the Partnership in connection with such sale; (ii) any portion of such proceeds applied by the General Partner toward the payment of indebtedness secured by a lien on or relating to the property sold; and (iii) any portion of such proceeds retained by the Partnership as reserves by decision of the General Partner.

ARTICLE II

FORMATION OF LIMITED PARTNERSHIP

The parties hereby form a Limited Partnership under the provisions of the Act. The rights and liabilities of the Partners shall be as provided in the Act except as herein otherwise provided.

ARTICLE III

NAME AND PRINCIPAL PLACE OF BUSINESS

The name of the Partnership shall be Fox Valley Auto Care Center Limited Partnership. The principal place of business of the Partnership shall be the General Partner's office located at 524 W. South Avenue, Chicago, Illinois. The General Partner may from time to time change the principal place of business, and shall notify the Limited Partners in writing within twenty (20) days of the effective date of any such change. The General Partner may in its discretion establish additional places of business of the Partnership.

ARTICLE IV

PURPOSE

The business of the Partnership is to acquire, develop and improve the Property as an auto service retail center, to continue to hold the center, after development, as an investment, to dispose of the center, and to engage in activities reasonably related or incidental thereto. The Parcel comprises both the Property and certain other adjacent real estate, which the Partnership is not acquiring. That balance of the Parcel, together with the Johnson Parcel, are being purchased by the General Partner for its own account; however, concurrently with the acquisition of the Property by the Partnership, the General Partner will sell the balance of the Parcel and the Johnson Parcel to a third party unaffiliated with the General Partner.

ARTICLE V

TERM

The term of the Partnership shall commence on the date hereof and shall terminate on December 31, 2013, unless sooner terminated as hereinafter provided.

ARTICLE VI

PARTNERSHIP CAPITAL; PARTNERS' NAMES, ADDRESSES AND CAPITAL CONTRIBUTIONS; CAPITAL ACCOUNTS

Section 6.1. The interests of the Partners in the Partnership shall be divided into General Partnership Interests and Limited Partnership Interests.

(a)   The General Partner shall have a 60% interest in the Partnership as a General Partner.

(b)   The Limited Partners, in the aggregate, shall have a 40% interest in the Partnership as Limited Partners.

The percentage interest of a Partner in the Partnership is referred to in this Agreement as such Partner's "Participating Percentage". The names, addresses and Participating Percentages of the Partners shall be as set forth in Exhibit B.

Section 6.2.

(a)   As its contribution to the capital of the Partnership, the General Partner shall contribute the sum of $1,000 to the capital of the Partnership.

(b)   The Limited Partners, in the aggregate, shall make the following contributions to the capital of the Partnership upon the formation of the Partnership:

    (i)   The sum of $50,000, which shall constitute working capital for the Partnership; and

    (ii)   Letters of Credit in the amount of $200,000.

(c)   For purposes of this Section 6.2,

    (i)   The term "Letter of Credit" means an irrevocable, unconditional letter of credit in form and substance satisfactory to Lender issued by a bank satisfactory to Lender and having an initial term of not less than one year, with such agreement to renew as Lender may reasonably require;

    (ii)   The term "Lender" means the construction lender for the development of the Property; and

    (iii)   The term "Loan" means the construction loan to be made by Lender to the Partnership.

(d)   At least thirty (30) days prior to the expiration date of a Letter of Credit or renewal thereof, and provided that the Letter of Credit has not been fully drawn against, the Limited Partner who procured such Letter of Credit shall cause such Letter of Credit (or undrawn portion thereof, if the Letter of Credit has been partially drawn against) to be renewed for an additional period of not less than one year or, if earlier, until the date the Loan is due (including any extensions and renewals of the Loan due date). This obligation shall expire upon the earlier to occur of (i) the dissolution of the Partnership and (ii) the repayment in full of the Loan.

(e)   If any Limited Partner ("Defaulting Partner") fails to comply with its capital contribution or Letter of Credit procurement or renewal obligations as set forth in Sections 6.2(b)(i), 6.2(b)(ii) and 6.2(d), the General Partner shall notify the other Limited Partners ("Non-Defaulting Partners"). The Non-Defaulting Partners shall thereupon be obligated, in proportion to their relative Participating Percentages, to provide capital contributions or additional Letters of Credit as the case may be in aggregate amount equal to the amount required to be provided by the Defaulting Partner. A Non-Defaulting Partner who fails to provide such capital contribution or Letter of Credit within fifteen days after receipt of such notice shall himself be treated as a Defaulting Partner and the provisions of this Section 6.2.(e) shall apply to such default.

A Defaulting Partner shall be subject to all of the sanctions and remedies provided in this Agreement and by law in cases of breach and default. The fact that Non-Defaulting Partners may supply capital contributions or Letters of Credit pursuant to this Section 6.2.(e) shall not cure or relieve the Defaulting Partner of the consequences of the Defaulting Partner's Default.

(f)   The Partnership shall return the Letters of Credit to the Limited Partners (or the undrawn portions thereof, if the Letters of Credit have been drawn against) upon repayment of the Loan.

Section 6.3. The General Partner, in addition to owning General Partnership Interests, shall have the right to acquire Limited Partnership Interests and with respect to such Limited Partnership Interests, the General Partner shall have the same rights and obligations and shall be subject to the same limitations as any Limited Partner. The Partnership shall separately account for such Limited Partnership Interests on its books and records for all purposes of this Agreement.

Section 6.4.

(a)   The Partnership shall create and maintain upon its books and records a Capital Account for each Partner. A Partner's Capital Account at any time shall be the sum of the Partner's contribution to the capital of the Partnership set forth in Section 6.2 hereof, subject to Section 6.4(b) hereof, plus all additional contributions by the Partner to the capital of the Partnership, plus all gains and net profits allocated to the Partner pursuant to Article VIII hereof, minus all distributions to the Partner with respect to its Partnership Interest pursuant to Article VII hereof, minus all losses allocated to the Partner pursuant to Article VIII hereof, and with all other adjustments required for the proper maintenance of capital accounts for Federal income tax purposes.

(b)   The Capital Accounts of the Partners shall be credited with the following amounts by virtue of the Capital Contributions described in Section 6.2:

    (i)   The General Partner has expended and will expend its own funds in the acquisition of the Property, the development of plans and programs for its development, the ownership of the Property until its transfer to the Partnership, and the formation of the Partnership. It is anticipated that all or a portion of these expenditures will be repaid to the General Partner out of the proceeds of the Loan. However, if and to the extent that the General Partner is not repaid all such expenditures in full out of the proceeds of the Loan, then the General Partner's Capital Account shall be credited with an amount equal to such unreimbursed expenditures.

    (ii)   At the time a Partner contributes cash to the capital of the Partnership, the Partner's Capital Account shall be credited with the amount of such cash contribution.

    (iii)   If and at the time that the Lender draws against a Partner's Letter of Credit, such Partner's Capital Account shall be credited with an amount equal to the amount so drawn, as though the Partner had made a cash contribution to the capital of the Partnership in amount equal to the amount so drawn.

Section 6.5. The Limited Partnership Interests are non-assessable.

Section 6.6. If a Limited Partner ("Defaulting Partner") shall fail timely to provide a Letter of Credit pursuant to Section 6.2(b), or shall fail timely to renew such Letter of Credit pursuant to Section 6.2(d), then the Partnership and the General Partner shall have the following remedies:

(a)   The General Partner, at its sole option, or its assigns shall have the right to purchase the Defaulting Partner's Partnership Interest or arrange for the sale of the Defaulting Partner's Partnership Interest on the terms and conditions set forth herein;

(b)   The General Partner, at its sole option, or its assigns shall have the right to purchase the Partnership Interest of the Defaulting Partner by (1) paying to the Defaulting Partner an amount equal to (A) the Defaulting Partner's cash contributions to the capital of the Partnership, plus (B) the amount (if any) drawn by the Lender upon the Defaulting Partner's Letter of Credit, minus (C) the aggregate cash distributions, if any, theretofore made to the Defaulting Partner by the Partnership, and (2) delivering to the Partnership a Letter of Credit in the amount which the Defaulting Partner was required to provide;

(c)   The General Partner may (on behalf of the Partnership and/or its assigns) offer the Partnership Interest to any other persons (including Partners other than the Defaulting Partner) at terms no less favorable to the Defaulting Partner than those set forth in Section 6.6(b). Any amounts so paid shall be applied, when (and to the extent) received, in the following order of priority:

(i)   To the expenses of the sale;

(ii)   To pledge with the Lender in lieu of a Letter of Credit, or to pledge with any financial institution in order to secure a Letter of Credit or to pledge for the benefit of a Limited Partner who provides a Letter of Credit pursuant to Section 6.2(e); and

(iii)   Any remainder including any funds released upon termination of a pledge pursuant to Section 6.6.(c)(ii) to the Defaulting Partner; or

(d)   The Partnership may pursue any remedy available to it as a secured party or otherwise under the Illinois Uniform Commercial Code.

Section 6.7. Each Limited Partner hereby pledges its Partnership Interest to the Partnership and grants to the Partnership a security interest in such Limited Partner's Partnership Interest as collateral security for the performance of the obligations of such Limited Partner pursuant to Sections 6.2(b) and (d).

Section 6.8.

(a)   In the event that the General Partner determines that the Partnership requires additional capital, the General Partner may raise such capital by offering additional Partnership Interests. The purchasers of such additional Partnership Interests may be granted such an interest or interests in the Partnership as may be determined by the General Partner. Any reduction in the Partners' Participating Percentages caused by such purchase shall occur pro rata between the General Partner, on the one hand, and the Limited Partners, on the other hand, all in accordance with their respective Participating Percentages, such that the ratio of the Participating Percentage of the General Partner to the Participating Percentage of each Limited Partner prior to the granting of any additional Partnership Interest equals the ratio of the Participating Percentage of the General Partner to the Participating Percentage (determined without regard to any additional Partnership Interest purchased by such Limited Partner) of each such Limited Partner after the granting of such additional Partnership Interest.

(b)   The Limited Partners shall have the first opportunity to purchase any additional Partnership Interests offered pursuant to Section 6.8(a) above. Before such Partnership Interests are sold, the General Partner shall deliver notice to each Limited Partner of its intent to offer such interests, which notice shall describe the terms and conditions of such offering. The Limited Partners shall have a period of thirty (30) days from the mailing of such notice by the General Partner to purchase the additional Partnership Interests on the terms and conditions described in the notice. Such option may be exercised by delivery of all (but not less than all) of the required consideration to the General Partner along with a document indicating the allocation of the additional Partnership Interests among the Limited Partners. The General Partner shall take such action as may be necessary or appropriate to issue the additional Partnership Interests promptly after receipt of such consideration and document from a Limited Partner. If the Limited Partners do not exercise the option provided for in this Section 6.8(b), the General Partner shall obtain the consent of a majority in interest of the Limited Partners as to the identity of the prospective purchaser or purchasers before selling the Partnership Interests.

ARTICLE VII

DISTRIBUTIONS

Section 7.1. Distributions of Financing Proceeds and Sale Proceeds, if any, shall be made in such amounts and at such times as the General Partner may determine.

Such distributions shall be allocated among the Partners in the following manner:

(a)   First, if the Lender has drawn against any Letter of Credit, distributions shall be made to those Partners whose Letters of Credit have been drawn against, in proportion to the amounts drawn against such Partners respectively, until each such Partner shall have received distributions pursuant to this Section 7.1(a) and pursuant to Section 7.2(a) in aggregate amount equal to the amount so drawn.

(b)   Next, if any Partner shall have made contributions to the capital of the Partnership in excess of those provided for in Section 6.2, distributions shall be made to such Partners, in proportion to the amounts so contributed by them, until each such Partner shall have received distributions pursuant to this Section 7.1(b) in aggregate amount equal to the amount so contributed.

(c)   Next, there shall be distributed to the General Partner the amount credited to the General Partner's capital account pursuant to Section 6.4(b)(i), if any, less the aggregate of all amounts theretofore distributed to the General Partner pursuant to this Section 7.1(c) and pursuant to Section 7.2(b).

(d)   Next, there shall be distributed to the Partners the amounts credited to their respective capital accounts pursuant to Sections 6.2(a)(i) and 6.2(b)(i), in proportion to the amounts so contributed by them respectively.

(e)   Any additional distributions shall be allocated among all Partners in proportion to their respective Participating Percentages.

Section 7.2. Distributions of Net Cash Receipts, if any, shall be made in such amounts and at such times as the General Partner may determine.

Such distributions shall be allocated among the Partners in the following manner:

(a)   First, if the Lender has drawn against any Letter of Credit, distributions shall be made to those Partners whose Letters of Credit have been drawn against, in proportion to the amounts drawn against such Partners respectively, until each such Partner shall have received distributions pursuant to Section 7.1(a) and pursuant to this Section 7.2(a) in an aggregate amount equal to the amount so drawn.

(b)   Next, there shall be distributed to the General Partner the amount credited to the General Partner's capital account pursuant to Section 6.4(b)(i), if any, less the aggregate of all amounts theretofore distributed to the General Partner pursuant to Section 7.1(c) and pursuant to this Section 7.2(b).

(c)   Any additional distributions shall be allocated among all Partners in proportion to their respective Participating Percentages.

ARTICLE VIII

ALLOCATION OF PROFITS AND LOSSES

Net profits and losses, credits and other tax items of the Partnership for each fiscal year shall be allocated among the Partners in proportion to their respective Participating Percentages; except that where and to the extent that Section 704(c) or other applicable provisions of the Internal Revenue Code of 1986 as amended may require a different allocation of any one or more items, such item or items shall be allocated in accordance with such requirements of the Internal Revenue Code of 1986 as amended.

ARTICLE IX

BOOKS OF ACCOUNT, RECORDS AND REPORTS

Section 9.1. Proper and complete records and books of account shall be kept by the General Partner at the principal office of the Partnership. Such books and records and all other Partnership documents (such as but not limited to Loan documents and land trust documents) shall be open to the reasonable inspection and examination of the Partners or their duly authorized representatives during reasonable business hours. Such books and records may be kept on the cash or accrual basis as the General Partner may determine. The General Partner shall furnish a list of the names and addresses of all the Partners to any Partner who requests such a list in writing for a legitimate and proper purpose.

The General Partner intends to engage Michael Corbley, CPA, an Affiliate of the General Partner, as the Partnership's accountant. Such accountant shall be paid as a Partnership expense reasonable fees for services rendered. The General Partner may select and change the Partnership's accountants at any time at its discretion.

Section 9.2. No later than ninety (90) days after the end of each Partnership fiscal year the General Partner shall furnish

(a)   A statement prepared by the Partnership's accountants in such form as the General Partner deems proper and as may be required by tax laws, which statement shall contain such information as is reasonably necessary for the preparation of the Limited and General Partners' federal and state income tax returns; and the General Partner will endeavor to provide the Limited Partners with copies of the tax returns proposed to be filed for the Partnership prior to the time that such tax returns are filed;

(b)   A report of the business and operations of the Partnership during the fiscal year, showing the Partnership's revenue and expenses, net profits and losses, Net Cash from operations and distributions made to Partners; and

(c)   Copies of any annual reports and showings required to be delivered to Lender.

Section 9.3. The General Partner shall send each Limited Partner a monthly written report of Partnership operations substantially in the form of Exhibit C.

Section 9.4. The fiscal year of the Partnership shall be the calendar year. The fiscal year may be changed from time to time by the General Partner, but only if such change is permissible under the then-applicable tax laws and regulations.

Section 9.5. The Partners will meet annually, commencing three years after the formation of the Partnership, to discuss the operations of the Property and the potential for sale. The meeting shall be advisory and informational in nature only and in no event shall the Limited Partners have the right or power to direct the General Partner or the Partnership to sell, or not to sell, the Property, such rights and powers being reserved exclusively to the General Partner.

ARTICLE X

POWERS, RIGHTS AND DUTIES OF THE GENERAL PARTNER

Section 10.1. (a) Except as otherwise provided herein, the General Partner shall have exclusive authority to manage the operations and affairs of the Partnership and to make all decisions regarding the business of the Partnership. The General Partner shall have all of the rights, powers and obligations of a General Partner as provided in the Act and as otherwise provided by law, and any action taken by the General Partner shall constitute the act of and serve to bind the Partnership. The exclusive authority of the General Partner shall not be limited to ordinary course of business matters, but shall include all matters relating to or affecting the business, affairs, assets, properties and obligations of the Partnership, including but not limited to the power, on behalf of the Partnership, to borrow or lend money, sell, mortgage, lease or otherwise transfer any interest in the assets of the Partnership, or execute any agreement with

10

respect to such borrowing, lending, or transfer. Persons dealing with the Partnership are entitled to rely conclusively on the power and authority of the General Partner.

(b) The General Partner is hereby granted the right, power and authority to do on behalf of the Partnership all things which, in its judgment, are necessary, proper or desirable to carry out the aforementioned duties and responsibilities, including but not limited to the right, power and authority to incur all reasonable expenditures; employ and dismiss from employment any and all Partnership employees, agents, independent contractors, real estate managers, brokers, attorneys and accountants; delegate the performance of duties and responsibilities to employees or agents subject to the supervision of the General Partner; sell all or any part of the Property; let or lease all or any portion of the Property for any purpose and without limit as to the term thereof, whether or not such term (including renewal terms) shall extend beyond the date of the termination of the Partnership and whether or not the portion so leased is to be occupied by the lessee or in turn subleased in whole or in part to others; create, by grant or otherwise, easements and servitudes, and it is specifically contemplated that the Partnership will grant easements in favor of the owners of that part of the Parcel other than the Property; borrow money and as security therefore mortgage all or any part of the Property; construct, alter, improve, repair, raze, replace or rebuild the Property, obtain replacements of any mortgages related in any way to the Property, and prepay in whole or in part, refinance, recast, modify, consolidate or extend any mortgages affecting the Property; do any and all of the foregoing at such price, rental or amounts, for cash, securities or other property and on such terms as the General Partner deems proper; place record title to the Property in the name of the Partnership or in the name of a trustee or land trust (provided that the Partnership is the beneficiary thereof, subject to the provisions of Section 18.10) for the purpose of mortgage financing or any other convenience or benefit of the Partnership and execute, acknowledge and deliver any and all instruments to effectuate any and all of the foregoing. The General Partner shall also be empowered to admit an assignee of a Limited Partner's interest to be a substituted Limited Partner, pursuant to and subject to the terms of Article XII of this Agreement.

Section 10.2.

(a) The General Partner shall use its best efforts, in good faith, in accordance with reasonable commercial practice and subject to events and agencies beyond the reasonable control of the General Partner,

(i) To cause the Partnership to complete the construction of the planned improvements upon the Property;

(ii) To cause the Partnership to comply with and perform its obligations under the Loan, any other construction loans or agreements and any mortgages upon the Property; and

(iii) To cause the Partnership to comply with all laws, ordinances, regulations and other governmental requirements applicable to the Partnership and the Property.

-11

(b)   If the Partnership requires more funds for the completion of the construction of the Property than are provided for in the Lender's loan commitment together with the capital contributions of the Partners, the General Partner shall use its best efforts to secure additional financing in amounts sufficient to permit completion.

(c)   Upon dissolution of the Partnership, if such dissolution constitutes a breach of this Agreement by the General Partner, the General Partner shall use its best efforts to attempt to secure the return to the Limited Partners of their Letters of Credit to the extent not theretofore drawn upon, such efforts to include offering to the Lender to substitute the General Partner's letter of credit, if and to the extent that the General Partner is able to secure a letter of credit upon normal and commercially reasonable terms and fees.

Section 10.3.   Every Partner shall at all times execute and deliver all documents, instruments and writings and do and perform all such other acts and deeds as may be necessary or appropriate in order to carry out the decisions of the General Partner, unless the decision is not authorized by this Agreement.

Section 10.4.   The General Partner shall devote such time to the Partnership business as it, in its discretion, shall deem to be necessary to manage and supervise the Partnership business in an efficient manner; but nothing in this Agreement shall preclude the employment, at the expense of the Partnership, of any agent or third party (whether or not such agent or third party is affiliated with or in any way related to any Partner) to manage or provide other services in respect of the Property subject to the control of the General Partner.

The General Partner is expressly empowered to engage the General Partner or any Affiliate of the General Partner to provide to the Partnership any or all of the services described in Exhibit D and to cause the Partnership to pay such General Partner or Affiliate reasonable and customary fees for such services.

Section 10.5.   The General Partner and any Affiliates may engage in or possess any interest in other business ventures of any kind, independently or with others, including but not limited to the acquisition, financing, construction, development, ownership, leasing, operation, management, syndication and brokerage of real and personal property, for their own account or for the accounts of others. The fact that any General Partner or Affiliate may encounter and take advantage of opportunities to do any of the foregoing personally or on behalf of others in whom the General Partner or Affiliate may or may not have an interest shall not subject the General Partner or Affiliate to any liability to the Partnership or any of the Partners on account of the lost opportunity. Neither the Partnership nor any Partner shall have any right by virtue of this Agreement or the partnership relationship created hereby in or to such ventures or activities or to the income or profits derived therefrom, and the pursuit of such ventures, even if competitive with the business of the Partnership, shall not be deemed wrongful or improper.

Section 10.6.   The Partnership may borrow funds from any General Partner or Affiliate; provided, however, that the interest rate shall not exceed two percentage points (2%) in excess of the prime rate of the First National Bank of Chicago at the date of the loan or any renewal thereof.

Section 10.7.   No General Partner shall be liable, responsible or accountable in damages or otherwise to the Partnership or to any Limited Partner for any action taken or failure to act on behalf of the Partnership within the scope of the authority conferred on the General Partner by this Agreement or by law unless such action or mission was performed or omitted in bad faith, recklessly, negligently, or in breach of the General Partner's obligations under this Agreement.

Section 10.8.   The Partnership, out of the Partnership's net assets, shall indemnify and hold harmless any person who was or is a General Partner or Affiliate of a General Partner and who was or is a party or is threatened to be made a party to any threatened, pending or completed action, suit or proceeding, whether civil, criminal, administrative or investigative (including any action by or in the right of the Partnership) by reason of any acts, omissions or alleged acts or omissions arising out such person's activities as a General Partner or Affiliate (collectively the "Indemnified Parties"), against any and all liabilities, losses and expenses for which such person has not otherwise been reimbursed (including but not limited to court costs, attorney's fees, judgments, fines and amounts paid in settlement) actually and reasonably incurred by such person in connection with such action, suit or proceeding so long as such person (i) did not act recklessly, in bad faith, or negligently or (ii) with respect to any criminal action or proceeding, had no reasonable cause to believe that the conduct was unlawful. The termination of any action, suit or proceeding by judgment, order, settlement, conviction, or upon a plea of nolo contendere or its equivalent, shall not of itself create a presumption that the person acted fraudulently, recklessly, negligently or in bad faith, or with respect to any criminal action or proceeding, had reasonable cause to believe that the conduct was unlawful.

To the extent that any of the Indemnified Parties has been successful on the merits or otherwise in defense of any action, suit or proceeding referred to in the first subparagraph of this Section 10.8 or in defense of any claim, issue or matter therein, such Indemnified Party shall be indemnified against expenses (including attorney's fees) actually and reasonably incurred in connection therewith.

Any indemnification under the first subparagraph of this Section 10.8 shall be made by the Partnership only as authorized in the specific case upon a determination that indemnification of the Indemnified Party is proper in the circumstances because the applicable standard of conduct set forth in such subparagraph has been met. Such determination shall be made by the written consent or affirmative vote of Limited Partners holding a majority of the then outstanding Participating Percentages held by all Limited Partners; or the party seeking indemnification may submit the matter to any court sitting in Cook County, Illinois for determination of whether the applicable standard of conduct has been met; or the Partnership and the party seeking indemnification may by mutual agreement submit the matter to arbitration.

Section 10.9.   The General Partner may, in its discretion, from time to time, make or revoke the election referred to in Section 754 of the Internal Revenue Code of 1986 as amended

13

or any similar provision enacted in lieu thereof. Each of the Partners will upon request supply the information necessary properly to give effect to such election. The General Partner will endeavor to make such election at the reasonable request of a Limited Partner, provided the Limited Partner agrees to pay the incremental costs of accounting and bookkeeping occasioned by such election.

Section 10.10.   The General Partner will, upon written request by any Limited Partner, endeavor to cooperate with the Limited Partner by assisting in the valuation of Partnership Property and Limited Partnership Interests for estate, inheritance and gift tax purposes and by preparing documents and reports and making adjustments to books required in connection with the death of a Partner or a transfer of a Limited Partnership Interest by the operation of such tax elections as may be in effect from time to time; provided, however, that (a) the Limited Partner requesting such services must pay the General Partner reasonable compensation on an hourly fee basis for rendering such services, together with all out of pocket expenses incurred by the General Partner in performing such services; and (b) the General Partner, prior to performing such services, may require the Limited Partner requesting such services to prepay to the General Partner the estimated fees and expenses for the rendering of such services.

ARTICLE XI

STATUS OF LIMITED PARTNERS

Section 11.1.   The Limited Partners shall not participate in the management or control of the Partnership's business, nor shall they transact any business for the Partnership, nor shall they have the power to act for or bind the Partnership, said powers being vested solely and exclusively in the General Partner.

Section 11.2.   No Limited Partner shall have any personal liability whatever, whether to the Partnership, to any of the Partners, to the creditors of the Partnership or otherwise, for any debt or obligation of the Partnership, other than to make such Partner's contribution to the capital of the Partnership as set forth herein.

Section 11.3.   The death or legal incapacity of a Limited Partners shall not cause a dissolution of the Partnership, but the rights of such Limited Partner to share in the profits and losses of the Partnership, to receive distributions of Partnership funds and to assign a Partnership interest pursuant to Article XII hereof shall, on the happening of such an event, devolve on the Partner's personal representative, or in the event of the death of whose limited partnership interest is held in joint tenancy, shall pass to the surviving joint tenant, subject to the terms and conditions of this Agreement, and the Partnership shall continue as a limited partnership. The estate of the deceased or incapacitated Limited Partner or such surviving joint tenant, as the case may be, shall be liable for all the obligations of the deceased Limited Partner. However, in no event shall such personal representative or surviving joint tenant become a substituted Limited Partner, except with the consent of the General Partner in accordance with Article XII hereof.

Section 11.4.   The Partnership and the General Partner shall indemnify, defend and hold harmless each Limited Partner from and against claims and liabilities asserted against such Limited Partner personally with respect to the Partnership and/or the activities of the Partnership with respect to the Property other than (a) the Limited Partner's obligations to make their agreed capital contributions as set forth herein, (b) any obligation a Limited Partner may have under partnership law to repay to the Partnership any amount distributed by the Partnership to such Limited Partner, and (c) liability of a Limited Partner who is held responsible as though a general partner by reason of participating in the control of the Partnership's business.

ARTICLE XII

TRANSFER OF PARTNERSHIP INTERESTS

Section 12.1.   No Limited Partner (including a substituted Limited Partner), nor any other holder of an interest in the Partnership as a Limited Partner ("Limited Partnership Interest") may sell, assign, transfer, hypothecate or otherwise alienate a Limited Partnership Interest or any interest therein unless all of the following conditions are met:

(a)   The transaction complies or is exempt from the registration requirements of Federal, Illinois and all other applicable securities laws and regulations (and the General Partner shall have the right to require that the Limited Partner or holder supply the Partnership with an opinion letter satisfactory to counsel for the Partnership directed to the Partnership from attorneys licensed to practice law in the State of Illinois or other jurisdiction the laws of which appear to be applicable stating that the transaction complies with or is exempt from the registration requirements of all applicable securities laws and regulations);

(b)   A duly executed and acknowledged counterpart instrument of assignment in form reasonably prescribed by or otherwise satisfactory to the General Partner is filed with the Partnership;

(c)   The terms of the instrument of assignment are not inconsistent with or contrary to the provisions of this Agreement;

(d)   The transferee files with the General Partner a written instrument in form reasonably prescribed by or otherwise satisfactory to the General Partner agreeing to be bound by all of the terms and provisions of this Agreement and all amendments and supplements thereto;

(e)   The Limited Partner or holder pays or causes to be paid to the Partnership in advance a fee not to exceed $500 to defray the Partnership's costs and expenses with respect to the transfer; and

(f)   The General Partner shall have determined that the transfer will not cause a termination of the Partnership for Federal income tax purposes.

Any such assignment shall be effective, and shall be recognized by the General Partner, as of the first day of the calendar month following the month during which all of the foregoing conditions are met, unless the General Partner consents to an earlier effective date.

Section 12.2.

(a)   No assignee of the whole or any part of a Limited Partner's interest shall have the right to become a substituted Limited Partner in place of the assignor unless all of the conditions Section 12.1 have been satisfied and all of the following additional conditions have been satisfied:

    (i)   The duly executed and acknowledged written instrument of assignment filed with the Partnership shall expressly state that it is the assignor's intention that the assignee become a substituted Limited Partner in place of the assignor;

    (ii)   The assignor and assignee shall have executed and acknowledged such other instruments as the General Partner may deem necessary or desirable to effect such admission, including the written acceptance and adoption by the assignee of all of the provisions of this Agreement and the assignee's execution, acknowledgment and delivery to the General Partner of a Power of Attorney in accordance with Article XV hereof; and

    (iii)   The General Partner shall have expressly consented in writing to such substitution, the granting or denial of which consent shall be in the sole and absolute discretion of the General Partner.

Notwithstanding the foregoing, the General Partner agrees that it will consent to a transfer by any of the Limited Partners named on page 1 of this Agreement ("Initial Limited Partner") to such Initial Limited Partner's spouse, parent, adult child, uncle, aunt, adult niece, adult nephew, or a trust the only beneficiaries of which are the Initial Limited Partner and/or such relatives, provided that (A) the Initial Limited Partner shall remain personally liable for the obligation to contribute capital and to provide and renew Letters of Credit described in Section 6.2., and (B) the transferee may not retransfer the Interest without the General Partner's consent, the granting or denial of which shall be in the sole and absolute discretion of the General Partner.

(b)   Any substitution of Limited Partners pursuant to this Section 12.2 shall be effective as of the first day of the month following the month in which all of the conditions herein have been satisfied, unless the General Partner consents to an earlier effective date.

(c)   The General Partner shall not have the right to assign all or any portion of its General Partnership Interest without the consent of all Limited Partners, except that:

(i)   The General Partner may assign all or any part of its General Partnership Interest as collateral security for Partnership loans or other Partnership obligations or otherwise for the benefit of the Partnership; and

(ii)   The General Partner may assign all or any part of its General Partnership Interest to an entity, which is wholly owned by Regent, or the owners of Regent;

in each case without the consent of any Limited Partner.

Section 12.3.   In no event shall any Partnership Interest be assigned to a minor or incompetent.

Section 12.4.   Anything in this Agreement to the contrary notwithstanding, no Limited Partner or other person who has become the holder of a Limited Partnership Interest shall transfer, assign or encumber all or any portion of his or her interest in the Partnership if such transfer, assignment or encumbrance would (in the sole and unreviewable opinion of the General Partner) result in the termination of the Partnership for purposes of the then applicable provisions of the Internal Revenue Code of 1986, as amended, or violate the provisions of the Securities Act of 1933, as amended, the Illinois Securities Act of 1953, as amended, or other applicable securities laws or regulations.

Section 12.5.   Any purported transfer or assignment of an interest in the Partnership made in contravention of the provisions of this Article XII shall be void and of no effect.

Section 12.6.   Any income Limited Partner and any transferee of any Limited Partner shall, as a condition of receiving an interest in the Partnership, agree to be bound by this Partnership Agreement and all Amendments thereto and other documents to the same extent and on the same terms as those who had an interest in the Partnership at the time of the execution of said Partnership Agreement and any Amendments thereto and other documents.

ARTICLE XIII

DISSOLUTION OF THE PARTNERSHIP –
WITHDRAWAL OF GENERAL PARTNER

Section 13.1.   The Partnership shall dissolve immediately on the first to occur of the following dates:

(a)   Ninety (90) days after the date of the bankruptcy, dissolution, removal or withdrawal from the Partnership of the last remaining General Partner, unless prior to the expiration of such ninety day period Limited Partners holding a majority in interest of Participating Percentages held by Limited Partners (if permitted by applicable law) agree to continue the Partnership business and select one or more new General Partners for the Partnership who agree to act as such.

(b)   The date of closing of the sale of all remaining interest in the Property owned by the Partnership and collection of all Sale Proceeds therefrom.

(c)   The date on which occurs the termination of the term of the Partnership pursuant to Article V of this agreement.

The bankruptcy, dissolution, removal or withdrawal of a General Partner shall not dissolve the Partnership if there are one or more remaining General Partners, unless the remaining General Partner or Partners expressly refuse to continue the Partnership business after the occurrence thereof.

Section 13.2.   For purposes of this Agreement, the "bankruptcy" of a General Partner shall be deemed to have occurred upon the happening of any of the following: (a) the filing of an application by such General Partner for, or a consent to, the appointment of a trustee of the General Partner's assets; (b) the filing by such General Partner of a voluntary petition in bankruptcy or the filing of a pleading in any court of record admitting in writing inability to pay debts as they come due; (c) the making by such General Partner of a general assignment for the benefit of creditors; (d) the filing by such General Partner of an answer admitting the material allegations of, or consenting to, or defaulting in answering, a bankruptcy petition filed against the General Partner in any bankruptcy proceeding; or (e) the entry of an order, judgment or decree by any court of competent jurisdiction adjudicating such General Partner a bankrupt or appointing a trustee of the General Partner's assets, and such order, judgment or decree continuing unstayed and in effect for any period of sixty (60) consecutive days.

Section 13.3.   In the event of the bankruptcy, withdrawal, dissolution or removal of a General Partner, such General Partner: (a) shall be and remain liable for all obligations and liabilities incurred as a General Partner during membership herein; and (b) shall be free of any obligation or liability incurred on account of the activities of the Partnership from and after the time of ceasing to be a General Partner of the Partnership.

If such event constitutes a wrongful dissolution of the Partnership, the General Partner shall be and remain liable to the Partnership for damages for such wrongful dissolution as provided by applicable law.

The General Partner agrees to execute such documents as may be necessary or appropriate to evidence its cessation to act as the Partnership's General Partner.

ARTICLE XIV

ADDITIONAL PROVISIONS CONCERNING
DISSOLUTION OF THE PARTNERSHIP

Section 14.1.   In the event of the dissolution of the Partnership for any reason, the General Partner shall commence to wind up the affairs of the Partnership and to liquidate its investments. The holders of Partnership Interests shall continue to share profits and losses

18

during the period of liquidation in the same manner as before the dissolution. The General Partner shall have full right and unlimited discretion to determine the time, manner and terms of any sale or sales of Partnership property pursuant to such liquidation, having due regard to the activity and condition of the relevant market and general financial and economic conditions.

Section 14.2.   Following the payment of, or provision for, all debts and liabilities of the Partnership and all expenses of liquidation, and subject to the right of the General Partner to set up reasonable cash reserves for contingent liabilities, post-liquidation winding up expenses and other proper purposes, the proceeds of the liquidation and any other funds of the Partnership shall be distributed in accordance with Article VII of this Agreement; provided, however, that in the event that the assets of the Partnership shall include any installment obligations, receivables, contingent rights to payment or other uncollected items, the General Partner may in its discretion assign such assets to itself or an Affiliate as trustee of a liquidating trust or other appropriate liquidating entity for the benefit of all Partners.

Section 14.3.   Within a reasonable time following the completion of the liquidation of the Partnership's assets, the General Partner shall supply to each Partner a statement which shall set forth the assets and the liabilities of the Partnership as of the date of complete liquidation and each Partner's pro rata share of distributions (and interest in any liquidating trust which may be established pursuant to Section 14.2) pursuant to Section 14.2.

Section 14.4.   Each Partner or holder of a Limited Partnership Interest shall look solely to the assets of the Partnership for all distributions with respect to the Partnership and such Partner's capital contributions thereto and share of profits or losses thereof and shall have no recourse therefore against any Partner. In no event shall the General Partner be personally liable to the Limited Partners for repayment of Capital Contributions or capital accounts.

No Partner or holder of a Partnership Interest shall have any right to demand or receive property other than cash upon dissolution and termination of the Partnership.

Section 14.5.   Upon the completion of the liquidation of the Partnership and the distribution of all Partnership funds, the Partnership shall terminate and the General Partner shall have the authority to execute and record one or more Certificates of Cancellation of the Partnership as well as any and all other documents required to effectuate the dissolution and termination of the Partnership.

ARTICLE XV

POWER OF ATTORNEY

Section 15.1.   Every Limited Partner, by the execution hereof, irrevocably constitutes and appoints the General Partner, with full power of substitution, as such Limited Partner's true and lawful attorney-in-fact in his, her or its name, place and stead to make, execute, sign, acknowledge, record and file, on behalf of such Limited Partner and on behalf of the Partnership, the following:

(a)   One or more Certificates of Limited Partnership, Certificates of Doing Business Under an Assumed Name, and any other certificates or instruments which may be required to be filed by the Partnership or the Partners under the laws of the State of Illinois or any other jurisdiction whose laws may be applicable;

(b)   One or more Certificates of Cancellation of the Partnership and such other instruments or documents as may be deemed necessary or desirable by the General Partner upon the termination of the Partnership business;

(c)   Any and all amendments of the instruments described in subsections 15.1(a) or 15.1(b) above, provided such amendments are either required by law to be filed or are consistent with this Agreement or have been authorized by the particular Partners;

(d)   With respect to a Defaulting Partner only, Uniform Commercial Code financing statements, continuation statements and similar documents necessary or appropriate to perfect, continue or otherwise evidence the security interests described in Section 6.7; and

(e)   Any and all such other instruments as may be deemed necessary by the General Partner to carry out fully the provisions of this Agreement in accordance with its terms.

Section 15.2.   The foregoing grant of authority:

(a)   Is a Special Power of Attorney coupled with an interest, is irrevocable and shall survive the death or incapacity of the Partner granting the power;

(b)   May be exercised by the General Partner on behalf of each Partner by a facsimile signature or by listing all of the Partners executing any instrument with a single signature as attorney-in-fact for all of them; and

(c)   Shall survive the delivery of an assignment by a Partner of the whole or any portion of the Partner's interest in the Partnership.

ARTICLE XVI

NOTICES

All notices and demands required or permitted under this Agreement shall be in writing and may be sent by certified, registered or first class mail, postage prepaid, or delivered to the Partners at their addresses as shown from time to time (on the records of the Partnership. Any Limited Partner may specify a new address for service of notice by notifying the General Partner in writing of such new address, which change shall become effective upon receipt of such notice by the General Partner. The General Partner may specify a new address for service of notice by notifying all Limited Partners.

ARTICLE XVII

AMENDMENT OF THE AGREEMENT

Section 17.1.   This Agreement may be amended in any respect only upon the written consent or the affirmative vote of all Partners.

Section 17.2.   Amendments to this Agreement may be proposed by the General Partner or by Limited Partners holding in the aggregate Participating Percentages of 25% or more.

Section 17.3.   In the event this Agreement shall be amended pursuant to this Article XVII or the Partnership capital shall change, the General Partner shall cause the Certificate of Limited Partnership to be amended (if required by applicable law) to reflect such change.

ARTICLE XVIII

MISCELLANEOUS

Section 18.1.   The Partners agree that the Property is not and will not be suitable for partition. Accordingly, each of the Partners hereby irrevocably waives any and all rights that such Partner might otherwise have to maintain any action for partition of the Property.

Section 18.2.   This Agreement constitutes the entire agreement among the parties. It supersedes any prior agreement or understanding among them, and it may not be modified or amended in any manner other than as set forth in this Agreement.

Section 18.3.   This Agreement and the rights and duties of the parties hereunder shall be governed by and interpreted in accordance with the laws of the State of Illinois.

Section 18.4.   Except as herein otherwise specifically provided, this Agreement shall be binding upon and inure to the benefit of the parties and their legal representatives, heirs, administrators, executors, successors and assigns.

Section 18.5.   Wherever from the context it appears appropriate, each term stated in either the singular or the plural shall include the singular and the plural, and pronouns stated in either the masculine, the feminine or the-neuter gender shall include the masculine, the feminine and the neuter.

Section 18.6.   Captions contained in this Agreement are inserted only as a matter of convenience and in no way define, limit or extend the scope or intent of this Agreement or any provision hereof.

Section 18.7.   Except with respect to matters as to which the General Partner is granted discretion under this Agreement, the opinion of the accountants retained by the Partnership from time to time shall be final and binding with respect to all computations, determinations or distributions made under Article VII, Article VIII or Article XIV of this Agreement.

Section 18.8.   Except as otherwise specifically provided in this Agreement, or unless specifically agreed to the contrary in writing in an individual case by the parties to the dispute, any dispute or controversy arising under or relating to this Agreement and the partnership relationship hereby formed shall be determined and settled only by court proceedings instituted in a court sitting in Chicago, Illinois which has jurisdiction of the subject matter. Every Partner hereby consents to venue in any court sitting in Chicago, Illinois.

Section 18.9.   If any provision of this Agreement or the application of such provision to any person or circumstance shall be held invalid, the remainder of this Agreement or the application of such provision to persons or circumstances other than those to which it is held invalid shall not be affected thereby and shall continue to be binding and in force.

Section 18.10.   The purchase price to the Partnership for the Property will be an average cost (on a square footage basis) based upon the total purchase price for the Parcel and the Johnson Parcel. The costs and expenses relating to the acquisition and ownership of the Parcel and the Johnson Parcel and improvements (such as road work) which benefit both the Property and the balance of the Parcel and/or the Johnson Parcel will be apportioned between the Partnership, the owner of the balance of the Parcel and the Johnson Parcel on a fair and equitable basis.

Regent and/or the Partnership will be entitled to reimbursement for a portion of certain improvement costs as is set forth in Paragraph 15 of the contract for purchase of the Parcel attached as Exhibit F.

Section 18.11.   The power of direction under the land trust holding title to the Property shall be exercised by the General Partner, upon the signature of David Delaney, or Richard Flamm or John Baxter (and the signature of only one of those three individuals shall be required), or any such other officers or agents as the General Partner may direct from time to time.

Section 18.12.   This Agreement may be executed in several counterparts, each of which shall be deemed an original but all of which shall constitute one and the same instrument. In addition, this Agreement may contain more than one counterpart of the signature page and this Agreement may be executed by the affixing of the signatures of each of the Partners to one of such counterpart signature pages; all of such counterpart signature pages shall be read as though one, and they shall have the same force and effect as though all of the signers had signed a single signature page.

Section 18.13.   For purposes of Internal Revenue Code Section 6231(a)(7), the General Partner shall be the tax matters partner of the Partnership. The General Partner will provide the Limited Partners with copies of communications from and to the Internal Revenue Service in connection with any Partnership tax audits.

ARTICLE XIX

LIMITED PARTNER REPRESENTATIONS AND WARRANTIES

Each Limited Partner by the execution of this Agreement acknowledges and agrees that the Limited Partnership Interests are not and will not be registered under the Securities Act of 1933 as amended and are being offered and sold in reliance upon the exemptions from registration provided in Sections 4(2) or 3(a)(11) of said Act as amended and Rule 147 and Regulation D thereunder for private placements and intrastate offerings, and that the Limited Partnership Interests have not been and will not be registered under the Illinois Securities Act of 1953 as amended, and are being offered and sold in reliance on the exemptions from registration provided in Section 4(G) and other applicable exemptions thereunder. Each Limited Partner makes the following agreements, representations, declarations, acknowledgements and warranties with the intent that the same may be relied upon in determining such person's suitability as a purchaser of Limited Partnership Interests and admission to the Partnership as a Limited Partner:

(a)   Such Limited Partner is acquiring the Limited Partnership Interests solely for his or her own personal account for investment and not for subdivision, fractionalization, resale, retransfer, pledge or distribution; he or she has no contract, undertaking, agreement or arrangement with any person to sell, transfer or pledge to such person or anyone else the Interests, or any part thereof or interest therein; he or she has no present plans or intentions to enter into any such contract, undertaking, agreement or arrangement; he or she has no present plans or intentions to transfer, alienate or dispose of the Interests or any interest therein whether for a valuable consideration or for no consideration; and he or she intends at this time to continue to hold the Interests as an investment for his or her own account for the foreseeable future.

(b)   He or she will not dispose of the Interests or any interest therein unless and until the General Partner shall have consented thereto and shall have determined as is provided in Article XII of this Agreement that the intended disposition is permissible under the Partnership Agreement, will not operate to terminate the Partnership for federal income tax purposes and does not violate the Federal Securities Act of 1933, the Illinois Securities Act of 1953, or any applicable state securities law or the rules and regulations of the Securities and Exchange Commission or any state securities commission. He or she further acknowledges and agrees that he or she is a bona fide permanent resident of the State of Illinois and that there is an absolute prohibition upon sale or transfer of the Interests or any interest therein to a non-resident of the State of Illinois prior to nine months from the date of the last sale by the Partnership of the Interests.

(c)   He or she understands that the General Partner and the Partnership have no obligation or intention to register the Interests under any federal or state securities act or law, either now or at any time in the future.

23

(d)   He or she, by reason of his or her knowledge and experience in financial and business matters in general, and real estate construction and operation activities in particular, is capable of evaluating the risks and merits of investment in the Interests. He or she has consulted with and been guided by his or her investment advisor, attorney or accountant or both ("Advisors") with respect to and concerning the advisability of the purchase of the Interests and has secured independent tax advice in respect to the investment contemplated hereby, on which he or she is solely relying, or he or she warrants that he or she is capable of evaluating an investment in the Interests without the assistance of such an advisor. No representations, warranties or other assurances of any kind have been made to him or her by or on behalf of the Partnership or the General Partner with respect to the present or future value of Interests or any income tax consequences of purchase, ownership or disposition of Interests.

(e)   He or she acknowledges that he or she has thoroughly reviewed this Agreement of Limited Partnership, that he or she is familiar with and understands the contents hereof, that he or she has discussed all questions or reservations which he or she might have had with the Advisors, if any, upon whom he or she is relying, that all such questions or reservations have been answered or resolved to his or her satisfaction, and that at the present time he or she has no questions or reservations concerning the Agreement of Limited Partnership, the Interests, the suitability of the Interests for purchase by him or her, or his or her ability to bear the loss of his or her entire investment in the Partnership.

(f)   He or she hereby agrees to, and shall, indemnify the Partnership, the General Partner and Affiliates and agents of each of them and hold them harmless from and against any and all loss, damage, judgment, liability, claim, cost or expense, including reasonable attorneys' fees, which they or any of them may sustain or incur by reason of or in connection with any misrepresentation or breach of warranty or agreement by him or her under this Article XIX or in connection with the sale or distribution by him or her of the Interests purchased by him or her pursuant hereto in violation of the Securities Act of 1933 as amended, the Illinois Securities Law of 1953 as amended, or other applicable laws.

(g)   No formal comprehensive offering memorandum or similar disclosure document has been or will be prepared for the Interests. Any written materials heretofore given or shown to the undersigned were intended and have been used by the undersigned only to provide general background information concerning the Partnership and its proposed business. He or she acknowledges that the General Partner has made available to him or her and his or her Advisors all documents, writings and information which he or she has requested pertaining to the Property, this Partnership, and any other matters whatsoever; that he or she and such Advisors have been given satisfactory opportunity to verify and clarify all information in respect thereof; and that he or she and such Advisor have no questions or reservations with respect to any of the same.

(h)   In order to ensure that the Interests are sold pursuant to an appropriate exemption from registration under the Securities Act of 1933 and appropriate state securities laws, each Limited Partner does hereby certify and represent that the following statements are true and correct:

(1)   He or she is of legal age and is legally competent to execute this Agreement.

(2)   He or she is not under any present or reasonably foreseeable future constraint to dispose of Interests to satisfy any existing or contemplated debt or undertaking.

(3)   He or she has adequate means, income and property exclusive of the Interests to provide for his and his dependents' current and reasonably foreseeable future needs and contingencies and has no need for liquidity of the Interests.

(4)   He or she is a bona fide permanent resident of the state of Illinois.

(5)   Each Limited Partner other than Acrosstown Partners Limited Partnership certifies and represents that he or she is a bona fide "accredited investor" within the meaning of Rule 501(a), Regulation D under the Securities Act of 1933 and satisfies both of the following criteria:

(A)   His or her net worth, or joint net worth with his or her spouse, exceeds $1,000,000; and

(B)   He or she had individual income in excess $200,000 in each of the last two completed calendar years and reasonably expects to have income in excess of $200,000 in the current year.

(6) Acrosstown Partners Limited Partnership certifies and represents:

(A)   That it was not formed primarily for the purpose of or in anticipation of participating in this Partnership, but rather has made other investments or engaged in other business prior to entering into this Partnership;

(B)   That its General Partner is owned or controlled by George A. Simmons;

(C)   That George A. Simmons is an "accredited investor" and satisfies all of the criteria set forth in Section (h)(5) of this Article XIX; and

(D)   That its net worth as of this date is

(i)   He or she expressly acknowledges and is aware of the following:

(1) The Partnership has no operating history. The Interests are speculative investments, which involve a high degree of risk of loss of his or her entire investment.

(2) No federal or state agency has made any findings or determination as to the fairness for investment or any recommendation or endorsement of the Interests as an investment.

(3) No federal or other tax benefits have been promised to him or her. He or she is not purchasing the Interests as a tax shelter or for other tax purposes, and the Interests are not a tax-oriented investment.

(j) He or she does hereby certify, under penalties of perjury, (i) that his or her Social Security Number shown on the signature page of this Agreement is true, correct and complete and (ii) that he or she is not subject to backup withholding, either because he or she has not been notified by the Internal Revenue Service that he or she is subject to backup withholding, or because the Internal Revenue Service has notified him or her that he or she is no longer subject to backup withholding.

ARTICLE XX

GENERAL PARTNER REPRESENTATIONS AND WARRANTIES

The General Partner represents and warrants to each Limited Partner as follows:

(a) Fee simple title to the Property will be held by First Mortgage Bank as Trustee under a trust agreement.

(b) The General Partner has no knowledge of any currently existing violation of any federal, state, county or municipal laws, ordinances, order, regulation or requirement affecting any portion of the Property, and no written notice of any such violation has been received by the General Partner from any governmental authority.

(c) There is no material action, suit or proceeding pending or, to the knowledge of General Partner, threatened against the General Partner or the Property relating to or arising out of the ownership, construction, management or operation of the Property, in any court or before or by any federal, state, county or municipal department, commission, board, bureau or agency or any other governmental institution.

(d) The Budget attached hereto as Exhibit E reflects the General Partner's best estimate of the cost of development of the Property including, but not limited to, the sums to be paid to the General Partner and Affiliates for services rendered or to be rendered and goods or other property provided or to be provided to the

Partnership.

ARTICLE XXI

MUTUAL REPRESENTATIONS AND WARRANTIES

Each Partner represents and warrants to each other Partner that such Partner has the full right and authority to enter into this Agreement, to perform all obligations of such Partner contained herein and to execute and deliver all documents herein provided, and that the entering into of this Agreement does not constitute a violation or breach of any of the terms of any contract or other instrument to which such Partner is a party or is subject or by which such Partner's assets or properties may be affected, the effect of which will materially and adversely impair the ability of such Partner to comply with the terms of this Agreement.

ARTICLE XXII

COVENANT OF THE GENERAL PARTNER

The General Partner agrees to use its best efforts to cause the Property to be developed in accordance with the Budget attached hereto as Exhibit E.

LIST OF EXHIBITS

Exhibit	Item
A	Development Site Plan
B	Names and Participatory Percentages of Partners
C	Sample Monthly Operations Report of Partnership
D	Listing of Services provided by General Partner
E	Proposed Development Budget
F	Regent-Metropolitan Purchase Agreement

[ed. note – all documents omitted, except for Exhibit B]

EXHIBIT B

Names and Participating Percentages of Partners

	Names	Participating Percentages
General Partner:	Regent Real Estate Development Corp.	60%
Limited Partners:	Samuel Wilkins	16%
	Acrosstown Partners Limited Partnership	16%
	Walter Simmons	8%

PURCHASE AGREEMENT

THIS PURCHASE AGREEMENT is made and entered into as of the 20th day of January, 1989, by and between Alan W. Johnson ("Mr. Johnson") and Barbara L. Johnson ("Mrs. Johnson") (Mr. Johnson and Mrs. Johnson are sometimes collectively referred to herein as "Seller") and REGENT REAL ESTATE DEVELOPMENT CORP., an Illinois corporation ("Buyer").

R E C I T A L S

A.   Seller owns fee simple title in and to the property described on Exhibit A hereto (the "Land"), together with an interest in the improvements and structures located on the Land (the "Improvements"). The Land and the Improvements are sometimes collectively referred to herein as the "Real Property" and are located in unincorporated DuPage County, Illinois.

[handwritten in right margin: there aren't any, but have it there anyway (want to make sure you get everything)]

B.   Buyer desires to purchase and Seller is willing to sell all of Seller's right, title and interest in and to the Real Property, together with all of Seller's right, title and interest in and to the other assets herein described.

NOW, THEREFORE, in consideration of the mutual undertakings and agreements herein contained, the parties hereby agree as follows:

1.   Purchase and Sale.

Seller agrees to sell to Buyer, and Buyer agrees to purchase from Seller, the Real Property, together with all right, title and interest of Seller in and to:

[handwritten in left margin: ...ngs ...xed to ...operty ...ually ...ilding]

All personal property, fixtures, furniture, furnishings, equipment and inventory owned by Seller and located on the Land and Improvements (the "Personalty") not removed by Seller as provided for in Paragraph 10 of this Agreement.

The Real Property, together with the assets and rights described above (being herein called the "Property"), all upon the terms, covenants and conditions hereinafter set forth.

2.   Purchase Price.

The purchase price for the Property (the "Purchase Price") shall be the sum of $580,000.00 (Five Hundred and Eighty Thousand Dollars), plus or minus prorations as provided for herein.

[handwritten at bottom: this K does not include easements - usually they do]

31

3.   Payment of Purchase Price.

The Purchase Price for the Property shall be paid to Seller by Buyer as follows:

A.   Upon the full execution of this Agreement by the Seller and the delivery thereof to Buyer, which shall occur no later than February 7, 1989:

(i)   Buyer shall deliver to Seller (by depositing same with the Escrow Agent (hereinafter defined)) the sum of $5,000.00 (Five Thousand Dollars) (said amount, together with the additional $80,000.00 (Eighty Thousand Dollars) deposited pursuant to Paragraph 15 hereof and all interest earned thereon, being herein called the "Deposit"), as a deposit against the Purchase Price in accordance with the terms and conditions of this Agreement, including Paragraph 15 hereof; and

(ii)   Seller shall deposit the Warranty Deed (hereinafter defined) with Title Services, Inc. pursuant to escrow instructions directing Title Services, Inc. to record same with the Recorder's Office of DuPage County only upon the joint direction of Buyer and Seller as provided for in Paragraph 8D of this Agreement or if Closing does not occur by August 24, 1989 or such later date as Buyer and Seller may agree to in writing to return same to Seller thereafter.

B.   The balance of the Purchase Price, plus or minus prorations as provided for herein, in cash or by cashier's or certified check.

4.   Conditions Precedent to Closing.

A.   The obligation of Buyer to purchase the Property shall be subject to satisfaction of the following conditions precedent:

(i)   On or before April 14, 1989, Buyer shall have procured a firm commitment for a loan to be secured by a mortgage or trust deed on the Property in the amount of $522.000.00 (Five Hundred and Twenty-Two Thousand Dollars), or such lesser amount as Buyer accepts, at a floating rate of interest with a cap at Eleven Percent (11%) per annum, for a term of 10 years to be amortized over 30 years and a fee not to exceed 1% of the loan amount.

(ii)   On or before the closing Date, the Real Property shall be annexed by the City of Aurora pursuant to an annexation agreement in form and substance satisfactory to Buyer, and shall be zoned to permit buyer to demolish the

Improvements and develop the Real Property as an auto care center as contemplated by Buyer, (including, without limitation, the development of a car wash). Buyer shall pay any and all costs incurred in connection with Buyer's attempts to obtain said annexation and zoning. Seller shall fully cooperate with Buyer in connection with the afore described annexation and zoning. Buyer covenants that Buyer shall not record such annexation agreement or zoning ordinance prior to Closing nor shall any such Agreements become binding or final with the City of Aurora or any other municipality, so that seller would be bound or in any way obligated should this transaction fail to close as per the terms of this Agreement.

this is a defined term + should not be used consistently

(iii)   On or before the Closing Date, no environmental health or safety problems shall exist with respect to the Real Property.

(iv)   On or before the Closing Date, Buyer shall have purchased the property for sale under that certain contract by and between Metropolitan Diversified Properties, Inc., a Connecticut corporation, and Buyer dated January __, 1989 (the "Other Contract"), a copy of which is attached hereto as Exhibit B.

B.   If any of conditions (i) through (iv) above are not satisfied, Buyer may terminate this Agreement by notifying Seller thereof and the Deposit shall be returned to Buyer. Buyer shall have the option to waive any of the conditions precedent set forth in this Paragraph 4 or elsewhere in this Agreement at any time prior to the Closing Date (hereinafter defined) by notice to Seller as provided for herein and in the event of such waiver, such condition shall be deemed to be satisfied.

5.   Delivery of Documents Prior to Closing and Exceptions to Title

A.   Within forty-five (45) days following the date hereof, Buyer, Buyer's attorney and Seller's attorney shall receive the items referred to in (i) and (ii) below provided that Buyer orders same. Seller shall reimburse Buyer for the costs and expenses of items (i) and (ii) below in an amount which shall not exceed the sum of One Thousand One Hundred Eighty Dollars ($1,180.00). Notwithstanding the foregoing to the contrary, if the Closing does not occur by August 24, 1989, or such later date as Buyer and Seller agree to in writing, then Seller shall not be required to reimburse Buyer for such costs and expenses unless the Closing does not occur due to Seller's default under this Agreement.

(i)   Three (3) copies of a current (dated within 30 days of the date hereof) plat of survey of the Real Property made and certified to Purchaser and Commonwealth Land Title Insurance Company ("Commonwealth") by the surveyor as having been made in compliance with applicable law and land survey standards and American Land Title Association ("ALTA") requirements for extended coverage owner's title insurance. Said survey shall locate all improvements on the Real Property (as of its date), set forth the common street address, show access to public roads or ways, show all encroachments, if any, and show, locate and describe all visible or recorded easements, building lines and utilities and show such other matter(s) as may be required by Commonwealth. All recorded easements shall be identified by the applicable recording information. Said survey shall contain the express certification that, except as specifically noted, there are no encroachments of lot or building lines or obstructed easements. The legal description on the survey shall coincide exactly with that on the title commitment to be furnished by Seller.

(ii)   A title commitment addressed to Purchaser (irrevocable for at least six months) for an owner's ALTA title insurance policy Form B, with full extended coverage over general exceptions 1 through 5, together with an endorsement insuring that the Real Property has access to a publicly dedicated highway or public street issued by Commonwealth, through Title Services, Inc., in the amount of the Purchase Price, covering the Seller's fee simple estate in the Land and Improvements on or after the date hereof, agreeing to insure marketable title to the Real Property in the Buyer with unobstructed rights of access to and from the Real Property, subject only to exceptions to title acceptable to Buyer. Concurrently, Commonwealth shall cause to be delivered to Buyer true copies of all recorded documents shown on said title commitment. If the title commitment discloses exceptions to title not acceptable to Buyer, or if the plat of survey discloses matters not conforming to the requirements of (i) above or any condition that renders the title unmarketable (herein referred to as "survey defects"), Seller in its sole discretion and at its sole cost and expense shall cause Commonwealth to either remove such exceptions from the title commitment or survey defects within ten (10) days from the date of delivery of the commitment by Commonwealth, and the time of Closing shall be extended to a date twenty (20) days after delivery of the title commitment (if Closing would otherwise be scheduled in accordance with the terms herein prior to said twenty (20) day extension). If Seller does not have the exceptions removed from the title commitment or does not correct such survey defects, Buyer may have a return of the Deposit and terminate this Agreement or, upon notice to Seller given within ten (10) days after the expiration of said ten (10) day period, elect to close with the title as it then is with the right to deduct from the Purchase Price and hold back from the funds dues at Closing, liens or encumbrance of a definite or ascertainable amount and, with respect to any title exceptions not referred to in the Preliminary Title Insurance Commitment attached hereto as Exhibit C, such further amounts as Buyer reasonably determines may be necessary to remove said exceptions or defects (any excess being remitted to Seller or deficiency being paid by Seller when all such exceptions or defects have been removed or settled to Buyer's reasonable satisfaction), the time of Closing being extended to a date five days after the date on which said notice shall have been given (if Closing would otherwise be scheduled in accordance with the terms hereof prior to said five (5) day extension).

B.   Title to the Real Property shall be conveyed to Buyer or its nominee by a recordable Warranty Deed (the "Warranty Deed"), with release of homestead rights, executed by the Seller, subject only to current general real estate taxes not yet due and payable, those exceptions shown on Exhibit "C" which do not interfere with Buyer's use of the Property as an auto service care center and car wash as contemplated by Buyer and other exceptions to title acceptable to Buyer in its reasonable judgment. As a condition to Closing, on the Closing Date, Commonwealth shall issue (and the willingness of Commonwealth to issue same shall be conclusive evidence of the availability of title to the Real Property as required hereby) to Buyer its standard ALTA owners policy ("Owner's Policy") form of title insurance in the amount of the Purchase Price showing title to the Real Property in Buyer, subject only to the exceptions to title permitted by Buyer and containing extended coverage, a 3.1 Zoning Endorsement insuring that the Real Property is zoned for use as an auto care center, including, without limitation, a car wash, and insuring that if the auto care center is constructed in accordance with Buyer's plans and specifications, the auto care center will comply with all zoning laws, an access endorsement as described in Paragraph 5A(ii) hereof and such other endorsements thereto as may be reasonably required by Buyer. Seller hereby agrees to pay the premiums for the above-referenced Owner's Policy and all such endorsements in an amount which, together with the costs of the survey described in Paragraph 5A(i) of this Agreement, shall not exceed the sum of One Thousand One Hundred Eighty Dollars ($1,180.00). Notwithstanding the foregoing to the contrary, if the Closing does not occur by August 24, 1989, or such later date as Buyer and Seller agree to in writing, then Seller shall not be required to reimburse Buyer for such costs and expenses unless the Closing does not occur due to Seller's default under this Agreement.

6. <u>Warranties.</u>

A. Seller hereby covenants, represents and warrants to Buyer as follows:

(i) Seller has full power and authority to execute and deliver this Agreement and all documents and instruments executed or to be executed by Seller pursuant hereto or in connection herewith, and to consummate the transactions provided for herein and therein. Seller owns fee simple title to the Real Property and Seller owns good title to the Property. Mr. Johnson and Mrs. Johnson own fee simple to the Real Property as joint tenants. Attached hereto, as Exhibit D is a true and correct copy of Seller's prior title insurance policy.

(ii) There are no leases of the Real Property or any part thereof. Seller has used the Property solely as a residence.

(iii) There are no written or oral agreements or commitments relating to the Property, including, without limitation, service contracts.

(iv) To the best of Seller's knowledge, Seller has received no written or oral notice from any governmental authority that the Improvements are in violation of any applicable laws, ordinances, rules or regulations.

(v) To the best of Seller's knowledge, as of the date hereof, there are no pending lawsuits relating to the Property.

(vi) Other than the representations and warranties expressly provided for herein with respect to the condition of the Real Property, including, without limitation, the representations and warranties contained in Paragraph 6A(4) hereof, Seller makes no representations or warranties as to the condition of the Real Property, and will deliver the Real Property to Buyer at Closing in the same condition as on the date hereof, subject to ordinary wear and tear and, subject to Paragraph 9 hereof, damage due to casualty or condemnation between the date hereof and the Closing Date.

B. Buyer hereby represents and warrants to Seller that Buyer has full power and authority to execute and deliver this Agreement and all documents and instruments executed or to be executed by Buyer pursuant hereto or in connection herewith, and to consummate the transactions provided for herein and therein.

C. The foregoing representations and warranties shall be deemed to be made as of the Closing Date and it is a condition to Closing that the foregoing representations and warranties be true as of the Closing Date or otherwise acceptable to Buyer or Seller, as the case may be, in their sole discretion. All of the representations, warranties and covenants contained in this Agreement shall survive the Closing and the delivery of the Trustee's Deed for a period of six (6) months. It is a condition to Closing that neither Seller nor Buyer shall be in default or in breach of any of their respective covenants or agreements herein.

problems

7. Seller's Covenants.

Seller hereby covenants and agrees that from and after the date hereof through the Closing Date, Seller will operate and maintain the Property in a prudent manner. Seller shall perform all of the covenants of Seller contained in this Agreement, including, without limitation, delivering to Buyer all documents and instruments required to be delivered under this Agreement, and the performance of all of said covenants is a condition to Closing. Seller shall not enter into any leases or contracts with respect to the Property without Buyer's prior written approval. Seller shall not incur any liabilities secured by any portion of the Property or suffer or permit any liens to be placed on the Real Property unless Seller causes, at its sole cost and expense, said liens to be removed or insured over, at Buyer's election, by

Commonwealth. Between the execution of this Agreement and Closing, Seller may permit a mortgage or trust deed to encumber the Property in an amount not to exceed the sum of $400,000.00 (Four Hundred Thousand Dollars) provided that said mortgage or trust deed secures a loan for Seller to purchase a new residence and Seller causes such lien to be fully paid and released at or prior to Closing. Seller hereby agrees to permit Buyer, its agents and employees, to enter upon the Real Property at all reasonable times and after reasonable notice to Seller in order for Buyer, its agents and employees, to conduct all necessary or appropriate (in the Buyer's sole judgment) investigations of all environmental, health and safety matters with respect to the Real Property, provided that such entries and investigations do not unreasonably interfere with Seller's use of the Property as a residence. The cost for such inspections on and any report issued in connection therewith shall be paid by Buyer and evidence of payment, including waivers of mechanic liens shall be provided to Seller and the Property returned to its original condition prior to the release of any earnest money to Buyer. In the event that such inspections or reports reveal in the Buyer's sole judgment any environmental, health or safety problems, Buyer may, at its election, (i) correct such problems to Buyer's satisfaction, or (ii) terminate this Agreement, in which case the Deposit shall be returned to Buyer, or (iii) accept the Real Property in such condition. Seller shall fully cooperate with Buyer with respect to Buyer's performance of the foregoing inspections and corrections. Notwithstanding the foregoing to the contrary, Buyer's entry upon the Real Property prior to Closing as provided for herein shall not be deemed to have delivered possession of the Real Property to Buyer prior to Closing.

8. Closing Conference.

A. The sale and purchase herein provided is conditioned upon final plan approval of the Fox Valley Auto Care Center ("Final Plan Approval") by the City of Aurora. In the event the City of Aurora does not approve the Final Plan on or before May 24, 1989, Buyer may at its election either (i) terminate this Agreement, in which case the Deposit shall be returned to Buyer and the Warranty Deed shall be returned to Seller, or (ii) elect to continue to attempt to obtain such approval after said date for a period not to exceed sixty (60) days.

B. The sale and purchase herein provided shall be closed (the "Closing") at a Closing conference ("Closing Conference") which shall be held on the Closing Date at 10:00 A.M. at the office of Title Services, Inc. As used herein, "Closing Date" means the date which is the earlier of (i) thirty (30) business days after Final Plan Approval, or (ii) August 24, 1989, both (i) and (ii) being subject to the satisfaction of all of the conditions to Closing provided for in this Agreement. If the conditions to Closing are not satisfied by August 24, 1989, or such later date as Buyer and Seller agree to in writing, this Agreement shall automatically terminate and the Deposit shall be returned to Buyer and the Warranty Deed shall be returned to Seller.

        C.   On or prior to the Closing Date, the parties shall deliver to Title Services, Inc. at its office in Chicago, Illinois, duly executed and acknowledged originals of the following: (1) by Seller, the Warranty Deed and (2) by Buyer, the Purchase Price, plus or minus prorations.

        D.   At the Closing Conference, each party shall satisfy itself that the other is then in a position to deliver the items specified in subparagraph E below and that Commonwealth is prepared to issue the Owner's Policy herein required. Upon being so satisfied, the parties shall instruct Commonwealth to record the Warranty Deed and to issue the Owner's Policy.

        E.   Upon receiving the advice from Commonwealth that it is issuing the Owner's Policy:

        (i)   Seller shall deliver to Buyer, in form and substance satisfactory to Buyer: (a) a Foreign Person Tax Affidavit pursuant to Section 1445 of the Internal Revenue Code (b) an affidavit of title covering the period from the date of the most currently dated title commitment issued by Commonwealth with respect to the Real Property to the Closing Date and (c) a Seller's attorney's opinion covering the Seller's power to do the transactions contemplated hereby, the due execution and delivery of the documents executed by Seller hereunder and the binding effect and enforceability of such documents.

        (ii)   Buyer shall deliver to Seller the Purchase Price.

        (iii)   The deed shall be delivered to Buyer by Commonwealth depositing the same for recordation in accordance with the requirements of the applicable law, with instructions to record the same as required and thereafter forward the same to Buyer at its address hereinafter specified in this Agreement.

        (iv)   Seller shall pay applicable state and county transfer taxes, payable in connection with the delivery and recording of the deed in an amount not to exceed the sum of $850.00 (Eight Hundred and Fifty Dollars). Additionally, Seller shall pay all costs and expenses of or related to the issuance of policies of title insurance herein required, including, but not limited to, the premiums for the same, and the costs of any preliminary title reports, commitments and surveys in connection with the same in an amount not to exceed the sum of Five Hundred Eighty Dollars ($580.00) and one-half (½) of all escrow charges and all other charges for or in connection with the Closing in an amount not to exceed the sum of Three Hundred Dollars ($300.00).

F.   Real estate taxes for the years 1988 and 1989 shall be prorated between Seller and Buyer as of the Closing Date. The amount of the real estate tax proration due Buyer shall be a credit against the Purchase Price, and shall be determined based upon 110% of the most recent bill. The prorations and payments shall be made on the basis of a written statement submitted to Buyer by Seller at least five (5) days prior to the Closing Date and approved by Buyer. Said real estate taxes shall not be reprorated when the final bills for same are received.

9.   Destruction of Property.

A.   In the event any of the improvements on the Real Property are damaged or destroyed by any casualty or taking prior to the Closing Date, Seller shall so notify Buyer, in writing. Seller shall either use the entire proceeds to make repairs or may, in their sole discretion, assign to Buyer at Closing one-half (½) of its interest in the insurance proceeds recoverable based upon said casualty or taking and shall promptly tender to Buyer one-half (½) of any and all insurance proceeds as, if and when Seller receives same. All proceeds recoverable concerning personal property, living expenses or other damages except the structure shall be retained in total by the Seller.

B.   In the event the Real Property or any portion thereof is condemned by any public authority, Seller shall promptly notify Buyer thereof and Buyer may, at its option, terminate this Agreement by notice to Seller given on or before the Closing Date, in which event the Deposit shall be returned to Buyer. If Buyer elects not to terminate this Agreement based upon said taking, Seller shall assign to Buyer at Closing all of Seller's interest in the condemnation award based upon said taking and shall promptly tender to Buyer any and all awards as, if and when Seller receives same.

10.   Possession.

A.   Seller may remain in possession of the Real Property for purposes of residing thereon for a period of sixty (60) days after Closing (the "Permitted Occupancy"), provided that (i) Seller notifies Buyer at least three (3) days before Closing of its intention to remain in possession after Closing and (ii) at Closing, Seller deposits the entire proceeds of the sale of the Property (the "Proceeds") into escrow, with James Mallory, Esq. as escrow agent, pursuant to escrow instructions satisfactory to Buyer. Buyer shall be entitled to, as consideration for the Permitted Occupancy, all of the interest which accrues on the Proceeds for each day that Seller remains in possession after Closing until Seller vacates the Real Property. The escrow instructions shall provide, among other things, that the proceeds deposited shall be invested in a money market account with Mid America Federal Savings and or Northern Trust Bank/Naperville, with interest accruing in favor of Buyer while Seller is in possession after Closing and that the escrow agent shall hold on to the proceeds deposited until Buyer notifies the escrow agent that Seller has vacated the Property. Buyer shall notify the Escrow Agent that Seller has vacated the Property once (a) Seller notifies Buyer that Seller has vacated the Property and delivers to Buyer a bill of sale and assignment in form and substance satisfactory to Buyer covering all items of Personalty described in Paragraph 1 of this Agreement not removed by Seller as provided for in this Paragraph 10, prior to Seller's vacation of the Property, and (b) Buyer confirms that Seller has indeed vacated the Property. Buyer or Buyer's agent shall confirm or shall give notice of Seller's failure to vacate within 24 hours of receipt of Seller's notice. Seller also agrees to pay to Buyer the sum of $250.00 for each day Seller remains in possession after the Permitted Occupancy until Seller vacates the Real Property and sole possession is delivered to Buyer. The escrow instructions shall also provide that the escrow agent shall pay to Buyer the amounts due Buyer pursuant to this Paragraph 10 upon written demand therefor by Buyer, notwithstanding any contrary directions from Seller. While Seller is in possession during the Permitted Occupancy, Buyer, its agents and employees, may enter upon the West one hundred fifty (150) feet of the Real Property for purposes of performing road work and excavation work, and such work and entries shall not constitute a nuisance or disturbance of Seller's possession. Seller may pledge the corpus of the Proceeds (but not the interest which has accrued thereon) as security for a loan to purchase a new residence. Seller may remove any structures, fixtures or personalty on the Property any time hereafter until the end of the Permitted Occupancy.

11.   Indemnification.

A.   Seller shall hold harmless, indemnify and defend Buyer from and against all loss, damage, claims, demands, actions or proceedings arising out of or relating to any of Seller's representations and warranties hereunder being untrue or incorrect in any material respect. Seller shall hold harmless, indemnify and defend Buyer from and against (1) any and all third party claims, suits, demands, actions or proceedings and any and all loss, liability and damage arising therefrom in any way related to the Property and arising out of events or omissions which occurred before the Closing Date (or after the Closing Date if arising due to the Permitted Occupancy) and (2) all costs and expenses, including attorneys' fees, related to any actions, suits or judgments incident to any of the foregoing. Buyer shall notify Seller of any such claim against Buyer within six (6) months after Closing and failure to notify Seller within said period shall terminate Buyer's rights under this Paragraph 11A.

B.   Buyer shall hold harmless, indemnify and defend Seller from and against all loss, damage, claims, demands, actions or proceedings arising out of or relating to any of Buyer's representations and warranties hereunder being untrue or incorrect in any material respect. Buyer shall hold harmless, indemnify and defend Seller from and against (1) any and all third party claims, suits, demands, actions or proceedings and any and all loss, liability and damage arising therefrom in any way related to the Property and arising out of events or omissions which occurred after the Closing Date, unless arising due to the Permitted Occupancy (or before the Closing Date if arising due to Buyer's entry upon the Real Property prior to Closing) and (2) all costs and expenses, including attorneys' fees, related to any actions, suits or judgments incident to any of the foregoing. Seller shall notify Buyer of any such claim against Seller within six (6) months after Closing and failure to notify Buyer within said period shall terminate Seller's rights under this Paragraph 11B.

12.   Notices.

Any notice, demand or document which either party is required or may desire to give or deliver to the other shall be in writing and may be personally delivered (including delivery by messenger) or given by overnight courier or by United States mail, certified, return receipt requested, postage prepaid, addressed as follows: to Seller, Alan and Barbara

Johnson, 7 S 780 Route 59,, Unincorporated DuPage County, Illinois, with a copy to James Mallory, Esq., 222 E Washington Ave., Naperville, Illinois, 60566, and to Buyer c/o The Regent Group, 524 West South Avenue, Chicago, Illinois, 60610 with a copy to: Kaplan & Miller, 450 Wacker Drive, Chicago, Illinois, 60606, Attention: Donna Smith, Esq., subject to the right of either party to designate a different address by notice similarly given. Any notice, demand or document so given shall be deemed delivered when delivered personally (including delivery by messenger) or by overnight courier or, if mailed as aforesaid, shall be deemed given on the day which is three (3) days after the day on which the same is deposited in the United States mail, as aforesaid.

13.   Miscellaneous.

This Agreement and the Exhibits hereto contain the entire agreement between the parties respecting the matters herein set forth and supersedes all prior agreements between the parties hereto respecting such matters. This Agreement cannot be amended except pursuant to a written instrument executed by both parties hereto. Time is of the essence of this Agreement. This Agreement shall be construed in accordance with the laws of the State of Illinois. Seller agrees at anytime from time to time, to execute any and all documents reasonably requested by Buyer to carry out the intent of this Agreement. The captions of this Agreement are intended for convenience of reference only and in no way define, describe or limit the scope or intent of this Agreement or of any of the provisions hereof. At any time hereafter, at the option of Buyer, the parties hereto shall execute a short form of this Agreement in recordable form for the purpose of placing third parties on notice of Buyer's interest in the Property. The terms, covenants and conditions contained herein shall be binding upon and inure to the benefit of the successors and assigns of the respective parties hereto. This Agreement shall become null and void if Seller fails to fully execute and deliver this Agreement to Buyer on or before February 7, 1989.

14.   Real Estate Commission.

Seller shall be responsible for and shall pay any and all real estate commissions and finder's fees payable to Proformance Realty in connection with this transaction. Each party hereunder shall indemnify, defend and hold the other party harmless from any claim made by any broker claiming to have been engaged by such party in connection with this transaction.

15. <u>Deposit: Termination Without Consummation.</u>

A.   On or before May 1, 1989, Buyer shall deliver to Seller (by depositing same with the Escrow Agent) the sum of Eighty Thousand Dollars ($80,000.00), provided that (i) Seller is not in default under this Agreement, and (ii) this Agreement is in full force and effect. The Deposit shall be held by Kaplan & Miller prior to the satisfaction of all of the conditions to Closing and shall be held by Title Services, Inc. thereafter (the "Escrow Agent") pursuant to the terms of this Agreement in an interest bearing account of the Escrow Agent's choice. Upon consummation of the Closing hereunder, the Escrow Agent shall simultaneously pay the deposit to Seller as part of the Purchase Price to be paid at the Closing. In the event the Closing is not consummated, the Escrow Agent shall deliver the Deposit in accordance with Paragraph B below and the other provisions of this Agreement.

B.   If the transaction herein provided shall not be closed by reason of Seller's default under this Agreement, then Buyer may, at its election, either (i) initiate a suit for specific performance with equitable adjustments or (ii) terminate this Agreement, in which event the Deposit shall be returned to Buyer. In the event the sale of the Property shall not be consummated solely on account of Buyer's default, then the Deposit shall be delivered to Seller as Seller's sole and exclusive remedy and shall be in lieu of any other monetary relief or, without limitation, any other relief, including the right to specific performance, to which Seller may otherwise be entitled by virtue of this Agreement, under law or in equity. In the event the sale of the Property shall not be consummated for any reason other than a default by Buyer or Seller hereunder, then the Deposit shall be returned to Buyer, and the parties shall have no further rights or remedies against each other. Notwithstanding anything to the contrary contained in this Agreement, the Escrow Agent shall hold on to the Deposit, deliver same to the Buyer or deliver same to the Seller only as directed in writing by the Buyer or pursuant to any court order. It is understood and agreed, however, that the previous sentence does not alter the rights of the Buyer and Seller to the Deposit which rights are governed by the other terms and conditions of this Agreement.

44

IN WITNESS WHEREOF, the parties hereto have executed this Agreement on the dates specified below.

SELLER:

Dated: January _____, 1989

_____
Alan W. Johnson

SS# _____

Dated: January _____, 1989

_____
Barbara L. Johnson

SS# _____

BUYER:

Regent Real Estate Development Corp.,

An Illinois corporation

Fed I.D. # 49-3146269

By: _____

Dated: January _____, 1989

Its: _____PRESIDENT_____

Attest: _____Sarah Martin_____

_____Secretary

EXHIBIT LIST

A   Land Description

B   Other Contract   (Regent-Metropolitan Contract)

C   Preliminary Title Insurance Commitment

D   Prior Title Policy

[ed. note – Exhibits B, C, and D are omitted. Exhibit B, the Regent-Metropolitan contract, in an executed version, is the next document.]

EXHIBIT A

THAT PART OF THE SOUTH EAST QUARTER OF SECTION TWENTY ONE (21),
TOWNSHIP THIRTY EIGHT (38) NORTH, RANGE NINE (9) EAST OF THE THIRD
PRINCIPAL MERIDIAN, DESCRIBED BY BEGINNING AT THE SOUTH EAST
CORNER OF SAID SECTION: THENCE NORTH 88° 48'SY WEST, 584.1 FEET;
THENCE NORTH 7° 58' WEST, 148.1 FEET; THENCE SOUTH 88° 48' EAST, 605.5
FEET TO THE EAST LINE OF SAID SECTION; THENCE SOUTH ON THE EAST LINE
OF SAID SECTION, 146.25 FEET TO THE PLACE OF BEGINNING, IN DUPAGE
COUNTY, ILLINOIS.

REAL ESTATE SALE AND PURCHASE AGREEMENT

(Fox Valley)

This Real Estate Sale and Purchase Agreement ("Agreement") is entered into as of this 21st day of February, 1989 by and between METROPOLITAN DIVERSIFIED PROPERTIES, INC., a Connecticut corporation ("Seller"), and REGENT REAL ESTATE DEVELOPMENT CORPORATION, an Illinois corporation ("Purchaser").

RECITALS

A.   LaSalle National Bank, not individually but as Trustee under that certain Trust Agreement dated December 26, 1984 and known as Trust No. 109000 ("Trustee"), is the record owner of the property shown and described on Exhibit A attached hereto and made a part hereof ("Property").

B.   Seller is the sole beneficiary of said Trust No. 109000.

C.   Seller desires to sell to Purchaser, and Purchaser desires to acquire from Seller, the Property, consisting of approximately 2.5 acres, under the terms and conditions hereinafter set forth.

NOW, THEREFORE, in consideration of the foregoing and the mutual covenants hereinafter contained, the parties agree as follows:

1.   PROPERTY.   Seller agrees to sell and cause to be conveyed to Purchaser or its nominee, and Purchaser agrees to acquire from Seller, the Property on the terms and conditions hereinafter set forth. Seller shall cause the Property to be conveyed by a recordable trustee's deed (the "Deed") in form as shown in Exhibit B attached hereto and made a part hereof. The Property shall be conveyed subject only to (i) the terms contained in the Deed, (ii) general real estate taxes not yet due and payable, (iii) utility and drainage easements and such other covenants, easements, restrictions and matters of record as shall not interfere with Purchaser's intended use of the Property and (iv) acts and deeds of Purchaser.

2.   PURCHASE PRICE.   The purchase price ("Purchase Price") shall be Three Hundred Sixty-Four Thousand Eight Hundred and 00/100 Dollars ($364,800.00) and shall be payable as follows:

(a)   Eighteen Thousand Two Hundred Forty and 00/100 Dollars ($18,240.00) earnest money deposit, one-half of which is due within ten (10) days of the execution of the Johnson Contract (as defined in Paragraph 14 hereof) by the parties thereto, and which shall be held by

49

Kaplan & Miller (at no cost to Seller) until the deposit of the second half of the earnest money deposit, pursuant to joint order escrow instructions satisfactory to Seller, and the other half of which is due on or before May 1, 1989. Upon the deposit of the second half of the earnest money, all of the earnest money will be held by Title Services, Inc. ("Escrowee") in an interest bearing account acceptable to Seller and Purchaser with the principal amount (i.e., interest less investment costs charged by Escrowee) payable on Closing to Purchaser or, if Seller is entitled to the earnest money because of Purchaser's default hereunder, to Seller. If Purchaser is in default under this Agreement, the earnest money plus all interest thereon shall be paid over to Seller upon joint order to Kaplan & Miller if it is holding the earnest money or upon Seller's sole demand to the Escrowee at such time as it is holding the earnest money. In the event that Purchaser is not in default under this Agreement, and this Agreement is terminated due to a condition upon which Purchaser's obligation to close is contingent not being satisfied, then the earnest money and net earnings thereon shall be returned to Purchaser. The escrow agreement shall be consistent with the foregoing and acceptable to the parties and Escrowee. The cost of establishing such escrow with Escrowee shall be divided evenly by the parties.

(b)   The balance of the Purchase Price, plus or minus prorations, by wire transfer, at Closing (as hereinafter described).

3.   SOIL INSPECTION AND TESTS.   Within 45 days from the date hereof Purchaser, its agents and its soil testing contractor, shall have the right to enter upon the Property for the purpose of performing soil test borings and such other investigations as to the condition of the real estate as it deems necessary. Purchaser agrees to give Seller 48 hours advance notice of its entry onto the Property pursuant to the terms of this Paragraph 3 and prior to such entry provide Seller's Designated Representative, which shall be The Daneman Company until further notice from Seller to Purchaser ("Seller's Designated Representative"), with evidence of insurance satisfactory to Seller for the coverages shown on Exhibit G attached hereto and made a part hereof and after any such entry shall restore the Property to its pre-existing condition. Purchaser agrees to save, defend, hold harmless and indemnify Seller, Trustee, and Seller's Designated Representative of and from all liabilities, losses, claims and expenses, including reasonable attorneys' fees, incurred by Seller, Trustee and/or Seller's Designated Representative by reason of the activities of Purchaser or its agents or contractors pursuant to this Paragraph 3. In the event within said period the results of such soil test borings or other investigations do not

indicate a capability of supporting a building of the type desired by Purchaser using construction methods which are usual and customary in the Chicago metropolitan area or otherwise indicate unsatisfactory soil conditions, including environmental conditions, then upon written notice to Seller within three (3) days following such period Purchaser shall have the right to terminate this Agreement, in which event the earnest money heretofore deposited shall be returned to Purchaser and all reports of such soil borings and other investigations shall be delivered to Seller. Purchaser agrees that other than the disclosure of the results of such soil test borings to Seller and to Purchaser's lender, Purchaser shall keep all information relating to such soil borings confidential, unless disclosure is otherwise required by law.

4.   SURVEY.   Within 45 days from the date hereof, Seller, at its own expense, shall cause to be furnished to Purchaser a survey of the Property, prepared by an Illinois licensed land surveyor (the "Surveyor"), properly describing the Property and showing the number of square feet or acreage contained therein. Prior to Closing, Seller shall deliver to Purchaser an ALTA or Illinois Land Survey Standards survey ("Survey") certified by the Surveyor to Purchaser, the Title Company (as hereinafter defined) and Purchaser's lender (provided that the name of Purchaser's lender is timely provided). The Survey shall be dated not earlier than forty-five (45) days before Closing and shall disclose no "Unpermitted Exceptions" (as hereinafter defined).

5.   TITLE EVIDENCE.   Not later than 45 days from the date hereof Seller shall procure and deliver to Purchaser an ALTA "Form B" commitment for an owner's title insurance policy issued by Commonwealth Land Title Insurance Company (the "Title Company") in the amount of the Purchase Price covering title to the Property and showing said title to be in Trustee, subject only to the general exceptions and conditions contained therein and the matters subject to which the Property is to be conveyed as described in Paragraph 1 herein. All title exceptions other than the foregoing are hereinafter referred to as the "Unpermitted Exceptions." The title commitment shall be conclusive evidence of good title as therein shown as to all matters insured by the policy, subject only to exceptions as stated therein. If the title commitment discloses Unpermitted Exceptions, Seller shall have 60 days from the date of Purchaser's written notice to Seller thereof which notice shall give within thirty (30) days of its receipt of the title commitment, to have the Title Company waive the Unpermitted Exceptions or commit to insure for the full amount of said policy against loss or damage that may be occasioned by such Unpermitted Exception. If Seller fails to have such Unpermitted Exceptions removed or, in the

alternative, to obtain the required commitment for title insurance within the specified time, Purchaser may (i) terminate this Agreement upon ten days prior written notice unless such failure is corrected or (ii) elect, upon notice given to Seller within 10 business days after the expiration of the 60 day period, to take title as it then is as aforesaid. Seller agrees that it will not willfully place any lien or encumbrance on the Property which is not released at Closing or fully insured over. The title policy delivered in connection with the Closing shall include extended coverage over the general printed exceptions. The cost of the title policy shall be paid by Seller, provided, however, the cost to Seller shall not exceed $300.00, including extended coverage over the printed general exceptions. Any additional cost of the title policy shall be paid by Purchaser.

Within 14 days after Seller's Designated Representative's approval of Purchaser's submittals made pursuant to 7.B, Purchaser may obtain at its own expense from the Title Company a commitment for the issuance of a so-called broad form zoning endorsement (ALTA Form 3.1 with parking) with the title policy. If, after using all reasonable efforts, a commitment for such zoning endorsement is not available to Purchaser subject only to Final Plan (as hereinafter defined) approval, and Purchaser gives written notice to Seller of such circumstance not later than three (3) days after the end of such 14 day period, then this Agreement shall be null and void and the earnest money shall be returned to the Purchaser; provided, however, that if within 10 days from receiving Purchaser's notice Seller causes Chicago Title Insurance Company to issue such commitment for such zoning endorsement, then this Agreement shall not so terminate and the parties shall use Chicago Title Insurance Company for this transaction with any cancellation fees of the Title Company to be paid by Purchaser. If Seller elects to try to cause Chicago Title Insurance Company to issue such endorsement, Purchaser shall fully cooperate with Seller.

6. UTILITIES. Sanitary sewer, storm sewer and water mains have been constructed to the Property line or in the adjacent roadway or right-of-way. Purchaser's subsequent connections to said utility lines shall be made in a good and workmanlike manner and in accordance with all applicable laws, ordinances and regulations imposed by governmental bodies having jurisdiction thereover. Where any of the said utility lines lie beneath or across roadways, Purchaser agrees to restore any property affected by such connections to its pre-existing condition and to save, defend, indemnify and hold harmless Seller, Trustee and Seller's Designated Representative from and against any and all losses, damages, claims, liabilities, costs

and expenses, including reasonable attorney's fees, suffered by Seller, Trustee and Seller's Designated Representative as a result of Purchaser's connection to said utility lines. Purchaser shall make its own arrangements for electrical, natural gas and telephone service directly with the appropriate utility company.

    7.   <u>CONSTRUCTION.</u>

    (a)   The right to a building permit does not exist until a Final Plan for the Property ("Final Plan") is approved by the City of Aurora ("City"). Therefore, closing is conditional on the approval by the City of a Final Plan acceptable to both Seller and Purchaser. Not later than March 22, 1989, Purchaser shall furnish to Seller's Designated Representative, at Purchaser's expense, all information relating to Purchaser's proposed improvements to the Property and Johnson Property (as hereinafter defined) as may be required for the Final Plan implementing the site plan depicted on Exhibit C ("Site Plan"). Approval of the median cut at South Road Access Drive shown on Exhibit C shall not be a contingency of this Agreement. Seller's Designated Representative shall approve or disapprove of such submittals within 10 business days after receipt and shall not unreasonably withhold its approval of such submittals provided that the improvements which Purchaser intends to construct are similar in quality and construction materials as other commercial buildings in the "Fox Valley Region I" Planned Unit Development. If Seller's Designated Representative fails to approve or disapprove of such submittals within such period, such submittals shall be deemed approved. Upon Seller's Designated Representative's approval of such submittals, Purchaser shall make prompt application to the City for its approval of a Final Plan. In the event the City does not approve the Final Plan on or before May 24, 1989, Seller or Purchaser shall have the option to terminate this Agreement and upon notices of the exercise of such option in writing Seller shall refund Purchaser's earnest money deposit; however, if the City has not approved the Purchaser's Final Plans and Purchaser has exercised diligent efforts and has initiated timely procedures to obtain such approval within such period, then either Seller or Purchaser may elect to extend the time within such approval must be obtained by a period not to exceed sixty (60) days, and provided, further, however, if Seller or Purchaser does not exercise their rights to so terminate this Agreement and thereafter approval of the Final Plan is obtained, Seller or Purchaser shall not thereafter have such right to terminate this Agreement.

(b)   Prior to Purchaser's application for governmental approvals and/or permits required for the commencement or continuation of any construction, Purchaser shall submit to Seller's Designated Representative complete final design documents consisting of building elevation drawings, site plan and landscape plan together with outline specifications describing materials to be used ("Construction Documents") for all improvements to be constructed by Purchaser on the Property. Seller's Designated Representative shall approve or disapprove of the Construction Documents within 10 business days after receipt and shall not unreasonably withhold its approval of such submittals provided that the Construction Documents are in substantial conformity with documents pursuant to Paragraph 7.A above previously approved by Seller's Designated Representative. If Seller's Designated Representative fails to so notify Purchaser of such approval or disapproval within such period, the Construction Documents shall be deemed approved. Approval by Seller's Designated Representative of the design documents or other submittals required hereby shall not be deemed to constitute a warranty or representation regarding the suitability of such submittals for the use therefor intended by Purchaser.

(c)   Purchaser agrees to commence construction of the facilities and improvements upon the Property within 12 months after the Closing, subject to Unavoidable Delays. Purchaser agrees that upon such commencement of construction, it will, with all due diligence, complete said facilities, such completion to be not later than 12 months thereafter, except for Unavoidable Delays. In the event of any such Unavoidable Delays, the time for completion shall be extended by the period of such Unavoidable Delays. Purchaser's construction shall be in a good and workmanlike manner and in substantial compliance with the approved Construction Documents and with all applicable laws and ordinances of governmental bodies having jurisdiction over the Property. As used in this Agreement "Unavoidable Delays" shall mean delays caused by governmental orders or edicts, governmental rationing or allocation of materials, strikes, lockouts, fires, acts of God, disasters, riots, delays in transportation, shortages of labor or materials or any other cause beyond the reasonable control of the party asserting such delays. In the event Purchaser shall fail to commence construction within the time period set forth above (or as extended by Unavoidable Delays), Purchaser agrees to exert its best efforts to sell the Property to a bona fide purchaser who will commit to commence development of the Property within a reasonable period of time.

8. USE. Purchaser represents that its intended use of the Property is for general commercial and retail uses consistent in character and quality with the commercial uses within the area developed under the name "Fox Valley East Region I" Planned Unit Development, including, but not limited to, for a retail automobile care center including a full service car wash and an insurance adjustment center. Purchaser agrees that for a period of 10 years the Property shall be used only for said purpose and for no other purpose without the prior written consent of the Seller which, in the case of proposed uses consistent in character and quality with other uses within the area developed under the name "Fox Valley East Region I" Planned Unit Development, shall not be unreasonably withheld. Such restrictions shall appear in the Deed.

9. BROKER. Purchaser represents and warrants to Seller that it dealt with no broker, licensed or otherwise, in connection with this transaction to whom a commission may be payable as a result of this transaction other than Seller's Designated Representative. Purchaser agrees that if any claim be made for brokerage commission or fee by any broker other than Seller's Designated Representative because of, or in connection with, any act of Purchaser or any of the individuals, firms or corporations affiliated with Purchaser, then Purchaser will indemnify, pay and hold Seller free and harmless from any and all liabilities, demands, losses, damages, costs and expenses (including reasonable legal fees and expenses) in connection therewith. Seller agrees that if any claim be made for brokerage commission or fee by any broker because of, or in connection with, any act of Seller or any of the individuals, firms or corporations affiliated with the Seller, then Seller will indemnify, pay and hold Purchaser free and harmless from any and all liabilities, demands, losses, damages, costs and expenses (including reasonable legal fee and expenses) in connection therewith.

10. CLOSING. The transaction contemplated hereby shall be closed through escrow with Title Services, Inc. as Escrowee in accordance with the general provisions of the usual deed and money escrow agreement then in use by the Escrowee, with such special provisions inserted therein as may be required to conform with this Agreement. At Seller's election, any such escrow shall provide that the Purchase Price, plus or minus prorations, shall be payable to Seller upon the recording of the deed in accordance with the foregoing escrow provisions and upon the Title Company assurance to the Purchaser that it will issue the Title Policy in accordance with the requirements of this Agreement. The cost of such escrow, if any, shall be divided equally between Seller and Purchaser.

The Closing shall take place at the office of the Escrowee in Chicago, Illinois no later than thirty (30) days after approval of the Final Plan by the City and the satisfaction of the other conditions of this Agreement. At Closing, Seller shall deposit the Deed, Purchaser shall deposit the balance of the Purchase Price in immediately available funds and the Deed for Johnson Residual (as defined in Paragraph 14 hereof) and Seller and Purchaser shall jointly deposit into the escrow, if any, such other documents, including an affidavit of title, a plat act affidavit (if a plat of subdivision is not being recorded pursuant to Paragraph 11), Foreign Investment in Real Property Tax Act, Section 145 I.R.C. ("FIRPTA") and ALTA Statements, as may be reasonably required to complete this transaction.

Seller shall pay the amount of any stamp tax imposed by the state or county in which the Property is located on the transfer of title and shall furnish a completed Real Estate Transfer Declaration signed by the Seller or the Seller's agent in the form required pursuant to the Real Estate Transfer Tax Act of the State of Illinois and the county in which the Property is located and shall furnish any declaration signed by the Seller or Seller's agent or meet other requirements as established by any municipal ordinance with regard to a transfer or transaction tax. Such tax required by ordinance shall be paid by the Purchaser. Purchaser shall pay for the cost of recording the Deed.

11.   REAL ESTATE TAXES; SUBDIVISION.

(a)   Seller shall pay all general real estate taxes which are due and payable at the date of Closing. Taxes for the current year shall be apportioned as of the date of Closing and all apportionments shall be based upon 110% of the latest tax bill. In the event that the Property is taxed as part of a larger parcel, the proration shall be determined on the basis that the acreage of the Property bears to the total acreage in such larger parcel. In such event, the parties shall cooperate in filing for a tax division.

(b)   If the City or County requires a plat of subdivision to be recorded or if the Westbrook Drive Extension is publicly dedicated, Seller agrees to execute a plat of subdivision covering all of (i) the Property, (ii) the Johnson Property and (iii) Seller's remaining property, described on Exhibit H attached hereto and made a part hereof, all as shown on Exhibit I attached hereto and made a part hereof and described in Exhibit I as Parcels 1, 2, 3, 4 and 5. If the recording of a plat of subdivision is not required and if the Westbrook Drive Extension is not publicly dedicated, Seller agrees to file a petition to divide Seller's and Purchaser's respective

56

properties into two separate taxable lots. Purchaser agrees to cooperate with Seller in its efforts to obtain approval for such plat of subdivision or tax division petition.

12. REMEDIES. In the event of a breach under this Agreement by either party prior to the Closing and provided the non-breaching party has previously given the breaching party 10 days notice specifying the nature of the breach (no such notice, however, shall be required in the event either party breaches its obligation to close this transaction pursuant to Paragraph 10 herein) and further provide the breaching party has failed to remedy the breach within said 10 day period, or, if the breach by its nature requires additional time to remedy, the breaching party fails to commence to remedy the breach or fails to diligently pursue the remedy thereafter, except with regard to the indemnification contained in Paragraph 3 hereof, the sole and exclusive remedy of the non-breaching party shall be, in the case of Seller, to retain the earnest money deposit as liquidated damages and, in the case of Purchaser, to receive a refund of its earnest money deposit or, if Seller's default is not as a result of matters beyond its control imposed by a third party or acts of God, either to receive a refund of its earnest money deposit or to seek specific performance of this Agreement.

In the event of any breach by either party subsequent to the Closing of any obligation hereunder which is specified herein as surviving the Closing, the non-breaching party shall have the right to pursue any and all remedies provided at law or in equity. The failure of either party to act upon a default of the other of any of the terms, conditions or obligations under this Agreement shall not be deemed a waiver of any subsequent breach or default under the terms, conditions or obligations hereof by such defaulting party.

13. FINANCING CONTINGENCY. This Agreement is contingent upon Purchaser obtaining a preliminary commitment for financing for the purchase of the Property and development thereof as contemplated by the March 22, 1989 submittals approved by Seller's Designated Representative pursuant to Paragraph 7.A hereof. If after using all reasonable efforts Purchaser is unable to obtain such commitment for financing and delivers written notice of such fact to Seller on or before April 14, 1989, this Agreement shall be null and void and the earnest money shall be returned to Purchaser. If Purchaser fails to deliver such notice to Seller by such date, it shall be conclusively presumed that Purchaser has satisfied or waived this contingency. Upon satisfaction of this contingency or waiver of this contingency, Purchaser shall pay the remainder of the earnest money deposit as contemplated by Paragraph 2.

14.   JOHNSON PROPERTY ACQUISITION, ANNEXATION AND ZONING.

(a)   The Closing of the transaction contemplated herein is contingent upon the consummation of the purchase and sale of the Johnson Property. Seller acknowledges that Purchaser has entered into a written contract in the form shown on Exhibit J attached hereto and made a part hereof, including a certain First Amendment thereto, (together, the "Johnson Contract") for the purchase of the property described in Exhibit D attached hereto and made a part hereof, which property is commonly known for the purposes hereof as the "Johnson Property". Purchaser shall obtain Seller's consent to any changes in the Johnson Contract from the form of Exhibit J, which consent shall not be unreasonably withheld or delayed provided that such change does not result in an extension of the outside date for the consummation of the transaction contemplated by the Johnson Contract. Notwithstanding anything in this Agreement to the contrary, a default by Purchaser under the Johnson Contract shall be an incurable default by Purchaser under this Agreement entitling Seller to retain the earnest money deposit.

(b)   It is a condition of Purchaser's obligations under the Johnson Contract that "On or before the Closing Date, no environmental, health or safety problems shall exist with respect to the Real Property." See Section 4.A (iii). For the purpose of satisfying this condition and the contingency set forth in Paragraph 3 of this Agreement, Purchaser agrees with Seller that it will conduct its investigations of all environmental, health and safety matters with regard to the Johnson Property (as permitted by Section 7 of the Johnson Contract) within 45 days from the date of this Agreement and that Purchaser shall either (i) waive or satisfy condition 4.a (iii) of the Johnson Contract or (ii) exercise its right to terminate the Johnson Contract because of the failure of such condition and give notice thereof to the Johnsons and Seller not later than the expiration of the contingency set forth in Paragraph 3 of this Agreement.

After the expiration of the contingency set forth in Paragraph 3 of this Agreement, Purchaser agrees that it shall have no right to terminate the Johnson Contract pursuant to Section 4.A (iii) thereof without Seller's written consent unless this Agreement is thereafter terminated on some other basis pursuant to its terms.

(c)   Commencing on the date hereof, Purchaser agrees to take any and all appropriate steps to request City to adopt the Fox Valley East Region I Plan Description (without any variances), and to use its best efforts to cause the City to annex into the City and zone of the Johnson Property, such that after the annexation and zoning, the Property and the Johnson

Property may be used for a unified commercial development as shown on the Site Plan. In the event that, despite the use of best efforts by Purchaser, the City will not annex and zone the Johnson Property on or before the outside date of the approval of the Final Plan, then upon written notice to Seller within such period, Purchaser will have the right to terminate this Agreement upon written notice to Seller in which event the earnest money heretofore deposited shall be returned to Purchaser.

(d)   At the time of Closing, subject to the provisions of Paragraph 14.E below, Purchaser will convey to Seller that portion of the Johnson Property described on Exhibit E attached hereto and made a part hereof ("Johnson Residual"), consisting of approximately 0.25 acres. Within 45 days of execution of the Johnson Contract, Purchaser will provide to Seller a copy of the title commitment for the Johnson Residual which shall name Seller as the insured therein and which shall be prepared according to the same specifications set forth in Paragraph 5 above, as well as a survey of the Johnson Residual prepared according to the same specifications set forth in Paragraph 4 above. Purchaser agrees to re-grade the Johnson Residual pursuant to the schematic drawings required under Paragraph 7.A of this Agreement and approved by Seller and to complete such work to Seller's satisfaction no later than November 15, 1989, subject to Unavoidable Delays.

(e)   Promptly upon Purchaser's receipt of the soil test borings and other investigations as Purchaser obtains with respect to the Johnson Property, but in any event within 45 days from the date hereof, Purchaser shall deliver to Seller's Designated Representative a true, correct and complete copy of the report of such borings and investigations as they relate to the Johnson connection with this transaction, Seller and Seller's Designated Representative shall keep all information relating to such reports confidential, unless disclosure is otherwise required by law. In the event that such reports indicate unsatisfactory soil conditions, including environmental conditions, then upon written notice to Purchaser within three (3) days following the expiration of such 45 day period Seller shall have the right at its option to either (i) terminate this Agreement, in which event the earnest money heretofore deposited shall be returned to the Purchaser or (ii) consummate this transaction pursuant to all the terms and conditions of this Agreement except that Purchaser shall not convey the Johnson Residual to Seller. Seller's notice to Purchaser shall specify the unsatisfactory soil conditions and, anything herein to the contrary notwithstanding, if Seller elects the option to terminate this Agreement on account thereof,

59

within 3 days of Purchaser's receipt of Seller's notice, Purchaser may give written notice to Seller that it covenants to correct such unsatisfactory soil conditions prior to closing (and as a condition thereto), in which event such termination shall be null and void (and the earnest money shall continue to be deposited in accordance with the requirements of this Agreement).

(f)   Seller agrees that Purchaser, its agents and/or its re-grading contractor, shall have the right to enter upon the Johnson Residual after closing for the purpose of performing such re-grading in accordance with the provisions hereof. Prior to such entry, Purchaser shall provide Seller's Designated Representative with evidence of insurance satisfactory to Seller for the coverages shown on Exhibit G attached hereto and made a part hereof, and after completion of such re-grading, shall restore the Johnson Residual to its pre-existing condition, except for the re-grading work. Purchaser agrees to save, defend, hold harmless and indemnify Seller, Trustee and Seller's Designated Representative of and from all liabilities, losses, claims and expenses, including reasonable attorney's fees, incurred by Seller, Trustee and/or Seller's Designated Representative by reason of the activities of Purchaser or its agents or contractors pursuant to this Paragraph 14.

15.   WESTBROOK DRIVE EXTENSION AND SOUTH ROAD ACCESS DRIVE. Purchaser agrees to construct the access drive referred to on the Site Plan as "South Road Access Drive". The pavement and roadway for South Road Access Drive shall be half on Purchaser's property and half on Seller's property adjacent thereto, as shown on the Site Plan. If approved as part of its Final Plan, Purchaser further agrees to construct a median cut in South Road ("South Road Median Cut") to permit entry onto the Property via South Road Access Drive. Purchaser further agrees to construct an extension of the pavement and utilities with respect to Westbrook Drive, from its present termination point to the highway commonly known as Route 59, as shown on the Site Plan. Seller and Purchaser shall jointly approve all design documents, budgets, construction and bidding documents, bidding lists, bids, contracts, change orders and contract invoices relating to all construction. Purchaser shall obtain waivers of liens and contractor's affidavits covering both Seller and Purchaser's respective properties, prior to making any payment to a contractor. At the election of Seller, Purchaser shall be required to use a construction escrow at its title company for payment of construction invoices. Costs of the respective roadways shall include preliminary and final engineering designs, construction, restoration of parkways, escrow fees and any punchlist items necessary to obtain the City's

approval or acceptance of work. All work shall be covered by a contractors' performance bond. Purchaser agrees that it shall complete its construction obligations no later than December 31, 1989, subject to Unavoidable Delays, except for the surface course of the pavements, which may at Purchaser's option be completed no later than one year after substantial completion of all other construction obligations. Seller reserves the right to construct either or both roadways contemplated above and be reimbursed by Purchaser for its proportionate share if Purchaser does not proceed to obtain necessary approvals, permits and commence construction within 60 days of Closing, subject to Unavoidable Delays. Seller agrees to provide 10 days notice to Purchaser of its intent to assume Purchaser's obligations for either or both roadways. Seller's costs in connection with said construction shall constitute a valid lien on the Property.

Purchaser agrees that, prior to Purchaser's entry onto the Property pursuant to the terms of this Paragraph 15, Purchaser will provide Seller's Designated Representative with evidence of insurance satisfactory to Seller for the coverage shown on Exhibit G attached hereto and made a part hereof and after completion of South Road Access Drive, shall restore the Property to its pre-existing condition, except for the South Road Access Drive improvement. Purchaser agrees to save, defend, hold harmless and indemnify Seller, Trustee and Seller's Designated Representative of and from all liabilities, losses, claims and expenses, including reasonable attorney's fees, incurred by Seller, Trustee and/or Seller's Designated Representative by reason of the activities of Purchaser or its agents or contractors pursuant to this Paragraph 15.

Seller will reimburse Purchaser for eighty percent (80%) of the costs of the Westbrook Drive Extension and fifty percent (50%) of the costs of the South Road Median Cut and the South Road Access Drive within 45 days after Purchaser makes a progress payment request accompanied by proper lien waivers, contractor affidavits, construction invoices, and certification by the engineer in charge of construction that the portion of the work which has been completed conforms to the requirements of the design documents. If either or both roadways are not publicly dedicated, Seller and Purchaser agree to grant and record at Closing reciprocal easements in their properties for the portion of the private roadway(s) which lies on their property and further agree to enter into an agreement in the form shown on Exhibit F attached hereto and made a part hereof to share the maintenance and repair costs of such private road(s) according to the construction cost allocation percentages described above.

16.   MISCELLANEOUS.

(a)   All notices or communications herein required or which either party desires to give to the other shall be in writing and sent by either Federal Express (or comparable overnight service) or hand delivery or registered or certified mail, postage prepaid, return receipt requested, and shall be mailed as follows:

If to Purchaser:

REGENT REAL ESTATE DEVELOPMENT CORPORATION

c/o The Regent Group

524 West South Avenue

Chicago, Illinois, 60610

With a copy to:

KAPLAN & MILLER

450 Wacker Drive

Chicago, Illinois, 60606

If to Seller:

METROPOLITAN DIVERSIFIED PROPERTIES, INC.

c/o The Daneman Company

1000 Barger Road

Oak Brook, Illinois, 60521

With Copies to:

AETNA REALTY INVESTORS, INC.

CitiCenter Plaza

Hartford, Connecticut, 06103

Notices given by Federal Express (or comparable overnight service) shall be effective the next business day: hand delivered notices shall be effective upon receipt; and notices given by certified or registered mail shall be effective two (2) business days after mailing. Upon written notice to the other party, either party may change their address for delivery of further notices or communications.

(b)   Purchaser may not assign its rights under this Agreement without the prior written consent of the Seller, except upon notice to Seller, Purchaser may assign its rights hereunder to a partnership of which Purchaser is the managing general partner. This Agreement shall insure to the benefit of and be binding upon the parties and their successors and permitted assigns.

(c)   The paragraph headings used herein are for convenience only and in no way are intended to define or limit the substantive provisions of this Agreement.

(d)   None of the provisions of this Agreement shall survive the Closing other than the provisions of Paragraphs 3, 6, 7, 8, 9, 11, 12, 14, 15 and this Paragraph 16.

(e)   Unless expressly contained herein, Seller has not made and does not make any representation or warranty as to any matter or thing affecting or related to the Property or this transaction, including but not limited to the physical condition (both surface and subsurface), zoning matters, anticipated income or expense, proposed operation or any other matter. Subject to the provisions hereof, Purchaser agrees to take the Property in its condition at Closing, Purchaser having made a thorough inspection and investigation. Seller shall not be liable or bound in any manner by any statements, representations, warranties or information furnished by any of Seller's employees, officers, agents, servants or any broker or other persons not expressly set forth herein. Purchaser hereby waives any and all rights of action it may have by statute or otherwise concerning the condition of the Property.

(f)   Time is of the essence hereof.

(g)   Seller represents to the Purchaser that this transaction is in the ordinary course of Seller's business and is not subject to the provisions of Section 902(d) of the Illinois Income Tax Act and similar provisions of the Retailer's Occupation Tax.

(h)   Purchaser and Seller each represent to the other that it has the requisite power and authority to enter into this Agreement, to perform the obligations created hereby and to consummate the transaction contemplated herein.

(i)   This Agreement shall be construed, governed and interpreted in accordance with Illinois law.

(j)   This Agreement may be executed in counterparts, each of which shall be considered an original and when taken together shall constitute one and the same instrument.

IN WITNESS WHEREOF, the parties hereto have executed this Agreement the date and year first above written.

SELLER:

Metropolitan Diversified Properties, Inc.

ATTEST:

Sharon McKenzie
Assistant Secretary

Joseph Sellers
Vice President

Regent Real Estate Development Corp.

ATTEST:

Sarah Martin
Secretary

David Delaney
President

EXHIBIT LIST

A   Legal Description

B   Trustee's Deed

C   Site Plan

D   Legal Description of Johnson Property

E   Parcel Identification Map

F   Declaration of Easement

G   Insurance

H   Parcel Maps

I   Parcel Maps

J   Regent-Johnson Purchase Agreement

[ed. note – Exhibits, C, D, E, H, I, and J are omitted. The Regent-Johnson Purchase Agreement is the previous document.]

EXHIBIT A
LEGAL DESCRIPTION

That part of the Southeast Quarter of Section 21, Township 38 North, Range 9 East of the Third Principal Meridian described as follows: Commencing at the most northerly corner of the Fox Valley East, Region 1, Unit No. 2, Aurora, DuPage, County, Illinois; thence easterly along the southerly line of South Road 428.64 feet for a point of beginning; thence southerly at right angles to the north line (as monumented) of a tract of land conveyed to Alan W. Johnson and Barbara L. Johnson by Document 747981 recorded March 2, 1955; thence easterly along said north line (as monumented) at right angles to the last described course 436.29 feet to the southwest corner of a tract of land described in Parcel 3 of Document R-75-34466; thence northerly along a westerly line of said Parcel 3 forming an angle of 88° 58' 28" with the last described course (measured clockwise therefrom) 263.47 feet to an angle in the westerly line of said Parcel 3; thence northwesterly along a southwesterly line of said Parcel 3 forming an angle of 210° 53' 06" with the last described course (measured counter-clockwise therefrom) 25.94 feet to an angle in said southwesterly line of said Parcel 3, being also the southerly line of said South Road; thence westerly along said southerly line 423.76 feet to the point of beginning, in the City of Aurora, DuPage County, Illinois and containing 2.534 acres.

66

EXHIBIT B

TRUSTEE'S DEED

THIS INDENTURE, made this _____ of _____, 1989, between LASALLE

NATIONAL BANK, a national banking association, as trustee under the provision of a Deed or

Deeds in Trust, duly recorded and delivered to said Bank in pursuance of a Trust Agreement

dated December 26, 1984, and known as Trust Number 109000 ("Grantor"), and

_____, ("Grantee").

WITNESSETH, that Grantor, in consideration of the sum of Ten and NO/100 Dollars

($10.00) and other good and valuable consideration in hand paid, does hereby grant, sell and

convey unto Grantee the following described real estate situated in Du Page County, Illinois, to

wit:

[To be inserted by Seller based on title commitment and survey legal description]

together with the tenements and appurtenances thereunto belonging (all hereinafter called the

"Premises".

TO HAVE AND TO HOLD the same unto Grantee and to the proper use and benefit

forever of Grantee.

This Deed is executed pursuant to and in the exercise of the power and authority granted

to and vested in said Trustee by the terms of said Deed or Deeds in Trust delivered to said

Trustee in pursuance of the trust agreement above mentioned.

The Premises are conveyed subject to each and every of the following terms, provisions,

conditions, covenants, restrictions and reservations (collectively called "Terms""):

1.   USE. For a period of ten (10) years from the date of recording hereof, the

Premises shall be used only for general commercial and retail uses consistent in character and

quality with the commercial uses within the area developed under the name "Fox Valley East

Region I" Planned Unit Development, including for a retail automobile care center including a

full service car wash and an insurance adjustment center and for no other purpose without the

prior written consent of Grantor, which, in the case of proposed uses consistent in character and

67

quality with other uses within the area developed under the name "Fox Valley East Region I" Planned Unit Development shall not be unreasonably withheld.

2. IMPROVEMENTS TO THE PREMISES.

A. Prior to construction of any building or other improvements on the Premises, Grantee shall deliver to Grantor's designated representative, which shall be The Daneman Company until further notice from Grantor to Grantee ("Grantor's Designated Representative"), 3 complete sets of schematic design documents showing, among other things, location of all buildings, parking facilities and areas, and other improvements intended for the Premises, including the means of ingress and egress, curb cuts, traffic flow, proposed signage and specifications thereof, parking ratio, area for shielded trash containers, setback lines, building height and building area, schematic architectural plans, grading and drainage plans, proposed utility connections, conceptual landscaping drawings and floor plans, which plans, drawings, and specifications shall show, among other things, elevations, rooftop screenings, aesthetic treatment of exterior surfaces, including exterior architectural design and decor, and other like pertinent data and outline specifications for the buildings and other facilities and improvements intended to be placed on or within the Premises, all of which are hereinafter called "Construction Documents." Within 15 business days after the submission of Construction Documents as aforesaid, Grantor's Designated Representative shall notify Grantee whether the Construction Documents are approved or disapproved. If Grantor's Designated Representative fails to approve or disapprove of such Construction Documents within 15 business days of submission, such Construction Documents shall be deemed approved. In no event will Construction Documents be approved which do not provide for underground installation of all utilities. Any disapproval of any part or portion of the Construction Documents shall generally set forth the reason or reasons for such disapproval. If Grantor's Designated Representative shall disapprove of any part or portion of the Construction Documents as above provided, Grantee shall revise its Construction Documents to incorporate such changes as may be requested to secure Grantor's Designated Representative's approval and shall deliver 3 completed sets of revised Construction Documents to Grantor's Designated Representative. Grantor's Designated Representative's approval of submitted Construction Documents shall be evidenced by its initialing of 1 copy thereof and returning same to Grantee.

68

B.   To the extent that any subsequent changes are made by Grantee in any approved Construction Documents which affect the exterior of any improvements, such changes shall be subject to the provisions of this Paragraph 2, and Grantee shall secure the approval of Grantor's Designated Representative in the manner herein provided.

C.   No signs of any type or nature shall be permitted on the Premises unless such signs have been first approved by Grantor's Designated Representative either separately or as part of approved Construction Documents, except for a reasonable temporary sign announcing the "grand opening" and reasonable sign announcing that space for lease is available on a portion of the Premises provided such signs shall be in conformity with all laws and Village ordinances and shall be subject to the approval of the Village in all respects. Except as otherwise provided in this Paragraph 2.C, no "for sale" or other temporary signs, flags, banners or streamers shall be permitted on the Premises.

3.   MAINTENANCE OF PREMISES.

A.   Grantee agrees that it shall maintain or cause to be maintained the Premises and all improvements located thereon, including the exterior of any building or buildings, pedestrian walks, parking lots and landscaped areas, in a clean, sightly and safe condition consistent with and similar to the Fox Valley Shopping Center in Aurora, Illinois, and further, that it will at all times and from time to time cause the prompt removal of all papers, debris, refuse, snow and ice and sweeping of paved areas within the Premises when and as required in order that the Premises be maintained as above provided. Unless otherwise approved by Grantor, all storage areas on the Premises shall be enclosed and the exterior display or storage of merchandise is prohibited. No parking or storage of automobiles, trailers or similar equipment shall be permitted on the Premises (except within enclosed improvements) for a period in excess of 24 hours. In the event of damage or destruction to any improvements upon the Premises by reason of fire or other casualty, Grantee shall thereafter either promptly restore such improvements to the condition existing prior to such damage or destruction or, in the alternative, raze and remove such improvements and landscape the Premises in a sightly manner.

B.   In the event Grantee shall fail or refuse to maintain the Premises as above provided, then Grantor's Designated Representative after 3 days written notice to Grantee specifying the manner in which Grantee has failed to maintain the Premises as above provided, and provided such failures have not been corrected within such 3 day period, or if such correction by its nature requires additional time, has not commenced correction, may enter upon the Premises and perform the maintenance set forth in said notice and neither Grantor nor Grantor's Designated Representative by reason of its doing so, shall be liable or responsible to Grantee for any losses or damages thereby sustained by Grantee or any occupants of the Premises or of anyone claiming by or under either an occupant or Grantee. In the event of damage or destruction to any improvements upon the Premises by reason of fire or other casualty, and Grantee fails or refuses either to restore promptly such improvements or raze and remove such improvements as above provided, then Grantor or Grantor's designated representative after 3 days written notice to Grantee, provided such failure has not been corrected within such 3 day period, may enter upon the Premises and raze and remove such improvements and landscape the Premises in a sightly manner. The cost of such work or razing and removing such improvements and so landscaping shall be paid by Grantee within 10 days of the date of rendering of a written statement from Grantor. Such statement shall specify the details of the maintenance performed and the costs thereof. Such costs shall be a lien on the Premises which may be enforced according to law.

4.   UNCOMPLETED VACANT BUILDING CONSTRUCTION.   In the event any buildings on the Premises are under construction for a period of more than 12 months subject to "Unavoidable Delays" and Grantee is not proceeding in a reasonable manner to complete construction with due diligence Grantee, upon written demand from Grantor, shall raze and remove such buildings from the Premises and shall landscape the Premises in a sightly manner. As used herein, "Unavoidable Delays" shall mean delays caused by governmental orders or edits, governmental rationing or allocation of materials, strikes, lockouts, fires, acts of God, disasters, riots, delays in transportation, shortages of labor or materials or any other cause beyond the reasonable control of Grantee. Grantor agrees that if required for the purposes of placing a bona fide mortgage from time to time upon the Premises, the proceeds of which are to be used for the construction of improvements which are in compliance with the terms hereof, it will execute such documents as may be necessary to subordinate the provisions of this Paragraph to the lien of the mortgage so that the lien of the mortgage will be superior to this Paragraph.

5. BENEFITS UNDER ANNEXATION AGREEMENT. Grantor expressly retains all benefits, including the right to receive any cash payments from governmental bodies and all rights, including certain rights of election with respect to water, roads and sewers, under that certain Annexation Agreement dated December 18, 1973 by and between the City of Aurora, Illinois, and other parties therein named, as amended (the "Annexation Agreement").

6. POWER OF ATTORNEY. Grantee hereby irrevocably appoints on behalf of itself, its grantees, successors and assigns, for the term of the Annexation Agreement, Metropolitan Diversified Properties, Inc. and its successors, assigns or designees, as its true and lawful attorney-in-fact and agent to execute and deliver (i) such amendments to the Annexation Agreement and/or planned development documents said attorney-in-fact, in its sole discretion, may from time to time deem necessary for the continuing development of the Fox Valley East Planned Development District; (ii) any and all documents relating to legal proceedings which said attorney-in-fact may from time to time deem necessary to maintain the Premises as territory annexed to the City of Aurora under the Annexation Agreement or any amendments thereto; and (iii) any and all documents relating to legal proceedings which said attorney-in-fact, in its sole discretion, may from time to time deem necessary in order to include the Premises as part of, to annex the Premises to, or to disconnect the Premises from any sanitary district, drainage district, park district, special taxing district, or any other unit of local government; provided that none of the foregoing actions may impose any greater financial or other obligation upon the Grantee or upon the Premises than is imposed on similar sites within the Fox Valley East Planned Development District.

7. ACCEPTANCE OF DEED. Grantee by accepting delivery of this Deed agrees to all the Terms and to all obligations by it to be performed hereunder. The Terms shall constitute covenants running with the land and bind every subsequent owner of all or a portion of the Premises.

8. TERM. The Terms hereof shall continue for so long as at least two major department stores shall be operated within the area commonly known as the Fox Valley Shopping Center, Aurora, Illinois; however, if any of the covenants, conditions, restrictions, easements, liens, charges, privileges, or rights created by this Deed would otherwise be unlawful

or void for violation of (a) the rule against perpetuities or some analogous statutory provisions, (b) the rule restricting restraints on alienation or (c) any other statutory or common law rules imposing time limits, then such provision shall continue only until twenty-one (21) years after the death of the last of the now living lawful descendants of Alan Dixon, United States Senator.

9.   MISCELLANEOUS

A.   No delay or omission in exercising any right accruing under the provisions of this Deed shall impair any such right or be construed to be a waiver thereof. A waiver of any of the covenants, conditions or agreements hereof shall not be construed to be a waiver of any subsequent breach thereof or of any other covenant, conditions or agreement therein contained.

B.   All rights, privileges and remedies afforded by this Deed shall be deemed cumulative, and the exercise of any one of such remedies shall not be deemed to be a waiver of any other right, remedy or privilege provided for herein.

C.   If any term, provision or condition contained in this Deed shall, to any extent, be invalid or unenforceable, the remainder of this Deed (or the application of such term, provision or condition to persons or circumstances other than those in respect of which it is invalid or unenforceable) shall not be affected thereby, and each and every other term, provision and condition of this Deed shall be valid and enforceable to the fullest extent possible permitted by law and the parties to the fullest extent possible modify such invalid or unenforceable term, provision or condition to the extent required to carry out the general intention of this Deed and to impart validity to such term, provision or condition.

D.   The captions of the sections of this Deed are for convenience only and shall not be considered nor referred to in resolving questions of interpretation or construction.

E.   All notices, waivers, statements, demands, approval or other communications (all of the same being referred to herein as "Notices") to be given under or pursuant to this Deed shall be in writing, addressed to the parties at their respective addresses as provided below, and will be delivered by Federal Express (or comparable overnight service) or hand delivery or certified or registered mail, postage prepaid. Notices given by Federal Express (or comparable overnight service) shall be effective the next business day; hand delivered Notices shall be effective upon receipt; and Notices given by certified or registered mail shall be effective two (2) business days after mailing.

The addresses of the parties to which such Notices are to be sent and the persons to whose attention said Notices are to be addressed will be those as provided herein, and until further notice are as follows:

If to Grantor:

METROPOLITAN DIVERSIFIED PROPERTIES, INC.

C/o The Daneman Company

1000 Barger Road

Oak Brook, Illinois, 60521

With Copies to:

AETNA REALTY INVESTORS, INC.

CitiCenter Plaza

Hartford, Connecticut, 06103

If to Grantee:

REGENT REAL ESTATE DEVELOPMENT CORPORATION

c/o The Regent Group

524 West South Avenue

Chicago, Illinois, 60610

F.   In the event that Grantor or its beneficiary shall institute any action or proceeding against Grantee or its beneficiary, or in the event the Grantee or its beneficiary shall institute any action or proceeding against Grantor or its beneficiary in either case relating to the provisions of this Deed, the unsuccessful party in such action or proceeding shall reimburse the successful party for the reasonable expenses, including attorney's fees and disbursements, incurred therein.

G.   This Deed is executed by LaSalle National Bank, not individually but as Trustee as aforesaid, in the exercise of the power and authority conferred upon and vested in it as such trustee, and under the express direction of the beneficiary or beneficiaries under a certain Trust Agreement known as Trust No. 109000 with LaSalle National Bank. It is expressly understood and agreed that nothing herein contained shall be construed as creating any liability whatsoever, expressed or implied, against said Trustee personally, and in particular, without limiting the generality of the foregoing, said Trustee shall have no personal liability to pay any indebtedness accruing under this Deed, either expressed or implied, herein contained, and that all personal liability of said LaSalle National Bank of any sort is hereby expressly waived by the Grantee, and by every person now and hereinafter claiming any right or security hereunder, and that so far as said LaSalle National Bank, is concerned, the owner of any indebtedness or liability accruing shall look solely to the property owned by the Trustee for the satisfaction of any such indebtedness or liability; further, that no duty shall rest upon LaSalle National Bank, either personally or as such trustee, to sequester trust assets, rentals, avails, or proceeds or any kind, or otherwise to see to the fulfillment or discharge of any obligation, expressed or implied, whether asserted as contract, tort liability or otherwise, arising under the terms of this Deed, except where said Trustee is acting pursuant to direction as provided by the terms of said Trust, and after the Trustee has first been supplied with funds required for the purpose.

IN WITNESS WHEREOF, Grantor has caused its corporate seal to be hereto affixed, and has caused its name to be signed to these presents by its Vice President and attested to by its Assistant Secretary, the day and year first above written.

LASALLE NATIONAL BANK, as Trustee
aforesaid

ATTEST:

_____   _____
Assistant Secretary   Vice President

EXHIBIT F

DECLARATION OF EASEMENT

This Declaration of Easement is made this _____ day of _____, 1989, by and between LA SALLE NATIONAL BANK, not individually but as Trustee under Trust Agreement dated December 26, 1984, and known as Trust No. 109000 ("LaSalle") , and REGENT REAL ESTATE DEVELOPMENT CORPORATION, an Illinois corporation ("Regent").

WITNESSETH:

WHEREAS, LaSalle is the record owner of the property legally described on Exhibit A attached hereto and made a part hereof, and shown as Parcels 1, 2, and 3 on Exhibit B attached hereto and made a part hereof; and

WHEREAS, Regent is the record owner of the property legally described on Exhibit C attached hereto and made a part hereof, and shown as Parcels 4 and 5 on Exhibit B; and

WHEREAS, LaSalle and Regent desire to create a non-exclusive perpetual easement over, across and upon the portion of their respective properties legally described on Exhibit D attached hereto and made a part hereof and shown on Exhibit B as "Access Road", for the benefit of Parcels 1, 2, 3, 4 and 5 as and for a roadway for the purpose of access, ingress and egress from said Parcels 1, 2, 3, 4 and 5 to South Road on the north and Westbrook Drive Extension on the south; and

WHEREAS, LaSalle and Regent desire to create a non-exclusive perpetual easement over, across and upon the portion of their respective properties legally described on Exhibit E attached hereto and made a part of hereof and shown on Exhibit B as "Westbrook Drive Extension", for the benefit of Parcels 1, 2, 3, 4 and 5 as and for a roadway for the purpose of access, ingress and egress from said Parcels 1, 2, 3, 4 and 5 to an existing easement providing access to Route 59 on the east, Westbrook Drive on the west and Access Road on the north.

NOW, THEREFORE, in consideration of the foregoing and the mutual covenants hereinafter contained, the parties agree as follows:

1.   LaSalle and Regent, for each of themselves and their respective successors and assigns, hereby grant to each of the other and their respective successors and assigns, for the benefit of Parcels 1, 2, 3, 4 and 5, a non-exclusive perpetual easement over, across and upon the Access Road, as legally described on Exhibit D and shown on Exhibit B; for purposes of constructing, reconstructing, repairing and maintaining a roadway for access, ingress and egress from Parcels 1, 2, 3, 4 and 5 to South Road, and the Westbrook Drive Extension, all as shown on Exhibit B.

2.   LaSalle and Regent, for each of themselves and their respective heirs and assigns, hereby grant to the other and their respective successors and assigns, for benefit of Parcels 1, 2, 3, 4, and 5 , a non-exclusive perpetual easement over, across and upon the Westbrook Drive Extension, as legally described on Exhibit E and shown on Exhibit B, for the purposes of constructing, reconstructing, repairing and maintaining a roadway for access, ingress or egress from Parcels 1, 2, 3, 4 and 5 to Westbrook Drive, Access Road and Route 59, all as shown on Exhibit B.

3.   Each of the parties agrees that no restrictions shall be imposed by any of them with respect to right-hand or left-hand turns to and from (i) the Access Road or (ii) Westbrook Drive Extension.

4.   The Access Road and the Westbrook Drive Extension shall be maintained in good condition and shall be repaired or reconstructed as needed. Such maintenance shall include, but not be limited to, surface repairs, striping, sign maintenance, and snow removal. As long as LaSalle or its successors remain the title holder of Parcels 1, 2 and 3 and LaSalle's present beneficiary or an affiliate of such beneficiary remains the beneficiary of LaSalle or its successors, Regent shall be responsible for maintaining, repairing and reconstructing the Access Road and the Westbrook Drive Extension and shall be reimbursed as provided for in Paragraphs 5, 6, and 7 hereof. As of such time as (a) LaSalle shall convey fee title to any part of Parcel 1, 2 or 3 (except in connection with a partial condemnation for road expansion purposes or a conveyance in lieu thereof) or (b) the beneficial interest in LaSalle is assigned to an entity unaffiliated with the present beneficiary of LaSalle or (c) construction of improvements (other than easements or roadways) in connection with the development of Parcels 1, 2, or 3 commences, then LaSalle and Regent (or their respective successors and assigns, as the case may be), will cooperate with each other as to the maintenance, repair and

reconstruction of the Access Road and Westbrook Drive Extension and shall mutually agree on contractors who will perform such maintenance work, but if the parties do not agree, then Regent (or its successors and assigns) shall have the right, upon thirty (30) days prior written notice to the owners of record of Parcels 1, 2 and 3 at their last known addresses, to contract for such maintenance, repair or reconstruction work with contractors of its choice and shall be reimbursed as provided for in Paragraphs 5, 6, and 7 hereof. The cost of such maintenance, repair or reconstruction work shall be paid as hereinafter set forth.

5.   The parties agree that the costs and expenses of repair, maintenance and reconstruction of the Access Road shall be apportioned among the various Parcels in the following manner:

      A.   Parcels 1, 2 & 3 - fifty percent (50%)

      B.   Parcels 4 & 5 - fifty percent (50%);

provided, however, that LaSalle, upon conveyances of any portion of Parcels 1, 2 or 3 shall have the right to assign to such portion, by document recorded in the Office of the DuPage County Recorder of Deeds, which document shall refer to this Agreement, the percentage of such costs and expenses to be allocated among Parcels 1, 2 and 3 to such portion, and from and after the recording of said document the portion of Parcels 1, 2 or 3 so conveyed by LaSalle shall be charged with the percentage so allocated to it, and the percentage chargeable to the remainder of Parcels 1, 2 or 3 shall thereupon be reduced by a like percentage.

Notwithstanding the foregoing, Regent shall bear one hundred percent (100%) of the cost of repair, maintenance and reconstruction of the Access Road (other than reconstruction related to the satisfactory completion of the original contract for the construction of the Access Road) until either (a) LaSalle conveys fee title to any portion of Parcels 1, 2 or 3 (except in connection with a partial condemnation for road expansion purposes or a conveyance in lieu thereof) or (b) the beneficial interest in LaSalle is assigned to any entity unaffiliated with the present beneficiary of LaSalle or (c) construction of improvements (other than easements or roadways) in connection with the development of Parcels 1, 2 or 3 commences.

Notwithstanding anything contained herein to the contrary, if there is any damage to the Access Road or the improvements in connection therewith caused by construction traffic in the course of developing the property benefited by the Access Road easement, the party having the construction work done shall bear one hundred percent (100%) of the cost for repairing such damage.

6.   The parties agree that the costs and expenses of repair, maintenance and reconstruction of the Westbrook Drive Extension shall be apportioned among the various Parcels in the following manner:

A.   Parcels 1, 2 & 3 - eighty percent (80%)

B.   Parcels 4 & 5 - twenty percent (20%);

provided, however, that LaSalle, upon conveyances of any portion of Parcels 1, 2 or 3 shall have the right to assign such portion, by document recorded in the Office of the DuPage County Recorder of Deeds, which document shall refer to this Agreement, the percentage of such costs and expenses to be allocated among Parcels 1, 2 and 3 to such portion, and from and after the recording of said document the portion of Parcels 1, 2 or 3 so conveyed by LaSalle shall be charged with the percentage so allocated to it, and the percentage chargeable to the remainder of Parcels 1, 2 or 3 shall thereupon be reduced by a like percentage.

7.   The costs and expenses of repair, maintenance and reconstruction described in Paragraphs 4 and 5 above shall be paid by the owner or owners of each of the Parcels in accordance with their respective percentages within thirty (30) days after written demand from the party having the responsibility for the repair or maintenance of (i) the Access Road or (ii) the Westbrook Drive Extension. Such costs shall be a lien on any Parcel (or portion thereof) whose owner fails to pay such costs when due, which lien may be enforced according to law.

8.   Each and all of the provisions of this Agreement (a) are made for the direct and mutual benefit of Parcels 1, 2, 3, 4 and 5 and shall constitute covenants running with the land in perpetuity, (b) will bind every owner of any portion of Parcels 1, 2, 3, 4 and 5 to the extent such portion is affected or bound hereby, and (c) will inure to the benefit of the parties and their respective transferees, successors and assigns.

9.   If at any time hereafter the Westbrook Drive Extension is publicly dedicated, the obligations of LaSalle and Regent hereunder shall no longer apply to the Westbrook Drive Extension as of the date that the dedication becomes effective.

IN WITNESS WHEREOF, the parties have executed this Agreement the date and year first above written.

LASALLE NATIONAL BANK, not individually but as Trustee under Trust Agreement dated December 26, 1984 and known as Trust No. 109000

ATTEST:

Elizabeth Keller

Assistant Secretary

[signature]

Vice President

Regent Real Estate Development Corp.

ATTEST:

Sarah Martin

Secretary

David Delaney

President

EXHIBIT G

<u>INSURANCE</u>

Prior to entry upon the Property described on Exhibit A attached hereto and made a part hereof, Regent Real Estate Development Corporation, an Illinois corporation, shall provide Metropolitan Diversified Properties, Inc., a Connecticut corporation ("MDP"), with a certificate of insurance in form and substance, and issued by a company, satisfactory to MDP, evidencing the following coverages and limits of insurance:

(a)   Worker's Compensation at statutory limits as required by the State in which the Job Site is located and Employers' Liability Insurance at a limit of not less than $100,000 for all damages arising from each accident or occupational disease.

(b)   Comprehensive General Liability Insurance:

Operations-Premises Liability

Products/Completed Operations Liability

(with 2 years residual coverage)

Contractual Liability

Broad Form Property Damage Endorsement

Independent Contractor's Liability

(if any work is subcontracted)

"X, C, U" Property Damage Liability

The limits of such liability insurance shall be no less than:

Bodily Injury Liability

$250,000 each occurrence

$500,000 aggregate

Property Damage Liability

$200,000 each occurrence

$200,000 aggregate

(c)   Comprehensive Automobile Liability Insurance covering all owned, hired, or non-owned vehicles including the loading or unloading thereof with limits no less than:

Bodily Injury Liability

$250,000 each person

$500,000 each occurrence

Property Damage Liability

$200,000 each occurrence

(d)   Umbrella Liability Insurance covering all operations with limits no less than:

Bodily Injury Liability

$1,000,000 each occurrence

$1,000,000 aggregate

Property Damage Liability

$1,000,000 each occurrence

$1,000,000 aggregate

Such certificate shall name MDP and LaSalle National Bank as Trustee under Trustee No. 109000 as additional insured under insurance coverage. Each policy and certificate shall provide that it will not be cancelled or materially altered except within thirty (30) days advance written notice by registered or certified mail to MDP.

ESCROW AGREEMENT

THIS ESCROW AGREEMENT is made this 10th day of July, 1989 by and among REGENT REAL ESTATE DEVELOPMENT CORP., an Illinois corporation ("Regent"), METROPOLITAN DIVERSIFIED PROPERTIES, INC., a Connecticut corporation ("Metropolitan"), ALAN W. JOHNSON and BABARA L. JOHNSON (the "Johnsons"), TURTLE WAX, INC., an Illinois corporation ("Turtle Wax") and TITLE SERVICES, INC., an Illinois corporation ("TSI").

WHEREAS, Regent and Metropolitan entered into that certain Real Estate Sale and Purchase Agreement dated February 21, 1989 (the "Metropolitan Contract") in which Regent agreed to purchase and Metropolitan agreed to sell to Regent certain property shown on Exhibit A attached hereto as "Parcel 4" and more particularly described in the Metropolitan Contract.

WHEREAS, Regent and the Johnsons entered into that certain Purchase Agreement, dated January 20, 1989, as amended by that certain First Amendment dated February 10, 1989 (the "Johnson Contract") in which Regent agreed to purchase and the Johnsons agreed to sell to Regent certain property located in unincorporated DuPage County shown on Exhibit A attached hereto as "Parcel 5" and "Parcel 3" and more particularly described in the Johnson Contract.

WHEREAS, pursuant to the Johnson Contract, the Johnsons have deposited into escrow the Warranty Deed, Plat Act Affidavit and Transfer Declaration with respect to Parcel 3 and Parcel 5 pursuant to escrow instructions agreed to by the Johnsons, Regent and TSI (the "First Escrow Agreement").

WHEREAS, Regent and Turtle Wax entered into that certain Real Estate Sale Contract, dated May 12, 1989 (the "Turtle Wax Contract") in which Regent agreed to sell and Turtle Wax agreed to purchase from Regent certain property located in Aurora and unincorporated DuPage County consisting of the southern portion (approximately 44 feet) of Parcel 4 and all of Parcel 5 more particularly described in the Turtle Wax Contract (the "Turtle Wax Property").

WHEREAS, in order to effectuate and coordinate the closings under the Metropolitan Contract, the Johnson Contract and the Turtle Wax Contract, (collectively, the "Contracts") the parties hereto have entered into this Escrow Agreement.

83

NOW, THEREFORE, in consideration of the foregoing and other good and valuable consideration, the receipt of which is hereby acknowledged, the parties hereto agree as follows:

1.   On or before 5:00 p.m. of the second business day after receipt of written notice from Regent that the closing under the contracts will occur:

   A.   Metropolitan shall deposit with TSI, in form and substance as required in the Metropolitan Contract:

      (1)   the Deed to Parcel 4;

      (2)   an Affidavit of Title;

      (3)   a FIRPTA Affidavit; and

      (4)   Wiring Instructions; and

      (5)   Pay Proceeds Letter.

   B.   Regent shall deposit with TSI, in form and substance as required in the Metropolitan Contract:

      (1)   The sum of $ [Amount to be agreed upon between Metropolitan and Regent prior to Metropolitan's obligation to make deposits] (the net purchase price under the Metropolitan Contract pursuant to item 1.C.1. hereof which shall be derived from the deposit by Turtle Wax provided for in Paragraph 1.I.(1) hereof, plus such additional amounts, which, notwithstanding anything to the contrary contained herein, shall be deposited by Regent, within fifteen business days after Turtle Wax makes said purchase price deposit, from the proceeds of loan [the "Loan"] to Regent from a lender [the "Lender"] selected by Regent); and

      (2)   the Deed to Parcel 3.

   C.   Metropolitan and Regent shall jointly deposit with TSI, in form and substance as required in the Metropolitan Contract:

      (1)   Closing Statements (3 originals) (which shall include among other things, a credit to Regent in the sum of $300.00 for title charges

and $18,240.00 for earnest money previously deposited by Regent with TSI and $365.00 for transfer stamps);

    (2)   ALTA Statements;

    (3)   State and County Transfer Declarations for the deeds deposited as items I.A.1. and I.B.2. hereof; and

    (4)   the Declaration of Easement.

    D.   Metropolitan and Regent shall also jointly deposit with TSI such other documents, including, without limitation, utility letters and GAP undertakings, as required by TSI to issue the "Regent Policy" and the "Metropolitan Policy" (as such terms are hereinafter defined).

    E.   Regent shall deposit with TSI the sum of $_____ (the net purchase price under the Johnson Contract pursuant to item 1.G.(1) hereof which shall be derived from the deposit by Turtle Wax provided for in Paragraph 1.I.(1) hereof, plus such additional amounts, which, notwithstanding anything to the contrary contained herein, shall be deposited by Regent within fifteen business days after Turtle Wax makes said purchase price deposit, from the proceeds of the Loan).

    F.   The Johnsons shall deposit with TSI in form and substance as required in the Johnson Contract:

    the Deed to Parcel 3 and Parcel 5 (previously deposited with TSI pursuant to the First Escrow Agreement);

    an Affidavit of Title;

    a FIRPTA Affidavit;

    a legal opinion from the Johnsons' Attorney; and

    the Johnson's forwarding address and social security numbers.

    G.   Regent and the Johnsons shall jointly deposit with TSI, in form and substance as required in the Johnson Contract:

    (1)   Closing Statements (3 originals) (which shall include among other things, a credit to Regent in the sum of $1,180.00, for title charges and survey costs, $580.00 for transfer stamps and $300.00 for the escrow fee hereunder);

(2)   ALTA Statements; and

(3)   State and County Transfer Declarations for the deed deposited as item 1.F.(1) hereof.

H.   Regent and the Johnsons shall also jointly deposit with TSI such other documents, including, without limitation, utility letters and GAP undertakings, as required by TSI to issue the Regent Policy.

I.   Turtle Wax shall deposit with TSI, in form and substance as required in the Turtle Wax Contract:

(1)   the sum of $_____ (the net purchase price under the Turtle Wax Contract pursuant to item 1.K.(1) hereof);

(2)   a Certified copy of Corporate Resolutions authorizing the purchase; and

(3)   a Certificate of Good Standing of Turtle Wax.

J.   Regent shall deposit with TSI, in form and substance as required in the Turtle Wax Contract:

(1)   a deed to the Turtle Wax Property;

(2)   a Certified Copy of Corporate Resolutions authorizing the sale;

(3)   a Certificate of Good Standing from Regent;

(4)   an Affidavit of Title; and

(5)   a FIRPTA Affidavit.

K.   Regent and Turtle Wax shall jointly deposit with TSI, in form and substance as required in the Turtle Wax Contract:

(1)   a Closing Statements (3 originals) (which shall include, among other things, a credit to Turtle Wax in the sum of $35,000.00 for earnest money previously deposited by Turtle Wax with TSI and $850.00 for transfer stamps);

(2)   ALTA Statements; and

(3)   State and County Transfer Declarations for the Turtle Wax Property.

L.   Regent and Turtle Wax shall also jointly deposit with TSI such other documents, including, without limitation, utility letters and GAP undertakings, as required by TSI to issue the "Turtle Wax Policy" (hereinafter defined).

2.   Upon receipt of all of the deposits to be made to TSI described in Paragraph 1 above (including notice from Metropolitan, Regent and Turtle Wax that the form of said deposits have been approved by them as in compliance with their respective Contracts) and when TSI, through Commonwealth Land Title Insurance Company, is prepared to issue the Regent Policy, the Metropolitan Policy, the Turtle Wax Policy and the "Loan Policy" (hereinafter defined) (subject only to "Regent's Notice" [hereinafter defined]), TSI shall notify Regent and its counsel, Kaplan & Miller ("K&M") by telecopy that all required deposits have been made, and upon receipt of a copy of the Plat of Subdivision for "Fox Valley East, Region 1, Unit No. 20, Aurora, DuPage County, Illinois" stamped by the Recorder's Office of DuPage County, Illinois, TSI is hereby authorized and directed to immediately:

A.   Record the following documents in the following order: (I) the deed deposited as item 1.A.(1) hereof; (ii) the deed deposited as item 1.F.(1) hereof; (iii) the deed deposited as item 1.B.(2) hereof, (iv) the Declaration of Easement; and (v) the deed to the Turtle Wax Property.

B.   Issue the Regent Policy to Regent, the Metropolitan Policy to Metropolitan, the Turtle Wax Policy to Turtle Wax and the Loan Policy to Lender (the closing to be a "New York style closing").

C.   Distribute the net purchase price to Metropolitan pursuant to the Closing Statement (item 1.C.(1) hereof) and disburse the net purchase price to the Johnson's pursuant to the Closing Statement (item 1.G.(1) hereof). The portion of the net purchase price to be disbursed to Regent pursuant to the Closing Statement (item 1.K.(1) hereof) and the portion of the net proceeds of the Loan to be disbursed to Regent pursuant to separate escrow instructions by and among Regent, Lender and TSI shall be applied to the purchase price deposits to be made by Regent pursuant to Paragraphs 1.B.(1) and 1.E. hereof, with any excess funds to be remitted to Regent.

D.   Deliver to Regent originals of items 1.A.(2), 1.A.(3), 1.C.(1), 1.F. (2), 1.F.(3), 1.F.(4), 1.G.(1), 1.I.(2), 1.I.(3), and 1.K.(1) deposited hereunder and photocopies of items 1.A.(1), 1.A.(4), 1.C.(2), 1.C.(3), 1.C.(4), 1.F.(1), 1.G.(2), 1.G.(3), 1.K.(2) and 1.K.(3) deposited hereunder.

E.   Deliver to Metropolitan an original of item 1.C.(1) deposited hereunder and photocopies of items 1.B.(2), 1.C.(2)., 1.C.(3) and 1.C.(4) deposited hereunder.

F.   Deliver to the Johnsons an original of item 1.G.(1) deposited hereunder and photocopies of items 1.G.(2) and 1.G.(3) deposited hereunder.

G.   Deliver to Turtle Wax originals of items 1.J.(2), 1.J.(3), 1.J.(4), 1.J.(5) and 1.K.(1) deposited hereunder and photocopies of items 1.A.(1), 1.C.(4), 1.J.(1), 1.K.(2) and 1.K.(3) deposited hereunder.

H.   Bill Regent for all title charges in connection with the Metropolitan Policy, the Regent Policy, the Turtle Wax Policy and the Loan Policy, $1,500.00 for its and the Johnson's portion of the "Escrow Fee" (hereinafter defined), and the charges for recording the deeds listed as items 1.A.(1) and 1.F.(1) hereof. Bill Metropolitan for the charges for recording the deed to Parcel 3 and $500.00 for its portion of the Escrow Fee. Bill Turtle Wax for the charges for recording the deed to the Turtle Wax Property and $500.00 for its portion of the Escrow Fee. The fee which TSI shall charge in connection with performing this Escrow Agreement shall equal the sum of $2,500.00 (the "Escrow Fee").

3.   If the closings under the Contracts do not occur within fifteen business days after any of the deposits referred to in Paragraph 1 hereof are made, then TSI shall return any deposits TSI has received to the party who has deposited same with TSI upon the written direction of such party after notifying the other parties hereto of such direction.

4.   The net purchase price deposited by Turtle Wax as item 1.I.(1) hereof shall be invested by TSI in a money market account with the interest thereon for the benefit of Turtle Wax, with the cost of investing such sum to be billed to Regent. The net proceeds of the Loan shall be invested as agreed to by Regent, Lender and TSI, with the interest thereof for the benefit of Regent or Lender as Regent and Lender directs TSI.

5.   Except as otherwise expressly provided for herein, all notices or deliveries to the parties hereto shall be made by hand delivery or by certified mail, postage prepaid,

return receipt requested, in the case of Regent to The Regent Group, 524 W. South Avenue, Chicago, Illinois 60610; in the case of Metropolitan to Metropolitan Diversified Properties, Inc., 1000 Barger Road, Oak Brook, Illinois; in the case of the Johnsons to Mr. and Mrs. Alan Johnson, 7S 780 Rt 59, Unincorporated DuPage County, Illinois; in the case of Turtle Wax to Turtle Wax, Inc., 5565 W. 72nd Street, Chicago, Illinois; and in the case of TSI to Title Services, Inc., 319 N. State Street, Chicago, Illinois.

6. As used herein, the term "Regent Policy" shall mean an Owner's Title Insurance Policy issued by Commonwealth Land Title Insurance Company in the form agreed to by Regent and TSI; the term "Metropolitan Policy" shall mean an Owner's Title Insurance Policy issued by Commonwealth Land Title Insurance Company in the form agreed to by Metropolitan and TSI; the term "Turtle Wax Policy" shall mean an Owner's Title Insurance Policy in the form agreed to by Turtle Wax and TSI; and the term "Lender's Policy" shall mean a Lender's Title Insurance Policy issued by Commonwealth Land Title Insurance in the form agreed to by Lender and TSI. The parties hereto expressly authorize Lender to receive a copy of this Escrow Agreement and authorize these instructions and any amendments hereto.

7. As used herein, the term "Regent's Notice" shall mean notice from K&M to the City of Aurora that all deposits necessary to effect the closings of the Contracts have been deposited pursuant to this Escrow Agreement, which notice shall be delivered in person or by facsimile machine addressed as follows: Mayor of Aurora, City of Aurora, 605 Downer Place, Aurora, Illinois.

8. Notwithstanding anything to the contrary contained in any of the Contracts, including, without limitation a statement in any of the Contracts that in the event of any inconsistency between the terms in the Contracts and any escrow agreement entered into that the terms of the Contracts shall control, the parties hereto agree that (i) the closings under the Contracts may occur no later than August 24, 1989, or such later date as agreed to in writing by all of the parties hereto, (ii) the mechanics of the closings shall occur as provided for in this Escrow Agreement and (iii) the Johnsons need not notify Regent of their intention to remain in possession of Parcel 3 and Parcel 5 until the day of closing under the Johnson Contract (the "Johnson Notice"). This Escrow Agreement shall not affect any of the agreements (except those relating to the date of

closing, the mechanics of closing and the Johnson Notice) between Regent and each of the other parties to the Metropolitan Contract, the Johnson Contract and the Turtle Wax Contract, all of which shall continue to be governed by the terms of the respective contracts. Nothing contained in this Escrow Agreement shall constitute any contract of agreement between or among Metropolitan, the Johnsons or Turtle Wax, each of which has executed this multi-party Escrow Agreement for the convenience of Regent in closing each of the transactions to which the other parties are party to.

9. This Escrow Agreement may be executed in counterparts, which taken together constitute one and the same instrument. Any amendment or supplement to this Escrow Agreement must be in writing and signed by the parties hereto.

IN WITNESS WHEREOF, the parties hereto have executed this Escrow Agreement on the date set forth above.

ESCROW TRUST INSTRUCTIONS

<u>TO</u>:

Title Services, Inc.   ("Escrowee")

319 N. State Street

Chicago, Illinois 60610

<u>FROM</u>:

First Mortgage Bank

423 N. Michigan Avenue

Chicago, Illinois 60690

First Mortgage Bank, (FMB), not personally but solely as Trustee of Trust No. 108049-04

("Trustee") and Fox Valley Auto Center Limited Partnership ("Beneficiary"), the sole

beneficiary thereof (collectively "Borrower")

By Kaplan & Miller

450 Wacker Drive

Chicago, Illinois 60606

A.   <u>Deposits of Borrower</u>

On or before August 2, 1989, Borrower will deposit:

     1.   Construction Mortgage and Security Agreement with Assignment of Rents from Trustee to FMB dated as of August 2, 1989 (the "Mortgage"), securing two notes in the aggregate face amount of $2,300,000 (the "Debt").

     2.   Assignment of Leases and Rents from Borrower to FMB (the "Assignment of Leases").

     3.   UCC-1 and UCC-2 Financing Statements from Borrower to FMB (the "Financing Statements").

     4.   Pay Proceeds Letter.

     5.   Such other documents as Commonwealth Land Title Insurance Company ("Commonwealth") requires of Borrower to issue the title insurance policy hereinafter described.

B.   <u>Deposits of FMB</u>

On or before August 2, 1989 FMB will deposit:

$491,300.00 being a portion of the proceeds of the Debt.

C. Recordation

When you are in receipt of all deposits you are instructed to record at once the Mortgage, the Assignment of Leases and the UCC-2 Financing Statements in the Office of the Recorder of DuPage County and to file the UCC-1 Financing Statements in the Office of the Secretary of State of Illinois.

D. Disbursement of Escrow

When you are unconditionally prepared to issue Commonwealth's ALTA Form Construction Loan Policy insuring FMB in the face amount of $2,300,000 insuring that the lien of the Mortgage is a first and prior lien on the premises described on Exhibit "A", subject only to the permitted exceptions set forth on Exhibit "B", containing the endorsements listed on Exhibit "C" (in form and substance satisfactory to FMB) and showing the matters described on Exhibit "D" as subordinate on Schedule B-Part II (the "Title Policy"), and FMB has advised you (which advice may be by telephone) that you may proceed as provided herein, you are authorized and directed to proceed as follows:

1. Deliver the Title Policy to FMB.

2. Deliver Deposits A1, A2, and A3, to FMB, after recordation.

3. Pay Borrower's title insurance, recording and escrow charges

3a. Pay FMB a Loan Fee in the amount of $23,000.00 [added by handwritten notation and initialed]

4. Pay FMB's attorney's fees, per invoice to be deposited with you on August 2, 1989.

5. Pay the balance of funds remaining herein pursuant to Borrower's instructions.

6. Issue yours and Commonwealth's bills, shown paid, for all title, escrow and recording charges, to Beneficiary.

E. Return of Deposits

In the event you are not prepared to disburse the said escrow funds pursuant to the above instructions on or before 1:00 p.m., August 4, 1989, then upon the written demand of FMB and without notice to any other party hereto, you are directed to return the total amount of funds deposited by FMB and all other deposits made herein to FMB. Upon your return of said funds to FMB (plus interest thereon), FMB will deliver to you duly executed releases of deposits nos. A1, A2 and A3.

In the absence of such written demand, you are directed to comply with these escrow instructions without reference to any date herein referred to unless directed otherwise by FMB.

F.   Business Day

Wherever under the terms and provisions of these Escrow Instructions the time for performance of a condition falls upon a Saturday, Sunday or holiday, such time for performance shall be extended to the next business day.

G.   Amendments

For the above purposes, amendments to these Escrow Instructions shall be considered the same as these Escrow Instructions.

H.   Investment

Except as to deposits of funds for which you have received express written direction concerning investment or other handling from FMB, you shall be under no duty to invest or reinvest any deposits at any time held by you hereunder you may commingle such deposits with other deposits or with your own funds in the manner provided for the administration of funds under Section 3 of the Illinois Trust Companies Act (Ch. 32, §289 Ill. Rev. Stat.), and you shall have no obligation to any party to pay any interest or earnings derived from such funds; provided, however, that nothing herein shall diminish your obligation to apply the full amount of the deposits in accordance with the terms of the Escrow Instructions, including interest thereon to the extent you have received express written direction from FMB for the investment thereof.

In the event you are requested to invest deposits hereunder, you are not responsible for any loss of principle or interest which may be incurred as a result of making the investments in accordance with such request or redeeming said investment for the purposes of this escrow.

I.   Entire Agreement; No Amendment of Agreement

These Escrow Trust Instructions constitute the entire agreement between Escrowee, on the one hand and Borrower and FMB on the other hand. It is understood and agreed upon among Borrower and FMB however, that the terms and provisions of these Escrow Trust Instructions shall in no event amend, or in any other respect modify, the rights and obligations of Borrower and FMB with respect to each other as set forth in the Construction Loan Agreement dated August 2, 1989 by and between FMB and Borrower, or the various documents evidencing or securing the Debt.

First Mortgage Bank

By: _____

Its Attorney

First Mortgage Bank, not personally but solely as Trustee of Trust No. 108049-04, and Fox

Valley Auto Center Limited Partnership, the sole beneficiary thereof

By: _____

Its Attorney

ACCEPTED AND AGREED TO:

TITLE SERVICES, INC.

Escrow Trustee

By: _____

Escrow Trustee Officer

94

EXHIBIT B

COMMONWEALTH
LAND TITLE INSURANCE COMPANY
MORTGAGE TITLE INSURANCE POLICY

SCHEDULE B

Part I

File: 111340   Policy Number: 411-978016

This policy does not insure against loss or damage by reason of the following:

1.   Taxes for 1989 and subsequent years, which are not yet due or payable.

PERMANENT REAL ESTATE TAX INDEX NO.   07-21-400-009

Affects: Premises in question and other property.   (Underlying land)

Total 1988 taxes – Paid

2.   Unrecorded easement for telephone facilities along the North line of Parcel 1 as disclosed by underground telephone lines as shown on Survey by Donahue and Thornhill, Inc. dated June 9, 1989 and by Utility Letter by Illinois Bell Telephone Company dated July 3, 1989.

3.   Possible easement for electric facilities along the North line of the land as disclosed by underground electric lines as shown on Survey by Donahue and Thornhill, Inc. dated June 9, 1989.

4.   Terms, provisions and conditions contained in Easement Grant:

Recorded: December 26, 1983

Document #: R33-94901

and Agreement:

Recorded: December 28, 1983

Document #: R83-94902

Relate to: Improvement of the Easement Parcel; construction and installation of water and sewer lines.

Affects: Parcel 2

5.   Terms, provisions and conditions contained in Declaration of Easement:

Recorded:

Document #:

Relate to: Maintenance, repair and reconstruction of the access road; costs of repair, maintenance and reconstruction of the access road.

Affects: Parcels 1 and 3

6. Rights of the adjoining owners to the concurrent use of said easement.

Affects: Parcels 2 and 3

7. Covenants, conditions and restrictions established by Trustee's

Deed;

Recorded:

Document #:

Relate to: Use of land; approval of construction plans; maintenance of premises and improvements; signs; uncompleted vacant building construction.

NOTE: Said covenants, conditions and restrictions do not provide for a reversion of title in the event of a breach thereof.

8. The land lies within the Aurora Sanitary District, which has accepted Federal Grants for sewage treatment works pursuant to Public Law 92-500. Federal law requires a user charge system separate from general ad valorem property taxes.

9. Pending disbursement of the full proceeds of the loan secured by the mortgage set forth under Item 4 of Schedule A hereof, this Policy insures only to the extent of the amount actually disbursed, but increases as each disbursement is made without knowledge of any defects in, or objection to, the title up to the face amount of the Policy.

10. Upon completion of the improvements in accordance with the plans and specifications prepared by _____ dated _____ the Company will issue its Comprehensive Form 100 Endorsement.

EXHIBIT C

Endorsements

Comprehensive

3.0 Zoning with Commitment to issue 3.1 (including parking).

Pending Disbursements.

Interim Certification for Mechanic's Liens.

Adjustable Interest Rate.

Access.

Usury.

Survey.

EXHIBIT D

1.   Assignment of Leases and Rents dated August 2, 1989 by and among Trustee, Beneficiary and FMB.

2.   Financing Statement: Debtor – Trustee

Secured Party – FMB

3.   Financing Statement: Debtor – Trustee

Secured Party – FMB

4.   An unrecorded lease dated _____, 1989, by and among Beneficiary, Trustee and Casey Muffler & Brake.

5.   An unrecorded lease dated _____, 1989, by and among Beneficiary, Trustee and Lube Pro's.

6.   An unrecorded lease dated _____, 1989, by and among Beneficiary, Trustee and Sparks Tune-Up.

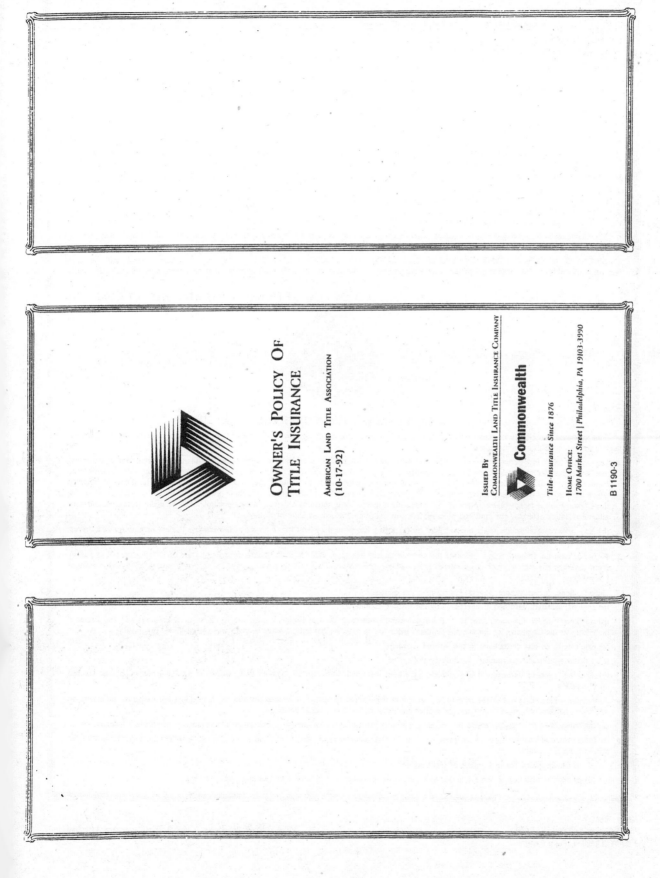

OWNER'S POLICY OF TITLE INSURANCE

AMERICAN LAND TITLE ASSOCIATION
(10-17-92)

ISSUED BY
COMMONWEALTH LAND TITLE INSURANCE COMPANY

Commonwealth

Title-Insurance Since 1876

HOME OFFICE:
1700 Market Street | Philadelphia, PA 19103-3990

B 1190-3

ISSUED BY
COMMONWEALTH LAND TITLE INSURANCE COMPANY

OWNER'S POLICY OF TITLE INSURANCE

Commonwealth

SUBJECT TO THE EXCLUSIONS FROM COVERAGE, THE EXCEPTIONS FROM COVERAGE CONTAINED IN SCHEDULE B AND THE CONDITIONS AND STIPULATIONS, COMMONWEALTH LAND TITLE INSURANCE COMPANY, a Pennsylvania corporation, herein called the Company, insures, as of Date of Policy shown in Schedule A, against loss or damage, not exceeding the Amount of Insurance stated in Schedule A, sustained or incurred by the insured by reason of:

1. Title to the estate or interest described in Schedule A being vested other than as stated therein;
2. Any defect in or lien or encumbrance on the title;
3. Unmarketability of the title;
4. Lack of a right of access to and from the land.

The Company will also pay the costs, attorneys' fees and expenses incurred in defense of the title, as insured, but only to the extent provided in the Conditions and Stipulations.

IN WITNESS WHEREOF, COMMONWEALTH LAND TITLE INSURANCE COMPANY has caused its corporate name and seal to be hereunto affixed by its duly authorized officers, the Policy to become valid when countersigned by an authorized officer or agent of the Company.

COMMONWEALTH LAND TITLE INSURANCE COMPANY

Attest: _James J. W. Lynch Jr._   By: _[signature]_

Secretary   President

EXCLUSIONS FROM COVERAGE

The following matters are expressly excluded from the coverage of this policy and the Company will not pay loss or damage, costs, attorneys' fees or expenses which arise by reason of:

1. (a) Any law, ordinance or governmental regulation (including but not limited to building and zoning laws, ordinances, or regulations) restricting, regulating, prohibiting or relating to (i) the occupancy, use, or enjoyment of the land; (ii) the character, dimensions or location of any improvement now or hereafter erected on the land; (iii) a separation in ownership or a change in the dimensions or area of the land or any parcel of which the land is or was a part; or (iv) environmental protection, or the affect of any violation of these laws, ordinances or governmental regulations, except to the extent that a notice of the enforcement thereof or a notice of a defect, lien or encumbrance resulting from a violation or alleged violation affecting the land has been recorded in the public records at Date of Policy.

   (b) Any governmental police power not excluded by (a) above, except to the extent that a notice of the exercise thereof or a notice of a defect, lien or encumbrance resulting from a violation or alleged violation affecting the land has been recorded in the public records at Date of Policy.

2. Rights of eminent domain unless notice of the exercise thereof has been recorded in the public records at Date of Policy, but not excluding from coverage any taking which has occurred prior to Date of Policy which would be binding on the rights of a purchaser for value without knowledge.

3. Defects, liens, encumbrances, adverse claims or other matters:

   (a) created, suffered, assumed or agreed to by the insured claimant;

   (b) not known to the Company, not recorded in the public records at Date of Policy, but known to the insured claimant and not disclosed in writing to the Company by the insured claimant prior to the date the insured claimant became an insured under this policy;

   (c) resulting in no loss or damage to the insured claimant;

   (d) attaching or created subsequent to Date of Policy; or

   (e) resulting in loss or damage which would not have been sustained if the insured claimant had paid value for the estate or interest insured by this policy.

4. Any claim, which arises out of the transaction vesting in the Insured the estate or interest insured by this policy, by reason of the operation of federal bankruptcy, state insolvency, or similar creditors' rights laws, that is based on:

   (a) the transaction creating the estate or interest insured by this policy being deemed a fraudulent conveyance or fraudulent transfer; or

   (b) the transaction creating the estate or interest insured by this policy being deemed a preferential transfer except where the preferential transfer results from the failure:

   (i) to timely record the instrument of transfer; or

   (ii) of such recordation to impart notice to a purchaser for value or a judgment or lien creditor.

NM 1   PA10
ALTA Owner's Policy (10-17-92)
Form 1190-1 Face Page

Valid Only If Schedules A and B and Cover Are Attached

ORIGINAL

CONDITIONS AND STIPULATIONS

1. DEFINITION OF TERMS.

The following terms when used in this policy mean:

(a) "insured": the insured named in Schedule A, and, subject to any rights or defenses the Company would have had against the named insured, those who succeed to the interest of the named insured by operation of law as distinguished from purchase including, but not limited to, heirs, distributees, devisees, survivors, personal representatives, next of kin, or corporate or fiduciary successors.

(b) "insured claimant": an insured claiming loss or damage.

(c) "knowledge" or "known": actual knowledge, not constructive knowledge or notice which may be imputed to an insured by reason of the public records as defined in this policy or any other records which impart constructive notice of matters affecting the land.

(d) "land": the land described or referred to in Schedule A, and improvements affixed thereto which by law constitute real property. The term "land" does not include any property beyond the lines of the area described or referred to in Schedule A, nor any right , title, interest, estate or easement in abutting streets, roads, avenues, alleys, lanes, ways or waterways, but nothing herein shall modify or limit the extent to which a right of access to and from the land is insured by this policy.

(e) "mortgage": mortgage, deed of trust, trust deed, or other security instrument.

(f) "public records": records established under state statutes at Date of Policy for the purpose of imparting constructive notice of matters relating to real property to purchasers for value and without knowledge. With respect to Section 1(a) (iv) of the Exclusions From Coverage, "public records" shall also include environmental protection liens filed in the records of the clerk of the United States district court for the district in which the land is located.

(g) "unmarketability of the title": an alleged or apparent matter affecting the title to the land, not excluded or excepted from coverage, which would entitle a purchaser of the estate or interest described in Schedule A to be released from the obligation to purchase by virtue of a contractual condition requiring the delivery of marketable title.

2. CONTINUATION OF INSURANCE AFTER CONVEYANCE OF TITLE.

The coverage of this policy shall continue in force as of Date of Policy in favor of an insured only so long as the insured retains an estate or interest in the land, or holds an indebtedness secured by a purchase money mortgage given by a purchaser from the insured, or only so long as the insured shall have liability by reason of covenants of warranty made by the insured in any transfer or conveyance of the estate or interest. This policy shall not continue in force in favor of any purchaser from the insured of either (i) an estate or interest in the land, or (ii) an indebtedness secured by a purchase money mortgage given to the insured.

3. NOTICE OF CLAIM TO BE GIVEN BY INSURED CLAIMANT.

The insured shall notify the Company promptly in writing (i) in case of any litigation as set forth in Section 4(a) below, (ii) in case knowledge shall come to an insured hereunder of any claim of title or interest which is adverse to the title to the estate or interest, as insured, and which might cause loss or damage for which the Company may be liable by virtue of this policy, or (iii) if title to the estate or interest, as insured, is rejected as unmarketable. If prompt notice shall not be given to the Company, then as to the insured all liability of the Company shall terminate with regard to the matter or matters for which prompt notice is required; provided, however, that failure to notify the Company shall in no case prejudice the rights of any insured under this policy unless the Company shall be prejudiced by the failure and then only to the extent of the prejudice.

4. DEFENSE AND PROSECUTION OF ACTIONS; DUTY OF INSURED CLAIMANT TO COOPERATE.

(a) Upon written request by the insured and subject to the options contained in Section 6 of these Conditions and Stipulations, the Company, at its own cost and without unreasonable delay, shall provide for the defense of an insured in litigation in which any third party asserts a claim adverse to the title or interest as insured, but only as to those stated causes of action alleging a defect, lien or encumbrance or other matter insured against by this policy. The Company shall have the right to select counsel of its choice (subject to the right of the insured to object for reasonable cause) to represent the insured as to those stated causes of action and shall not be liable for and will not pay the fees of any other counsel. The Company will not pay any fees, costs or expenses incurred by the insured in the defense of those causes of action which allege matters not insured against by this policy.

(b) The Company shall have the right, at its own cost, to institute and prosecute any action or proceeding or to do any other act which in its opinion may be necessary or desirable to establish the title to the estate or interest, as insured, or to prevent or reduce loss or damage to the insured. The Company may take any appropriate action under the terms of this policy, whether or not it shall be liable hereunder, and shall not thereby concede liability or waive any provision of this policy. If the Company shall exercise its rights under this paragraph, it shall do so diligently.

(c) Whenever the Company shall have brought an action or interposed a defense as required or permitted by the provisions of this policy, the Company may pursue any litigation to final determination by a court of competent jurisdiction and expressly reserves the right, in its sole discretion, to appeal from any adverse judgment or order.

(d) In all cases where this policy permits or requires the Company to prosecute or provide for the defense of any action or proceeding, the insured shall secure to the Company the right to so prosecute or provide defense in the action or proceeding, and all appeals therein, and permit the Company to use, at its option, the name of the insured for this purpose. Whenever requested by the Company, the insured, at the Company's expense, shall give the Company all reasonable aid (i) in any action or proceeding, securing evidence, obtaining witnesses, prosecuting or defending the action or proceeding, or effecting settlement, and (ii) in any other lawful act which in the opinion of the Company may be necessary or desirable to establish the title to the estate or interest as insured. If the Company is prejudiced by the failure of the insured to furnish the required cooperation, the Company's obligations to the insured under the policy shall terminate, including any liability or obligation to defend, prosecute, or continue any litigation, with regard to the matter or matters requiring such cooperation.

5. PROOF OF LOSS OR DAMAGE.

In addition to and after the notices required under Section 3 of these Conditions and Stipulations have been provided the Company, a proof of loss or damage signed and sworn to by the insured claimant shall be furnished to the Company within 90 days after the insured claimant shall ascertain the facts giving rise to the loss or damage. The proof of loss or damage shall describe the defect in, or lien or encumbrance on the title, or other matter insured against by this policy which constitutes the basis of loss or damage and shall state, to the extent possible, the basis of calculating the amount of the loss or damage. If the Company is prejudiced by the failure of the insured claimant to provide the required proof of loss or damage, the Company's obligations to the insured under the policy shall terminate, including any liability or obligation to defend, prosecute, or continue any litigation, with regard to the matter or matters requiring such proof of loss or damage.

In addition, the insured claimant may reasonably be required to submit to examination under oath by any authorized representative of the Company and shall produce for examination, inspection and copying, at such reasonable times and places as may be designated by any authorized representative of the Company, all records, books, ledgers, checks, correspondence and memoranda, whether bearing a date before or after Date of Policy, which reasonably pertain to the loss or damage. Further, if requested by any authorized representative of the Company , the insured claimant shall grant its permission, in writing, for any authorized representative of the Company to examine , inspect and copy all records, books, ledgers, checks, correspondence and memoranda in the custody or control of a third party, which reasonably pertain to the loss or damage. All information designated as confidential by the insured claimant provided to the Company pursuant to this Section shall not be disclosed to others unless, in the reasonable judgement of the Company, it is necessary in the administration of the claim. Failure of the insured claimant to submit for examination under oath, produce other reasonably requested information or grant permission to secure reasonably necessary information from third parties as required in this paragraph shall terminate any liability of the Company under this policy as to that claim.

6. OPTIONS TO PAY OR OTHERWISE SETTLE CLAIMS; TERMINATION OF LIABILITY.

In case of a claim under this policy, the Company shall have the following additional options:

(a)To Pay or Tender Payment of the Amount of Insurance.

To pay or tender payment of the amount of insurance under this policy together with any costs, attorneys' fees and expenses incurred by the insured claimant, which were authorized by the Company, up to the time of payment or tender of payment and which the Company is obligated to pay.

Upon the exercise by the Company of this option, all liability and obligations to the insured under this policy, other than to make the payment required, shall terminate, including any liability or obligation to defend, prosecute, or continue any litigation, and the policy shall be surrendered to the Company for cancellation.

(b) To Pay or Otherwise Settle With Parties Other than the Insured or With the Insured Claimant.

(i) to pay or otherwise settle with other parties for or in the name of an insured claimant any claim insured against under this policy, together with any costs, attorneys' fees and expenses incurred by the insured claimant which were authorized by the Company up to time of payment and which the Company is obligated to pay; or

(ii) to pay or otherwise settle with the insured claimant the loss or damage provided for under this policy, together with any costs, attorneys' fees and expenses incurred by the insured claimant which were authorized by the Company up to the time of payment and which the Company is obligated to pay.

Upon the exercise by the Company of either of the options provided for in paragraphs (b)(i) or (ii), the Company's obligations to the insured under this policy for the claimed loss or damage, other than the payments required to be made, shall terminate, including any liability or obligation to defend, prosecute or continue any litigation.

Conditions and Stipulations Continued Inside Cover

B 1190-1

CONTROL NO. 206-168672

61711

CONDITIONS AND STIPULATIONS

7. DETERMINATION, EXTENT OF LIABILITY AND COINSURANCE.

This policy is a contract of indemnity against actual monetary loss or damage sustained or incurred by the insured claimant who has suffered loss or damage by reason of matters insured against by this policy and only to the extent herein described.

(a) The liability of the Company under this policy shall not exceed the least of:

(i) the Amount of Insurance stated in Schedule A; or,

(ii) the difference between the value of the insured estate or interest as insured and the value of the insured estate or interest subject to the defect, lien or encumbrance insured against by this policy.

(b) In the event the Amount of Insurance stated in Schedule A at the Date of Policy is less than 80 percent of the value of the insured estate or interest or the full consideration paid for the land, whichever is less, or if subsequent to the Date of Policy an improvement is erected on the land which increases the value of the insured estate or interest by at least 20 percent over the Amount of Insurance stated in Schedule A, then this Policy is subject to the following:

(i) where no subsequent improvement has been made, as to any partial loss, the Company shall only pay the loss pro rata in the proportion that the amount of insurance at Date of Policy bears to the total value of the insured estate or interest at Date of Policy; or

(ii) where a subsequent improvement has been made, as to any partial loss, the Company shall only pay the loss pro rata in the proportion that 120 percent of the Amount of Insurance stated in Schedule A bears to the sum of the Amount of Insurance stated in Schedule A and the amount expended for the improvement.

The provisions of this paragraph shall not apply to costs, attorneys' fees and expenses for which the Company is liable under this policy, and shall only apply to that portion of any loss which exceeds, in the aggregate, 10 percent of the Amount of Insurance stated in Schedule A.

(c) The Company will pay only those costs, attorneys' fees and expenses incurred in accordance with Section 4 of these Conditions and Stipulations.

8. APPORTIONMENT.

If the land described in Schedule A consists of two or more parcels which are not used as a single site, and a loss is established affecting one or more of the parcels but not all, the loss shall be computed and settled on a pro rata basis as if the amount of insurance under this policy was divided pro rata as to the value on Date of Policy of each separate parcel to the whole, exclusive of any improvements made subsequent to Date of Policy, unless a liability or value has otherwise been agreed upon as to each parcel by the Company and the insured at the time of the issuance of this policy and shown by an express statement or by an endorsement attached to this policy.

9. LIMITATION OF LIABILITY.

(a) If the Company establishes the title, or removes the alleged defect, lien or encumbrance, or cures the lack of a right of access to or from the land, or cures the claim of unmarketability of title, all as insured, in a reasonably diligent manner by any method, including litigation and the completion of any appeals therefrom, it shall have fully performed its obligations with respect to that matter and shall not be liable for any loss or damage caused thereby.

(b) In the event of any litigation, including litigation by the Company or with the Company's consent, the Company shall have no liability for loss or damage until there has been a final determination by a court of competent jurisdiction, and disposition of all appeals therefrom, adverse to the title as insured.

(c) The Company shall not be liable for loss or damage to any insured for liability voluntarily assumed by the insured in settling any claim or suit without the prior written consent of the Company.

10. REDUCTION OF INSURANCE; REDUCTION OR TERMINATION OF LIABILITY.

All payments under this policy, except payments made for costs, attorneys' fees and expenses, shall reduce the amount of the insurance pro tanto.

11. LIABILITY NONCUMULATIVE

It is expressly understood that the amount of insurance under this policy shall be reduced by any amount the Company may pay under any policy insuring a mortgage to which exception is taken in Schedule B or to which the insured has agreed, assumed, or taken subject, or which is hereafter executed by an insured and which is a charge or lien on the estate or interest described or referred to in Schedule A, and the amount so paid shall be deemed a payment under this policy to the insured owner.

12. PAYMENT OF LOSS.

(a) No payment shall be made without producing this policy for endorsement of the payment unless the policy has been lost or destroyed, in which case proof of loss or destruction shall be furnished to the satisfaction of the Company.

(b) When liability and the extent of loss or damage has been definitely fixed in accordance with these Conditions and Stipulations, the loss or damage shall be payable within 30 days thereafter.

13. SUBROGATION UPON PAYMENT OR SETTLEMENT.

(a) The Company's Right of Subrogation.

Whenever the Company shall have settled and paid a claim under this policy, all right of subrogation shall vest in the Company unaffected by any act of the insured claimant.

The Company shall be subrogated to and be entitled to all rights and remedies which the insured claimant would have had against any person or property in respect to the claim had this policy not been issued. If requested by the Company, the insured claimant shall transfer to the Company all rights and remedies against any person or property necessary in order to perfect this right of subrogation. The insured claimant shall permit the Company to sue, compromise or settle in the name of the insured claimant and to use the name of the insured claimant in any transaction or litigation involving these rights or remedies.

If a payment on account of a claim does not fully cover the loss of the insured claimant, the Company shall be subrogated to these rights and remedies in the proportion which the Company's payment bears to the whole amount of the loss.

If loss should result from any act of the insured claimant, as stated above, that act shall not void this policy, but the Company, in that event, shall be required to pay only that part of any losses insured against by this policy which shall exceed the amount, if any, lost to the Company by reason of the impairment by the insured claimant of the Company's right of subrogation.

(b) The Company's Rights Against Non-insured Obligors.

The Company's right of subrogation against non-insured obligors shall exist and shall include, without limitation, the rights of the insured to indemnities, guaranties, other policies of insurance or bonds, notwithstanding any terms or conditions contained in those instruments which provide for subrogation rights by reason of this policy.

14. ARBITRATION

Unless prohibited by applicable law, either the Company or the insured may demand arbitration pursuant to the Title Insurance Arbitration Rules of the American Arbitration Association. Arbitrable matters may include, but are not limited to, any controversy or claim between the Company and the insured arising out of or relating to this policy, any service of the Company in connection with its issuance or the breach of a policy provision or other obligation. All arbitrable matters when the Amount of Insurance is $1,000,000 or less shall be arbitrated at the option of either the Company or the insured. All arbitrable matters when the Amount of Insurance is in excess of $1,000,000 shall be arbitrated only when agreed to by both the Company and the insured. Arbitration pursuant to this policy and under the Rules in effect on the date the demand for arbitration is made or, at the option of the insured, the Rules in effect at Date of Policy shall be binding upon the parties. The award may include attorneys' fees only if the laws of the state in which the land is located permit a court to award attorneys' fees to a prevailing party. Judgment upon the award rendered by the Arbitrator(s) may be entered in any court having jurisdiction thereof.

The law of the situs of the land shall apply to an arbitration under the Title Insurance Arbitration Rules.

A copy of the Rules may be obtained from the Company upon request.

15. LIABILITY LIMITED TO THIS POLICY; POLICY ENTIRE CONTRACT.

(a) This policy together with all endorsements, if any, attached hereto by the Company is the entire policy and contract between the insured and the Company. In interpreting any provision of this policy, this policy shall be construed as a whole.

(b) Any claim of loss or damage, whether or not based on negligence, and which arises out of the status of the title to the estate or interest covered hereby or by any action asserting such claim, shall be restricted to this policy.

(c) No amendment of or endorsement to this policy can be made except by a writing endorsed hereon or attached hereto signed by either the President, a Vice President, the Secretary, an Assistant Secretary, or validating officer or authorized signatory of the Company.

16. SEVERABILITY.

In the event any provision of the policy is held invalid or unenforceable under applicable law, the policy shall be deemed not to include that provision and all other provisions shall remain in full force and effect.

17. NOTICES, WHERE SENT.

All notices required to be given the Company and any statement in writing required to be furnished the Company shall include the number of this policy and shall be addressed to COMMONWEALTH LAND TITLE INSURANCE COMPANY, 1700 Market Street, Philadelphia, PA 19103-3990.

NM 1 PA 10
ALTA Owner's Policy (10-17-92)
Form 1190-3 Cover Page

ORIGINAL

Valid Only If Face Page, Schedules A and B Are Attached

Commonwealth

TITLE SERVICES, INC.

610 E. Roosevelt Road
P.O. Box 430
Wheaton, IL. 60189—0430
(312) —690—9130

OWNER'S TITLE INSURANCE POLICY
SCHEDULE A

File: 111340

Date of Policy: August 3, 1989

Policy Number: 107—330846

Amount of Policy: $2,300,000.00

1.   Name of Insured:

 ***FIRST MORTGAGE BANK , AS TRUSTEE UNDER TRUST AGREEMENT
 DATED APRIL 11, 1989 AND KNOWN AS TRUST #1O8O49-O4***

2.   The estate or interest in the land covered by this policy is fee simple, except as
indicated at Item #4 below.

3.   Title to the estate or interest covered by this policy at the date hereof is vested in
the Insured.

4.   The land referred to in this policy is described as follows:

(SEE ATTACHED)

This policy valid only if Schedule B is attached.

SCHEDULE A LEGAL DESCRIPTION

***PARCEL 1:

LOT 1 IN FOX VALLEY EAST, REGION 1, UNIT NO. 20, BEING A SUBDIVISION OF
PART OF THE SOUTHEAST QUARTER OF SECTION 21, AND PART OF THE NORTH EAST
QUARTER OF SECTION 28, TOWNSHIP 38 NORTH, RANGE 9, EAST OF THE THIRD
PRINCIPAL MERIDIAN, ACCORDING TO THE PLAT THEREOF RECORDED AUGUST 2, 1989
AS DOCUMENT R89-093679, IN DUPAGE COUNTY, ILLINOIS.

PARCEL 2:

EASEMENT APPURTENANT TO PARCEL 1 FOR INGRESS AND EGRESS AS CREATED BY
EASEMENT GRANT RECORDED DECEMBER 28, 1983 AS DOCUMENT R83-94901 AND
AGREEMENT RECORDED DECEMBER 28, 1983 AS DOCUMENT R83-94902. SAID
EASEMENT DESCRIBED AS FOLLOWS:

THAT PART OF THE NORTHEAST QUARTER OF SECTION 28, TOWNSHIP 38 NORTH,
RANGE 9 EAST OF THE THIRD PRINCIPAL MERIDIAN DESCRIBED AS FOLLOWS:
COMMENCING AT THE NORTHEAST CORNER OF SAID SECTION 28; THENCE NORTH 86
DEGREES 57 MINUTES 52 SECONDS WEST ALONG THE NORTH LINE OF SAID SECTION
28 AS MONUMENTED AND OCCUPIED 48.83 FEET TO THE WESTERLY RIGHT OF WAY
LINE OF ILLINOIS STATE ROUTE NO. 59; THENCE SOUTH 4 DEGREES 55 MINUTES 49
SECONDS WEST ALONG SAID RIGHT OF WAY LINE 33.0 FEET FOR A POINT OF
BEGINNING; THENCE NORTH 84 DEGREES 31 MINUTES 30 SECONDS WEST 310.35 FEET
TO A POINT ON THE WESTERLY LINE (AS MONUMENTED AND OCCUPIED) OF A TRACT
-OF LAND CONVEYED TO THE SCHOOL TRUSTEES OF DUPAGE COUNTY THAT IS 20.0
FEET SOUTHERLY OF THE NORTHWEST CORNER OF SAID TRACT (AS MONUMENTED AND
OCCUPIED); THENCE SOUTH 5 DEGREES 37 MINUTES 28 SECONDS EAST ALONG SAID
WESTERLY LINE 40.76 FEET TO A LINE DRAWN PARALLEL WITH AND 40.0 FEET
SOUTHERLY OF THE LAST DESCRIBED COURSE (MEASURED AT RIGHT ANGLES
THERETO); THENCE SOUTH 84 DEGREES 31 MINUTES 30 SECONDS EAST ALONG SAID
PARALLEL LINE 302.88 FEET TO SAID WESTERLY RIGHT OF WAY LINE; THENCE
NORTH 4 DEGREES 55 MINUTES 49 SECONDS EAST ALONG SAID RIGHT OF WAY LINE
40.0 FEET TO THE POINT OF BEGINNING IN NAPERVILLE TOWNSHIP, DUPAGE COUNTY,
ILLINOIS.

This policy valid only if Schedule B is attached.

page 2

PARCEL 3:

EASEMENT APPURTENANT TO PARCEL 1 OVER, ACROSS AND UPON THE ACCESS ROAD FOR
ACCESS, INGRESS AND EGRESS FROM PARCEL 1 TO SOUTH ROAD ON THE NORTH AND
WESTBROOK DRIVE EXTENSION TO THE SOUTH AS CREATED BY DECLARATION OF
EASEMENT RECORDED AUGUST 3, 1989 AS DOCUMENT R89-093712. SAID
ACCESS ROAD DESCRIBED AS FOLLOWS:

THAT PART OF THE SOUTHEAST QUARTER OF SECTION 21, TOWNSHIP 38 NORTH.
RANGE 9 EAST OF THE THIRD PRINCIPAL MERIDIAN DESCRIBED AS FOLLOWS:
COMMENCING AT THE MOST NORTHERLY CORNER OF FOX VALLEY EAST, REGION 1,
UNIT NO. 2, AURORA, DUPAGE COUNTY, ILLINOIS; THENCE EASTERLY ALONG THE
SOUTHERLY LINE OF SOUTH ROAD 425.40 FEET FOR A POINT OF BEGINNING; THENCE
SOUTHERLY AT RIGHT ANGLES TO THE SOUTH LINE (AS MONUMENTED) OF A TRACT OF
LAND CONVEYED TO LA VERNE W. JACKSON AND CLARA L. JACKSON BY DOCUMENT
747981 RECORDED MARCH 2, 1955, 361.54 FEET TO SAID SOUTH LINE; THENCE
WESTERLY ALONG SAID SOUTH LINE AT RIGHT ANGLES TO THE LAST DESCRIBED
COURSE 15.0 FEET; THENCE NORTHERLY PARALLEL WITH THE PENULTIMATE
DESCRIBED COURSE 358.29 FEET TO THE SOUTHERLY LINE OF SAID SOUTH ROAD;
THENCE EASTERLY ALONG SAID SOUTHERLY LINE 15.35 FEET TO THE POINT OF
BEGINNING, IN THE CITY OF AURORA, DUPAGE COUNTY, ILLINOIS.

ALSO

THAT PART OF THE SOUTHEAST QUARTER OF SECTION 21, TOWNSHIP 38 NORTH,
RANGE 9 EAST OF THE THIRD PRINCIPAL MERIDIAN DESCRIBED AS FOLLOWS:
COMMENCING AT THE MOST NORTHERLY CORNER OF FOX VALLEY EAST, REGION 1,
UNIT NO.- 2, AURORA, DUPAGE COUNTY, ILLINOIS; THENCE EASTERLY ALONG THE
SOUTHERLY LINE OF SOUTH ROAD 425.40 FEET FOR A POINT OF BEGINNING; THENCE
SOUTHERLY AT RIGHT ANGLES TO THE SOUTH LINE (AS MONUMENTED) OF A TRACT OF
LAND CONVEYED TO LA VERNE W. JACKSON AND CLARA L. JACKSON BY DOCUMENT
747981 RECORDED MARCH 2, 1955, 361.54 FEET TO SAID SOUTH LINE; THENCE
EASTERLY ALONG SAID SOUTH LINE AT RIGHT ANGLES TO THE LAST DESCRIBED
COURSE 15.0 FEET; THENCE NORTHERLY PARALLEL WITH THE PENULTIMATE
DESCRIBED COURSE 364.75 FEET TO THE SOUTHERLY LINE OF SAID SOUTH ROAD;
THENCE WESTERLY ALONG SAID SOUTHERLY LINE 15.34 FEET TO THE POINT OF
BEGINNING, IN THE CITY OF AURORA, DUPAGE COUNTY, ILLINOIS.

This policy valid only if Schedule B is attached.

page 3

SCHEDULE A - LEGAL DESCRIPTION CONTINUED... PARCEL 4:

EASEMENT APPURTENANT TO PARCEL 1 FOR INGRESS AND EGRESS AS CREATED BY
EASEMENT GRANT RECORDED AUGUST 3, 1989 AS DOCUMENT NUMBER R89-093714.
SAID EASEMENT DESCRIBED AS FOLLOWS:

THAT PART OF LOT 1, FOX VALLEY EAST, REGION 1, UNIT NO. 20, AURORA,
DUPAGE COUNTY, ILLINOIS DESCRIBED AS FOLLOWS: COMMENCING AT THE
SOUTHWEST CORNER OF SAID LOT; THENCE EASTERLY ALONG THE SOUTH LINE OF
SAID LOT 15.0 FEET FOR A POINT OF BEGINNING; THENCE NORTHERLY PARALLEL
WITH THE WEST LINE OF SAID LOT 15.0 FEET; THENCE EASTERLY TO A POINT ON
THE EAST LINE OF SAID LOT THAT IS 13.0 FEET NORTHERLY OF THE SOUTHEAST
CORNER OF SAID LOT; THENCE SOUTHERLY ALONG SAID EAST LINE 13.0 FEET TO
SAID SOUTHEAST CORNER; THENCE WESTERLY ALONG THE SOUTH LINE OF SAID LOT
424.24 FEET TO THE POINT OF BEGINNING, IN THE CITY OF AURORA, DU PAGE
COUNTY, ILLINOIS.

                         AND ALSO;

THAT PART OF LOT 2, FOX VALLEY EAST, REGION 1, UNIT NO. 20 AURORA, DUPAGE
COUNTY, ILLINOIS DESCRIBED AS FOLLOWS: COMMENCING AT THE NORTHWEST
CORNER OF SAID LOT; THENCE EASTERLY ALONG THE NORTH LINE OF SAID LOT 15.0
FEET FOR A POINT OF BEGINNING; THENCE SOUTHERLY PARALLEL WITH THE WEST
LINE OF SAID LOT 15.0 FEET; THENCE EASTERLY TO A POINT ON THE EAST LINE
OF SAID LOT THAT IS 16.0 FEET SOUTHERLY OF THE NORTHEAST CORNER OF SAID
LOT; THENCE NORTHERLY ALONG SAID EAST LINE 16.0 FEET TO SAID NORTHEAST
CORNER; THENCE WESTERLY ALONG SAID NORTH LINE 424.24 FEET TO THE POINT OF
BEGINNING, IN THE CITY OF AURORA, DUPAGE COUNTY, ILLINOIS.***

This policy valid only if Schedule B is attached.

Commonwealth

OWNER'S TITLE INSURANCE POLICY

SCHEDULE B

File: 111340   Policy Number: 107-330846

This policy does not insure against loss or damage by reason of the following:
1.:   Taxes for 1989 and subsequent years, which are not yet due or payable

PERMANENT REAL ESTATE TAX INDEX NO.   07-21-400-009
Affects: Premises in question and other property. (Underlying land)
Total 1988 taxes – Paid

2.:   Unrecorded easement for telephone facilities along the North line of Parcel 1 as disclosed
by underground telephone lines as shown on Survey by Donahue and Thornhill, Inc. dated
June 9, 1989 and by Utility Letter by Illinois Bell Telephone Company dated July 3, 1989.

3.:   Possible easement for electric facilities along the North line of the land as disclosed by
underground electric lines as shown on Survey by Donahue and Thornhill, Inc. dated June
9, 1989.

4.:   Terms, provisions and conditions contained in Easement Grant:
Recorded: December 28, 1983
Document #: R83-94901
and Agreement:
Recorded: December 28, 1983
Document #: R83-94902
Relate to: Improvement of the Easement Parcel; construction and installation of water and
sewer lines.
Affects: Parcel 2

5.:   Terms, provisions and conditions contained in Declaration of Easement:
Easement:
Recorded: August 3, 1989
Document #: R89-093712
Relate to: Maintenance, repair and reconstruction of the access road; costs
of repair, maintenance and reconstruction of the access road.
Affects: Parcels 1 and 3
6.:   Rights of the adjoining owners to the concurrent use of said easement.
Affects: Parcels 2 and 3

7.:   Covenants, conditions and restrictions established by Trustee's
Deed:
Recorded: August 3, 1989

Document #:   R89-093709
Relate to: Use of land; approval of construction plans; maintenance of premises and
improvements; signs; uncompleted vacant building construction.
NOTE: Said covenants, conditions and restrictions do not provide for a
reversion of title in the event of a breach thereof.

8.:   The land lies within the Aurora Sanitary District which has accepted Federal Grants for
       sewage treatment works pursuant to Public Law 92-500. Federal law requires a user
       charge system separate from general ad valorem property taxes.

9.:   Terms, powers, provisions and limitations of the Trust under which title to
       Insured premises is held.

10.: Any lien or right to lien for improvements furnished to the property on or
       after the effective date of this Policy.

11.   A Construction Mortgage and Security Agreement with Assignment of Rents to secure an
       indebtedness in the amount state herein:
       Mortgagor: First Mortgage Bank, as Trustee under Trust Agreement
       dated April 11, 1989 and known as Trust #108049-04.
       Mortgagee: First Mortgage Bank
       Dated: August 2, 1989
       Recorded:August 3, 1989
       Document #:R89-093715
       Original amount $ 2,300,000.00

12.: An Assignment of Leases and Rents to further secure an indebtedness:
       Assignor: First Mortgage Bank, as Trustee under Trust Agreement dated
       April 11, 1989 and known as Trust #108049-04 and Fox Valley Auto Care
       Center Limited Partnership
       Designee: First Mortgage Bank
       Dated: August 3, 1989
       Document # : R89-093716

13. Financing Statement:
    Debtor: First Mortgage Bank, as Trustee under Trust Agreement dated
    April 11, 1989 and known as Trust #108049-04
    Secured Party: First Mortgage Bank
    Filed: August 3, 1989
    Document #:89U-4281
    Recorded:August 3, 1989
    Document #:R89-93717

14. Financing Statement:
    Debtor: Fox Valley Auto Care Center Limited
    Secured Party: First Mortgage Bank
    Filed: August 3, 1989
    Document #:89U-4281
    Recorded:August 3, 1989

15. Terms, provisions and conditions contained in Easement Grant:
    Recorded:August 3, 1989
    Document #:R89-093714
    Relate to Use, maintenance and repair of the easement premises; parking,
    stacking and loading
    Affects: Parcels 1 and 4

ENDORSEMENT #1

To be annexed to and form a part of Policy No. 107-330846 insuring

***FIRST MORTGAGE BANK, AS TRUSTEE UNDER TRUST AGREEMENT DATED
APRIL 11, 1989 AND KNOWN AS TRUST #108049-04***
as set forth in said Policy.

The said Policy is hereby amended in the following manner:

This Policy insures the Insured that the property depicted in the survey by
Donahue and Thornhill, Inc. dated June 10, 1989 is the same property described
in Schedule A herein.

IN WITNESS WHEREOF COMMONWEALTH LAND TITLE INSURANCE COMPANY has
caused its corporate name and seal to be hereunto affixed on August 3, 1989.

Commonwealth

ENDORSEMENT #2

To be annexed to and form a part of Policy No.   107-330846 insuring

*** FIRST MORTGAGE BANK, AS TRUSTEE UNDER TRUST
AGREEMENT DATED APRIL 11, 1989 AND KNOWN AS TRUST #108049-
04***
as set forth in said Policy.

The said Policy is hereby amended in the following manner:

The Company hereby insures the insured that any tax sale of the general real estate taxes
affecting the land underlying the easements insured herein, or any tax deed issued pursuant to
any such tax sale, will not result in the loss or termination of said easements.

The coverage extended by this endorsement is not applicable if the land underlying the
easements insured herein becomes a separately taxed parcel of property and a tax deed is issued
solely because of the non-payment of such separate tax.

IN WITNESS WHEREOF COMMONWEALTH LAND TITLE INSURANCE COMPANY has
caused its corporate name and seal to be hereunto affixed on August 3, 1989

ISSUED BY
COMMONWEALTH LAND TITLE INSURANCE COMPANY

Commonwealth

ENDORSEMENT #3

To be annexed to and form a part of Policy No.   107-330846 insuring

*** FIRST MORTGAGE BANK, AS TRUSTEE UNDER TRUST
AGREEMENT DATED APRIL 11, 1989 AND KNOWN AS TRUST #108049-
04***
as set forth in said Policy.

The said Policy is hereby amended in the following manner:

The Policy insures that the sewer lines, water lines and street paving as contained in Grant and
Agreement shown in Schedule B as Item 4 have been installed in accordance with the plans and
specifications as specified in said instruments and the terms and provisions contained therein
have complied with.

IN WITNESS WHEREOF COMMONWEALTH LAND TITLE INSURANCE COMPANY has
caused its corporate name and seal to be hereunto affixed on August 3, 1989

Commonwealth

ENDORSEMENT #4 - ALTA ENDORSEMENT FORM – 3.1

Attached to and made a part of Policy Number 107-330846

1. The Company insures the insured against loss or damage sustained by reason of any incorrectness in the assurance that, at Date of Policy:
   (a) According to applicable zoning ordinances and amendments thereto, the land is classified Zone Planned Development District.
   (b) The following use or uses are allowed under that classification:
   An approximately 18,900 square foot automobile care center, to house a mixture of retail and automotive services uses.

2. The Company further insures against loss or damage arising from a final decree of a court of competent jurisdiction.
   (a) prohibiting the use of the land, with the construction thereon of any structure in accordance with the plans and specifications described in Paragraph 2(b) below, as specified in Paragraph 1(b): or
   (b) requiring the removal or alteration of said structure on the basis that, the construction of said structure violates said ordinances and amendments thereto as said ordinances and amendments appear on the Date of Policy with respect to any of the following matters:
   (i)   Area, width or depth of the land as a building site for the structure;
   (ii)   Floor space area of the structure;
   (iii)   Setback of the structure from the property lines of the land;
   (iv)   Height of the structure; or
   (v)   Parking. Provided, however, that the proposed structure is built in substantial compliance with plans and specifications by Fox Valley Auto Care Center Site and Architectural Drawings prepared July 24, 1989 by MFH and Associates and Fox Valley Auto Care Center Grading and Utility Plan prepared March 20, 1989 by Haeger and Associates with respect to the matter set forth in 2(b)   (i) —(v).

There shall be no liability under this endorsement based on the invalidity of the ordinance and amendments thereto until after a final decree of a court of competent jurisdiction adjudicating the invalidity, the effect of which is to prohibit the use or uses.

Loss or damage as to the matters insured against this endorsement shall not include loss or damage sustained or incurred by reason of the refusal of any person to purchase, lease or lend money on the estate or interest covered by this policy.

This endorsement is made a part of the policy and is subject to all of the terms and provisions thereof and of any prior endorsements thereto. Except to the extent expressly stated, it neither modifies any of the terms and provisions of the policy and any prior endorsements nor does it extend the effective date of the policy and prior endorsements, nor does it increase the face amount thereof.

113

ISSUED BY
COMMONWEALTH LAND TITLE INSURANCE COMPANY

Commonwealth

ENDORSEMENT #5

To be annexed to and form a part of Policy No.   107-330846 insuring

*** FIRST MORTGAGE BANK, AS TRUSTEE UNDER TRUST
AGREEMENT DATED APRIL 11, 1989 AND KNOWN AS TRUST #108049-
04***
as set forth in said Policy.

The said Policy is hereby amended in the following manner:

This Policy insures the Insured that Access to and from South Road, Westbrook Drive and
Illinois State Route 59 is via the Easements shown as Parcels 2 and 3 in Schedule A herein.

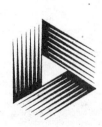

LOAN POLICY OF TITLE INSURANCE

AMERICAN LAND TITLE ASSOCIATION
(10-17-92)

ISSUED BY
COMMONWEALTH LAND TITLE INSURANCE COMPANY

Commonwealth
A LANDAMERICA COMPANY

Title Insurance Since 1876

HOME OFFICE:
101 Gateway Centre Parkway, Gateway One
Richmond, Virginia 23235-5153

B 1191-3

Commonwealth
A LANDAMERICA COMPANY

SUBJECT TO THE EXCLUSIONS FROM COVERAGE, THE EXCEPTIONS FROM COVERAGE CONTAINED IN SCHEDULE B AND THE CONDITIONS AND STIPULATIONS, COMMONWEALTH LAND TITLE INSURANCE COMPANY, a Pennsylvania corporation, herein called the Company, insures, as of Date of Policy shown in Schedule A, against loss or damage, not exceeding the Amount of Insurance stated in Schedule A, sustained or incurred by the insured by reason of:

1. Title to the estate or interest described in Schedule A being vested other than as stated therein;
2. Any defect in or lien or encumbrance on the title;
3. Unmarketability of the title;
4. Lack of a right of access to and from the land;
5. The invalidity or unenforceability of the lien of the insured mortgage upon the title;
6. The priority of any lien or encumbrance over the lien of the insured mortgage;
7. Lack of priority of the lien of the insured mortgage over any statutory lien for services, labor or material:
   (a) arising from an improvement or work related to the land which is contracted for or commenced prior to Date of Policy; or (b) arising from an improvement or work related to the land which is contracted for or commenced subsequent to Date of Policy and which is financed in whole or in part by proceeds of the indebtedness secured by the insured mortgage which at Date of Policy the insured has advanced or is obligated to advance;
8. The invalidity or unenforceability of any assignment of the insured mortgage, provided the assignment is shown in Schedule A, or the failure of the assignment shown in Schedule A to vest title to the insured mortgage in the named insured assignee free and clear of all liens.

The Company will also pay the costs, attorneys' fees and expenses incurred in defense of the title or the lien of the insured mortgage, as insured, but only to the extent provided in the Conditions and Stipulations.

IN WITNESS WHEREOF, COMMONWEALTH LAND TITLE INSURANCE COMPANY has caused its corporate name and seal to be hereunto affixed by its duly authorized officers, the Policy to become valid when countersigned by an authorized officer or agent of the Company.

COMMONWEALTH LAND TITLE INSURANCE COMPANY

Attest: *Wm. Chadwick Perrine*
Secretary

By: *Janet A. Alpert*
President

EXCLUSIONS FROM COVERAGE

The following matters are expressly excluded from the coverage of this policy and the Company will not pay loss or damage, costs, attorneys' fees or expenses which arise by reason of:

1. (a) Any law, ordinance or governmental regulation (including but not limited to building and zoning laws, ordinances, or regulations) restricting, regulating, prohibiting or relating to (i) the occupancy, use, or enjoyment of the land; (ii) the character, dimensions or location of any improvement now or hereafter erected on the land; (iii) a separation in ownership or a change in the dimensions or area of the land or any parcel of which the land is or was a part; or (iv) environmental protection, or the effect of any violation of these laws, ordinances or governmental regulations, except to the extent that a notice of the enforcement thereof or a notice of a defect, lien or encumbrance resulting from a violation or alleged violation affecting the land has been recorded in the public records at Date of Policy. (b) Any governmental police power not excluded by (a) above, except to the extent that a notice of the exercise thereof or a notice of a defect, lien or encumbrance resulting from a violation or alleged violation affecting the land has been recorded in the public records at Date of Policy.
2. Rights of eminent domain unless notice of the exercise thereof has been recorded in the public records at Date of Policy, but not excluding from coverage any taking which has occurred prior to Date of Policy which would be binding on the rights of a purchaser for value without knowledge.
3. Defects, liens, encumbrances, adverse claims or other matters: (a) created, suffered, assumed or agreed to by the insured claimant; (b) not known to the Company, not recorded in the public records at Date of Policy, but known to the insured claimant and not disclosed in writing to the Company by the insured claimant prior to the date the insured claimant became an insured under this policy; (c) resulting in no loss or damage to the insured claimant; (d) attaching or created subsequent to Date of Policy (except to the extent that this policy insures the priority of the lien of the insured mortgage over any statutory lien for services, labor or material); or (e) resulting in loss or damage which would not have been sustained if the insured claimant had paid value for the insured mortgage.
4. Unenforceability of the lien of the insured mortgage because of the inability or failure of the insured at Date of Policy, or the inability or failure of any subsequent owner of the indebtedness, to comply with applicable doing business laws of the state in which the land is situated.
5. Invalidity or unenforceability of the lien of the insured mortgage, or claim thereof, which arises out of the transaction evidenced by the insured mortgage and is based upon usury or any consumer credit protection or truth in lending law.
6. Any statutory lien for services, labor or materials (or the claim of priority of any statutory lien for services, labor or materials over the lien of the insured mortgage) arising from an improvement or work related to the land which is contracted for and commenced subsequent to Date of Policy and is not financed in whole or in part by proceeds of the indebtedness secured by the insured mortgage which at Date of Policy the insured has advanced or is obligated to advance.
7. Any claim, which arises out of the transaction creating the interest of the mortgagee insured by this policy, by reason of the operation of federal bankruptcy, state insolvency, or similar creditors' rights laws, that is based on:
   (a) the transaction creating the interest of the insured mortgagee being deemed a fraudulent conveyance or fraudulent transfer; or
   (b) the subordination of the interest of the insured mortgagee as a result of the application of the doctrine of equitable subordination; or
   (c) the transaction creating the interest of the insured mortgagee being deemed a preferential transfer except where the preferential transfer results from the failure:
      (i) to timely record the instrument of transfer; or
      (ii) of such recordation to impart notice to a purchaser for value or a judgment or lien creditor.

NM 2 PA 20
ALTA Loan Policy (10-17-92)
Form 1191-1 Face Page

Valid Only If Schedules A and B and Cover Are Attached

ORIGINAL

116

CONDITIONS AND STIPULATIONS

1. DEFINITION OF TERMS.

The following terms when used in this policy mean:

(a) "insured": the insured named in Schedule A. The term "insured" also includes

(i) the owner of the indebtedness secured by the insured mortgage and each successor in ownership of the indebtedness except a successor who is an obligor under the provisions of Section 12(c) of these Conditions and Stipulations (reserving, however, all rights and defenses as to any successor that the Company would have had against any predecessor insured, unless the successor acquired the indebtedness as a purchaser for value without knowledge of the asserted defect, lien, encumbrance, adverse claim or other matter insured against by this policy as affecting title to the estate or interest in the land);

(ii) any governmental agency or governmental instrumentality which is an insurer or guarantor under an insurance contract or guaranty insuring or guaranteeing the indebtedness secured by the insured mortgage, or any part thereof, whether named as an insured herein or not;

(iii) the parties designated in Section 2(a) of these Conditions and Stipulations.

(b) "insured claimant": an insured claiming loss or damage.

(c) "knowledge" or "known": actual knowledge, not constructive knowledge or notice which may be imputed to an insured by reason of the public records as defined in this policy or any other records which impart constructive notice of matters affecting the land.

(d) "land": the land described or referred to in Schedule A, and improvements affixed thereto which by law constitute real property. The term "land" does not include any property beyond the lines of the area described or referred to in Schedule A, nor any right, title, interest, estate or easement in abutting streets, roads, avenues, alleys, lanes, ways or waterways, but nothing herein shall modify or limit the extent to which a right of access to and from the land is insured by this policy.

(e) "mortgage": mortgage, deed of trust, trust deed, or other security instrument.

(f) "public records": records established under state statutes at Date of Policy for the purpose of imparting constructive notice of matters relating to real property to purchasers for value and without knowledge. With respect to Section 1 (a) (iv) of the Exclusions From Coverage, "public records" shall also include environmental protection liens filed in the records of the clerk of the United States district court for the district in which the land is located.

(g) "unmarketability of the title": an alleged or apparent matter affecting the title to the land, not excluded or excepted from coverage, which would entitle a purchaser of the estate or interest described in Schedule A or the insured mortgage to be released from the obligation to purchase by virtue of a contractual condition requiring the delivery of marketable title.

2. CONTINUATION OF INSURANCE.

(a) After Acquisition of Title. The coverage of this policy shall continue in force as of Date of Policy in favor of (i) an insured who acquires all or any part of the estate or interest in the land by foreclosure, trustee's sale, conveyance in lieu of foreclosure, or other legal manner which discharges the lien of the insured mortgage; (ii) a transferee of the estate or interest so acquired from an insured corporation, provided the transferee is the parent or wholly-owned subsidiary of the insured corporation, and their corporate successors by operation of law and not by purchase, subject to any rights or defenses the Company may have against any predecessor insureds; and (iii) any governmental agency or governmental instrumentality which acquires all or any part of the estate or interest pursuant to a contract of insurance or guaranty insuring or guaranteeing the indebtedness secured by the insured mortgage.

(b) After Conveyance of Title. The coverage of this policy shall continue in force as of Date of Policy in favor of an insured only so long as the insured retains an estate or interest in the land, or holds an indebtedness secured by a purchase money mortgage given by a purchaser from the insured, or only so long as the insured shall have liability by reason of covenants of warranty made by the insured in any transfer or conveyance of the estate or interest. This policy shall not continue in force in favor of any purchaser from the insured of either (i) an estate or interest in the land, or (ii) an indebtedness secured by a purchase money mortgage given to the insured.

(c) Amount of Insurance: The amount of insurance after the acquisition or after the conveyance shall in neither event exceed the least of:

(i) the Amount of Insurance stated in Schedule A;

(ii) the amount of the principal of the indebtedness secured by the insured mortgage as of Date of Policy, interest thereon, expenses of foreclosure, amounts advanced pursuant to the insured mortgage to assure compliance with laws or to protect the lien of the insured mortgage prior to the time of acquisition of the estate or interest in the land and secured thereby and reasonable amounts expended to prevent deterioration of improvements, but reduced by the amount of all payments made; or

(iii) the amount paid by any governmental agency or governmental instrumentality, if the agency or instrumentality is the insured claimant, in the acquisition of the estate or interest in satisfaction of its insurance contract or guaranty.

3. NOTICE OF CLAIM TO BE GIVEN BY INSURED CLAIMANT.

The insured shall notify the Company promptly in writing (i) in case of any litigation as set forth in Section 4(a) below, (ii) in case knowledge shall come to an insured hereunder of any claim of title or interest which is adverse to the title to the estate or interest or the lien of the insured mortgage, as insured, and which might cause loss or damage for which the Company may be liable by virtue of this policy, or (iii) if title to the estate or interest or the lien of the insured mortgage, as insured, is rejected as unmarketable. If prompt notice shall not be given to the Company, then as to the insured all liability of the Company shall terminate with regard to the matter or matters for which prompt notice is required; provided, however, that failure to notify the Company shall in no case prejudice the rights of any insured under this policy unless the Company shall be prejudiced by the failure and then only to the extent of the prejudice.

4. DEFENSE AND PROSECUTION OF ACTIONS; DUTY OF INSURED CLAIMANT TO COOPERATE.

(a) Upon written request by the insured and subject to the options contained in Section 6 of these Conditions and Stipulations, the Company, at its own cost and without unreasonable delay, shall provide for the defense of an insured in litigation in which any third party asserts a claim adverse to the title or interest as insured, but only as to those stated causes of action alleging a defect, lien or encumbrance or other matter insured against by this policy. The Company shall have the right to select counsel of its choice (subject to the right of the insured to object for reasonable cause) to represent the insured as to those stated causes of action and shall not be liable for and will not pay the fees of any other counsel. The Company will not pay any fees, costs or expenses incurred by the insured in the defense of those causes of action which allege matters not insured against by this policy.

(b) The Company shall have the right, at its own cost, to institute and prosecute any action or proceeding or to do any other act which in its opinion may be necessary or desirable to establish the title to the estate or interest or the lien of the insured mortgage, as insured, or to prevent or reduce loss or damage to the insured. The Company may take any appropriate action under the terms of this policy, whether or not it shall be liable hereunder, and shall not thereby concede liability or waive any provision of this policy. If the Company shall exercise its rights under this paragraph, it shall do so diligently.

(c) Whenever the Company shall have brought an action or interposed a defense as required or permitted by the provisions of this policy, the Company may pursue any litigation to final determination by a court of competent jurisdiction and expressly reserves the right, in its sole discretion to appeal from any adverse judgement or order.

(d) In all cases where this policy permits or requires the Company to prosecute or provide for the defense of any action or proceeding, the insured shall secure to the Company the right to so prosecute or provide defense in the action or proceeding, and all appeals therein, and permit the Company to use, at its option, the name of the insured for this purpose. Whenever requested by the Company, the insured, at the Company's expense, shall give the Company all reasonable aid (i) in any action or proceeding, securing evidence, obtaining witnesses, prosecuting or defending the action or proceeding, or effecting settlement, and (ii) in any other lawful act which in the opinion of the Company may be necessary or desirable to establish the title to the estate or interest or the lien of the insured mortgage, as insured. If the Company is prejudiced by the failure of the insured to furnish the required cooperation, the Company's obligations to the insured under the policy shall terminate, including any liability or obligation to defend, prosecute, or continue any litigation, with regard to the matter or matters requiring such cooperation.

Conditions and Stipulations Continued Inside Cover

271604

CONDITIONS AND STIPULATIONS
(Continued)

5. PROOF OF LOSS OR DAMAGE.

In addition to and after the notices required under Section 3 of these Conditions and Stipulations have been provided the Company, a proof of loss or damage signed and sworn to by the insured claimant shall be furnished to the Company within 90 days after the insured claimant shall ascertain the facts giving rise to the loss or damage. The proof of loss or damage shall describe the defect in, or lien or encumbrance on the title, or other matter insured against by this policy which constitutes the basis of loss or damage and shall state, to the extent possible, the basis of calculating the amount of the loss or damage. If the Company is prejudiced by the failure of the insured claimant to provide the required proof of loss or damage, the Company's obligations to the insured under the policy shall terminate, including any liability or obligation to defend, prosecute, or continue any litigation, with regard to the matter or matters requiring such proof of loss or damage.

In addition, the insured claimant may reasonably be required to submit to examination under oath by any authorized representative of the Company and shall produce for examination, inspection and copying, at such reasonable times and places as may be designated by any authorized representative of the Company, all records, books, ledgers, checks, correspondence and memoranda, whether bearing a date before or after Date of Policy, which reasonably pertain to the loss or damage. Further, if requested by any authorized representative of the Company, the insured claimant shall grant its permission, in writing, for any authorized representative of the Company to examine, inspect and copy all records, books, ledgers, checks, correspondence and memoranda in the custody or control of a third party, which reasonably pertain to the loss or damage. All information designated as confidential by the insured claimant provided to the Company pursuant to this Section shall not be disclosed to others unless, in the reasonable judgment of the Company, it is necessary in the administration of the claim. Failure of the insured claimant to submit for examination under oath, produce other reasonably requested information or grant permission to secure reasonably necessary information from third parties as required in this paragraph, unless prohibited by law or governmental regulations, shall terminate any liability of the Company under this policy as to that claim.

6. OPTIONS TO PAY OR OTHERWISE SETTLE CLAIMS; TERMINATION OF LIABILITY.

In case of a claim under this policy, the Company shall have the additional options:

(a) To Pay or Tender Payment of the Amount of Insurance or to Purchase the Indebtedness.

(i) to pay or tender payment of the amount of insurance under this policy together with any costs, attorneys' fees and expenses incurred by the insured claimant, which were authorized by the Company, up to the time of payment or tender of payment and which the Company is obligated to pay; or

(ii) to purchase the indebtedness secured by the insured mortgage for the amount owing thereon together with any costs, attorneys' fees and expenses incurred by the insured claimant which were authorized by the Company up to the time of purchase and which the Company is obligated to pay.

If the Company offers to purchase the indebtedness as herein provided, the owner of the indebtedness shall transfer, assign, and convey the indebtedness and the insured mortgage, together with any collateral security, to the Company upon payment therefor.

Upon the exercise by the Company of either of the options provided for in paragraphs a(i) or (ii), all liability and obligations to the insured under this policy, other than to make the payment required in those paragraphs, shall terminate, including any liability or obligation to defend, prosecute, or continue any litigation, and the policy shall be surrendered to the Company for cancellation.

(b) To Pay or Otherwise Settle With Parties Other than the Insured or With the Insured Claimant.

(i) to pay or otherwise settle with other parties for or in the name of an insured claimant any claim insured against under this policy, together with any costs, attorneys' fees and expenses incurred by the insured claimant which were authorized by the Company up to the time of payment and which the Company is obligated to pay; or

(ii) to pay or otherwise settle with the insured claimant the loss or damage provided for under this policy, together with any costs, attorneys' fees and expenses incurred by the insured claimant which were authorized by the Company up to the time of payment and which the Company is obligated to pay.

Upon the exercise by the Company of either of the options provided for in paragraphs b(i) or (ii), the Company's obligations to the insured under this policy for the claimed loss or damage, other than the payments required to be made, shall terminate, including any liability or obligation to defend, prosecute or continue any litigation.

7. DETERMINATION AND EXTENT OF LIABILITY.

This policy is a contract of indemnity against actual monetary loss or damage sustained or incurred by the insured claimant who has suffered loss or damage by reason of matters insured against by this policy and only to the extent herein described.

(a) The liability of the Company under this policy shall not exceed the least of:

(i) the Amount of Insurance stated in Schedule A, or, if applicable, the amount of insurance as defined in Section 2 (c) of these Conditions and Stipulations;

(ii) the amount of the unpaid principal indebtedness secured by the insured mortgage as limited or provided under Section 8 of these Conditions and Stipulations or as reduced under Section 9 of these Conditions and Stipulations, at the time of loss or damage insured against by this policy occurs, together with interest thereon; or

(iii) the difference between the value of the insured estate or interest as insured and the value of the insured estate or interest subject to the defect, lien or encumbrance insured against by this policy.

(b) In the event the insured has acquired the estate or interest in the manner described in Section 2(a) of these Conditions and Stipulations or has conveyed the title, then the liability of the Company shall continue as set forth in Section 7(a) of these Conditions and Stipulations.

(c) The Company will pay only those costs, attorneys' fees and expenses incurred in accordance with Section 4 of these Conditions and Stipulations.

8. LIMITATION OF LIABILITY.

(a) If the Company establishes the title, or removes the alleged defect, lien or encumbrance, or cures the lack of a right of access to or from the land, or cures the claim of unmarketability of title, or otherwise establishes the lien of the insured mortgage, all as insured, in a reasonably diligent manner by any method, including litigation and the completion of any appeals therefrom, it shall have fully performed its obligations with respect to that matter and shall not be liable for any loss or damage caused thereby.

(b) In the event of any litigation, including litigation by the Company or with the Company's consent, the Company shall have no liability for loss or damage until there has been a final determination by a court of competent jurisdiction, and disposition of all appeals therefrom, adverse to the title or to the lien of the insured mortgage, as insured.

(c) The Company shall not be liable for loss or damage to any insured for liability voluntarily assumed by the insured in settling any claim or suit without the prior written consent of the Company.

(d) The Company shall not be liable for: (i) any indebtedness created subsequent to Date of Policy except for advances made to protect the lien of the insured mortgage and secured thereby and reasonable amounts extended to prevent deterioration of improvements; or (ii) construction loan advances made subsequent to Date of Policy, except construction loan advances made subsequent to Date of Policy for the purpose of financing in whole or in part the construction of an improvement to the land which at Date of Policy were secured by the insured mortgage and which the insured was and continued to be obligated to advance at and after Date of Policy.

9. REDUCTION OF INSURANCE; REDUCTION OR TERMINATION OF LIABILITY.

(a) All payments under this policy, except payments made for costs, attorneys' fees and expenses, shall reduce the amount of the insurance pro tanto. However, any payments made prior to the acquisition of title to the estate or interest as provided in Section 2(a) of these Conditions and Stipulations shall not reduce pro tanto the amount of the insurance afforded under this policy except to the extent that the payments reduce the amount of the indebtedness secured by the insured mortgage.

(b) Payment in part by any person of the principal of the indebtedness, or any other obligation secured by the insured mortgage, or any voluntary partial satisfaction or release of the insured mortgage, to the extent of the payment, satisfaction or release, shall reduce the amount of insurance pro tanto. The amount of insurance may thereafter be increased by accruing interest and advances made to protect the lien of the insured mortgage and secured thereby, with interest thereon, provided in no event shall the amount of insurance be greater than the Amount of Insurance stated in Schedule A.

(c) Payment in full by any person or the voluntary satisfaction or release of the insured mortgage shall terminate all liability of the Company except as provided in Section 2(a) of these Conditions and Stipulations.

10. LIABILITY NONCUMULATIVE.

If the insured acquires title to the estate or interest in satisfaction of the indebtedness secured by the insured mortgage, or any part thereof, it is expressly understood that the amount of insurance under this policy shall be reduced by any amount the Company may pay under any policy insuring a mortgage to which exception is taken in Schedule B or to which the insured has agreed, assumed, or taken subject, or which is hereafter executed by an insured and, which is a charge or lien on the estate or interest described or referred to in Schedule A, and the amount so paid shall be deemed a payment under this policy.

11. PAYMENT OF LOSS.

(a) No payment shall be made without producing this policy for endorsement of the payment unless the policy has been lost or destroyed, in which case proof of loss or destruction shall be furnished to the satisfaction of the Company.

(b) When liability and the extent of loss or damage has been definitely fixed in accordance with these Conditions and Stipulations, the loss or damage shall be payable within 30 days thereafter.

12. SUBROGATION UPON PAYMENT OR SETTLEMENT.

(a) The Company's Right of Subrogation.

Whenever the Company shall have settled and paid a claim under this policy, all right of subrogation shall vest in the Company unaffected by any act of the insured claimant.

The Company shall be subrogated to and be entitled to all rights and remedies which the insured claimant would have had against any person or property in respect to the claim had this policy not been issued. If requested by the Company, the insured claimant shall transfer to the Company all rights and remedies against any person or property necessary in order to perfect this right of subrogation. The insured claimant shall permit the Company to sue, compromise or settle in the name of the insured claimant and to use the name of the insured claimant in any transaction or litigation involving these rights or remedies.

If a payment on account of a claim does not fully cover the loss of the insured claimant, the Company shall be subrogated to all rights and remedies of the insured claimant after the insured claimant shall have recovered its principal, interest, and costs of collection.

(b) The Insured's Rights and Limitations.

Notwithstanding the foregoing, the owner of the indebtedness secured by the insured mortgage, provided the priority of the lien of the insured mortgage or its enforceability is not affected, may release or substitute the personal liability of any debtor or guarantor, or extend or otherwise modify the terms of payment, or release a portion of the estate or interest from the lien of the insured mortgage, or release any collateral security for the indebtedness.

When the permitted acts of the insured claimant occur and the insured has knowledge of any claim of title or interest adverse to the title to the estate or interest or the priority or enforceability of the lien of the insured mortgage, as insured, the Company shall be required to pay only that part of any losses insured against by this policy which shall exceed the amount, if any, lost to the Company by reason of the impairment by the insured claimant of the Company's right of subrogation.

(c) The Company's Rights Against Non-insured Obligors.

The Company's right of subrogation against non-insured obligors shall exist and shall include, without limitation, the rights of the insured to indemnities, guaranties, other policies of insurance or bonds, notwithstanding any terms or conditions contained in those instruments which provide for subrogation rights by reason of this policy.

The Company's right of subrogation shall not be avoided by acquisition of the insured mortgage by an obligor (except an obligor described in Section 1(a) (i) of these Conditions and Stipulations) who acquires the insured mortgage as a result of an indemnity, guarantee, other policy of insurance, or bond and the obligor will not be an insured under this policy, notwithstanding Section 1(a)(i) of these Conditions and Stipulations.

13. ARBITRATION.

Unless prohibited by applicable law, either the Company or the insured may demand arbitration pursuant to the Title Insurance Arbitration Rules of the American Arbitration Association. Arbitrable matters may include, but are not limited to, any controversy or claim between the Company and the insured arising out of or relating to this policy, any service of the Company in connection with its issuance or the breach of a policy provision or other obligation. All arbitrable matters when the Amount of Insurance is $1,000,000 or less shall be arbitrated at the option of either the Company or the insured. All arbitrable matters when the Amount of Insurance is in excess of $1,000,000 shall be arbitrated only when agreed to by both the Company and the insured. Arbitration pursuant to this policy and under the Rules in effect on the date the demand for arbitration is made or, at the option of the insured, the Rules in effect at Date of Policy shall be binding upon the parties. The award may include attorneys' fees only if the laws of the state in which the land is located permit a court to award attorneys' fees to a prevailing party. Judgment upon the award rendered by the Arbitrator(s) may be entered in any court having jurisdiction thereof.

The law of the situs of the land shall apply to an arbitration under the Title Insurance Arbitration Rules.

A copy of the Rules may be obtained from the Company upon request.

14. LIABILITY LIMITED TO THIS POLICY; POLICY ENTIRE CONTRACT.

(a) This policy together with all endorsements, if any, attached hereto by the Company is the entire policy and contract between the insured and the Company. In interpreting any provision of this policy, this policy shall be construed as a whole.

(b) Any claim of loss or damage, whether or not based on negligence, and which arises out of the status of the lien of the insured mortgage or of the title to the estate or interest covered hereby or by any action asserting such claim, shall be restricted to this policy.

(c) No amendment of or endorsement to this policy can be made except by a writing endorsed hereon or attached hereto signed by either the President, a Vice President, the Secretary, an Assistant Secretary, or a validating officer or authorized signatory of the Company.

15. SEVERABILITY.

In the event any provision of this policy is held invalid or unenforceable under applicable law, the policy shall be deemed not to include that provision and all other provisions shall remain in full force and effect.

16. NOTICES, WHERE SENT.

All notices required to be given the Company and any statement in writing required to be furnished the Company shall include the number of this policy and shall be addressed to its Corporate Headquarters, 101 Gateway Centre Parkway, Gateway One, Richmond, Virginia 23235-5153. Mailing address: P.O. Box 27567, Richmond, Virginia 23261-7567.

NM2 PA 20
ALTA Loan Policy (10-17-92)
Cover Page
Form 1191-3

ORIGINAL

Valid Only If Face Page and Schedules A and B Are Attached

118

ISSUED BY
COMMONWEALTH LAND TITLE INSURANCE COMPANY

Commonwealth

TITLE SERVICES, INC.

610 E. Roosevelt Road
P.O. Box 430
Wheaton, IL. 60189—0430
(312) —690—9130

MORTGAGE TITLE INSURANCE POLICY
SCHEDULE A

File: 111340

Date of Policy: August 3, 1989

Policy Number: 411-978016

Amount of Policy: $2,300,000.00

1.   Name of Insured: ***FIRST MORTGAGE BANK ***

2.   The estate or interest in the land described in this Schedule and which is encumbered by the insured mortgage is fee simple, except as indicated at Item #5 below.

3.   The estate or interest referred to herein is at date of policy vested in:
     FIRST MORTGAGE BANK, AS TRUSTEE UNDER TREST AGREEMENT DATED APRIL 11, 1989 AND KNOW AS TRUST #108049-04

4.   The mortgage, herein referred to as the insure mortgage, and the assignments thereof, if any, are described as follows:
A mortgage to secure an indebtedness in the amount stated herein:
Mortgagor: First Mortgage Bank, as Trustee under Trust Agreement date April 11, 1989 and know as Trust #108049-04
Mortgagee: First Mortgage Bank
Dated:
Recorded:
Document #:
Original Amount: $2,300,000

5.   The land referred to in this Policy is described as follows:

(SEE ATTACHED)

This policy valid only if Schedule B is attached.

SCHEDULE A LEGAL DESCRIPTION

***PARCEL 1:

LOT 1 IN FOX VALLEY EAST, REGION 1, UNIT NO. 20, BEING A SUBDIVISION OF
PART OF THE SOUTHEAST QUARTER OF SECTION 21, AND PART OF THE NORTH EAST
QUARTER OF SECTION 28, TOWNSHIP 38 NORTH, RANGE 9, EAST OF THE THIRD
PRINCIPAL MERIDIAN, ACCORDING TO THE PLAT THEREOF RECORDED AUGUST 2, 1989
AS DOCUMENT R89-093679, IN DUPAGE COUNTY, ILLINOIS.

PARCEL 2:

EASEMENT APPURTENANT TO PARCEL 1 FOR INGRESS AND EGRESS AS CREATED BY
EASEMENT GRANT RECORDED DECEMBER 28, 1983 AS DOCUMENT R83-94901 AND
AGREEMENT RECORDED DECEMBER 28, 1983 AS DOCUMENT R83-94902. SAID
EASEMENT DESCRIBED AS FOLLOWS:

THAT PART OF THE NORTHEAST QUARTER OF SECTION 28, TOWNSHIP 38 NORTH,
RANGE 9 EAST OF THE THIRD PRINCIPAL MERIDIAN DESCRIBED AS FOLLOWS:
COMMENCING AT THE NORTHEAST CORNER OF SAID SECTION 28; THENCE NORTH 86
DEGREES 57 MINUTES 52 SECONDS WEST ALONG THE NORTH LINE OF SAID SECTION
28 AS MONUMENTED AND OCCUPIED 48.83 FEET TO THE WESTERLY RIGHT OF WAY
LINE OF ILLINOIS STATE ROUTE NO. 59; THENCE SOUTH 4 DEGREES 55 MINUTES 49
SECONDS WEST ALONG SAID RIGHT OF WAY LINE 33.0 FEET FOR A POINT OF
BEGINNING; THENCE NORTH 84 DEGREES 31 MINUTES 30 SECONDS WEST 310.35 FEET
TO A POINT ON THE WESTERLY LINE (AS MONUMENTED AND OCCUPIED) OF A TRACT
-OF LAND CONVEYED TO THE SCHOOL TRUSTEES OF DUPAGE COUNTY THAT IS 20.0
FEET SOUTHERLY OF THE NORTHWEST CORNER OF SAID TRACT (AS MONUMENTED AND
OCCUPIED); THENCE SOUTH 5 DEGREES 37 MINUTES 28 SECONDS EAST ALONG SAID
WESTERLY LINE 40.76 FEET TO A LINE DRAWN PARALLEL WITH AND 40.0 FEET
SOUTHERLY OF THE LAST DESCRIBED COURSE (MEASURED AT RIGHT ANGLES
THERETO); THENCE SOUTH 84 DEGREES 31 MINUTES 30 SECONDS EAST ALONG SAID
PARALLEL LINE 302.88 FEET TO SAID WESTERLY RIGHT OF WAY LINE; THENCE
NORTH 4 DEGREES 55 MINUTES 49 SECONDS EAST ALONG SAID RIGHT OF WAY LINE
40.0 FEET TO THE POINT OF BEGINNING IN NAPERVILLE TOWNSHIP, DUPAGE COUNTY,
ILLINOIS.

This policy valid only if Schedule B is attached.

page 2

PARCEL 3:

EASEMENT APPURTENANT TO PARCEL 1 OVER, ACROSS AND UPON THE ACCESS ROAD FOR
ACCESS, INGRESS AND EGRESS FROM PARCEL 1 TO SOUTH ROAD ON THE NORTH AND
WESTBROOK DRIVE EXTENSION TO THE SOUTH AS CREATED BY DECLARATION OF
EASEMENT RECORDED AUGUST 3, 1989 AS DOCUMENT R89-093712. SAID
ACCESS ROAD DESCRIBED AS FOLLOWS:

THAT PART OF THE SOUTHEAST QUARTER OF SECTION 21, TOWNSHIP 38 NORTH.
RANGE 9 EAST OF THE THIRD PRINCIPAL MERIDIAN DESCRIBED AS FOLLOWS:
COMMENCING AT THE MOST NORTHERLY CORNER OF FOX VALLEY EAST, REGION 1,
UNIT NO. 2, AURORA, DUPAGE COUNTY, ILLINOIS; THENCE EASTERLY ALONG THE
SOUTHERLY LINE OF SOUTH ROAD 425.40 FEET FOR A POINT OF BEGINNING; THENCE
SOUTHERLY AT RIGHT ANGLES TO THE SOUTH LINE (AS MONUMENTED) OF A TRACT OF
LAND CONVEYED TO LA VERNE W. JACKSON AND CLARA L. JACKSON BY DOCUMENT
747981 RECORDED MARCH 2, 1955, 361.54 FEET TO SAID SOUTH LINE; THENCE
WESTERLY ALONG SAID SOUTH LINE AT RIGHT ANGLES TO THE LAST DESCRIBED
COURSE 15.0 FEET; THENCE NORTHERLY PARALLEL WITH THE PENULTIMATE
DESCRIBED COURSE 358.29 FEET TO THE SOUTHERLY LINE OF SAID SOUTH ROAD;
THENCE EASTERLY ALONG SAID SOUTHERLY LINE 15.35 FEET TO THE POINT OF
BEGINNING, IN THE CITY OF AURORA, DUPAGE COUNTY, ILLINOIS.

                                   ALSO

THAT PART OF THE SOUTHEAST QUARTER OF SECTION 21, TOWNSHIP 38 NORTH,
RANGE 9 EAST OF THE THIRD PRINCIPAL MERIDIAN DESCRIBED AS FOLLOWS:
COMMENCING AT THE MOST NORTHERLY CORNER OF FOX VALLEY EAST, REGION 1,
UNIT NO.- 2, AURORA, DUPAGE COUNTY, ILLINOIS; THENCE EASTERLY ALONG THE
SOUTHERLY LINE OF SOUTH ROAD 425.40 FEET FOR A POINT OF BEGINNING; THENCE
SOUTHERLY AT RIGHT ANGLES TO THE SOUTH LINE (AS MONUMENTED) OF A TRACT OF
LAND CONVEYED TO LA VERNE W. JACKSON AND CLARA L. JACKSON BY DOCUMENT
747981 RECORDED MARCH 2, 1955, 361.54 FEET TO SAID SOUTH LINE; THENCE
EASTERLY ALONG SAID SOUTH LINE AT RIGHT ANGLES TO THE LAST DESCRIBED
COURSE 15.0 FEET; THENCE NORTHERLY PARALLEL WITH THE PENULTIMATE
DESCRIBED COURSE 364.75 FEET TO THE SOUTHERLY LINE OF SAID SOUTH ROAD;
THENCE WESTERLY ALONG SAID SOUTHERLY LINE 15.34 FEET TO THE POINT OF
BEGINNING, IN THE CITY OF AURORA, DUPAGE COUNTY, ILLINOIS.

This policy valid only if Schedule B is attached.

                                                        page 3

MORTGAGE TITLE INSURANCE POLICY

SCHEDULE B
Part I

File: 111340

Policy Number: 411-978016

This policy does not insure against loss or damage by reason of the following:

1.:   Taxes for 1989 and subsequent years, which are not yet due or payable PERMANENT
      REAL ESTATE TAX INDEX NO.   07-21-400-009
      Affects: Premises in question and other property.   (Underlying land)
      Total 1988 taxes – Paid

2.:   Unrecorded easement for telephone facilities along the North line of Parcel 1 as disclosed
      by underground telephone lines as shown on Survey by Donahue and Thornhill, Inc. dated
      June 9, 1989 and by Utility Letter by Illinois Bell Telephone Company dated July 3, 1989.

3.:   Possible easement for electric facilities along the North line of the land as
      disclosed by underground electric lines as shown on Survey by Donahue and
      Thornhill, Inc. dated June 9, 1989.

4.:   Terms, provisions and conditions contained in Easement Grant:
      Recorded: December 28, 1983
      Document #: R83-94901
      and Agreement:
      Recorded: December 28, 1983
      Document #: R83-94902
      Relate to: Improvement of the Easement Parcel; construction and
      installation of water and sewer lines.
      Affects: Parcel 2

5.:   Terms, provisions and conditions contained in Declaration of Easement:
      Easement:
      Recorded: August 3, 1989
      Document #: R89-093712
      Relate to: Maintenance, repair and reconstruction of the access road; costs
      of repair, maintenance and reconstruction of the access road.
      Affects: Parcels 1 and 3

6.:   Rights of the adjoining owners to the concurrent use of said easement.
          Affects: Parcels 2 and 3

7.: Covenants, conditions and restrictions established by Trustee's
Deed:
Recorded: August 3, 1989
Document #:   R89-093709
Relate to: Use of land; approval of construction plans; maintenance of premises and improvements; signs; uncompleted vacant building construction.
NOTE: Said covenants, conditions and restrictions do not provide for a reversion of title in the event of a breach thereof.

8.: The land lies within the Aurora Sanitary District, which has accepted Federal Grants for sewage treatment works pursuant to Public Law 92-500. Federal law requires a user charge system separate from general ad valorem property taxes.

9.: Pending disbursement of the full proceeds of the loan secured by the mortgage set forth under Item 4 of Schedule A hereof, this Policy insures only to the extent of the amount actually disbursed, but increases as each disbursement is made without knowledge of any defects in, or objection to, the title up to the face amount of the Policy.

10. Upon completion of the improvements in accordance with the plans and specifications prepared by _____ dated _____ the Company will issue its Comprehensive Form 100 Endorsement.]

Commonwealth

SCHEDULE B

Part II

In addition to the matters set forth in Part I of this Schedule, the title to the estate or interest in the land described or referred to in Schedule A is subject to the following matters, but the Company insures that such matters are subordinate to the lien or charge of the insured mortgage upon said estate or interest.

1. An Assignment of Leases and Rents to further secure an indebtedness:
   Assignor: First Mortgage Bank, as Trustee under Trust Agreement dated April 11, 1989 and known as Trust #108049-04 and Fox Valley Auto Care Center Limited Partnership
   Designee: First Mortgage Bank
   Dated: August 3, 1989
   Document #:R89-093716

2. Financing Statement:
   Debtor: First Mortgage Bank, as Trustee under Trust Agreement dated April 11, 1989 and known as Trust #108049-04
   Secured Party: First Mortgage Bank
   Filed: August 3, 1989
   Document #:89U-4281
   Recorded:August 3, 1989
   Document #:R89-93717

3. Financing Statement:
   Debtor: Fox Valley Auto Care Center Limited
   Secured Party: First Mortgage Bank
   Filed: August 3, 1989
   Document #:89U-4281
   Recorded:August 3, 1989

File No.   111340

ENDORSEMENT

To be annexed to and form a part of Policy No.   411-978016 insuring
FIRST MORTGAGE BANK
as set forth in said Policy.

The said Policy is hereby amended in the following manner:

The Company hereby insures against loss or damage by reason of:

(1) The invalidity or unenforceability of the lien of the insured mortgage resulting from the provisions therein, which provide for changes in the rate of interest.

(2) Loss of priority of the lien of the insured mortgage as security for the unpaid principal balance of the loan, together with interest as changed in accordance with the insured mortgage, which loss of priority is caused by said changes in the rate of interest.

This endorsement does not insure against loss or damage by reason of the failure of the insured to comply with the Regulations of the Office of the Comptroller of the Currency, Treasury concerning Adjustable Rate Mortgages (12 C.F.R. Part 29 and any amendments thereto).

This endorsement does not insure against loss or damage based upon (a) usury, or (b) any consumer credit protection or truth in lending law.

The insurance afforded by this endorsement is not subject to paragraph 3(d) of the Exclusions From Coverage. Except to the extent expressly stated, it neither modifies any of the terms and provisions of any prior endorsements, nor does it increase the face amount of the policy.

ISSUED BY
COMMONWEALTH LAND TITLE INSURANCE COMPANY

Commonwealth

File No. 111340
Endorsement No. 770-002787
Premium $ Standard

ALTA ENDORSEMENT FORM – 3.1

Attached to and made a part of Policy Number 107-330846

1. The Company insures the insured against loss or damage sustained by reason of any incorrectness in the assurance that, at Date of Policy:
    (a) According to applicable zoning ordinances and amendments thereto, the land is classified Zone Planned Development District.
    (b) The following use or uses are allowed under that classification:
    An approximately 18,900 square foot automobile care center, to house a mixture of retail and automotive services uses.

2. The Company further insures against loss or damage arising from a final decree of a court of competent jurisdiction.
    (a) Prohibiting the use of the land, with the construction thereon of any structure in accordance with the plans and specifications described in Paragraph 2(b) below, as specified in Paragraph 1(b): or
    (b) Requiring the removal or alteration of said structure on the basis that, the construction of said structure violates said ordinances and amendments thereto as said ordinances and amendments appear on the Date of Policy with respect to any of the following matters:
    (i)   Area, width or depth of the land as a building site for the structure;
    (ii)   Floor space area of the structure;
    (iii)   Setback of the structure from the property lines of the land;
    (iv)   Height of the structure; or
    (v)   Parking. Provided, however, that the proposed structure is built in substantial compliance with plans and specifications by Fox Valley Auto Care Center Site and Architectural Drawings prepared July 24, 1989 by MFH and Associates and Fox Valley Auto Care Center Grading and Utility Plan prepared March 20, 1989 by Haeger and Associates with respect to the matter set forth in 2(b) (i) —(v).

There shall be no liability under this endorsement based on the invalidity of the ordinance and amendments thereto until after a final decree of a court of competent jurisdiction adjudicating the invalidity, the effect of which is to prohibit the use or uses.

Loss or damage as to the matters insured against this endorsement shall not include loss or damage sustained or incurred by reason of the refusal of any person to purchase, lease or lend money on the estate or interest covered by this policy.

This endorsement is made a part of the policy and is subject to all of the terms and provisions thereof and of any prior endorsements thereto. Except to the extent expressly stated, it neither modifies any of the terms and provisions of the policy and any prior endorsements nor does it extend the effective date of the policy and prior endorsements, nor does it increase the face amount thereof.

This Trust Agreement, dated this ___11th___, of ___April___

19_89_ and known as Trust Number ___1080494___ is to certify that FIRST MORTGAGE BANK, a corporation duly organized and existing as a national banking association under the laws of the United States of America, and duly authorized to accept and execute trusts within the State of Illinois, as Trustee hereunder, is about to take title to the following described real estate in _____ County, Illinois, to-wit:

See Exhibit A attached hereto and made a part hereof.

Otherwise known as No. ___Route 59 and South Road, Aurora, Illinois___
Improvements: ___commercial___
And that when it has taken the title thereto or to any other real estate deeded to it as Trustee hereunder, it will hold it for the uses and purposes and upon the trusts herein set forth. The following named persons shall be entitled to the earnings, avails and proceeds of said real estate according to the respective interests herein set forth, to-wit:

Fox Valley Auto Care Center Limited Partnership, a limited partnership

THIS IS TO CERTIFY that the within Document, Consisting of _1_ pages, Is a TRUE COPY OF THE ORIGINAL Trust Agreement (and assignments). This certification makes no representation as to title to real estate contained in said Trust on file with this Company. FIRST MORTGAGE BANK as Trustee under Trust No. _108 049-04_

By _[signature]_
            Authorized Officer

Date _4/11/89_

    IT IS UNDERSTOOD AND AGREED between the parties hereto, and by any person or persons who may become entitled to pay interest under this trust, that the interest of any beneficiary hereunder shall consist solely of a power of direction to deal with the title to said real estate and to manage and control said real estate as hereinafter provided, and the right to receive the proceeds from rentals and from mortgages, sales or other disposition of said real estate, and that such right in the avails of said real estate shall be deemed to be personal property, and may be assigned and transferred as such : that in case of the death of any beneficiary hereunder during the existence of this trust, his or her right and interest hereunder shall, except as herein otherwise specifically provided, pass to his or her executor or administrator, and not to his or her heirs at law : and that no beneficiary now has and that no beneficiary hereunder at any time shall have any right, title or interest in or to any portion of said real estate as such either legal or equitable, but only an interest in the earnings, avails and proceeds as aforesaid. Nothing herein contained shall be construed as imposing any obligation on the Trustee to file any income, profit or other tax reports or schedules, it being expressly understood that the beneficiaries hereunder from time to time will individually make all such reports and pay any and all taxes growing out of their interest under this Trust Agreement The death of any beneficiary hereunder shall not terminate the trust nor in any manner affect the powers of the Trustee hereunder. No assignment of any interest hereunder shall be binding on the Trustee until the original or a duplicate of the assignment is lodged with the Trustee, and its acceptance indicated thereon.

In case said Trustee shall make any advances of money or account of this trust or shall be made a party to any litigation on account of holding title to said real estate or in connection with this trust, or in case said Trustee shall be compelled to pay any sum of money on account of this trust, whether on account of breach of contract, injury to person or property, fines or penalties under any law, judgments or decrees, or otherwise, the beneficiaries hereunder do hereby jointly and severally agree as follows: (1) that they will on demand pay to the said Trustee, with interest thereon at the rate of 7 % per annum, all such disbursements or advances or payments made by said Trustee, together with its expenses, including reasonable attorneys' fees: (2) that the said Trustee shall not be required to convey or otherwise deal with said property at any time held hereunder until all of said disbursements, payments, and (3) that in case of non-payment within ten (10) days after demand said Trustee may sell all or any part of said real estate at public or private sale on such terms as it may see fit, and retain from the proceeds of said sale a sufficient sum to reimburse itself for all such disbursements, payments, advances and interest thereon and expenses, including the expenses of such sale and attorneys fees, rendering the overplus, if any, to the then beneficiaries. However, nothing herein contained shall be construed as requiring the Trustee to advance or pay out any money on account of this trust or to prosecute or defend any legal proceeding involving this trust or any property or interest thereunder unless it shall be furnished with funds sufficient therefor or be satisfactorily indemnified in respect thereto. In the event the Trustee is served with process or notice of legal proceedings or of any other matter concerning the trust or the trust property, the sole duty of the Trustee in connection therewith shall be to forward the process or notice by first class mail to the person designated as the person to whom inquires or notices shall be sent or, in the absence of such designation, to any person having a beneficial interest herein. The last address appearing in the records of the Trustee shall be used for such mailing.

It is further understood and agreed that neither First Mortgage Bank, individually or as Trustee, nor its successor or successors in trust, shall incur any personal liability or be subjected to any claim, judgment or decree for anything it or they or its or their agents or attorneys may do or omit to do in or about the said real estate or under the provisions of said deed or deeds in trust or this Trust Agreement, or any amendment thereof, or for injury to person or property obligations or indebtedness incurred or entered into by the Trustee in connection with said real estate may be entered into by it in the name of the then beneficiaries hereunder, as their attorney-in-fact hereby irrevocably appointed for such purposes, or, at the election of the Trustee, in its own name, as trustee of an express trust and not individually (and the Trustee shall have no obligation whatsoever with respect to any such contract, obligation or indebtedness except only so far as the trust property and funds in the actual possession of the Trustee shall be applicable to the payment and discharge thereof).

In no case shall any party dealing with said Trustee, or any successor in trust, in relation to said real estate or to whom said real estate or any part thereof shall be conveyed, contracted to be sold, leased or mortgaged by said Trustee, or successor in trust be obliged to see to the application of any purchase money, rent or money borrowed or advanced on said real estate, or be obliged to see that the terms of this trust have been complied with, or be obliged to inquire into the authority, necessity or expediency of any act of said Trustee, or successor in trust, or be obliged or privileged to inquire into any of the terms of this Trust Agreement, and every deed, trust deed, mortgage, lease or other instrument executed by said Trustee, or successor in trust, in relation to said real estate shall be conclusive evidence in favor of every person (including the Registrar of Titles of said County) relying upon or claiming under any such conveyance, lease or other instrument, (a) that at the time of the delivery thereof, the trust created by this Trust Agreement was in full force and effect, (b) that such conveyance or other instrument was executed in accordance with the trusts, conditions and limitations contained in this Trust Agreement and all amendments hereof. If any and binding upon all beneficiaries under this Trust Agreement: (c) that said Trustee, or successor in Trust, was duly authorized and empowered to execute and deliver every such deed, trust deed, lease, mortgage or other instrument: and (d) if a conveyance has been made to a successor or successors in trust, that such successor or successors in trust have been properly appointed and are fully vested with all the title, estate, rights, powers authorities, duties and obligations of its, his or their predecessor in trust.

This Trust Agreement shall not be placed on record in the Recorder's Office of the county in which the real estate is situated, or elsewhere and the recording of the same shall not be considered as notice of the rights of any person hereunder, derogatory to the title or powers of said Trustee.

Trustee may at any time resign by sending a notice of its intention so to do by registered or certified mail to each of the then beneficiaries hereunder at his or her address last known to the Trustee. Such resignation shall become effective ten days after the mailing of the notices by the Trustee in the event of his resignation, a successor or successors may be appointed by the person or persons then entitled thereunder to direct the Trustee in the disposition of the Trust property, and the Trustee shall thereupon convey the trust property to such successor or successors in trust in the event that no successor in trust is named as above provided within ten days after the mailing of such notices by the Trustee, then, the Trustee may convey the trust property to the beneficiaries in accordance with their respective interest thereunder or the Trustee may at its option, file a bill for appropriate relief in any court of competent jurisdiction. The Trustee may at its option, cause any such Deed of conveyance to be recorded or registered. The Trustee, notwithstanding such resignation, shall continue to have a first lien on the trust property for its costs, expenses and attorney's fees and for its reasonable compensation.

Every successor Trustee or trustees appointed hereunder shall become fully vested with all the estate properties, rights, powers, trusts, duties and obligations of its, his or their predecessor.

While First Mortgage Bank is the sole owner of record of the real estate referred to herein, and, so far as the public is concerned, has full power to deal therewith, it is understood and agreed by the parties hereto and by any person who may hereafter become a party hereto or a beneficiary hereunder, that said First Mortgage Bank will (subject to its rights as Trustee as aforesaid) convey title to said real estate, execute and deliver deeds including deeds conveying directly to a trust grantee or otherwise deal with said trust estate only when authorized to do so in writing and that, (notwithstanding any change in the beneficiary of beneficiaries hereunder), it will, on the written direction of

Any one of:

David Delaney, Richard Flamm, Steven Matthews

Or will, on the written direction of such other person or persons as shall be from time to time named in writing by the beneficiary or beneficiaries, or on the written direction of such person or persons as may be beneficiary or beneficiaries at the time, make deeds for, pay the proceeds of any mortgage sale or conveyance of, or otherwise deal with said trust estate, or proceeds thereof, in the manner so directed provided, however, that the Trustee shall not be required to enter into any personal obligation or liability in dealing with said real estate or to make itself liable for any damages, costs, expenses, fines or penalties, or to deal with the title so long as any money is due to it hereunder. Otherwise, the Trustee shall not be required to inquire into the propriety of any such direction. Mortgage or Trust Deeds made and executed by the Trustee may include waiver of any and all rights of redemption from sale under any order or decree of foreclosure of such Mortgage or Trust Deed.

The beneficiary or beneficiaries hereunder shall in his, her or their own right have the full management of said real estate and control of the selling, renting and handling thereof, and any beneficiary or his or her agent shall handle the rents thereof and the proceeds of any sales of said property, and said Trustee shall not be required to do anything in the management or control of said real estate or in respect to the payment of taxes or assessments or in respect to insurance, litigation or otherwise, except on written direction as hereinabove provided, and after the payment to it or all moneys necessary to carry out said instructions. The beneficiaries hereunder agree to operate and maintain said real estate in accordance with all laws, codes, regulations and ordinances respecting the use, occupancy, maintenance or control thereof. No beneficiary hereunder shall have any authority to contract for or in the name of the Trustee or to bind the Trustee personally. If any property remains in this trust twenty years from this date it shall be sold at public sale by the Trustee on reasonable notice, and the proceeds of the sales shall be divided among those who are entitled thereto.

First Mortgage Bank shall receive for its services in accepting this trust and in taking title hereunder the sum of $ ___390___ ; also the sum of $ ___195___ : per year for holding title after the ___10th___ day of ___April___, ___1990___ subject to adjustment in accordance with its schedule of fees from time to time in effect, so long as any property remains in the trust: also its regular schedule of fees for making deeds, mortgages, leases and/or other instruments as may be required hereunder, from time to time, and it shall receive reasonable compensation for any special services which may be rendered by it hereunder, and for taking and holding any other property or improvement which may hereafter be deeded to or acquired by it hereunder, and in the event, the value of the property held hereunder is increased by reason of title thereto for each year after the year in which such improvement is made, which fees, charges or other compensation, the beneficiaries hereunder jointly and severally agree to pay, and it is hereby understood and agreed that all such fees and compensations shall constitute a first lien on the real estate and property held hereunder.

IN TESTIMONY WHEREOF, said First Mortgage Bank has caused these presents to be signed by its Vice President or Assistant Vice President, attested by its Assistant Secretary, and has caused its corporate seal to be hereto affixed as and for the act and deed of said association, the day and year first above written.

FIRST MORTAGE BANK

ATTEST: *Julie A. Arnold* By *[signature]*
       Assistant Secretary   Vice President

       And on said day the said beneficiaries have signed this Declaration of Trust and Trust Agreement in order to signify their assent to the terms hereof.

FOX VALLEY AUTO CARE CENTER LTD. PARTNERSHIP, an
   Illinois Limited Partnership

By: Regent Real Estate Development Corp., Gen. Partner

	[seal]	Address c/o The Regent Group
By: David Delaney, President	[seal]	524 W. South Avenue
	[seal]	Address Chicago, Illinois 60610
_____	[seal]	Address _____
_____	[seal]	Address _____
_____	[seal]	Address _____

May the name of any beneficiary be disclosed to the public?   No

To whom shall inquiries, notices and other matters be referred David Delaney

    Address _____   Phone _____

May oral inquiries be referred directly? _____ Phone _____

To whom shall bills be mailed _____ David Delaney

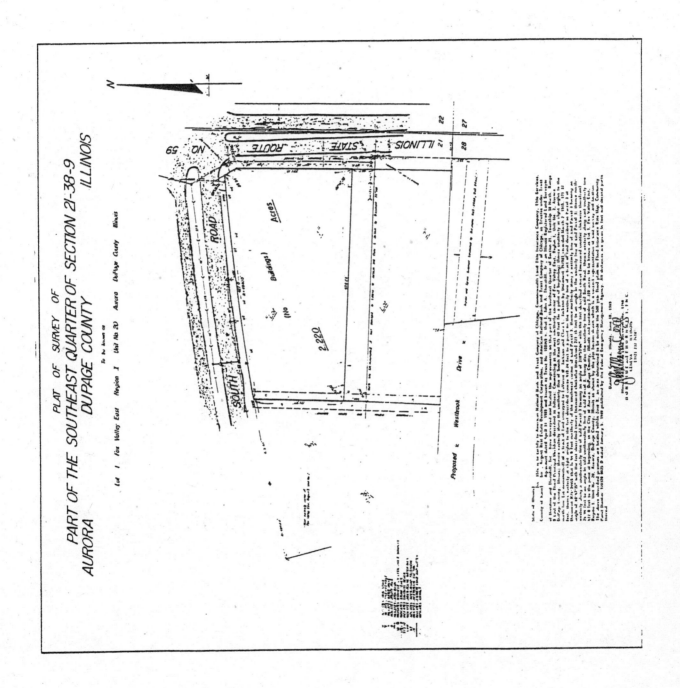

PLAT OF SURVEY OF

PART OF THE SOUTHEAST QUARTER OF SECTION 21-38-9
AURORA   DUPAGE COUNTY   ILLINOIS

To be known as

Lot 1   Fox Valley East   Region I   Unit No 20   Aurora   DuPage County   Illinois

EASEMENT GRANT

This EASEMENT GRANT is made between FIRST MORTGAGE BANK, not personally but as Trustee under a Trust Agreement dated April 11, 1989 and known as Trust No. 108049-4 (hereinafter referred to as "FMB") and Turtle Wax Inc., an Illinois corporation (hereinafter referred to as "Turtle Wax").

The following recitals of fact are a material part of this instrument:

A.   FMB is the owner of a tract of land described in Exhibit A attached hereto and made a part hereof (hereinafter referred to as "Parcel 1").

B.   Turtle Wax is the owner of a tract of land described in Exhibit B attached hereto and made a part hereof (hereinafter referred to as "Parcel 2").

C.   FMB and Turtle Wax wish to grant and to receive from each other an easement over, under and across that part of Parcel 1 and Parcel 2 legally described in Exhibit C attached hereto and made a part hereof (hereinafter referred to as the "Easement Premises").

NOW, THEREFORE, in consideration of the sum of Ten and no/100 ($10.00) Dollars, the foregoing recitals and other valuable consideration, the receipt and sufficiency of which are hereby acknowledged, the following grants, agreements, and covenants and restrictions are made:

1.   GRANT OF EASEMENT. FMB and Turtle Wax hereby grant, sell, bargain and convey to each other, their successors and assigns, as an easement appurtenant to Parcel 1 and Parcel 2, a reciprocal, perpetual easement for ingress and egress over, under and across the Easement Premises.

2.   USE OF EASEMENT PREMISES. The installation or maintenance by FMB or Turtle Wax of pipes, conduits, or wires, under, upon or over the Easement Premises is forbidden, except for storm sewer lines and connections and such other exceptions agreed to in writing by FMB and Turtle Wax. FMB and Turtle Wax, however, reserve the right to use the portion of the Easement Premises which they each own for purposes, which do not unreasonably interfere with or obstruct the operation of the easement herein granted to each other.

3.   MAINTENANCE AND REPAIR. FMB shall pave the Easement Premises and shall maintain and repair the Easement Premises as it deems necessary or desirable in its reasonable judgment. Turtle Wax hereby grants, sells, bargains and conveys to FMB a perpetual

easement over that portion of the Easement Premises which Turtle Wax owns for purposes of paving the Easement Premises and maintaining and repairing the Easement Premises as provided for herein. Turtle Wax shall reimburse FMB for fifty percent (50%) of the costs for such maintenance and repair work within ten (10) days after Turtle Wax is notified of the cost thereof, which notice shall be accompanied by paid receipts or other evidence of cost and written breakdown of the work. Said maintenance and repair shall include, without limitation, the costs of repaving, patching, and refilling the Easement Premises and removing any trash or debris therefrom. If FMB fails to commence to make any necessary repairs to the Easement Premises or fails to commence to maintain the Easement Premises within thirty (30) days after notice by Turtle Wax of the need for repair or maintenance of the Easement Premises or fails to diligently pursue such repair or maintenance work, then Turtle Wax may, after notice to FMB, perform such work and upon completion thereof be reimbursed for fifty percent (50%) of the cost thereof within ten (10) days after FMB is notified of the cost thereof, which notice shall be accompanied by paid receipts or other evidence of cost and written breakdown of the work. Notwithstanding anything contained herein to the contrary, if there is any damage to the Easement Premises or the improvements in connection therewith caused by construction traffic in the course of developing the property benefited by the Easement Premises, the party having the construction work done shall bear one hundred percent (100%) of the cost for repairing such damage. The costs and expenses for repair and maintenance of the Easement Premises shall be a lien on Parcel 1 for the amounts FMB fails to pay when due and shall be a lien on Parcel 2 for the amounts Turtle Wax fails to pay when due, which liens may be enforced according to law.

4.   PARKING, STACKING AND LOADING. Except as hereinafter provided, FMB and Turtle Wax agree that they shall not use the Easement Premises for parking, stacking, loading or unloading and shall not permit any of their tenants, employees, invitees or customers to so use the Easement Premises. FMB and Turtle Wax acknowledge that stacking occurs in rare circumstances and in such circumstances FMB or Turtle Wax, as the case may be, will use reasonable efforts to reduce the level of such stacking.

5.   TITLE. This Easement Grant is made and executed by FMB and Turtle Wax subject to the permitted exceptions described in Exhibit D attached hereto and made a part hereof. The mortgagee(s) of the mortgage(s) described in Exhibit D shall subordinate such mortgage to this Easement Grant.

6.   RUNNING OF BENEFITS AND BURDENS. All provisions of this instrument, including the benefits and burdens, run with the land are binding upon and enure to the successors, assigns, and tenants of the parties hereto.

7.   ATTORNEY'S FEES. Either party may enforce this instrument by appropriate action and the party which prevails in such litigation shall recover as part of its costs a reasonable attorney's fee.

8.   NOTICE. FMB's address is First Mortgage Bank as Trustee under Trust No. 10849-4, c/o Regent Group,. Chicago, Illinois and Turtle Wax's address is Chicago, Illinois. Either party may lodge written notice of change of address with the other. All notices shall be sent by U. S. mail, registered or certified mail, return receipt requested, to the addresses provided for in this paragraph and shall be deemed given when placed in the mail.

IN WITNESS WHEREOF, FMB and Turtle Wax have executed this Easement Grant this _____ day of _____.

FIRST MORTGAGE BANK, as Trustee as

aforesaid

By: ~~Brad Peterson~~

Its: ~~Vice President~~

_____ an Illinois corporation

By: ~~Julie A. Arnold~~

Its: ~~Assistant Secretary~~

This instrument is executed by the undersigned Land Trustee, not personally but solely as Trustee in the exercise of the power and authority conferred upon and vested in it as such Trustee. It is expressly understood and agreed that all of the warranties, indemnities, presentations, covenants, undertakings and agreements herein made on the part of Trustee are undertaken by it solely in its capacity as Trustee and not personally. No personal liability or personal responsibility is assumed by or shall at any time be asserted or enforceable against the Trustee on account of any warranty, indemnity, representation, undertaking or agreement of the Trustee in this instrument.

EXHIBIT A

[ed. note - Legal description of Regent's parcel.]

EXHIBIT B

[ed. note - Legal description of Turtle Wax's parcel.]

EXHIBIT C

COMMON BOUNDARY EASEMENT BETWEEN LOTS 1 AND 2

That part of Lot 1, Fox Valley East, Region 1, Unit No. 20, Aurora, DuPage County, Illinois described as follows: Commencing at the southwest corner of said Lot; thence easterly along the south line of said Lot 15.0 feet for a point of beginning; thence northerly parallel with the west line of said Lot 15.0 feet; thence easterly to a point on the east line of said Lot that is 13.0 feet northerly of the southeast corner of said Lot: thence southerly along said east line 13.0 feet to said southeast corner; thence westerly along the south line of said Lot 424.24 feet to the point of beginning, in the City of Aurora, DuPage County, Illinois.

and also;

That part of Lot 2, Fox Valley East, Region 1, Unit No. 20, Aurora, DuPage County, Illinois described as follows: Commencing at the northwest corner of said Lot; thence easterly along the north line of said Lot 15.0 feet for a point of beginning; thence southerly parallel with the west line of said Lot 15.0 feet; thence easterly to a point on the east line of said Lot that is 16.0 feet southerly of the northeast corner of said Lot; thence northerly along said east line 16.0 feet to said northeast corner; thence westerly along said north line 424.24 feet to the point of beginning, in the City of Aurora, DuPage County, Illinois.

EXHIBIT D

1.   Taxes for 1989 and subsequent years, which are not yet due or payable.

2.   Terms, provisions, and conditions contained in Easement Grant:

Recorded: December 28, 1983

Document #: R83-94901

and Agreement:

Recorded: December 28, 1983

Document #: R83-94902

Relate to: Improvement of the Easement Parcel; construction and installation of water and sewer lines.

3.   Terms, provisions and conditions contained in Declaration of Easement:

Recorded:

Document #:

Relate to: Maintenance, repair and reconstruction of the access road; costs of repair, maintenance and reconstruction of the access road

4.   Rights of the adjoining owners to the concurrent use of said easement.

5.   Covenants, conditions and restrictions established by Trustee's Deed:

Recorded:

Document #:

Relate to: Use of land; approval of construction plans; maintenance of premises and improvements; signs; uncompleted vacant building construction.

6.   The land lies within the Aurora Sanitary District which has accepted Federal grants for sewage treatment works pursuant to Public Law 92-500.

ANNEXATION AGREEMENT

FOR

FOX VALLEY AUTO MALL

THIS ANNEXATION AGREEMENT ("AGREEMENT"), made and entered into this 6th day of June, 1989, by and between the CITY OF AURORA, ILLINOIS, a municipal corporation ("CITY"), Alan W. and Barbara L. Johnson ("OWNERS"), and Regent Real Estate Development Corp. (the "CONTRACT PURCHASER").

WITNESSETH:

1.   The Owners collectively are record title holders of the premises legally described in Attachment "A", attached hereto (the "Subject Property").

2.   The Owners have attached hereto in Attachment "B" a disclosure of the beneficial owners of any land trusts holding title to the Subject Property.

3.   The parties to this Agreement desire that the Subject Property be annexed to the City of Aurora with the benefits to the Subject Property being as follows:

    a.   Full development potential of the Subject Property.

    b.   Establishment of high quality development standards that will elevate, support and stabilize property values for the proposed land uses.

    c.   Provision of a water supply system that has been engineered to supply water services to the Subject Property through the year 2020 and beyond.

    d.   Provision of a sanitary sewer system that has been engineered to supply services to the Subject Property through the Aurora Sanitary District's Facilities Planning Area.

    e   Provision of police protection by the City's fully trained, staffed and equipped Police Department.

    f.   Provision of fire protection by the City's fully trained, staffed and equipped Fire Department.

    g.   Reduced insurance rates due to the City's Fire Department having a Class 3 rating.

4.   The Subject Property is contiguous to the city limits of the City of Aurora, Kane/DuPage Counties, Illinois, and is not within the corporate limits of any other municipality.

5.   The Owners have contracted to sell the Subject Property to Regent Real Estate Development Corp. (the "Contract Purchaser") and the Contract Purchaser, or its successors and assigns, intends to develop a portion of the Subject Property along with a certain parcel (the "Daneman Parcel") located to the north of the Subject Property, which is legally described upon Attachment "C". The portion of the Subject Property to be developed by the Contract Purchaser and the Daneman Parcel, taken together, are legally described upon Attachment "D" and shall be known as the "Development Tract".

6.   This Agreement is made pursuant to Chapter 24, Sections 11-15.1-1 et seq. and 7-1-1 et seq., Illinois Revised Statutes (1985).

7.   All notices, publications, public hearings, and all other matters attendant to said Agreement as required by State statute and the ordinances, regulations, and procedures of the City have been met.

NOW, THEREFORE, it is agreed by and between the parties hereto as follows:

SECTION A.   Recitals

The recitals set forth above are incorporated herein as if fully set forth.

SECTION B.   Annexation and Zoning

1)   The City is in receipt of a properly executed annexation petition ("Annexation Petition") pursuant to this Agreement covering the Subject Property. Upon receipt of notice from the Contract Purchaser's attorney that all deposits necessary to effect the closings of (i) the Subject Property from the Owners to the Contract Purchaser or its nominee, (ii) the Daneman Parcel to the Contract Purchaser or its nominee, and (iii) that portion of the Development Tract legally described upon Attachment K (the "Turtle Wax Tract") to Turtle Wax, Inc. or its nominee (the "Closings") have been deposited into an escrow established for the purpose of effecting the Closings, the City shall, at the next meeting of the City Council following receipt of said notice, adopt an ordinance annexing the

142

Subject Property to the City pursuant to the Annexation Petition. Said notice shall be in recordable form and Contract Purchaser shall record a copy of same within thirty (30) days of delivery of said notice to the City.

2)   Immediately subsequent to the passage of the ordinance annexing the Subject Property, as described in paragraph B(1) above, the City shall adopt an ordinance and/or resolution, as appropriate (i) classifying the Subject Property as being in the Planned Development District; (ii) rendering the Subject Property subject to the plan description ("Plan Description") governing the Planned Development District, which was approved on August 15, 1973 pursuant to Ordinance Number 4330; (iii) adopting a preliminary plan designating the Subject Property as a Business classification; (iv) granting a special use permit for an auto laundry or car wash; (v) approving a preliminary and final plat of subdivision for a larger parcel of land, of which the Subject Property is a part, a copy of which is attached hereto as Attachments "E" and "F" respectively; (vi) approving the Final Plan in the form as set forth on Attachment "G"; (vii) granting the variation(s) as set forth in Section E herein; (viii) approving a left turn lane on South Road for traffic traveling westbound on South Road and turning south onto a road to be created along the border of the Daneman Parcel and the property located directly west of said Parcel; and (ix) accepting the dedication of the extension of Westbrook Drive from its current terminus to Route 59, if such a dedication is tendered to the City.

3)   Within 90 days of annexation to the City, Owners agree to petition the Fox Valley Park District and Aurora Sanitary District for annexation of the Subject Property, if applicable.

SECTION C.   Duration, Applicability and Owner Responsibility

1)   This Agreement shall be binding upon and inure to the benefit of the parties hereto, successor owners of record of the Subject Property, or any part thereof, which is the subject of this Agreement, heirs, executors, administrators, successors, assignees, lessees, devises and upon any

143

successor municipalities for a period from the date of execution hereof through July 27, 1993, unless changed in accordance with law.

2)   It is understood and agreed by the parties hereto that, in the event all or any portion of the Subject Property is sold or conveyed at any time during the term of this Agreement, all the obligations and responsibilities of the then-current owner shall devolve upon and be assumed by such purchaser or grantee, and said owner shall be released from all obligations which relate to any portion of the Subject Property as may have been sold or conveyed.

3)   In the event that the City has not received the notice referenced in paragraph B(1) above within ninety (90) days of execution of this Agreement, this Agreement shall be null and void. Nothing herein shall prevent the city from extending the time period for the filing of said notice in the event Contract Purchaser petitions the City for such an extension.

SECTION D.   Development Review

1)   Owners agree that no portion of the Subject Property shall be developed unless and until such development has been approved by the City in accordance with the conditions hereinafter set forth and that the development plat attached hereto as Attachment "H" be used as a general guideline in the development of the Subject Property.

2)   The provisions of the Aurora Subdivision Control Ordinance shall govern all development of the Subject Property regardless of the size of a parcel being developed at any one time. If no subdivision plats for the Subject Property are required, then Owners agree that the public improvements and other subdivision control requirements of the Aurora Subdivision Control Ordinance shall be applicable to the Subject Property.

3)   That the Subject Property shall be governed only by the Plan Description and to the extent any City zoning or subdivision ordinance, code or regulation is inconsistent with the terms of the Plan Description, the terms of the Plan Description shall control, except as provided for in this Agreement.

4) In the event Owners desire to develop the Development Tract other than in substantial compliance with the approved Final Plan described in subparagraph B(2) above, the following shall apply:

(a) A preliminary plan is required to be approved by the City Council on the total property described in Attachment "A" prior to the approval of any preliminary plats and final plats.

(b) A preliminary plat is required to be approved as per the Aurora Subdivision Control Ordinance prior to the approval of any final plats.

(c) The parties agree that no part of the Subject Property shall be developed unless an acceptable site plan for the tract to be developed has been submitted to and approved by the City in accordance with the Required Components of Final Site Plans attached hereto as Attachment "J".

(d) Should the City, after the execution of this Agreement, amend Attachment "J". The amended Required Components of Final Site Plans shall apply at the time development occurs.

(e) Final site plans shall be accompanied by final engineering and landscape plans as required by the City.

(f) Preliminary plans and plats shall be submitted by Owners to the City and shall be referred to the Aurora Planning Council for technical review; to the Aurora Planning Commission for recommendation; and to the Planning and Development Committee of the Aurora City Council which shall review the findings of the Planning Council and recommendation of the Planning Commission to make a final recommendation to the City Council which shall take final action on the plan or plat. Public notice and public hearings shall not be required.

(g) Final plats and plans shall be submitted by Owners to the City and shall be referred to the Aurora Planning Council for technical review; to the Aurora Planning Commission for recommendation;

and to the Planning and Development Committee for final disposition. Public notice and public hearings shall not be required. The decision of the Planning and Development Committee may be appealed to the Aurora City Council by the Owners, any member of the Aurora City Council, or any official of the City of Aurora, within four (4) business days from the date of the decision by the Aurora Planning and Development Committee. All appeals shall be filed by 5:00 p.m. on the fourth day as described above with the Aurora City Clerk on the form prescribed as a petition for appeal to the City Council. The decision of the Planning and Development Committee shall serve as recommendation to the Aurora City Council in the event of an appeal being filed.

(i) Preliminary plats and plans, and final plats and plans may be submitted and approved simultaneously.

SECTION E.   Variations

1) A variation from the twenty foot (20') setback from the south boundary of the Subject Property, as set forth at Section III.A.3.b., to permit and allow a setback of two feet seven inches (2' 7") for pavement for vehicular access.

2) The parties hereto agree that the preferred method for the stormwater management system to be provided for the proposed development should be located off-site at the Spring Lake and Willow Lake facilities. In the event that on-site detention is required, the City Engineer may consider a variation of the building foundation elevation above the 100 year water elevation, as provided for in Aurora's Stormwater Control Ordinance.

SECTION F.   Roads, Public Utilities and Storm Water Retention

1) Owners agree to participate in all future, lawfully approved special assessment projects for public improvements concerning the Subject Property.

2) Owners agree to enter into cross-easement agreements with contiguous and adjoining property owners to the west of the property with regard to

roads when said actions are necessary in the opinion of the City Engineer of the City of Aurora, Illinois. Owners agree that such cross-easement agreements shall include the rights of access by contiguous and adjoining property owners to access points onto the public right of way that are located upon the Subject Property; said access to be accomplished by crossing such portions of the Subject Property as are necessary. The obligation of the Owners to enter into cross-easement agreements as contemplated herein shall be contingent upon the owners of adjoining property granting similar cross-easement agreements to the Owners.

3) Owners agree to do all that is necessary to dedicate and shall dedicate to the City that portion of the Subject Property located east of a line seventy-five feet (75') west of the center line of Illinois State Route 59 for right-of-way. A Plat of said Dedication shall be submitted to the City at the time the Owners petition the City for annexation of the Subject Property.

4) The Owners agree to construct and install a double-fed water main system to provide adequate fire protection and water service for the Subject Property, and to connect said water mains to the existing City water system, as approved by the City.

5) Owners agree to connect to the sanitary sewer system and shall pay such charges for sewer service as are prescribed by City ordinances or by the Aurora Sanitary District.

6) Any and all field tiles on the Subject Property must be protected during construction and shall be re-routed so as to not run under any building. Any filling operations must be done in such a manner so as not to raise the overland emergency routing from adjacent properties. When, as and if said field tile is rerouted, Owners shall not be required to use any tile of a type, kind or character other than is the same or equal to that presently used in the field tile in question. If the tile is run under any paved area, concrete tile must be used.

7) The parties hereto agree that no development of the Subject Property shall occur until and unless adequate storm and sanitary discharge plans

and other related plans have been approved by the appropriate City of Aurora Department or Departments, or agency, in charge, which approval shall not be unreasonably withheld. Any storm water control facilities shall conform to the design criteria specified in Attachment "I" of this Annexation Agreement. Notwithstanding any provision to the contrary within the Plan Description referenced in paragraph B(2) of this Agreement, the parties hereto agree that the City's storm water control ordinance in effect at the time of development shall apply to the Subject Property.

SECTION G.   General Provisions

1)   Owners agree that the construction of buildings on the Subject Property and all fees related to said construction shall be in accordance with the Aurora Building Code requirements in force at the time of application for building permit.

2)   All codes and ordinances of the City of Aurora not amended herein by this Agreement and all codes and ordinances adopted by said City after the execution and entering into of this Agreement by the parties hereto shall apply to the Subject Property.

3)   Owners shall make City impact fee payments totaling $5,197.50 but shall make no other City contributions, donations, gifts or impact fees in connection with the development of the Subject Property.

4)   Owners agree that all existing structures on the Subject Property, including signage, shall be razed and removed within one (1) year of annexation.

5)   Owners and all successors and assigns in interest shall be limited in development of the Subject Property to the uses, and only those uses, permitted by the Plan Description.

6)   That no off premises signs be erected on the Subject Property

7)   If any section, subsection or paragraph of this Agreement shall be held invalid, the invalidity of such section, subsection or paragraph shall not affect any of the other provisions of this Agreement.

8)   Notice. Any notice or demand hereunder from any party hereto to another

148

party hereto shall be in writing and shall be deemed served if delivered in person, by facsimile machine ("fax") or mailed by prepaid, registered or certified mail addressed as follows:

If to the City: Mayor of Aurora

If to the "Owners":   Alan W. and Barbara L. Johnson

If to the Contract Purchaser: Regent Real Estate Development Corp.

PHASE I ENVIRONMENTAL

PROPERTY TRANSFER ASSESSMENT

PARCELS LOCATED AT

7S 780 ROUTE 59

NAPERVILLE, ILLINOIS

Prepared For:

THE REGENT GROUP

CHICAGO, ILLINOIS

Prepared By:

VERSAR, INC.

OAK BROOK, ILLINOIS

JULY 1989

1.0   INTRODUCTION

Versar, Inc. was retained by the Regent Group to perform a limited Phase I property transfer environmental assessment of two adjacent parcels located south of Fox Valley Shopping Center in Aurora, Illinois. The southern parcel is commonly known as 7S 780 Route 59, Naperville, Illinois 60540. No street address or plat number was identified for the northern parcel.

The purpose of the Phase I assessment is to identify major environmental concerns and potential environmental liabilities that could significantly affect the value of the property as an asset.

As agreed, our scope of services on this project was limited to the following tasks:

i)   An onsite physical inspection of the land areas and building interior areas that are the subject of this transaction.

ii)   Interviews with available persons who have knowledge related to the history and development of the land parcel to identify potential concerns related to potential environmental contamination from previous land uses.

iii) Review of historic aerial photographs and other data available to assess the potential for historic environmental contamination of the property.

iv) Review of on site chemical storage, handling and disposal practices, and of the heating oil storage tank.

v) Review of the surrounding land uses to assess the potential for environmental contamination and liability.

vi) Limited sampling to determine the presence of asbestos containing materials.

vii) Contact with regulatory agencies and review of regulatory lists to establish if there are known environmental concerns for the property.

Excluded from our scope of work was any soil, ground water, or air sampling or testing.

The site visit was performed on July 21, 1989. Versar representatives were accompanied by Alan and Barbara Johnson, property owners of the southern parcel, who provided information about the property and access to the buildings.

2.0 PHYSICAL INSPECTION

The subject parcels are located at the southwest corner of the intersection of South Road and Illinois State Route 59 on the eastern edge of Aurora, DuPage County, Illinois. The two parcels comprise 4.557 acres, according to plat surveys supplied by the Regent Group.

The northern parcel is unimproved grassland, which previously was used for agricultural purposes. The southern parcel includes a two-story house, a garage, and four outbuildings (two small barns, a chicken coop, and a lawn mower shed). A tree line, or hedgerow, separates the two parcels. An underground storm sewer is located along this tree line. The basement drains in the house discharge into the storm sewer. In the past these drains were connected to a septic tank located on the north side of the garage. The septic tank and associated drain tiles are currently unused. A second, larger septic tank and drain tiles for domestic sanitary wastewater are located in the front yard area on the east side of the house. The larger septic tank was pumped out approximately 5 years ago, while the smaller, unused septic tank has never been pumped out, according to the current property owner.

Potable water from the house is supplied by a 120 foot deep domestic well located on the western side of the house in the back yard. The current property owners, Alan and

Barbara Johnson stated that they have no complaints about the water quality from the well. The well water has never been sampled.

The house is heated by a fuel oil burning furnace in the basement. Fuel oil #2 is supplied by a 275 gallon aboveground tank located adjacent to the furnace in the basement. The fill and vent pipes for the tank are located in the flower bed outside the basement wall closest to the tank. Approximately two feet of fill and/or vent pipe run underground from the flower bed to the basement wall.

A small, 300 square foot vegetable garden is located in the back yard to the west of the house on the south parcel.

Two small barns (one is currently in use as a chicken coop), an abandoned chicken coop, and a lawn mower shed are located north of the garden along the tree line at the northern edge of the parcel.

Farther west of the garden and outbuildings on the southern parcel is a former soybean and oat field which is no longer farmed, and is currently grown over with weeds. No improvements are located on this section of the parcel which extends to the property boundary.

During the physical inspection no indications or signs of potential chemical contamination such as stained soils, distressed vegetation, or odors were noted.

3.0   SITE HISTORY

The property owners of the southern parcel, Alan and Barbara Johnson, were interviewed to determine the history of the parcel and any potential concerns related to previous land uses. A review of historic aerial photographs and maps is included in the next section.

The Johnsons purchased an existing house in 1955 and have occupied the southern parcel since that time. The northern parcel has been undeveloped during this time. The Johnsons did not know the age of the house. The property was used primarily for cattle grazing until the Fox Valley mall was built to the north approximately 10 years ago. In addition to cattle grazing, a section of the southern parcel was used for soybean and oat farming. No fertilizers, herbicides or other pesticides were used or stored on the property for farming, according to Barbara Johnson. Ms. Johnson pointed out that household quantities of pesticides have been used on the 300 square foot vegetable garden in the back yard.

The Johnsons stated that there have not been any spills associated with filling the heating oil tanks in the basement, and that they have always been able to grow flowers around the outdoor fill pipe for the tank. No evidence of soil staining was noted in this area during the physical inspection of the property.

4.0   REVIEW OF HISTORIC AERIAL PHOTOGRAPHS AND MAPS

Aerial photographs from 1963, 1970, 1975, and 1988 and the topographic map from 1962 (Naperville Quad, photo revised in 1972 and 1980) were reviewed in order to assess the potential for historic environmental contamination of the property. The aerials are included as Attachment 1 [Omitted. Eds.]. This map and the aerials confirm that the property use has been agricultural/vacant since at least 1962. The land use at the two subject parcels does not appear to have changed much in the last 30 years. No structures are present at the northern parcel in any of the aerials. The house and farm outbuildings are present at the southern parcel in all of the aerials. Surrounding land uses are agricultural until the 1975 aerial where the mall is under construction, and preconstruction soil excavation is occurring at properties to the west of the site. The gasoline station at the southwest corner of Ogden and Route 59 appears to have been built between 1970 and 1975. The gasoline station at the northeast corner of Ogden and Route 59 is not present until the 1988 aerial.

Based on a review of site history and historic aerial photographs, the potential for site contamination and corresponding liability from prior land uses appears negligible.

5.0   REVIEW OF ONSITE CHEMICALS AND THE HEATING OIL STORAGE TANK

Several gallons of household paints and several small containers of garden pesticides were in storage in the garage connected to the house. These chemicals are consumed during use. The small quantities of paints and pesticides in storage will be removed when the property is vacated, according to the Johnsons. No significant chemical use or storage was identified during the assessment.

A 275 gallon aboveground heating oil tank is located in the basement of the house adjacent to the oil fueled furnace. The tank contained approximately 70 gallons of #2 fuel oil at the time of the site visit. The floor around the tank was very clean and there was no evidence of any type of floor staining from potential past spills or leaks associated with the tank. However several open drains located on the basement floor discharge to the city storm sewer. These drains discharged to an abandoned septic tank in the past. There have been no leaks or spills associated with the tank or filling the tank, according to the Johnsons. The fill pipe and vent pipe for tank are located outside the house in the flower garden along the basement wall closest to the tank (the northeast side of the basement). Several feet of fill pipe and vent pipe run underground and through the basement wall to the tank. Because these pipes do not normally hold any heating oil, there is little potential for any soil contamination from potential leaks in the pipe runs.

The surface soil area around fill pipe is unstained and there are no indications that major spills have occurred during past filling of the tank.

6.0   REVIEW OF SURROUNDING LAND USES

The subject parcels are located in a commercial / retail area of Aurora, Illinois. The Fox Valley Shopping Center is located approximately 2000 feet northwest of the site across South Road. Retail stores such as Lion Photo, Carpetland, and Poolorama are located on adjacent properties west of the site. A vacant field currently being excavated for a future WalMart store is located east across Route 59. The Indian Plains School administrative building is adjacent and south of the site. Farther south, approximately 600 feet south of this site, is the intersection of Ogden Avenue and Illinois State Route 59. Mobil gasoline service stations are located at both the northeast and southwest corners of this intersection. The Mobil station at the northeast corner is under the Naperville Fire Department jurisdiction while the Mobil at the southwest corner is under Aurora jurisdiction. Representatives of Naperville and Aurora fire departments were contacted and both stated that they were not aware of any leaks or spills associated with underground tanks at either gasoline station. Potential leaks or spills from underground tanks at these stations could impact the groundwater from the well at the property which is used for drinking water.

7.0   ASBESTOS INSPECTION

The following section briefly describes the Versar asbestos inspection procedure used by Versar and the selective testing and sampling performed at the site. The scope of the asbestos sampling and testing was limited to preliminary screening for potential

155

asbestos-containing materials (ACM). U.S. EPA defines ACM as those materials containing greater than 1% asbestos by weight.

7.1 Inspection

The inspection for ACM included all area of the house that Versar was permitted to inspect, and that could be inspected without the disassembly of complicated mechanical or rigid structural components of the house. Areas inspected included interior floors, walls, ceilings, areas above suspended ceilings, mechanical piping exteriors, and equipment exteriors. Areas not inspected include the air handling equipment and vent interiors, door interiors, and areas behind solid walls (including pipe insulation for water pipes which runs along the outside wall from the upstairs bathroom). Materials which were clearly labeled, or easily identified as non-ACM were not sampled for ACM.

7.2 Results

Ten (10) bulk samples were collected from potential ACM of the following types:

- floor coverings and mastic
- ceiling tile
- roofing materials
- paper insulation on hot air ducts and risers

Bulk sample analysis results and a summary of sample locations and materials is included as Table 1. Non-friable transite roof shingles containing ACM were discovered on the house and garage, comprising approximately 1500 square feet. In addition, some replacement shingles are in storage in the garage. Friable paper insulation ACM was identified on hot air ductwork exteriors and as an interior seal at joints where hot air ducts vent inside various rooms in the house. All other materials sampled were determined not to contain ACM. A detailed analytical report for each bulk samples is included in Attachment 2 [Omitted. Eds.].

8.0 REGULATORY / RECORDS REVIEW

The EPA CERCLIS, National Priority List (NPL), and Illinois State Priority List were reviewed to determine if the site or any other nearby properties are listed for inclusion. EPA's CERCLA Program (or Superfund Program) identifies hazardous waste disposal sites that may require remedial action to mitigate potential negative impacts to human health or the environment. Sites with potential contamination or abandoned hazardous waste disposal are included in the EPA inventory, which is designated the CERCLIS. Sites that have undergone evaluation and are subsequently determined to be above a specified level of threat to human health or the environment are included on the NPL (Superfund) list. Sites that have undergone evaluation and are determined to be above a specified level of threat, but are less of a risk than the level required for inclusion on the NPL, may be listed on the Illinois State priority list. The site and adjacent properties are not listed on the NPL, CERCLIS, or State priority lists.

The DuPage County Public Health Department, Division of Environmental health, was contacted to determine the existence of health department inspection records, citizen complaints, or water well information. According to a representative of the health department, no file exists for the site.

The Aurora Fire Bureau Fire Marshall, Mr. John Kerns, was contacted and stated that his fire department has no record of chemical spills, fires, or underground tanks at the site. The Aurora Fire Bureau has jurisdiction over the Mobil gas station located at the southwest corner of Ogden Avenue and Illinois State Route 59, approximately 600 feet south of the site. Mr. Kerns stated that he believed there have been no leaks or spills associated with the underground tanks at this station.

8.0   CONCLUSION

Versar performed a Phase I Property Transfer Environmental Assessment of two parcels located at South Road and Illinois State Route 59 in Aurora, Illinois. Based on the site inspection, discussion with knowledgeable officials, review of available information and historical aerial photos and maps, and on the results of asbestos material sampling, no major environmental concerns were identified and the potential that the property presents any significant environmental liability is judged to be extremely unlikely. However, paper insulation on heating ducts and transite roof shingles on the house were determined to include asbestos containing materials. The 1500 square feet of ACM roof shingles are non-friable materials, and as such, would not be subject to regulated procedures for removal and disposal.

DISCLAIMER

The purpose of this preliminary environmental assessment is to review existing documentation and to evaluate the current environmental status of the property. Versar, Inc. does not assume responsibility for the elimination of hazards that could possibly cause accidents, injuries, damage, or liabilities. Compliance with submitted recommendations and/or suggestions in no way assures elimination of hazards or the fulfillment of a property owner's obligation under any local, state, or federal laws, or any modifications or changes thereto. It is the responsibility of the property owner to notify authorities of any conditions that are reportable under law.

Information regarding operations, practices, conditions, and test data were obtained, in part, from site personnel, and have been assumed to be correct and complete. Versar is relying on the accuracy of this information in preparing this report. Versar assumes no liability for misrepresentation or information withheld by the site personnel, or for items not visible, accessible, or present at the site at the time of the survey.

Since the facts stated in this report are subject to a professional interpretation, they could result in differing conclusions.

Versar makes no warranty and assumes no liability with respect to the use of information contained in this report. No changes to its form or content may be made without Versar's express written approval.

[ed. note – the following are omitted: site map, aerial photographs, (taken in 1963, 1970, 1975, and 1988), "Chain of Custody Form" and "Bulk Asbestos Analysis Laboratory Reports" (how and from where the asbestos samples were gathered.]

CONSTRUCTION LOAN AGREEMENT

THIS CONSTRUCTION LOAN AGREEMENT ("Agreement") made as of this 2nd day of August, 1989 by and among FIRST MORTGAGE BANK, a national banking association ("Lender"), FIRST MORTGAGE BANK, not personally but as Trustee under Trust Agreement dated April 11, 1989, and known as Trust No. 108049-04 (the "Trust"), and FOX VALLEY AUTO CARE CENTER LIMITED PARTNERSHIP, an Illinois limited partnership (the "Beneficiary") (the Trust and Beneficiary are referred to herein collectively as the "Borrower").

RECITALS

1.   The Trust is about to acquire fee simple title to an approximately 2.22 acre site located in the City of Aurora, DuPage County, Illinois and legally described in Exhibit "All attached hereto (the "Real Estate") upon which Borrower intends to construct an auto care center development in which SPARKS TUNE-UP ("Sparks"), LUBE PRO'S ("Lube") and CASEY MUFFLER & BRAKE ("Casey") are major tenants.

2.   Borrower shall make or cause to be made all necessary on-site and off-site improvements, including, without limitation, roads and utilities on the Real Estate and shall construct on the Real Estate an auto care center development and all related facilities and improvements (all of the foregoing improvements being referred to collectively as the "Improvements") . The Real Estate and Improvements, together with all fixtures, fittings, apparatus, machinery, equipment and furnishings and any other personal property and any replacements thereof or substitutes therefor, now or hereafter located in or used in any way in connection with the sale or operation of the Improvements or the Real Estate and not owned by contractors or subcontractors are herein sometimes together referred to as the "Project".

3.   Borrower desires to borrow from Lender an aggregate amount not to exceed Two Million Three Hundred Thousand Dollars ($2,300,000.00) (the "Loan"), the proceeds of which are to be used for the acquisition of the Real Estate and payment of the construction costs of the Improvements, all as set forth in the Project Budget (as hereinafter defined).

NOW THEREFORE, in consideration of the mutual covenants and agreements herein contained, the parties agree as follows:

ARTICLE 1

1.1   The foregoing Preambles and all other recitals set forth herein are made a part of this Agreement.

1.2   The Exhibits referred to in this Agreement are incorporated herein and expressly made a part hereof.

ARTICLE 2

DEFINITIONS AND EXHIBITS

2.1   DEFINITIONS. The following terms as used in this Agreement shall have the following meanings (such meanings to be equally applicable in both the singular and plural forms of the terms defined):

AFFILIATE - shall mean any person, firm, corporation or entity (herein collectively called a "Person") directly or indirectly controlling or controlled by, or under direct or indirect common control with, another Person. A Person shall be deemed to control another Person for the purposes of this definition if such first Person possesses, directly or indirectly, the power to direct, or cause the direction of, the management and policies of the second Person, whether through the ownership of voting securities, common directors, trustees or officers, by contract or otherwise.

ARCHITECT'S AGREEMENT - The agreement between the General Partner and Borrower's Architect assigned to the Beneficiary dated April 26, 1989 for preparation by Borrower's Architect of the Plans and Specifications.

BENEFICIARY - Fox Valley Auto Care Center Limited Partnership, an Illinois limited partnership.

BORROWER - First Mortgage Bank, not personally but solely as Trustee under Trust Agreement dated April 11, 1989 and known as Trust No. 108049-04 and Beneficiary.

BORROWER'S ARCHITECT - MFH Associates.

BORROWER'S LIABILITIES - The Loan, all interest from time to time accruing thereon, and all liabilities and indebtedness of any and every kind and nature now or hereafter owing, arising, due or payable from Borrower to Lender whether under this Agreement or under any of the Loan Documents.

CASEY - Casey Muffler & Brake.

CASEY LEASE - A lease between Borrower and Casey which shall be subject to the Lender's prior approval and the execution of which shall be a condition precedent to Lender's obligation to make the Loan and disburse the proceeds thereof.

CHANGE ORDER - Any change in the Construction Contract or Plans and Specifications which materially affects the quality or intended use of the Project or increases the cost of construction by more than $10,000 as to any single change order or $50,000 as to the entire Project.

CONSTRUCTION COMMENCEMENT DATE - October 30, 1989.

CONSTRUCTION COMPLETION DATE - June 30, 1990.

DEFAULT - An Event of Default or any event, which upon the passage of time or giving of notice (or both) would constitute an Event of Default.

DEFAULT INTEREST RATE - That rate of interest set forth and payable, as provided in the Notes.

DUE DATE - The date set forth in the Notes by which full payment under the Notes is due.

ENGINEER - MFH Associates.

ENGINEER'S AGREEMENT - The contract dated April 26, 1989 between the General Partner and the Engineer, assigned to the Beneficiary.

ESTIMATED TOTAL COST OF COMPLETING THE IMPROVEMENTS - shall mean as of any given date, the then total cost of completing construction of the Improvements pursuant to the Plans and Specifications and any Change Orders permitted under the terms of this Agreement. The Estimated Total Cost of Completing the Improvements shall be determined by the Lender except where expressly otherwise indicated herein.

EVENT OF DEFAULT - The occurrence of any one or more of the events described in Section 10.1 hereof.

FORCE MAJEURE - Acts of God, unusual weather conditions, strikes, lockouts or labor disputes, inability to obtain an adequate supply of materials, fuel, water, electricity, labor or other supplies, casualty, governmental action, accidents, breakage, repairs, or other conditions, matters or events which are not within the reasonable control of Borrower and not attributable to the bad faith of Borrower or its agents, excluding the lack of funds to, perform any obligation hereunder.

GENERAL CONTRACT - The contract dated July 15, 1989 between Regent Construction Corporation, as general contractor, and General Partner, assigned to Beneficiary, for the construction of the Improvements.

GENERAL CONTRACTOR - Regent Construction Corporation.

GENERAL PARTNER - Regent Real Estate Development Corp., an Illinois corporation.

GOVERNMENTAL APPROVALS - All authorizations, approvals, waivers, exemptions, variances, franchises, permits and. licenses or federal, state, municipal or other governmental authorizations required for the acquisition, construction, development ownership and operation of all or any part of the Project.

GOVERNMENTAL AUTHORITIES - Any and all federal, state, municipal or other governmental bodies having jurisdiction over Borrower, Beneficiary or all or any part of the Project.

GUARANTORS – David Delaney and Steven Matthews.

GUARANTY - The Guaranty of Payment and Performance to be executed by the Guarantors.

HARD COSTS - The costs of the labor and materials for construction of the Project.

HAZARDOUS SUBSTANCES - means any toxic or hazardous wastes, pollutants, or substances, including without limitation, asbestos, PCBs, petroleum products and by-products, substances defined as "hazardous substances" or "toxic substances" or similarly identified in the Comprehensive Environmental Response, Compensation and Liability Act of 1980, as amended, 42 U.S.C. Sec. 9061 et seq., Hazardous Materials Transportation Act, 49 U.S.C. Sec. 1802, et seq., The Resource Conservation and Recovery Act, 42 U.S.C. Sec. 6901 et seq., The Toxic Substance Control Act of 1976, as amended, 15 U.S.C. Sec. 2601 et seq., Clean water Act, 33 U.S.C. Sec. 466 et seq., as amended, and Clean Air Act, 42 U.S.C. Sec. 7401 et seq., or in any other applicable federal, state or local Environmental Laws.

IMPROVEMENTS - All improvements heretofore or hereafter constructed by Borrower on the Real Estate including, without limitation, roads, storm sewers, detention and retention facilities, sanitary sewers, curbs, gutters and utility systems.

INTEREST RATE - That rate of interest specified in the Notes.

LEASES - All leases, subleases, licenses, concessions, grants, tenancies or other possessory interests in all or any part of the Project, now or hereafter existing.

LENDER - First Mortgage Bank.

LENDER'S CONSTRUCTION CONSULTANT - The architect, engineer or other professional consultant retained by Lender to supervise and/or inspect the Real Estate and/or the construction of the Project, the cost of whose services shall be borne by Borrower.

LETTER OF CREDIT - The irrevocable and unconditional direct pay letter of credit in the sum of $200,000 issued by Harris Trust and Savings Bank for the benefit of Lender to secure the Notes and this Agreement.

LIEN - Any encumbrance, lien, mortgage, pledge, charge, lease, easement, servitude, right of others or security interest of any kind.

162

LOAN - The loan being made by Lender to Borrower pursuant to the terms of this Agreement, together with all further or future advances made pursuant to or under this Agreement.

LOAN AMOUNT - Not to exceed $2,300,000.00.

LOAN CLOSING DATE - August 2, 1989.

LOAN DOCUMENTS - All documents and instruments executed by Borrower or by Guarantors evidencing or securing the Borrower's Liabilities including without limitation those described in Exhibit "B" attached hereto.

LOAN EXPENSES -.Any and all of Lender's expenses relating to the Loan, including, without limitation, recording, registration and filing charges and taxes, mortgage taxes, charges of the Title Company, photocopying, printing and Photostatting expenses, costs of surveys, escrow charges, costs of all studies of the Real Estate's soil, including, without limitation, toxic waste studies, costs of certified copies of instruments and other documents, fees of any construction services, all costs, fees and expenses of Lender's Construction Consultant, and all attorney's fees relative to the preparation and delivery of this Agreement, the Loan Documents and the disbursement of the Loan.

LUBE - Lube Pro's

LUBE LEASE - A lease between Borrower and Lube which shall be subject to the Lender's prior approval and the execution of which shall be a condition precedent to Lender's obligations to make the Loan and disburse the proceeds thereof.

MORTGAGE - That certain Construction Mortgage and Security Agreement with Assignment of Rents encumbering the Project to be made by Borrower in favor of Lender to secure Borrower's Liabilities.

MORTGAGED PREMISES - The Real Estate and all other property conveyed to Lender as security for the Loan as more fully described in the Mortgage together with the Improvements.

MUNICIPALITY - The City of Aurora.

NOTES - The Borrower's Notes delivered to Lender with principal amounts of $2,100,000 and $200,000.

PERMITTED EXCEPTIONS - The exceptions to title contained in Exhibit "C" attached hereto.

PLANS AND SPECIFICATIONS - The plans and specifications for the Improvements as approved by Lender, prepared by the Engineer and the Borrower's Architect.

PRIME RATE - As defined in the Notes.

PROJECT - The Real Estate and Improvements developed in accordance with the terms of this Agreement.

PROJECT BUDGET - The budget attached hereto as Exhibit "D" setting forth all expenses and costs of the Project.

REAL ESTATE - The real estate legally described on Exhibit "A" attached hereto.

RECIPROCAL EASEMENT AGREEMENT OR REA - That certain Declaration of Easement dated July 28, 1989, and recorded August 2, 1989 as Document No. _____, between the Trust and LaSalle National Bank as Trustee under Trust Agreement dated December 26, 1984 and Known as Trust No. 109000.

SOFT COSTS - Expenses, fees and other costs of development of the Real Estate other than costs for labor and materials.

SPARKS - Sparks Tune-Up.

SPARKS LEASE - A lease between Borrower and Sparks, which shall be subject to the Lender's prior approval and the execution of which shall be a condition precedent to Lender's obligation to make the Loan and disburse the proceeds thereof.

TITLE COMPANY - Commonwealth Land Title Insurance Company.

TOXIC WASTE REPORT - A toxic waste report showing that the Real Estate and adjacent land conform to all applicable federal, state and local environmental laws, statutes, ordinances, rules and regulations and contains no Hazardous Substances.

TRUST - First Mortgage Bank, not personally but as Trustee under Trust Agreement dated April 11, 1989 and known as Trust No. 108049-04

WORK - The labor and materials to be furnished for the construction of the Improvements.

ARTICLE 3

REPRESENTATIONS, WARRANTIES AND COVENANTS

3.1   In order to induce Lender to execute this Agreement and to make the Loan, the Trust represents and the Beneficiary represents and warrants as follows:

(a)   The Trust owns good and marketable fee simple title to the Real Estate. The Real Estate is free and clear of all liens, claims and encumbrances except the Permitted Exceptions. Subject to the terms and conditions contained in this Agreement, Borrower intends to develop an auto care center containing approximately 18,500 square feet, more or less, on the Real Estate.

(b)   The Beneficiary is the owner of the entire beneficial interest in the Trust and any one of David Delaney and Steven Matthews hold the sole power of direction thereunder, free and clear of all liens, claims and encumbrances, other than a collateral assignment in favor of Lender.

(c)   Beneficiary is a limited partnership duly formed and in good standing under the laws of the state of Illinois and all partnership action required to authorize the execution and performance of the obligations in this Agreement and in the other Loan Documents by Beneficiary has been taken.

(d)   General Partner is an Illinois corporation duly formed and in good standing under the laws of the state of Illinois, all corporate action required to authorize the execution and performance of the obligations in this Agreement and in the other Loan Documents by General Partner has been taken and General Partner's execution and delivery of this Agreement and the other Loan Documents and performance thereunder do not and will not contravene or conflict, violate or constitute a default under its articles of incorporation, bylaws, any applicable law, rule, regulation, judgment, decree or order or any agreement, indenture or instrument to which it is a party or is bound.

(e)   Each of Borrower and General Partner has full power and authority to execute and deliver this Agreement and the other Loan Documents to be executed and delivered by Borrower pursuant to this Agreement and to perform their respective obligations hereunder and thereunder. Upon the execution and delivery thereof, this Agreement and all such Loan Documents will be valid, binding and enforceable upon Borrower in accordance with their respective terms. Execution and delivery of this Agreement and the other Loan Documents to be executed and delivered by Borrower, do not and will not contravene, conflict with, violate or constitute a default under the partnership agreement governing Beneficiary, any applicable law, rule, regulation, judgment, decree or order or any agreement, indenture or instrument to which either Borrower is a party or is bound or which is binding upon or applicable to the Project or any portion thereof.

(f)   There is not any condition, event or circumstance existing, or any litigation, arbitration, governmental or administrative proceedings, actions, examinations, claims or demands pending, or to Borrower's knowledge, threatened, affecting either Borrower, the Project or the use or operation thereof, or which would prevent either Borrower from complying with or performing its respective obligations under this Agreement, the Notes or any of the other Loan Documents within the time limits set forth therein for such compliance or performance, and to the best of Beneficiary's knowledge no basis for any such matter exists.

(g)   Upon completion of the Improvements as contemplated by the Plans and Specifications, all utilities necessary for use, operation and occupancy of the Project will be available and all requirements then required by applicable law for unrestricted use of such utilities will be fulfilled. All building, zoning, safety, health, fire, water district, sewerage and environmental protection agency permits and other licenses and permits which are required by any governmental authority for construction of the Improvements and the use, occupancy and operation thereof in accordance with the Plans and Specifications therefor will be obtained by or furnished to Borrower prior to commencement of construction, as may be required by any governmental authority, and will be obtained and maintained in full force and effect by Borrower when and as required by any governmental authority.

(h)   All financial statements submitted to Lender relating to each of Borrower and the Guarantors are true and correct in all material respects, fairly present the financial condition of the person or entity to which they pertain and the other information therein described and do not contain any untrue statement of a material fact or omit to state a fact material to the financial statements submitted or this Agreement. No adverse change has occurred in the financial condition of either "Borrower or the Guarantors since the dates of the most recent financial statements furnished to Lender.

(i)   Upon completion of construction of the Improvements in accordance with the Plans and Specifications, the Improvements and the use, occupancy and operation of thereof will not, violate any contractual arrangements with third parties, violate any laws, statutes, ordinances, rules, orders or regulations of any kind whatsoever (including without limitation, those relating to environmental protection, water use, zoning, building, fire, health or safety), any contractual arrangements with third parties or any covenants, conditions, easements, rights of way or restrictions of record and neither Borrower nor any agent thereof has received any notice, written or otherwise, alleging any such violation. No right to any off-site facilities will be necessary to insure compliance by the Project with all environmental protection, public highway, water use, zoning, building, fire, health, safety or similar statutes, laws, ordinances, codes, rules, regulations, orders and decrees, except as previously disclosed to Lender.

(j)   The General Partner has entered into the Architect's Agreement and the Engineer's Agreement with Borrower's Architect and the Engineer pursuant to which the Borrower's Architect and Engineer have agreed to perform architectural and engineering services in connection with the design and construction of the Improvements. The Architect's Agreement and Engineer's Agreement have been assigned by General Partner to Beneficiary, are in full force and effect, unamended, and no default exists thereunder by either party thereto.

(k)   The General Contractor has agreed to act as general contractor and to perform all general contracting services in connection with the construction of the Project.

(l)   The General Contractor has prior to the date hereof and will hereafter enter into subcontracts (all of said subcontracts being hereinafter collectively referred to as the "Subcontracts") for the performance of portions of the Work. Borrower will deliver to Lender upon request true, complete and correct copies of all Subcontracts that have been entered into prior to the date hereof, or are hereafter executed, together with all amendments thereto made prior to the date hereof.

(m)   Attached hereto as Exhibit "D" is the Project Budget, which is a true, complete and correct budget and forecast of the projected sources and uses of funds and projected revenues and expenses with respect to the ownership of the Project and the construction of the Improvements.

(n)   Prior to and as a condition to the first disbursement of the proceeds of the Loan, Borrower shall have a minimum of $200,000 of equity invested in the Project represented by the Letter of Credit to be delivered to Lender.

(o)   All permits, consents, approvals or authorizations by, or registrations, declarations, withholdings of objection or filings with and Governmental Authorities necessary in connection with the valid execution, delivery and performance of this Agreement, the Note, the Mortgage, the Loan Documents, or necessary for the construction of the Improvements have been obtained, are valid, adequate and in full force and effect or will be obtained prior to the commencement of construction of the Improvements.

(p)   All utility services necessary and adequate for construction and for the operation of the Improvements for their intended purpose are available at the boundaries of the Real Estate which abut on a public way, including, sanitary and storm sewer facilities, gas and electric and telephone facilities; and the providing of all such utility services necessary for the construction and operation of the Improvements are not subject to the consent or withholding of objection of any Governmental Authorities or, if so subject, such consent or withholding of objection shall have been obtained prior to commencement of construction.

(q)   All roads, easements and other necessary modes of ingress or egress to the Mortgaged Premises necessary for the full utilization of the Improvements for their intended purpose or for the construction thereof have been completed or obtained or the necessary rights of way therefore have been acquired and all necessary steps (except for building permits prior to land acquisition) have been taken by the Borrower or the appropriate Governmental Authorities to insure the complete construction and installation thereof.

(r)   (i) Except as disclosed in the Toxic Waste Report, the Project and the use and operation thereof are currently in compliance and will remain in compliance with all applicable environmental, health and safety laws, rules and regulations; and to the best of the Borrower's knowledge after diligent inquiry: (ii) the Real Estate has never been used for a sanitary land fill, dump or for the disposal, generation or storage of Hazardous Substances; (iii) no Hazardous Substances have been deposited or are located in, under or upon the Real Estate or property adjacent thereto and no part of the Real Estate is presently contaminated by any Hazardous Substances; and (iv) no underground storage tanks are or have been located on the Real Estate. No notice has been received by Borrower of any Hazardous Substance in, under or upon the Real Estate or any parcels adjacent thereto or of any violation of any environmental protection laws or regulations with respect to the Real Estate or any parcels adjacent thereto and no facts exist which would provide a basis for any such violation with respect to the Real Estate or any parcels adjacent thereto.

(s)   Except as otherwise disclosed in writing to Lender, no part of the Real Estate contains "waters of the United States," as defined in 33 CFR 328, and the Project will not include the discharging of dredged or fill material into waters of the United States as such activity is described and regulated by Section 404 of the Clean Water Act 33 U.S.C. § 1344.

(t)   The Casey Lease, Lube Lease and Sparks Lease are unmodified and in full force and effect and the copies thereof delivered to Lender are true, correct and complete copies of the originals.

(u) The REA is unmodified, in full force and effect and no default or claim of default exists thereunder.

3.2   SURVIVAL OF REPRESENTATIONS, WARRANTIES AND COVENANTS. The foregoing representations, warranties and covenants will be true and correct on the date of the initial disbursement of the Loan hereunder and at the dates of all subsequent disbursements of the Loan. It shall be a condition to Borrowers right to receive a disbursement of the Loan that all of the foregoing representations, warranties and covenants be true and correct on the date of such disbursement and with the same force and effect as of the date of this Agreement. All representations, warranties, acknowledgments, covenants and agreements made in this Agreement or in any certificate or other document delivered to the Lender by Borrower pursuant to or in connection with this Agreement shall be deemed to have been relied upon by Lender, notwithstanding any investigation heretofore or hereafter made by Lender or on its behalf (and Borrower hereby acknowledges such reliance by Lender in making the Loan and all disbursements thereof) and shall survive the making of any or all of the disbursements contemplated hereby and shall continue in full force and effect as long as there remains unperformed any obligations to Lender hereunder or under the Note, the Mortgage or Guaranty, or any of the other Loan Documents; provided, however, that all representations and warranties in respect to Hazardous Substances shall survive repayment of the Loan and discharge of Borrower's liabilities.

ARTICLE 4

AGREEMENT TO MAKE LOAN AND REPAYMENT THEREOF

4.1   AGREEMENT TO BORROW AND LEND. On the basis of the covenants, agreements, warranties and representations of Borrower contained in this Agreement and subject to the terms and conditions herein set forth, Lender agrees to lend to Borrower a sum not to exceed the Loan Amount, the proceeds of which are to be disbursed by Lender as herein provided solely for the payment of costs and expenses shown on the Project Budget actually incurred by Borrower.

4.2   DISBURSEMENT OF THE LOAN AMOUNT. Subject to the satisfaction of the terms and conditions herein contained, the proceeds of the Loan shall be disbursed as follows:

(a)   The first disbursement of the Loan shall be made at such time as all of the conditions set forth in Section 5.1 hereof have been satisfied by Borrower. Each subsequent disbursement shall be made only at such time as all applicable conditions set forth in Article 5 hereof have been satisfied by Borrower.

(b)   All disbursements (including the first) for construction of the Improvements will be made, at Lender's option (i) through a construction loan escrow trust established with the Title Company, (ii) to the Borrower or (iii) directly to the General Contractor or subcontractors. The execution of this Agreement constitutes an irrevocable direction and authorization by Borrower to Lender to disburse the Loan proceeds in the above manner. Except for payment of fees for permits and other governmental requirements each disbursement to pay construction costs shall in no event exceed the amount then due the General Contractor or any subcontractors for Work completed and in place, less a 10% retainage which retainage shall be reduced to 5% when the value of the Work completed and in place for the applicable subcontractor exceeds fifty percent (50%) of the value of such subcontractor's subcontract, which retainage shall not be paid until completion of all Improvements, the work of such General Contractor or subcontractor has been accepted by Borrower's Architect and approved by Lender's Construction Consultant and Lender determines such release of retainage is appropriate in its reasonable judgment.

(c)   Without limitation of any other provision hereof, with respect to any particular item or category shown on the Project Budget, in no event shall Lender be required to disburse any portion of the Loan in excess of the portion of the Loan allocated to such item or category of the Project as shown on the Project Budget. Borrower shall be permitted to reallocate amounts set forth in the Project Budget for specific line items to offset cost savings on one line item against cost overruns on another line item and vice versa with Lender's prior written consent which shall not be unreasonably withheld or delayed.

4.3   DISBURSEMENT PROCEDURES.

(a)   Borrower shall request and Lender shall be required to make disbursements of the Loan not more frequently than once each calendar month. Lender may at any time take such action as it deems appropriate to verify that the conditions precedent to each disbursement have been satisfied, including but not limited to, verification of the amounts due under any construction contract relative to the Work. Borrower agrees to cooperate with Lender in any such action. If in the course of any such verification, any amount shown on any construction contract, application for payment, sworn statement or waiver of lien is subject to a possible discrepancy, such discrepancy shall be eliminated by Borrower to Lender's satisfaction. Each request for disbursement shall be made by a notice delivered from Borrower to Lender not less than two (2) days prior to the date of requested disbursement specifying in detail the amount and mode of each disbursement and accompanied by the documents listed in Section 5.2(a) hereof.

(b)   For purposes of this Agreement (i) the cost of labor and material furnished for the Work shall be deemed to be incurred by Borrower when the labor and material have been incorporated into the Improvements, (ii) the cost of services (other than labor included in the work) shall be deemed to be incurred by Borrower when the services are actually rendered, and (iii) any other costs shall be deemed to be incurred by Borrower when due and payable, but not before the value to be received in return for such cost has been received by Borrower.

(c)   No disbursement for materials purchased by Borrower but not yet installed or incorporated into the Project shall be made without Lender's prior approval of the conditions under which such materials are purchased and stored. In no event shall any such disbursement be made unless the materials involved have been delivered to the Real Estate or stored with a bonded warehouseman, with satisfactory evidence of security, insurance and suitable storage. Borrower shall provide Lender, in connection with such materials, a copy of a bill of sale or other evidence of title in Borrower, together with a copy of UCC Searches against Borrower and the warehouseman, if applicable indicating no liens or claims which may affect such materials.

(d)   If at any time the Lender reasonably determines that the Estimated Total Cost of Completing the Improvements is more than the Loan Amount plus the amount of any funds of Borrower then on deposit with the Lender pursuant to this Section or otherwise on deposit and pledged to the Lender or available as additional collateral excluding the Letter of Credit, or that the amounts advanced for any cost item shown on the Project Budget exceeds or would if disbursed exceed, the amount shown therefor on the Project Budget the Lender shall have no obligation to make any further advances hereunder and Borrower covenants and agrees that within ten (10) days of the mailing of written notice of such deficiency it will deposit funds with the Lender in an amount sufficient to cure the deficiency (provided; however, in no circumstance shall the Letter of Credit be utilized to cure such deficiency), all funds so deposited with the Lender to be held by it as collateral security for the Loan and disbursed for the payment of costs for which Loan proceeds may be requested hereunder prior to the disbursement of any further proceeds of the Loan.

(e)   Borrower hereby authorizes Lender to make advances of Loan proceeds directly to itself for payment and reimbursement of all interest due hereunder and under the Note and all other charges, costs and expenses (including Loan Expenses) required to be paid by Borrower hereunder which interest and other charges, costs and expenses are not paid within fifteen (15) days following delivery of statements therefor to Borrower.

4.4   INTEREST ON AND REPAYMENT OF LOAN.

(a)   Prior to a Default, interest on all funds advanced under this Agreement, shall accrue from and after the date of each such advance at the Interest Rate and be payable monthly commencing on the first day of the month following the initial disbursement of the Loan by the Lender;

(b)   The Interest Rate shall be computed for actual days on the basis of the number of days elapsed and a three hundred sixty (360) day year;

(c)   Interest on all funds advanced under this Agreement shall accrue at the Default Interest Rate subsequent to the occurrence of Default or as otherwise provided in the Note;

(d)   Borrower agrees to pay to Lender interest on all funds advanced under this Agreement from time to time to, or for the benefit of, Borrower at the Interest Rate or the Default Interest Rate in accordance with the terms of the Note; and

(e)   Notwithstanding any provisions of this Agreement or any instrument securing payment of the Loan to the contrary, it is the intent of Lender and Borrower that Lender shall never be entitled to receive, collect or apply, as interest on principal of the indebtedness, any amounts in excess of the maximum rate of interest permitted to be charged by applicable law; and if under any circumstances whatsoever, fulfillment of any provision of this Agreement, at the time performance of such provision shall be due, shall involve transcending the limit of validity prescribed by applicable law, then, ipso facto, the obligation to be fulfilled shall be reduced to the limit of such validity; and in. the event Lender ever receives, collects or applies as interest any such excess, such amount which would be excess interest shall be deemed a permitted partial prepayment of principal and treated hereunder as such; and if the principal of the indebtedness under this Agreement is paid in full, any remaining excess funds shall forthwith be paid to Borrower. In determining whether or not interest of any kind payable hereunder, under any specific contingency, exceeds the highest lawful rate, Lender and Borrower shall, to the maximum extent permitted under applicable law, (1) characterize any non-principal payment as an expense, fee or premium rather than as interest and (2) amortize, prorate, allocate and spread to the end that the interest on account of such indebtedness does not exceed the maximum amount permitted by applicable law; provided that if the amount of interest received for the actual period of existence thereof exceeds the maximum lawful rate, Lender shall refund to Borrower the amount of such excess. Lender shall not be subject to any penalties provided by any laws for contracting for, charging or receiving interest in excess of the maximum lawful rate.

4.5   INTEREST RESERVE. The Lender shall establish and maintain an interest reserve as provided in the Project Budget and shall have the right to disburse payments therefrom to pay interest on the Loan. Lender agrees that so long as no Default exists hereunder or under the Loan Documents, Lender shall apply the interest reserve to pay interest due and owing on the Loan at Borrower's request. Such disbursements shall be added to the principal balance of the Loan and shall bear interest at the Interest Rate.

4.6   NOTES. Borrower's obligations to repay Lender the Loan Amount shall be evidenced by the Notes of the Borrower payable to the order of Lender.

4.7   SECURITY FOR BORROWER'S.OBLIGATIONS. Payment of all sums to be paid by Borrower to Lender under this Agreement shall be secured, inter alia, by the Mortgage, the Letter of Credit and all other Loan Documents.

ARTICLE 5

GENERAL CONDITIONS OF LOAN

5.1   CONDITIONS TO FIRST ADVANCES FOR CONSTRUCTION AND FOR NONCONSTRUCTION COSTS. Lender shall not be obligated to make the first advance for construction costs hereunder unless it has received all of the following prior to the requested disbursement date for the first advance for construction costs:

(a)   the Notes;

(b)   the Mortgage;

(c)   the Loan Documents;

(d)   a commitment from the Title Company to issue its standard form of ALTA mortgagee's construction loan title policy (the "Title Policy") in the Loan Amount with Pending Disbursement Endorsement, a 3.0 Zoning Endorsement with a commitment to issue a 3.1 Zoning Endorsement with Parking Coverage, a Comprehensive 1 Endorsement, affirmative coverage insuring Borrower's rights under the REA and such other endorsements as the Lender shall specify, such policy showing title to the Real Estate in the Trust and insuring the Mortgage as a first lien without encroachments or prior right of others on the Real Estate, subject only to the Permitted Exceptions listed on Exhibit "C" attached hereto, the disbursement of the Loan, standard objections which cannot be cured until completion of the Improvements (but no exception for matters of survey or mechanic's or materialmen's liens or rights to liens shall appear), and such other exceptions and objections as are satisfactory to the Lender in its discretion;

(e)   A Plat of Survey of the Real Estate made by a Surveyor licensed in the State of Illinois showing the legal description and area of the Real Estate, all discrepancies, conflicts, encroachments, improvements, overlapping of improvements, setback lines, roadways, easements, fences, apparent travel ways, water courses and apparent disposal sites, that are either of record, apparent or may be discovered by visible inspection. Such survey shall be updated as of the date upon which the foundation has been laid and completion of framing of the Improvements to show all improvements then in place so placed that the Project is within the lot lines and in compliance with any restrictions of record or ordinances relating to the location thereof. Such surveys shall be certified to Lender, Borrower and Title Company as having been prepared in accordance with the Minimum Standard Detail Requirements for Land Title Surveys jointly established and adopted by the American Land Title Association and the American Congress on Surveying and Mapping in 1988 and shall further certify that no portion of the Real Estate lies within the 100 year flood plan or any area having special flood hazards as designated by Federal Emergency Management Agency. Said Plat of Survey shall be updated following completion of foundations to show such foundations within applicable lot and building lines. In addition, Borrower shall provide a Surveyor's drawing showing the proposed access to and from the Real Estate to a dedicated roadway.

(f)   such documents, opinions, acknowledgments, consents and assurances, trust agreements and opinions of counsel - as the Lender shall deem reasonably necessary or appropriate to evidence the capacity and authority of the Borrower, General Partner, and all other parties to the transactions contemplated hereby to enter into said transactions and be bound by the terms and conditions of this Agreement and all other agreements delivered to the Lender in connection with the transactions contemplated hereby and evidencing the fact that all such documents shall be the valid and binding obligations of the parties thereto, enforceable in accordance with their terms;

(g)   such documents, opinions, withholdings of objection and assurances as the Lender shall reasonably deem necessary or appropriate to evidence the truthfulness of the representations and warranties contained in Article 3 hereof and the observance of the covenants contained in Article 7 hereof, including without limitation such evidence as the Lender deems reasonably necessary to indicate complete compliance with all requirements of Governmental Bodies with respect to the construction of the Improvements and the use thereof for their intended purposes to the extent that such consents or withholdings of objection may be obtained prior to completion of construction and such evidence as the Lender may deem necessary or appropriate to evidence - the availability of all utilities, including water, sewers, gas and electricity, may be necessary to construct the Improvements in accordance with the Plans and Specifications and to use said Improvements in accordance with their intended purposes;

(h)   such additional documents, opinions, comments or withholdings of objection as may be required by the Title Company in order to provide the insurance to be afforded to the Lender pursuant to subsections (d) of this Section 5.1;

(i)   soil tests and engineering studies confirming that the soil type and compatibility, sub-soil conditions and water levels are suitable and sufficient for construction of the Project in accordance with the Plans and Specifications and no special preparation of any nature will be required with respect to any of the Real Estate except as contemplated by the Project Budget;

(j)   insurance certificates together with copies of policies, with prepaid premiums, from companies, with coverage and in amounts and containing mortgagee's loss payable clauses, all satisfactory to Lender and each such policy shall provide that such policy may not be cancelled or amended by any party for any reason whatsoever without first giving Lender at least thirty (30) days' prior written notice of any proposed cancellation or amendment;

(k)   a satisfactory appraisal of the Project made by an appraiser belonging to the American Institute of Real Estate Appraisers, which will be provided no later than September 30, 1989;

(1)   evidence satisfactory to Lender that sufficient sanitary sewer lines and treatment plant capacity, electric service, water service, gas service and telephone service are available for the Improvements;

(m)   a toxic waste report showing that the Real Estate and adjacent land conform to all applicable federal, state and local environmental laws, statutes, ordinances, rules and regulations and contains no Hazardous Substances;

(n)   satisfactory evidence that the Real Estate is properly zoned to permit the construction and operation of the Project as contemplated by this Agreement;

(o)   satisfactory evidence that the Real Estate has been platted;

(p)   a copy of the fully executed Architect's Agreement Engineer's Agreement and General Contract;

(q)   on Lender's request such documents as Borrower has provided the Title Company in connection with the issuance of the Title Policy;

(r)   copies of all licenses and building permits necessary for construction and completion of the Improvements and all other permits and licenses required for construction, use and operation of the Improvements (except those permits and licenses which by their nature cannot be obtained until completion of the Work), all of which shall be unconditional, together with a collateral assignment of all licenses, permits, consents, authorizations and utility installation and service agreements;

(s)   certificates executed by the Engineer and Architect containing the following: (1) a detailed list of the final Plans and Specifications for the Improvements,, (2) a statement that such Plans and Specifications are complete in all respects and show all work and materials required for construction and completion of the Improvements, which when completed in accordance therewith, shall be in compliance with all applicable laws, regulations and ordinances; (3) a statement that the Plans and Specifications for the Improvements were prepared in a manner consistent with accepted architectural practices and in full compliance with all applicable zoning,. building, environmental protection, safety and health laws, ordinances and regulations applicable to the construction, use and operation of the Project; (4) a list of all certificates, permits, licenses, consents and authorizations of governmental authorities which are necessary to permit the commencement of the construction of the Improvements either have been obtained and are in full force and effect or there are no impediments to obtaining such certificates, permits, licenses and other authorizations, and that they will be promptly obtained prior to commencement of the construction of the Improvements; and (5) a statement that adequate water, sewer, electrical power and other public and private utilities are available to the site in such capacities as to adequately Service the Project and, after the completion of the construction of the Improvements;

(t)   An opinion of the attorney for Borrower and the Guarantors in form and substance satisfactory to Lender;

(u)   Copies of all applicable ordinances and all zoning proceedings relating to the Project, if any, certified as being true, correct and complete by the applicable governmental authority, and such other evidence as Lender requires that the Project will conform to all applicable building, zoning and use laws And ordinances and may be lawfully occupied for its intended purposes;

(v)   Evidence satisfactory to Lender that the Project is not located in an area designated as a wetland or by the Secretary of Housing and Urban Development as having special flood hazards, or if it is so located (as to flood hazards), satisfactory evidence that flood insurance is in effect;

(w)   Uniform Commercial Code, federal and state tax lien and judgment searches covering each party comprising Borrower and the Guarantors, disclosing no matters objectionable to Lender;

(x)   Such payment and performance bonds as Lender may reasonably require for the Contractor and any subcontractors;

(y)   Two sets of final, detailed Plans and Specifications for the Improvements, which shall be subject to prior approval by Lender and Lender's Construction Consultant, together with evidence satisfactory to Lender that the appropriate local authorities have approved such Plans and Specifications as satisfying the terms of any agreements, ordinances, regulations or requirements, applicable to the Project. Borrower will not cause or allow any changes or modifications in the Plans and specifications or any deviations therefrom which would materially adversely affect the scope or quality of the Project without the prior written consent of Lender and all necessary governmental authorities;

(z)   A subordination, non-disturbance and attornment agreement from Casey, Lube and Sparks in form and substance satisfactory to Lender;

(aa)   An Owner's Affidavit and Sworn Contractor's Statement, waivers of lien and an Application for Payment in the form prescribed by Lender together with a statement of the General Contractor that all items of construction cost have been incorporated into the Project in accordance with the Plans and Specifications;

(ab)   A certificate of the Lender's Construction Consultant and the Borrower's Architect in form and substance reasonably satisfactory to Lender, to the effect that each has made diligent investigation and that, based on such investigation, all construction to the date of the request for disbursement has been completed in accordance with the Plans and Specifications and certifying the approval of the request for disbursement;

(ac)   The Letter of Credit in form and substance satisfactory to Lender; and

(ad)   Such other documents, instruments and opinions of counsel as may be reasonably required by Lender and are not otherwise described in this Agreement. Lender shall not be obligated to make the first advance for nonconstruction costs until it has received the preceding documents and approvals stated in subparagraphs (a) - (j) , (1), (n)-(q), (s)(5), (t)-(x), (ac) and (ad).

5.2   CONDITIONS TO SUBSEQUENT ADVANCES. The Lender's obligation to make any advance after the first advance for nonconstruction costs and the first advance for construction costs shall be subject to the continued satisfaction of the conditions set forth in Section 5.1 hereof and to the satisfaction of the following conditions:

(a)   The Lender shall have received the following, in form and content acceptable to the Lender, at least two (2) days prior to the requested disbursement date:

(i)   A written request from the Borrower or its agent (the Borrower hereby appoints the Beneficiary as its agent for such purpose only) requesting the advance and approving the affidavits, certificates and 'contractor's statements tendered in support of such advance,, and either stating that no additional contracts have been entered into by the Borrower or the Beneficiary for items payable from the Loan since the date of the sworn statement furnished pursuant to Section 5.1(aa) hereof or describing all such additional contracts in the manner required by said Section;

(ii)   current sworn Contractor's statements in conformance with the requirements of Section 5.1 hereof;

(iii)   waivers of lien from each contractor, subcontractor and materialman on whose behalf funds are sought for payment, all of which waivers shall comply with the mechanic's lien law of the State of Illinois and shall conform to the requirements of the Title Company;

(iv)   invoices for all costs and expenses for which funds are sought for reimbursement and which are attributable to other than work done or materials supplied by contractors, subcontractors or materialmen;

(v)   Written certification from the Borrower's Architect and Lender's Construction Consultant setting forth the following:

   (1)   That the amount of all disbursements for labor, services, work and materials (including the disbursement then requested) is fair and does not exceed 90% of the value or 95% of the value if the applicable work and materials in place exceed fifty percent of the applicable contract value, based upon contract prices and including contractor overhead and profit, of the labor, services, work and materials rendered to and incorporated in the Improvements and materials stored on the Real Estate, and that such onsite materials are reasonably necessary for the progress of construction;

   (2)   That the workmanship of all work on the Improvements is good and the materials in place are of good quality;

   (3)   That the Improvements are being constructed in accordance with the Plans and Specifications; and

   (4)   That the construction, to the date of the issuance of the certificate, complies with all applicable building codes, regulations and ordinances;

(vi)   A Date Down Endorsement to the Title Policy to cover such advance, which endorsement shall show no encumbrances other than Permitted Encumbrances;

(vii)   An Interim Mechanic's Lien Endorsement to the Title Policy to cover such advance;

(viii)   Such evidence (including architect's certificates) as may be requested by the Lender to demonstrate that the reserves established in the Project Budget are adequate for the purposes for which they were established, and that the Loan is in balance in accordance with Section 4.3(d) hereof;

(ix)   Such additional certificates and documents, opinions, withholdings of objection and assurances as the Lender shall reasonably deem necessary or appropriate to evidence the continued accuracy of the representations and warranties contained in Section 3.1 hereof and the observance and performance of the covenants contained in Article 7 hereof; and

(b)   No Event of Default shall have occurred and be continuing under the Loan Documents, and no event shall have occurred and no condition shall exist which with the passage of time or the giving of notice, or both, would constitute an Event of Default under the Loan Documents. Each request for disbursement by Borrower shall constitute Borrower's certification that the representations and warranties contained in Article 3 hereof are true and correct as of the date of such request, Borrower's certification that Borrower is in compliance with the terms and conditions of this Agreement, and Borrower's representation and warranty to Lender, with respect to the Work, materials and other items for which payment is requested that (except as otherwise permitted); such Work and materials have been incorporated into the Project, free of liens and encumbrances; the value thereof is as estimated therein; such Work and materials substantially conform to the approved Plans and Specifications or Plans and Specifications, as applicable, this Agreement, and all applicable statutes, laws, ordinances, rules and regulations; and the requisitioned value of such Work and materials and the amounts of all other items of cost for which payment is requested by Borrower have theretofore been in fact paid for in cash by Borrower or the same are then due and owing by Borrower. Approval by Lender of requests for advances shall not constitute an acceptance by Lender of the Work, materials or other items of cost for which payment is requested by the Borrower except to the extent that the facts contained in the Borrower's requests for advances are actually as so represented and warranted.

5.3   CONDITIONS PRECEDENT TO FINAL ADVANCE. The Lender shall not be obligated to make the final advance hereunder until the following conditions have been satisfied:

(a)   All conditions precedent to subsequent advances specified in Section 5.2 hereof shall be satisfied with respect to said last advance;

(b)   The Lender's Construction Consultant and the Borrower's Architect shall have certified that the Improvements have been completed in accordance with the Plans and Specifications;

(c) The Lender shall have received a final plat of survey showing the completed Improvements and satisfying the requirements with respect to the initial survey specified in Section 5.1(e) hereof;

(d) The Lender shall have received such evidence as it shall reasonably request of the approval of all Governmental Bodies of the Improvements (except tenant finish work not preventing occupancy of areas in which tenant finish work has been completed) in their entirety for permanent occupancy; and

(e) The Lender shall have received a final Title Policy conforming to the requirements of Section 5.1(d) hereof, except that any endorsements previously issued in modified form by reason of the fact that construction of the Improvements was not complete shall be issued in standard unmodified form.

ARTICLE 6

LOAN EXPENSES AND ADVANCES BY LENDER

6.1 LOAN EXPENSES. Borrower shall pay, according to invoices provided by Lender, all of Lender's Loan Expenses.

6.2 RIGHT OF LENDER TO MAKE ADVANCES TO CURE DEFAULT. In the event that Borrower shall fail to perform any of Borrower's covenants and agreements herein contained, or make any payments required by this Agreement, Lender may (but shall not be obligated to) perform any one or all of such covenants and agreements after notice and the expiration of any applicable cure periods, make any such payments (including those due Lender) or advance funds in excess of , the f ace amount of the Notes, and any amounts expended by Lender in so doing plus interest thereon at the Default Interest Rate shall be secured by the Loan Documents and, shall be due and payable by Borrower to lender, on demand.

6.3 INDEBTEDNESS SECURED BY LOAN DOCUMENTS Any and all advances and payments made by Lender under this Agreement and all Loan Expenses set forth in Section 6.1 above as and when advanced or incurred by Lender, shall be and become secured by the Loan Documents to the same extent as if all terms and provisions of this Agreement were set forth in the Loan Documents, whether or not the aggregate amount of such advances, payments and Loan expenses exceed the face amount of the Note; provided, however, that the total indebtedness secured by the Loan Documents shall not in any event exceed $10,000,000.00.

6.4 LOAN FEES. Upon the opening of the Loan, Borrower shall pay Lender a loan fee in the amount of one percent (1%) of the amount of the Loan.

ARTICLE 7

BORROWER'S COVENANTS AND AGREEMENTS

7.1   PROJECT COMMENCEMENT AND COMPLETION. Unless the Project is delayed by Force Majeure, the Loan shall remain in balance including payment of all interest and costs and all tenants shall continue their leases in full force and effect with all payments required thereunder being made, Borrower shall commence construction of the Project on or before the Construction Commencement Date and shall cause the construction of the Improvements to be diligently and expeditiously carried out to completion on or before the Construction Completion Date, in a good and workmanlike manner, in accordance with the Plans and specifications, as applicable, and all applicable laws, ordinances and regulations. Without limiting the generality of the foregoing, Borrower shall cause construction of the Project to continue without interruption (subject to the above-stated Force Majeure exception) until completion, and to be completed in accordance with the Plans and Specifications on or before the Construction Completion Date. Construction of the Project shall not be deemed to be complete until the Lender's Construction Consultant is prepared to certify that all space located within the Project can be used and occupied in accordance with all applicable laws, ordinances and regulations.

7.2   DELIVERY OF CERTIFICATE OF OCCUPANCY. Upon completion of the Improvements and as a condition to final disbursement, Borrower shall deliver to Lender a copy of an unconditional certificate of occupancy for the Improvements, if such certificate would be customarily issued by the Municipality.

7.3   CHANGE ORDER. Borrower shall not, without the prior written approval of Lender, such approval not to be unreasonably withheld, make or permit any "material change" in the Plans and Specifications. Borrower shall furnish to Lender with each request for approval of a "material change" in the Plans and Specifications, a certificate of the Borrower to the effect that such change is in compliance with all applicable laws and ordinances. For purposes hereof, "material change" shall mean any single change having an estimated cost of more than $10,000 or any group or series of changes having an aggregate cost of more than $50,000.

7.4   COMPLIANCE WITH REGULATIONS. Borrower shall comply or cause compliance with all applicable building codes, zoning ordinances, environmental protection, health and safety laws and regulations, and other laws, ordinances and regulations governing construction, use and operation of the Project.

7.5   LENDER'S RIGHT TO INSPECT. Borrower shall permit inspection of the Improvements at all times by Lender, Lender's Construction Consultant or its representatives.

7.6   INSURANCE. Borrower shall pay all premiums on all insurance policies required under Section 5.1(j) and the Mortgage from time to time during the progress of construction, as such premiums are billed and become due, and thirty (30) days before any such policies of insurance expire Borrower shall furnish to Lender with premiums paid as due, additional and renewal insurance policies in form, and with companies, coverage, deductibles and amounts satisfactory to Lender. Borrower shall pay prior to the due date thereof all real estate tax bills covering all or any portion of the Project. In the event of failure by Borrower to provide such insurance or pay such taxes, Lender may place insurance and pay such taxes and treat the amounts expended therefor as disbursements of Loan proceeds and such amounts from the date so expended until paid shall bear interest at the Default Interest Rate.

7.7   DELIVERY OF REPORTS AND FINANCIAL STATEMENTS. Borrower will from time to time furnish to Lender such information and reports, financial and otherwise, concerning Borrower and Guarantor, the construction of the Work, and the operation of such Project as Lender reasonably requires, including without limitation (i) within thirty (30) days after the end of each calendar year, annual financial statements of the Guarantor certified by Guarantor to be true, complete and correct and (ii) on or before June 1 and December 1 of each year, semi-annual financial statements of the Beneficiary and the Project on Lender's standard form or on such other form as Lender shall approve setting forth the information therein required as of the six month periods ending March 31 and September 30 of each year containing income and expense statements, a balance sheet and a statement of Borrower's equity in the Project, prepared by the Beneficiary, certified to be true, complete and correct by an officer of the Beneficiary.

7.8   REPRESENTATIONS AND WARRANTIES REMAIN TRUE. Borrower agrees that all representations and warranties of Borrower contained in Article 3 hereof shall remain true at all times until the Loan is repaid in full.

7.9   TITLE TO PROJECT FREE OF LIENS. Except for (i) the Mortgage and other security for the Loan, (ii) the, lien of general real estate taxes payments of which is not yet due, (iii) mechanic's liens which are bonded against to the satisfaction of Lender, (iv) the Permitted Exceptions, Borrower shall keep title to the Project free of all liens, claims and encumbrances, whether senior or junior to the Mortgage, and (v) easements to utility companies necessary to the operation of the improvements which easements have been reasonably approved by Lender.

7.10   DEFENSE OF LITIGATION WITH RESPECT TO PROJECT. If any proceedings are filed seeking to enjoin or otherwise prevent or declare invalid or unlawful the construction occupancy, maintenance or operation of the Improvements or any portion thereof, Borrower will cause such proceedings to be vigorously contested in good faith, and in the event of any adverse ruling or decision, prosecute all allowable appeals therefrom, and will, without limiting the generality of the foregoing, resist the entry or seek the stay of any temporary or permanent injunction that may be entered, and use its best efforts to bring about a favorable and speedy disposition of all such proceedings. Costs of all such proceedings, including without limitation, all of Lender's costs, and reasonable fees and disbursements of Lender's counsel in connection with any such proceedings, whether or not Lender is a party thereto, shall be at Borrower's expense, such expenses, including reasonable attorneys' fees and fees and charges for court costs, bonds and the like to be deemed to be Loan Expenses hereunder, shall bear interest from the date so incurred until paid at the Default Interest Rate and shall be payable to Lender on demand.

7.11   NO TRANSFER OF ANY PORTION OF PROJECT. Except as expressly permitted pursuant to Article 10 below, Borrower shall not, without Lender's prior written consent, suffer, permit or enter into any agreement for any sale, lease, transfer, or in any way encumber or dispose of or grant or suffer any security or other assignment (collateral or otherwise) of or in all or any portion of the Project, or the beneficial interest or power of direction in, to or under the Trust or any interest in Beneficiary or stock in General, Partner, provided that (i) limited partnership interests in the Beneficiary may be transferred if the General Partner shall remain in control of Beneficiary subsequent to such transfer and the Lender is notified and grants its approval prior to such transfer, such approval not to be unreasonably delayed or withheld and (ii) stock in General Partner may be transferred if Guarantors shall remain in control of General Partner subsequent to such transfer and the Lender is notified and grants its approval prior to such transfer, such approval not to be unreasonably delayed or withheld. Any consent by Lender, or any waiver of an Event of Default under this Paragraph 7.11, shall not constitute a consent to, or waiver of any right, remedy or power of Lender under any subsequent Event of Default hereunder.

7.12   NO MATERIAL CHANGES IN AGREEMENT. Borrower shall not, without the prior written approval of Lender and Borrower's Architect (to the extent and in cases where necessary), make any material changes or consent to any material changes in the Architect's Agreement or the Engineer's Agreement.

7.13   COMPLIANCE WITH LOAN DOCUMENTS. Borrower shall promptly and fully perform and comply in all respects with the obligations, covenants, agreements, terms, provisions and requirements of the Loan Documents.

7.14   SATISFACTION OF CONDITIONS FOR DISBURSEMENT. If Borrower does not apply for a disbursement of the Loan within sixty (60) days after the date of the most recent disbursement of the Loan, Borrower shall nevertheless cause all of the conditions precedent to disbursement set forth in Article 5 to be satisfied as of the expiration of said sixty (60) day period, and every thirty (30) days thereafter, until another disbursement is applied for.

7.15   MAINTENANCE OF LENDER'S LIEN AND APPOINTMENT OF LENDER AS ATTORNEY IN FACT. Borrower shall execute and deliver or cause to be executed and delivered to Lender now, and at any time or times hereafter, all documents, instruments, letters of direction, notices, authorizations, reports, acceptances, receipts, consents, waivers, affidavits and certificates as Lender may reasonably request, in form satisfactory to Lender, to perfect and maintain perfected the Liens granted by Borrower to Lender upon the Project or other collateral securing the Borrower's Liabilities pursuant to the terms of this Agreement and the Loan Documents or in order to consummate fully all of the transactions contemplated hereunder; and in connection therewith, Borrower hereby irrevocably makes, constitutes and appoints Lender and any of its officers, employees or agents, as its true and lawful attorney with power to sign the name of Borrower to any such document, instrument, letter of direction, notice, report, acceptance, receipt, consent, waiver, affidavit or certificate if Borrower have not complied with Lender's request to execute such document within seven (7) days from date of Borrower's receipt of such written request.

7.16   USE OF LOAN PROCEEDS. No portion of the proceeds of the Loan shall be used for any purpose other than that specified in this Agreement or as consented to in writing by Lender.

7.17   INDEMNIFICATION OF LENDER. To the fullest extent permitted by law, Borrower shall indemnify, save and keep the Lender harmless from any damage, claims or causes of action brought by third parties arising out of or related to a known or alleged design or construction defect of the Project, or otherwise arising out of or related to Borrower's operations and management or other activities of or in connection with the Project. Borrower hereby acknowledges that Lender shall not be deemed to have assumed any responsibility or liability in respect to the design of the Project, or the adequacy of the Plans and Specifications, on account of Lender's receipt or review of the Plans and Specifications or delivered pursuant to this Agreement.

7.18   DEFENSE OF LENDER. If Lender, by virtue of its undertaking of this financing and for no specific act or failure to act on its own part, is made a party to any suit or suits involving the Borrower or any other party relating to this financing or to the Project, other than suits between the parties hereto, Borrower herewith agrees that it will employ competent, experienced attorneys satisfactory to the Lender to defend Lender in such action at Borrower's own cost and, failing to do so, Lender may make use of attorneys employed by it and any amount so expended by Lender shall be additional liability owing by Borrower to Lender with interest therein at the Default Interest Rate, payable on demand and secured by the Loan Documents.

7.19   ALLOCATION OF PAYMENTS. Lender shall have the continuing right to allocate and reallocate all payments or funds which may be received by, Lender at any time or times hereafter towards repayment of any portion of Borrower's Liabilities in such manner as Lender deems advisable.

7.20   WAIVER OF NOTICES. Except for the written notices specifically provided herein, if any, Borrower waives to the fullest extent permitted by law: (i) any and all notice or demand which Borrower might be entitled to receive with respect to this Agreement or the Loan Documents by virtue of any applicable statute or law; and (ii) any demand, protest, notice of payments and non-payments, or any default, release, compromise, settlement, extension or renewal of all notes, instruments or documents at any time held by Lender on which Borrower may in any way be liable; and (iii) notice of any action taken by Lender unless expressly required by this Agreement or by any other Loan Document.

7.21   REPRESENTATIONS AND WARRANTIES SURVIVE CLOSING. All representations and warranties of Borrower and all terms, provisions, conditions and agreements to be performed by Borrower contained herein or in any of the Loan Documents executed heretofore and concurrently herewith by Borrower and delivered to Lender, or in any documents, instruments, certificates or agreements executed by Borrower shall be true and satisfied at the time of the execution of this Agreement, and as between Lender and Borrower shall survive the closing hereof and the execution and delivery of this Agreement and any and all of the Loan Documents.

7.22   PROVIDING OF INFORMATION AND NOTICE TO LENDER OF EVENTS OF DEFAULT. So long as Borrower's Liabilities remain unpaid, Borrower will: promptly supply Lender with such information concerning its affairs and property as Lender may reasonably request from time to time hereafter; promptly notify Lender of any condition or event which constitutes a breach, Default or Event of Default of any term, condition, warranty, representation or provision of this Agreement or any of the Loan Documents and of any material adverse change in the financial condition of Borrower or Guarantor; maintain a standard and modern system of accounting in accordance with generally accepted accounting principles; within the time periods provided in the Loan Documents furnish to Lender true and correct copies of accounting statements relating to the Project and financial statements of Borrower, in form satisfactory to Lender; permit Lender or any of its agents or representatives to have access to and to examine all of its books and records regarding this transaction at any time or times hereafter during business hours and permit Lender to copy and make abstracts from any and all of said books and records. Lender will not disclose such information to parties other than Lender's officers and agents except when legally required to do so.

7.23   REMEDY VIOLATION OF GOVERNMENTAL REGULATIONS. Borrower shall remedy, in a manner reasonably satisfactory to all Governmental Authorities and the Lender, such portions or aspects of the construction contemplated herein as may be determined to be not substantially in compliance with the approved Plans and Specifications or any governmental laws, ordinances, rules and regulations affecting the Project.

7.24   LENDER'S INSPECTIONS. Borrower shall cooperate with Lender in arranging for inspections from time to time of the Project by Lender's Construction Consultant and any other representatives of Lender. Borrower acknowledges and agrees that (i) all of such inspections. and reports shall be made for the sole benefit of Lender and not for the benefit of Borrower or any third party, and neither Lender nor Lender's Construction Consultant or any other of its representatives, agents or contractors assume any responsibility or liability except to Lender, by reason of such inspections or reports, (ii) Borrower will not rely upon any of such inspections or reports for any purpose whatsoever, and (iii) such inspections and reports will not constitute a waiver of any of the provisions of this Agreement or any of the obligations of Borrower hereunder. Borrower further acknowledges and agrees that neither Lender nor Lender's Construction Consultant or any other of Lender's representatives, agents or contractors shall be deemed in any way responsible for any matters related to design or construction of the Improvements.

7.25   ACCESS TO BORROWER'S BOOKS AND RECORDS. Borrower shall allow Lender, its representatives or agents, at any time during normal business hours, access to the records and books of account, including any supporting or related vouchers or papers, kept by or on behalf of Borrower, its representatives or agents in connection with the Project, such access to include the right to make abstracts or copies thereof.

7.26   NOTICE OF LITIGATION. Borrower shall promptly furnish Lender a written notice of any litigation in which Borrower or any of Guarantors named as defendant or affecting or relating to the Project, which may materially adversely affect the Project or the parties' ability to perform their respective obligations hereunder or under the Loan Documents.

7.27   COMPLIANCE AND INDEMNITY WITH RESPECT TO HAZARDOUS SUBSTANCES. Borrower at its sole cost and expense shall (i) comply with and shall cause its agents and representatives to comply with all federal, state and local laws, rules, regulations and orders with respect to the use, discharge or removal of Hazardous Substances, (ii) pay immediately when due the cost of removal of any Hazardous Substances, and (iii) keep the Project free of any lien imposed pursuant to such laws, rules, regulations and orders. To the fullest extent permitted by law, Borrower indemnities and saves Lender harmless from and against all loss, cost, including reasonable attorneys' fees, liability and damage whatsoever, including all foreseeable and unforeseeable consequential damages,, directly or indirectly arising out of the use, generation, storage or disposal of Hazardous Substances in, on, under or in the proximate vicinity of the Project and the cost of any required or necessary repair, cleanup or detoxification and the preparation of any closure or other required plans, incurred by Lender by reason of any violation of any applicable statute or regulation for the protection of the environment which occurs or has occurred upon the Project, or by reason of the imposition of any governmental lien for the recovery of environmental cleanup costs expended by reason of such violation. It is expressly understood and agreed that to the extent that Lender is strictly liable under any such statute, Borrower's obligation to Lender under this indemnity shall likewise be without regard to fault on the part of Borrower with respect to the violation of law which results in liability to Lender. It is also expressly understood that this indemnification shall not terminate when the Loan is paid in full but rather shall survive the term of the indebtedness secured hereby.

7.28   MAINTENANCE OF BENEFICIARY'S AND GENERAL PARTNER'S EXISTENCE. General Partner shall at all times maintain its existence as a corporation in good standing under the laws of the State of Illinois, and Beneficiary shall at all times maintain its existence as a - limited partnership duly existing under the laws of the State of Illinois.

ARTICLE 8

INSURANCE
FIRE AND CASUALTY

8.1   INSURANCE. The Borrower will, at its expense, maintain the following insurance with good and responsible insurance companies reasonably satisfactory to the Lender:

(a)   Builder's Risk. It will insure the Improvements, all property (whether real, personal or mixed) incorporated therein and all materials and supplies delivered to the Project for use in connection with construction of the Improvements and all equipment to be used for that purpose under insurance policies in builder's risk form with standard non-contributory mortgage clauses providing that any loss is to be adjusted with, and any recovery payable to, the Lender as its interest may appear. All such policies shall be in such amounts, contain such coverage and insure against such risks as shall be reasonably satisfactory to the Lender. Without limiting the generality of the foregoing, the Improvements and all materials, supplies and equipment shall be insured to an amount equal to 100% of the full insurable value thereof (actual replacement value without deduction for depreciation) at all times against loss or damage by fire, lightning,

184

windstorm, explosion, theft and such other risks as are usually included under extended coverage.

(b)   Other Insurance. It will procure and maintain or cause to be procured and maintained insurance with respect to the Project against such other perils and risks (exclusive of the perils and risks insured against under the coverage provided in subsection (a) of this Section 8.1) as the Lender shall reasonably request and, without any such request, will procure and maintain or cause to be procured and maintained comprehensive general liability insurance, statutory workmen's compensation insurance, insurance against statutory structural work act liability and flood insurance (if the Project is in an area designated by a Governmental Body as having special flood hazards). All such insurance shall be maintained under policies containing such provisions and coverage and being in such amounts as are approved by the Lender, which policies shall name the Lender as a mortgagee and as a named additional insured thereunder.

(c)   Policy Provisions. All insurance maintained by Borrower shall be maintained with good and responsible insurance companies, shall provide that no cancellation thereof shall be effective until at least 30 days after receipt by the Lender of written notice thereof, shall provide that losses are payable notwithstanding any acts or omissions of Borrower, shall contain no deductible provisions which have not been approved by Lender and shall be satisfactory to Lender in all other respects.

(d)   Renewal Policies. Borrower will deliver to the Lender the original of any policy required under the provisions of this Section 8.1 (or, if coverage is provided under a master policy, a photocopy of such policy and an assigned certificate of insurance) and will cause renewal policies to be delivered thereto at least 15 days prior to the expiration of any such policies.

(e)   Adjustment of Loss. Borrower is hereby authorized to adjust and compromise any losses under any insurance afforded, subject to prior approval of the Lender in the case of losses exceeding $25,000.00. In the case of losses exceeding $150,000 in the aggregate, Lender shall have the sole right to adjust and compromise any such losses, and such adjustment and compromise shall be made by Lender in good faith.

(f)   Additional Policies. Borrower shall not take out or maintain separate insurance concurrent in kind or form or contributing in the event of loss with any insurance required hereinabove.

8.2   APPLICATION OF INSURANCE AND CONDEMNATION PROCEEDS ON INDEBTEDNESS. In case of loss or damage by fire or other casualty to the Project, or condemnation of all or any part of the Project, insurance or condemnation proceeds, as the case may be, shall be applied as provided in the Mortgage. Unless otherwise directed in writing by Lender, in the event of damage or destruction of the Project, or condemnation of all or any portion of the Project, Borrower shall rebuild, repair, replace or restore the Project to the extent such insurance or condemnation proceeds are made available to do so pursuant to the Mortgage.

ARTICLE 9

TAXES AND LIENS

9.1 TAXES. Borrower shall. promptly pay when due and payable, all sales, use, excise, real and personal property, income, corporate, franchise and other taxes, assessments and governmental charges of every kind and nature, which are now or shall hereafter be levied or assessed against Borrower or Borrower's interest in the Project or which may otherwise be or become a Lien upon the Project. In the event Borrower shall fail to pay any such tax, assessment, claim, levy or charge or to discharge any such Lien, the Lender, without waiving or-releasing any obligation or Event of Default of Borrower hereunder, may at any time or times hereafter, but shall be under no obligation to do so, make such payment, settlement, compromise, or release or cause to be released any such Lien and take any other action with respect thereto which Lender deems advisable, and all sums paid by Lender in satisfaction of, or on account of any such claims, taxes, levies, or assessments or governmental charges, or to discharge or release any' of such Liens, and any expenses, including reasonable attorneys' fees, court costs and other charges relating thereto, shall be an additional liability of Borrower owing to Lender with interest at the Default Interest Rate and payable on demand and secured by the Loan Documents.

9.2 LIENS. Borrower agrees not to suffer or permit any Liens or claims for Liens to be filed or otherwise asserted against the Project or any funds due contractor(s), or any subcontractors of sub-subcontractors, including, without limitation, any tax, mechanics' or materialmen's Liens and promptly to discharge such Liens in case of the filing of any claims for Lien or proceedings for the enforcement thereof, except for the Liens granted by the Loan Documents to secure the Loan; provided, however, that Borrower shall have the right to contest in good faith and with reasonable diligence the validity of any such Lien or claimed Lien upon either (i) deposit with the Title Company or the Lender, of a sum or other security in an amount determined by Lender in its sole discretion to be adequate to insure payment thereof and to prevent any sale, foreclosure or forfeiture of the Project by reason of non-payment thereof or (ii) cause such Title Company to insure the liens granted to Lender to be superior to any such Lien or claim for Lien as to all disbursements of the Loans theretofore or thereafter made by Lender. Upon the conclusion of any such contest and in the event of an adverse result, the Borrower immediately will satisfy any judgment rendered or decree entered and will at its expense cause such Lien or Liens to be released. In case Borrower shall fail promptly either to discharge or to contest claims asserted and give security in the manner above provided, or having commenced to contest the same, and having given such security, shall fail to prosecute such contest with diligence, or to maintain such deposit for its full amount, or upon adverse conclusion of any such contest to cause any judgment or decree thereon to be satisfied and such Lien to be released then and in any such event the Lender may, at its discretion, after notice to Borrower procure the release and discharge of any such Lien claim and any judgment or decree thereunder and, further may in its sole discretion effect any settlement or compromise of the same, and any amounts- so expended by Lender shall be an additional liability owing by Borrower to Lender with interest at the Default Interest Rate, and payable on demand, secured by the Loan Documents. In settling, compromising or discharging any Liens or claims for Lien, Lender is hereby authorized to use any sums or security deposited with Lender or the Title Company pursuant to the terms of this Paragraph, to settle, compromise or discharge any such Liens or claims for Lien, and Lender shall not be required to inquire into the validity or amount of any such Liens or claims for Lien.

ARTICLE 10

DEFAULTS BY BORROWER
AND LENDER'S REMEDIES

10.1   DEFAULT BY BORROWER. The occurrence of any one or more of the following shall constitute an "Event of Default", as such term is used herein:

(a)   The failure of Borrower to make any principal or interest payment due under any of the Notes or any other payment under the Loan Documents when such payment is due and the failure to cure such default within five (5) days after notice thereof;

(b)   The failure of Borrower to observe or perform any of the conditions, provisions or obligations under this Agreement and to fail to cure the same within thirty (30) days after giving of written notice thereof; provided, however, that if such event cannot be cured within such thirty (30) day period and Borrower promptly commences and thereafter diligently proceeds to cure such event, the time period for curing such event shall be extended for a period not to exceed thirty (30) additional days;

(c) The occurrence of any Event of Default under any of the Loan Documents;

(d)   Either Beneficiary, Trust or any of the Guarantors, shall: be adjudicated a bankrupt or insolvent; file a voluntary petition in bankruptcy, or admit (by answer, by default or otherwise) the material allegations of a petition filed against them in bankruptcy, or take or omit to take any action for the purpose of, or with the result of, effecting or permitting any of the foregoing; allow a substantial part of their property to be attached, seized, levied upon, or be taken possession of by any receiver custodian or assignee for the benefit of creditors; be enjoined, restrained, or in any way prevented by court order from conducting all or a substantial portion of their business affairs, or from performing any of their obligations as set forth in this Agreement; provided, however, that if any of the events described in this subsection occur without the consent of the Beneficiary, general partner of the Beneficiary, Trust or Guarantors, then such party shall have the right to cure such event within sixty (60) days after the event occurs; and provided further that if any of the events stated in this subparagraph (d) shall occur with respect to any Guarantors, such event may be cured by the substitution within 30 days following such event of another guarantor acceptable to Lender in Lender's sole reasonable discretion;

(e)   The sale, assignment, pledge, transfer, grant of a security interest in, or other hypothecation (except as otherwise herein provided, or as consented to in advance by Lender) of (i) any interest in the Trust, (ii) any of Borrower's interest in the Project or any interest therein,

(iii) any partnership interest in Beneficiary; or (iv) any stock in General Partner, for security purposes or otherwise other than pursuant to this Agreement or the Loan Documents;

(f)   Construction of the Improvements is so delayed for any reason whatsoever (whether within or outside the control of Borrower or any other person), including, without limitation, on account of damage or destruction by fire or other casualty (whether or not covered by insurance), so that in the reasonable judgment of Lender, the Improvements will not be substantially completed on or before the Construction Completion Date, as may be extended as otherwise provided by this Agreement, unless such delay is caused by Force Majeure and at all times during such delay the Loan remains in balance including payment of all interest and costs and all tenants remain obligated on their leases and continue making all payments due thereunder;

(g)   Any material, inaccuracy or untruth in any representation, covenant or warranty contained in this Agreement, any other Loan Documents or any document securing the Note or the Guaranty, or of any statement or certification as to facts delivered to Lender pursuant to any Loan Documents;

(h)   The disapproval by Lender at any time of any Work for failure to comply with this Agreement, the Plans and Specifications, and failure to cause the same to be corrected to the satisfaction of Lender within twenty (20) days after the date of written notice of such disapproval;

(i)   Failure of Borrower for a period of sixty (60) days after Lender's demand to procure the dismissal or disposition to Lender's satisfaction of any proceedings seeking to enjoin or otherwise prevent or declare invalid or unlawful the construction, occupancy, maintenance or operation of the Project, or any portion thereof, as called for by the terms of this Agreement, or of any proceedings which could or might affect the validity or priority of the lien of the Mortgage or other security for the Loan or which could materially affect Borrower's ability to perform its obligations under this Agreement;

(j)   A material adverse change in the financial conditions of the Beneficiary or any of the Guarantors and the failure of the Beneficiary or Guarantors to deliver to Lender other collateral satisfactory to Lender within fifteen (15) days following notice by Lender to Borrower of such adverse change;

(k)   The bankruptcy or insolvency of the General Contractor or any general contractor who is a substitute for the General Contractor, or the withdrawal of any of the foregoing from proceeding with the Work, and failure of Borrower to procure a contract with a new general contractor satisfactory to Lender within thirty (30) days from the occurrence of such bankruptcy, insolvency or withdrawal;

(l)   The attachment, seizure, levy upon or taking of possession by any receiver, custodian or assignee for the benefit of creditors of all or a substantial part of the property of any Borrower or any of the Guarantors;

(m)   The incompetency or death of any of the Guarantors, unless in the event of the Guarantor's death, the Guarantor's estate assumes the liabilities of the Guarantor under the Guaranty by an instrument satisfactory to Lender within thirty
(30) days of the Guarantor's death;

(n)   The insolvency of the issuer of the Letter of Credit, the expiration of the Letter of Credit for any reason whatsoever, or the occurrence of any event which in Lender's reasonable opinion impairs the Letter of Credit issuer's ability to make payment upon the Letter of Credit, and the failure of Borrower to obtain a substitute Letter of Credit within fifteen (15) days after notice from Lender;

Upon occurrence of any Event of Default, Borrower's Liabilities howsoever evidenced and secured shall, at the option of Lender and without notice (except as specifically set forth in this Article 10), become immediately due and payable and thereafter shall bear interest at the Default Interest Rate until cured.

10.2   LENDER'S OBLIGATIONS AFTER A DEFAULT. Upon the occurrence of a Default, Lender shall have no further obligations thereafter to advance money or extend credit to or for the benefit of Borrower under this Agreement, or any Loan Document.

10.3   LENDER'S REMEDIES UPON AN EVENT OF DEFAULT.

Upon   the occurrence of an Event of Default hereunder:

(a)   Lender may, declare the principal of and interest on the Note to be forthwith due and payable and thereupon the Note, including both principal and interest, shall be and becomes immediately due and payable without presentment, demand or further notice of any kind.

(b)   Lender may offset any indebtedness, obligations or liabilities owed to the Borrower against any indebtedness, obligations or liabilities of the Borrower to it.

(c)   Lender shall have the right, but not the obligation, to take possession of the Property together with all materials, equipment and improvements thereon, whether affixed or not, and perform any and all work and labor necessary to complete the Improvements substantially in accordance with the Plans and Specifications or with such changes therein as the Lender deems appropriate to complete the work or protect and preserve the Improvements and for that purpose. the Lender shall have the right to expend sums in addition to the Loan Amount and all such additional sums shall constitute indebtedness of the Borrower to the Lender and shall be entitled to the benefit of the security afforded by the Mortgage and Loan Documents. and the guaranty of the Guarantor. Borrower, to implement the rights of the Lender hereunder. irrevocably constitutes and appoints the Lender its true and lawful attorney in fact with full power of substitution for it and in its name, place and stead to take any and all actions the Lender deems necessary or appropriate to complete construction of the Improvements and to protect and preserve same and, without limiting the generality of the foregoing, irrevocably authorizes the Lender as follows: to use the funds of Borrower at any time coming into its hands, including any balance which may be held in escrow, any funds which may remain unadvanced hereunder and any funds then on deposit with the Lender pursuant to Section 4.3(d) hereof, for the purpose of completing the Improvements in the manner contemplated hereby or in such manner as the Lender deems appropriate to enhance the value of the Project; to employ such contractors, subcontractors, agents, architects and inspectors as shall be necessary or appropriate for said purposes; to enter into, alter, amend or modify any and all contracts, agreements or documents in connection with the construction of the Improvements or the furnishing of labor and materials in connection therewith; to pay, settle, compromise or collect all existing accounts or claims arising in connection with the construction of the Improvements, including all claims which are or may become liens against the Project; to take all actions it may deem necessary or appropriate in connection with title to the Property; to execute all applications, certificates or instruments which may be requested or required under any contract or by any Governmental Body; to prosecute and defend all actions or proceedings in connection with the construction of the Improvements; and to do any and every act with respect to construction of the Improvements and the operation, use and maintenance thereof which Borrower may do in its own behalf.

(d)   Lender may exercise any right or remedy set forth in the Mortgage or Loan Documents or available at law or in equity.

10.4 WAIVER OF BORROWER"S PERFORMANCE BY LENDER. Lender reserves the right under this Agreement to waive, or extend time for, performance of any provisions, warranties, terms and conditions hereof, and the failure at any time or times hereafter to require strict performance by Borrower of any of the provisions, warranties, terms and conditions contained in this Agreement, or the Loan Documents, and such failure shall not waive, affect or diminish any right of Lender thereafter to demand strict compliance and performance therewith and with respect to any other provisions, warranties, terms and conditions contained in such agreements, and any waiver or any Event of Default, whether prior or subsequent thereto, and whether of the same or a different type. None of the warranties, conditions, provisions and terms contained in this Agreement, or any Loan Document, shall be deemed to have been waived by any act or knowledge of Lender, its agents, officers or employees, except by an instrument in writing signed by an officer of Lender and directed to Borrower specifying such waiver.

10.5   LENDER'S EXPENSES WITH RESPECT TO PROJECT. If at any time or times Lender employs counsel for advice or other representation with respect to the Project, this Agreement or any Loan Document, or to protect, collect, lease, sell, take possession of, or liquidate any portion or all of the Project, or to attempt to enforce any security interest or lien in any portion or all of the Project, or to collect Borrower's Liabilities or to enforce any right of Lender against any other person, firm or corporation which may be obligated to Lender by virtue of this Agreement, or any Loan Document, heretofore, now or hereafter delivered to Lender by or for the benefit of Borrower, then in any of such events all of the reasonable attorneys' fees arising from such services, and any expenses, costs and charges relating thereto, shall constitute an additional liability owing by Borrower to Lender, payable on demand, with interest at the Default Interest Rate and secured by the Loan Documents.

ARTICLE 11

NOTICES

11.1   GENERAL. All notices or other communications required or permitted hereunder shall be (a) in writing and shall be deemed to be given when either (i) delivered in person, (ii) received after deposit in a regularly maintained receptacle of the United States mail as registered or certified mail, postage prepaid, (iii) received if sent by private courier service, (iv) on the day on which the party to whom such notice is addressed refuses delivery by mail or by private courier service or (v) three (3) days have elapsed after mailing by certified or registered mail postage prepaid, return receipt requested, and (b) addressed as follows:

To Lender:	c/o	First Mortgage Bank
		423 North Michigan Avenue
		Chicago, Illinois 60690
		Attn: Gerald Peterson

With copy to:		Jack Halloman
		Suite 900
		228 North LaSalle Street
		Chicago, Illinois 60604

To Borrower:	c/o	David Delaney
		524 West South Avenue
		Chicago, Illinois 60610

With copy to:		Donna Smith
		Kaplan & Miller
		450 Wacker Drive
		Chicago, Illinois 60606

or to each such party at such other addresses as such party may designate in a written notice to the other parties.

ARTICLE 12

GENERAL

12.1   ASSIGNMENT. Lender may assign, negotiate, pledge or otherwise hypothecate all or any portion of this Agreement or grant participation herein, or in any of its rights and security hereunder, including, without limitation, the Mortgage, Notes, and all other Loan Documents; and, in case of such assignment, Borrower will accord full recognition thereto and agree that all rights and remedies of Lender in connection with the interest so assigned shall be enforceable against Borrower by such assignee with the same force and effect and to the same extent as the same would have been enforceable by Lender but for such assignment. Borrower may not assign or hypothecate its rights under this Agreement.

12.2   BINDING EFFECT. This Agreement shall be binding upon and shall inure to the benefit of, all parties hereto and their respective successors, assigns, executors and personal representatives; provided, however, that Borrower may not assign its rights under this Agreement.

12.3   SINGULAR, PLURAL, ETC. Wherever in this Agreement the context so requires, the singular number shall include the plural number and vice versa, and any gender herein shall be deemed to include the feminine, masculine or neuter gender, as the context so requires.

12.4   RELATIONSHIP OF PARTIES. The relationship between Lender and Borrower shall be only that of creditor-debtor and no relationship of agency, partner or joint or co-venturer shall be created by or inferred from this Agreement and the Loan.

12.5   PUBLICIZING LOAN. If Lender so requires and if permitted by the Municipality, Borrower shall install a sign on the Project stating that Lender is providing financing for the Project. Such sign will. be located so as to comply with all zoning ordinances. Lender may publicize the Loan if it so elects.

12.6   SEVERABILITY. If any provision of this Agreement shall be held invalid or unenforceable to any extent, the remainder of this Agreement shall not be affected thereby and shall be enforceable to the greatest extent permitted by law.

12.7   RIGHTS ARE CUMULATIVE. The rights and remedies granted to the Lender hereunder shall be in addition to and cumulative of any other rights or remedies it may have under the Notes, Mortgage, Loan Documents or any document or documents executed in connection therewith or available under applicable law. No delay or failure on the part of the Lender in the exercise of any power or right shall operate as a waiver thereof nor as an acquiescence in any default, nor shall any single or partial exercise of any power or right preclude any other or further exercise thereof or the exercise of any other power or right.

12.8   WAIVER AND AMENDMENT. Neither this Agreement nor any provision hereof may be amended, changed, waived, terminated or discharged orally, but only by an instrument in writing signed by the party against whom enforcement of the change, waiver, termination or discharge is sought and, without limiting the generality of the foregoing, no advance of loan proceeds hereunder shall constitute a waiver of any of the conditions of the Lender's obligation to make further advances nor in the event the Borrower is unable to satisfy any such condition shall any such waiver have the effect of precluding the Lender from thereafter declaring such inability to be a Default or an Event of Default hereunder.

12.9   NO BENEFIT TO THIRD PARTIES. This Agreement is for the sole and exclusive benefit of the Borrower and the Lender and all conditions of the obligation of the Lender to make advances hereunder are imposed solely and exclusively for the benefit of the Borrower and no other person shall have standing to require satisfaction of such conditions in accordance with their terms or be entitled to assume that the Lender will refuse to make advances in the absence of strict compliance with any and all thereof and no other person shall under any circumstances be deemed to be a beneficiary of such conditions, any or all of which may be freely waived in whole or in part by t-he Lender at any time if it in its sole discretion deems it advisable to do So. Without limiting the generality of the foregoing, the Lender shall not have any duty or obligation to anyone to ascertain that funds advanced hereunder are used to pay the cost of constructing the Improvements or to acquire materials and supplies to be used in connection therewith or to pay costs of owning, operating and maintaining same.

12.10   TIME IS OF THE ESSENCE. Time is of the essence of this Agreement.

12.11   HOLIDAYS. If any payment required to be made hereunder or in respect of the Notes shall fall due on a Saturday, Sunday or other day which is a legal holiday for banks in the State of Illinois, such payment shall be made on the next succeeding bank business day and interest at the rate the Notes bear for the period prior to maturity shall continue to accrue on any principal installment thereon from the stated due date thereof to and including the next succeeding bank business day on which the payment is payable.

12.12   GOVERNING LAW. This Agreement and the rights and duties of the parties hereto shall be construed and determined in accordance with the laws of the State of Illinois.

12.13   VENUE AND JURY TRIAL. TO INDUCE LENDER TO ACCEPT THIS AGREEMENT AND THE OTHER LOAN DOCUMENTS, BORROWER IRREVOCABLY, AGREES THAT, SUBJECT TO LENDER'S SOLE AND ABSOLUTE ELECTION, ALL ACTIONS OR PROCEEDINGS IN ANY WAY, MANNER OR RESPECT, ARISING OUT OF OR FROM OR RELATED TO THIS AGREEMENT OR THE OTHER LOAN DOCUMENTS SHALL BE LITIGATED ONLY IN COURTS HAVING SITUS WITHIN THE CITY OF CHICAGO, OR COUNTY OF DUPAGE, STATE OF ILLINOIS. BORROWER HEREBY CONSENTS AND SUBMITS TO THE JURISDICTION OF ANY LOCAL, STATE OR FEDERAL COURT LOCATED WITHIN SAID CITY OR COUNTY, AND STATE. BORROWER HEREBY WAIVES ANY RIGHT IT MAY HAVE TO TRANSFER OR CHANGE THE VENUE OF ANY LITIGATION BROUGHT IN ACCORDANCE WITH THIS PARAGRAPH. BORROWER AND LENDER HEREBY IRREVOCABLY WAIVE THE RIGHT TO TRIAL BY JURY WITH RESPECT TO ANY ACTION IN WHICH BORROWER AND LENDER ARE PARTIES.

12.14   COUNTERPARTS. This Agreement may be executed in any number of counterparts and all such counterparts taken together shall be deemed to constitute one instrument.

12.15   NO OTHER AGREEMENTS. This Agreement, together with the Notes, Mortgage and the Loan Documents, constitutes the entire understanding of the parties with respect to the transactions contemplated hereby, and all prior understandings with respect thereto, whether written or oral, shall be of no force and effect.

12.16 JOINT AND SEVERAL LIABILITY. The covenants, agreements, representations and warranties contained herein shall constitute the joint and several covenants, agreements, representations and warranties of the Beneficiary and the Trust except as otherwise specifically provided herein and the occurrence of any event of default with respect to the Beneficiary or such Trust shall constitute an event entitling Lender to invoke the remedies herein provided for.

12.17 SURVIVAL OF COVENANTS, ETC. All covenants, representations and warranties made herein or in any statement or certificate delivered to the Lender pursuant to any of the provisions hereof shall survive the making of the Loan and shall continue in full force and effect until the obligations of Borrower; hereunder and the indebtedness evidenced by the Notes have been fully paid and satisfied and the Mortgage has been released of record by the Lender.

12.18 ORDERS AND INSTRUCTIONS. The Beneficiary is hereby authorized to deal with the Lender in connection with all matters concerning the Loan and the Lender shall be fully protected in acting on any orders or instructions (including requests for advances of Loan proceeds) received from the Beneficiary thereof and all disbursements so made shall be a good receipt and acquittance against the Beneficiary.

12.19 HEADINGS. The descriptive headings of the paragraphs herein are for convenience only and shall not affect the meaning or construction of any of the provisions hereof.

12.20 NO AMENDMENT EXCEPT IN WRITING. This Agreement may not be altered or amended, except by an agreement in writing signed by the parties hereto.

12.21 CONFLICTS WITH LOAN DOCUMENTS. In the event of any conflict between the provisions of this Agreement and the Loan Documents the provisions of this Agreement shall prevail; provided, however, that neither this provision nor any other provision of this Agreement shall be deemed to limit, abrogate or impair any provision in any one or more of the Loan Documents, Letter of Credit or other documents related to the Loan providing more extensive restrictions or requirements upon Borrower, or more extensive or expansive rights or remedies on behalf of Lender, or less burdensome requirements or restrictions on Lender, than are contained in this Agreement.

12.22 TRUSTEE EXCULPATION. This instrument is executed by the undersigned Trustee, not personally but as Trustee under the terms of that certain Trust Agreement dated the 11th day of April, 1989, and known as Trust No. 108049-04 and it is expressly understood and agreed between the parties hereto, anything herein to the contrary notwithstanding, that each and all of the covenants, undertakings, agreements, representations and warranties herein contained are made and intended not as personal covenants, undertakings, agreements, representations and warranties of the Trustee individually or for the purpose of binding it personally but only of the Trustee as such Trustee and this instrument is executed and delivered by First Mortgage Bank, as Trustee solely in the exercise of the power conferred upon it as such Trustee and no personal liability or personal responsibility is assumed by nor at any time shall be asserted or enforced against said Bank on account hereto or on account of any covenant, undertaking, agreement, representation or warranty herein contained either express or implied, all such personal liability, if any, being hereby expressly waived and released by the parties hereto and by all persons claiming by, through or under said parties and so far as said Bank is concerned, the Lender shall look solely to the Real Estate, to other collateral security herefor and to Guarantors hereof for payment and performance of the obligations of the Trustee hereunder. Nothing herein contained shall, however, operate or be deemed to impair,, invalidate, avoid or negate the covenants, undertakings, agreements and representations of the Trustee as such Trustee.

IN WITNESS WHEREOF, the parties have caused this presents to be executed by their respective partners and officers on the date and year first set forth above.

TRUSTEE:
ATTEST:
FIRST MORTGAGE BANK, as
Trustee as aforesaid

By: _____   By: _____
Its: _VICE PRESIDENT_   Its: _Assistant Secretary_

BENEFICIARY:
ATTEST:
FOX VALLEY AUTO CARE CENTER
LIMITED PARTNERSHIP

By:
REGENT REAL ESTATE DEVELOPMENT CORP.,
General Partner

By: _____   By: _Sarah Martin_
Its: _PRESIDENT_   Its: _Secretary_

LENDER:
ATTEST:
FIRST MORTGAGE BANK

By: _____   By: _____
Its: _VICE PRESIDENT_   Its: _Assistant Secretary_

195

PROMISSORY NOTE

THIS NOTE, made in Chicago, Illinois on August 2, 1989, for Two Hundred Thousand and no/100 Dollars ($200,000.00), or so much thereof as shall be disbursed to or for the benefit of the Maker and outstanding hereunder with interest as provided herein.

1.   Recitals.

(a)   This Note is made by First Mortgage Bank, not personally but as Trustee under Trust Agreement dated April 11, 1989 and known as Trust No. 108049-04 ("Trustee"), and Fox Valley Auto Care Center Limited Partnership, a limited partnership, an Illinois limited partnership ("Fox Valley" jointly with the Trustee, the "Maker") and is payable to FIRST MORTGAGE BANK ("Lender"). Lender and any subsequent holder from time to time of this Note is referred to as "Payee." The amount disbursed by Lender to Maker, repayment of which is evidenced by this Note and a certain other Promissory Note of even date herewith in the amount of $2,100,000 from Maker to Lender (the "Other Note") is referred to as the "Loan".

(b)   This Note and the Other Note are issued pursuant to the terms of a Construction Loan Agreement of even date herewith between Maker and Lender (the "Loan Agreement") and is secured, among other items, (i) by a certain Construction Mortgage and Security Agreement with Assignment of Rents ("Mortgage"), dated of even date herewith, executed and delivered by Trustee to Lender, encumbering certain interests in real and personal property located in DuPage County, Illinois, as more particularly described as the Mortgaged Premises in the Mortgage (the "Property"), (ii) by certain other documents securing repayment of this Note (the "Loan Documents", as defined in the Loan Agreement); and (iii) by a Letter of Credit in the amount of $200,000 issued by Harris Bank and Trust Company for the benefit of Lender. All of the agreements, conditions, covenants, provisions and stipulations contained in the Loan Agreement, Mortgage and other Loan Documents are hereby made a part of this Note to the same extent and with the same force and effect as if they were fully set forth herein and Maker covenants and agrees to keep and perform them, or cause them to be kept and performed, strictly in accordance with their terms.

2.   Payments of Principal and Interest.

(a)   Fox Valley and Trustee, jointly and severally, hereby promise to pay to the order of Payee the principal sum of Two Hundred Thousand Dollars and no/100 ($200,000.00), or so much thereof as is from time to time advanced', in lawful money of the United States of America, and to pay interest at said office of the Lender on the balance of principal from time to time outstanding and unpaid hereon from the date hereof until the maturity hereof (whether by lapse of time, acceleration or otherwise) together with interest at the rate per annum equal to the "Prime Rate" of the Lender as announced by the Lender from time to time in effect plus one percent (1%) (the "Interest Rate"). Said rate shall fluctuate and be effective when and as said "Prime Rate" fluctuates. "Prime Rate" means such rate as the Lender announces periodically to be its Prime Rate and may not necessarily be the best rate charged by the Lender. Lender shall have no obligation to notify Maker of changes in the Prime Rate. Interest shall be paid monthly in arrears commencing on the 1st day of September, 1989 and on the first of each successive month thereafter through and including the 1st day of January, 1991 with a final payment of all accrued, unpaid interest, together with the entire principal balance of the indebtedness evidenced hereby due and payable on January 31, 1991 (the "Maturity Date").

(b)   Interest shall be computed for actual days on the basis of a three hundred sixty (360) day year. All payments on account of the indebtedness evidencing the Note shall first be applied to late charges and costs and fees incurred by Payee in enforcing its rights hereunder or under the Mortgage, next to interest on the unpaid principal balance and the remainder to reduce unpaid principal.

(c)   After an Event of Default hereunder (as hereinafter defined), any sums remaining unpaid hereunder shall bear interest at the "Default Interest Rate" until such event of default is cured unless the Payee has commenced any of the remedies of Payee described in paragraph 4(a) of this Note in which case the Default Interest Rate shall remain in effect until such action is dismissed. The "Default Interest Rate" shall mean four percent (4%) per annum in excess of the Interest Rate.

(d)   If any installment of principal or interest due hereunder, or any monthly deposit for taxes or insurance if required under the Mortgage, shall become overdue the undersigned shall pay to the holder hereof on demand a "late charge" of five cents ($.05) for each dollar so overdue, in order to defray part of the increased cost of collection occasioned by any such late payment, as liquidated damages and not as a penalty.

(e)   Payment of all amounts due under this Note shall be made at the office of Lender, 423 North Michigan Avenue, Chicago, Illinois 60690 or such other place as Payee may from time to time designate in writing.

(f)   Notwithstanding any provisions of this Note or any instrument securing payment of the indebtedness evidenced by this Note to the contrary, it is the intent of Maker and Payee that Payee shall never be entitled to receive, collect or apply, as interest on principal of the indebtedness, any amount in excess of the maximum rate of interest permitted to be charged by applicable law; and if under any circumstance whatsoever, fulfillment of any provision of this Note, at the time performance of such provision shall be due, shall involve transcending the limit of validity prescribed by applicable law, then, ipso facto, the obligation to be fulfilled shall be reduced to the limit of such validity; and in the event Payee ever receives, collects or applies as interest any such excess, such amount which would be excess interest shall be deemed a "permitted partial prepayment" of principal without penalty or premium and treated hereunder as such; and if the principal of the indebtedness secured hereby is paid in full, any remaining excess funds shall forthwith be paid to Maker. In determining whether or not interest of any kind payable hereunder, under any specific contingency, exceeds the highest lawful rate, Maker and Payee shall, to the maximum extent permitted under applicable law, (1) characterize any non-principal payment as an expense, fee or premium rather than as interest and (2) amortize, prorate, allocate and spread to the end such payment so that the interest on account of such indebtedness does not exceed the maximum amount permitted by applicable law; provided that if the amount of interest received for the actual period of existence thereof exceeds the maximum lawful rate, Payee shall refund to Maker the amount of such excess. Payee shall not be subject to any penalties provided by any laws for contracting for, charging or receiving interest in excess of the maximum lawful rate.

3. Prepayment and Repayment.

Maker reserves the privilege, without cost or penalty, to prepay all or any part of the principal balance of this Note upon three (3) days prior written notice to Payee of its intention to do so.

4. Default and Remedies.

(a) In the event (i) default is made in the payment of any part of the principal or interest due pursuant to this Note as the same becomes due and payable, or of any sums advanced pursuant to the terms of this Note, the Other Note, the Loan Agreement, the Mortgage or other Loan Documents, and such default is not fully cured within five (5) days after notice thereof, or (ii) default is made in the performance or observance of any covenant, agreement, term or condition contained in this Note (other than as specified in clause (i) above), and such default is not fully cured within the time stated in paragraph 10.1(b) of the Loan Agreement, or (iii) there shall be an Event of Default under the Loan Agreement, the Other Note, or an Event of Default under any of the other Loan Documents, then in the case of the defaults set forth above (collectively "Events of Default"), Payee shall have the option, without demand or notice, to declare the unpaid principal of this Note, together with all accrued interest, prepayment premium, if any, and other sums secured by the Mortgage or such other Loan Documents, at once due and payable to the extent permitted by law, to foreclose the Mortgage and the liens or security interests securing the payment of the Note, and to exercise any and all other rights and remedies available at law or in equity or under the Mortgage or the other Loan Documents.

(b) The remedies of Payee, as provided herein or in the Mortgage or any of the other Loan Documents shall be cumulative and concurrent, and may be pursued singularly, successively or together, at the sole discretion of Payee, and may be exercised as often as occasion therefor shall arise. No act of omission or commission of Payee, including specifically any failure to exercise any right, remedy or recourse, shall be deemed to be a waiver or release of the same, such waiver or release to be effected only through a written document executed by Payee and then only to the extent specifically recited therein. A waiver or release with reference to any one event shall not be construed as continuing, as a bar to, or as a waiver or release of, any subsequent right, remedy or recourse as to a subsequent event.

5.   Costs and Attorneys' Fees.

If any Event of Default under this Note shall occur, Maker promises to pay all costs of collection of every kind, including but not limited to all appraisal costs, reasonable attorneys' fees, court costs, and expenses of every kind, incurred by Payee in connection with such collection or the protection or enforcement of any or all of the security for this Note, whether or not any lawsuit is filed with respect thereto.

6.   Use of Proceeds

Fox Valley represents, warrants, covenants and agrees and Trustee represents, covenants and agrees that all proceeds of the Loan evidenced by this Note will be used for the purposes specified in Paragraph 6404 (1)(C) of Chapter 17 of the Illinois Revised Statutes, and that the indebtedness secured hereby constitutes a business loan which comes within the purview of Paragraph 6404 (1)(C).

7.   Waiver.

Except as otherwise expressly provided herein, or in the Mortgage or other Loan Documents, each maker, surety and endorser hereon waives grace, notice, notice of intent to accelerate, notice of default, protest, demand, presentment for payment and diligence in the collection of this Note, and in the filing of suit hereon, and agrees that his or its liability and the liability of his or its heirs, beneficiaries, successors and assigns for the payment hereof shall not be affected or impaired by any release or change in the security or by any increase, modification, renewal or extension of the indebtedness or its mode and time of payment. Except as otherwise expressly provided herein, or in the Mortgage or other Loan Documents, it is specifically agreed by the undersigned that the Lender shall have the right at all times to decline to make any such release or change in any security given to secure the payment hereof and to decline to make any such increase, modification, renewal or extension of the indebtedness or its mode and time of payment.

8.   Nonpermitted Transfers.

Section 20 of the Mortgage provides that any sale, transfer, other alienation or further encumbrance of the Property, other than as expressly permitted therein, constitutes an Event of Default thereunder. In such event, the holder of this Note shall have the right to invoke any remedies therein provided including, without limitation, the right to declare immediately due and payable the entire outstanding principal balance of this Note, together with all accrued interest, prepayment premium, if any, and all other sums secured by the Mortgage or other Security Documents.

9.   Notices.

All notices or other communications required or permitted hereunder shall be (a) in writing and shall be deemed to be given when either (i) delivered in person, (ii) three days after deposit in a regularly maintained receptacle of the United States mail as registered or certified mail, postage prepaid, (iii) when received if sent by private courier service, or (iv) on the day on which Maker or Lender refuses delivery by mail or by private courier service, and (b) addressed as follows:

To Lender:
c/o   First Mortgage Bank
       423 N. Michigan Avenue
       Chicago, Illinois

To Borrower:
Attn: David Delaney
       Regent Real Estate Development Corp.
       524 W. South Avenue
       Chicago, Illinois 60610

With copy to:
       Donna Smith, Esq.
       Kaplan & Miller
       450 Wacker Drive
       Chicago, Illinois 60606

or to each such party at such other addresses as such party may designate in a written notice to the other parties.

10.   Miscellaneous.

(a)   The headings of the paragraphs of this Note are inserted for convenience only and shall not be deemed to constitute a part hereof.

(b)   All payments under this Note shall be payable in lawful money of the United States which shall be legal tender for public and private debts at the time of payment; provided that a check will be deemed sufficient payment so long as it clears when presented for payment. Each payment of principal or interest under this Note shall be paid not later than 2:00 P.M. Central Standard Time on the date due therefor and funds received after that hour shall be deemed to have been received by Payee on the following day. Except as otherwise provided herein, all payments (whether of principal, interest or other amounts) which are applied at any time by Payee to indebtedness evidenced by this Note may be allocated by Payee to principal, interest or other amounts as Payee may determine in Payee's sole discretion.

(c)   This Note has been made and delivered at Chicago, Illinois and all funds disbursed to or for the benefit of Maker will be disbursed in Chicago, Illinois.

(d)   The obligations and liabilities under this Note of the Trust and Fox Valley in their capacity as such shall be joint and several and shall be binding upon and enforceable against the Trust and Fox Valley in their capacity as such and their respective heirs, legatees, legal representatives, successors and assigns. Any action to enforce this Note may be brought against either of the Trust and Fox Valley in their capacity as such without any reimbursement or joinder of the other party in such action. This Note shall inure to the benefit of and may be enforced by Lender, its successors and assigns.

11.   Severability.

If any provision of this Note or any payments pursuant, to the terms hereof shall be invalid or unenforceable to any extent, the remainder of this Note and any other payments hereunder shall not be affected thereby and shall be enforceable to the greatest extent permitted by law.

12.   Exculpation.

This Note is executed by First Mortgage Bank, not personally but as Trustee as aforesaid in the exercise of the power and authority conferred upon and vested in it as such Trustee (and said Trustee hereby warrants that it possesses full power and authority to execute this instrument), and it is expressly understood and agreed that nothing herein contained shall be construed as creating any liability on said Trustee personally to pay this Note or any interest that may accrue thereon, or any indebtedness accruing hereunder, or to perform any covenant, either express or implied, herein contained, all such liability, if any being expressly waived by Payee and by every person now or hereafter claiming any right or security hereunder, and that so far as said Trustee personally is concerned, the legal holder or holders of this Note and the owners or owners of any indebtedness accruing hereunder shall look solely to the premises hereby conveyed for the payment thereof, by the enforcement of the lien hereby created, in the manner herein and in this Note provided or by action to enforce the personal liability of any guarantors of the indebtedness hereby secured or by proceeding against any other collateral security therefor.

IN WITNESS WHEREOF, Maker has executed, sealed and delivered this Note as of the date and year first above written.

ATTEST:

FIRST MORTGAGE BANK, as
Trustee as aforesaid

By: _~~Don Peters~~_   By: _Julie A. Arnold_
     Its: ~~VICE PRESIDENT~~   Its: ~~Assistant Secretary~~

FOX VALLEY AUTO CARE CENTER
LIMITED PARTNERSHIP

By: Regent Real Estate
Development Corp.,
General Partner

By: _David Delaney_
     Its: _PRESIDENT_

CONSTRUCTION MORTGAGE AND SECURITY AGREEMENT
WITH ASSIGNMENT OF RENTS

This Construction Mortgage and Security Agreement with Assignment of Rents dated as of August 2, 1989, from FIRST MORTGAGE BANK, not personally but as Trustee under Trust Agreement dated April 11, 1989, and known as Trust No. 108049-04 whose address is 423 N. Michigan Avenue, Chicago, Illinois 60690, (hereinafter referred to as "Mortgagor") to FIRST MORTGAGE BANK with its office at 423 N. Michigan Avenue Chicago, Illinois 60690 (hereinafter referred to as "Mortgagee");

WITNESSETH THAT:

WHEREAS, Mortgagor and Fox Valley Auto Care Center Limited Partnership, an Illinois limited partnership ("Beneficiary") have executed and delivered to Mortgagee two promissory notes payable to Mortgagee bearing even date herewith in the principal amounts of $2,100,000.00 and $200,000.00 (said notes and any and all extensions and renewals thereof, amendments thereto and substitutions or replacements therefor are referred to herein as the "Notes") by which Mortgagor and Beneficiary promise to pay said principal sum (or so much thereof as may be outstanding at the maturity thereof) on January 31, 1991, together with interest on the balance of principal from time to time outstanding and unpaid thereon at the rate and at the time specified in the Notes; and

WHEREAS, the Notes have been issued under and subject to the provisions of a Construction Loan Agreement bearing even date herewith between Mortgagor, Beneficiary and Mortgagee (such Construction Loan Agreement being hereinafter referred to as the "Loan Agreement");

NOW, THEREFORE, to secure (i) the payment when and as due and payable of the principal of and interest on the Notes or so much thereof as may be advanced from time to time under and pursuant to the Loan Agreement, (ii) the payment of all other indebtedness which this Mortgage by its terms secures and (iii) the performance and observance of the covenants and agreements contained in this Mortgage, the Loan Agreement, the Notes and any other instrument or document securing the Notes, (all of such indebtedness, obligations and liabilities identified in (i), (ii) and (iii) above being hereinafter referred to as the "indebtedness hereby secured"), the Mortgagor does hereby grant, sell, convey, mortgage and assign unto the Mortgagee, its successors and assigns and does hereby grant to Mortgagee, its successors and assigns a security interest in all and singular the properties, rights, interests and privileges described in Granting Clauses I, II, III, IV, V and VI below all of same being collectively referred to herein as the "Mortgaged Premises":

GRANTING CLAUSE I

That certain real estate lying and being in the County of DuPage and State of Illinois, more particularly described in Exhibit "All attached hereto and made a part hereof.

GRANTING CLAUSE II

All buildings and improvements of every kind and description heretofore or hereafter erected or placed on the property described in Granting Clause I and all materials intended for construction, reconstruction, alteration and repairs of the buildings and improvements now or hereafter erected thereon, all of which materials shall be deemed to be included within the premises immediately upon the delivery thereof to the said real estate, and, except for any sales trailer and construction trailer not owned by Mortgagor, all fixtures, machinery, apparatus, equipment, fittings and articles of personal property of every kind and nature whatsoever now or hereafter attached to or contained in or used in connection with said real estate and the buildings and improvements now or hereafter located thereon and the operation, maintenance and protection thereof (but excluding any of such items as are owned by tenants), including but not limited to all, machinery, motors, fittings, radiators, awnings, shades, screens, all gas, coal, steam, electric, oil and other heating, cooking, power and lighting apparatus and fixtures, all fire prevention and extinguishing equipment and apparatus, all cooling and ventilating apparatus and systems, all plumbing, incinerating, sprinkler equipment and fixtures, all elevators and escalators, all communication and electronic monitoring equipment, all window and structural cleaning rigs and all other machinery and other equipment of every nature and fixtures and appurtenances thereto and all items of furniture, appliances, draperies, carpets, other furnishings, equipment and personal property used or useful in the operation, maintenance and protection of the said real estate and the buildings and improvements now or hereafter located thereon and all renewals or replacements thereof or articles in substitution therefor, whether or not the same are or shall be attached to said buildings or improvements in any manner; it being mutually agreed, intended and declared that all the aforesaid property shall, so far as permitted by law, be deemed to form a part and parcel of the real estate and for the purpose of this Mortgage to be real estate and covered by this Mortgage,- and as to the balance of the property aforesaid, this Mortgage is hereby deemed to be as well a Security Agreement under the provisions of the Uniform Commercial Code for the purpose of creating hereby a security interest in said property, which is hereby granted by Mortgagor as debtor to Mortgagee as secured party, securing the indebtedness hereby secured. The addresses of Mortgagor (debtor) and Mortgagee (secured party) appear at the beginning hereof.

GRANTING CLAUSE III

All right, title and interest of Mortgagor now owned or hereafter acquired in and to all and singular the estates, tenements, hereditaments, privileges, easements, licenses, franchises, appurtenances and royalties, mineral, oil and water rights belonging or in any wise appertaining to the property described in the preceding Granting Clause I and the buildings and improvements now or hereafter located hereon and the reversions, rents, issues, revenues and profits thereof, including all interest of Mortgagor in all rents, issues and profits of the aforementioned property

206

and all rents, issues, profits, revenues, royalties, bonuses, rights and benefits due, payable or accruing (including all deposits of money as advanced rent or for security) under any and all leases and renewals thereof or under any contracts or options for the sale of all or any part of, said property (including during any period allowed by law for the redemption of said property after any foreclosure or other sale), together with the right, but not the obligation, to collect, receive and receipt for all such rents and other sums and apply them to the indebtedness hereby secured and to demand, sue for and recover the same when due or payable; provided that the assignments made hereby shall not impair or diminish the obligations of Mortgagor under the provisions of such leases or other agreements nor shall such obligations be imposed upon Mortgagee. By acceptance of this Mortgage, Mortgagee agrees, that until an Event of Default (as hereinafter defined) shall occur giving Mortgagee the right to foreclose this Mortgage, Mortgagor may collect, receive (but not more than 30 days in advance) and enjoy such rents.

GRANTING CLAUSE IV

All judgments, awards of damages, settlements and other compensation hereafter made resulting from condemnation proceedings or the taking of the property described in Granting Clause I or any part thereof or any building or other improvements now or at any time hereafter located thereon or any easement or other appurtenance thereto under the power of eminent domain, or any similar power or right (including any award from the United States Government at any time after the allowance of the claim therefor, the ascertainment of the amount thereof and the issuance of the warrant for the payment thereof), whether permanent or temporary, or for any damage (whether caused by such taking or otherwise) to said property or any part thereof or the improvements thereon or any part thereof, or to any rights appurtenant thereto, including severance and consequential damage, and any award for change of grade of streets (collectively "Condemnation Awards").

GRANTING CLAUSE V

All property and rights, if any, which are by the express provisions of this instrument required to be subjected to the lien hereof and any additional property and rights that may from time to time hereafter by installation or writing of any kind, be subjected to the lien hereof.

GRANTING CLAUSE VI

All rights in and to common areas and access roads on adjacent properties heretofore or hereafter granted to Mortgagor and any after-acquired title or reversion in and to the beds of any ways, roads, streets, avenues and alleys adjoining the property described in Granting Clause I or any part thereof.

TO HAVE AND TO HOLD the Mortgaged Premises and the properties, rights and privileges hereby granted, bargained, sold, conveyed, mortgaged, pledged and assigned, and in which a security interest is granted, unto Mortgagee, its successors and assigns, forever; provided, however, that this instrument is upon the express condition that if the principal of and interest on the Notes shall be paid in full and all other indebtedness hereby secured shall be fully paid and

207

performed and any commitment to advance funds contained in the Loan Agreement shall have been terminated, then this instrument and the estate and rights hereby granted shall cease, determine and be void and this instrument shall be released by Mortgagee upon the written request and at the expense of Mortgagor, otherwise to remain in full force and effect.

Mortgagor hereby covenants and agrees with Mortgagee as follows:

1.   Payment of the Indebtedness. The indebtedness hereby secured will be promptly paid as and when the same becomes due.

2.   Representation of Title and Further Assurances. Mortgagor will execute and deliver such further instruments and do such further acts as may be reasonably necessary or proper to carry out more effectively the purpose of this instrument and, without limiting the foregoing, to make subject to the lien hereof any property agreed to be subjected hereto or covered by the Granting Clauses hereof or intended so to be. At the time of delivery of these presents, the Mortgagor is well seized of an indefeasible estate in fee simple in the portion of the Premises which constitutes real property subject only to the matters set forth in Exhibit "B" attached hereto and hereby made a part hereof (the "Permitted Exceptions"), and Mortgagor has good right, full power and lawful authority to convey, mortgage and create a security interest in the same, in the manner and form aforesaid; except as set forth in Exhibit "B" hereto, the same is free and clear of all liens, charges, easements, covenants, conditions, restrictions and encumbrances whatsoever, including as to the personal property and fixtures, security agreements, conditional sales contracts and anything of a similar nature, and the Mortgagor shall and will forever defend the title to the Mortgaged Premises against the claims of all persons whomsoever.

3.   Mortgage Constitutes Construction Mortgage. This Mortgage, in part, secures an obligation for the construction of improvements on the real property herein described, and constitutes a construction mortgage for the purpose of Article Nine of the Uniform Commercial Code of Illinois and is entitled to all of the benefits afforded construction mortgages thereunder.

4.   Compliance with Loan Agreement. Mortgagor will abide by and comply with and be governed and restricted by all of the terms, covenants, provisions, restrictions and agreements contained in the Loan Agreement, and in each and every supplement thereto or amendment thereof which may at any time or from time to time be executed and delivered by the parties thereto or their successors and assigns.

5.   Provisions of Loan Agreement. The proceeds of the Notes are to be disbursed by the Mortgagee in accordance with the terms contained in the Loan Agreement, the provisions of which are incorporated herein by reference to the same extent as if fully set forth herein. Mortgagor covenants that any and all monetary disbursements made in accord with the Loan Agreement shall constitute adequate consideration to Mortgagor for the enforceability of this Mortgage and the Notes, and that all advances and indebtedness arising and accruing under the Loan Agreement from time to time, whether or not the total amount thereof may exceed the face amount of the Notes, shall be secured by this Mortgage. Upon default in any of the terms, provisions or covenants in the Loan Agreement contained, which default is not cured within the

time permitted by the Loan Agreement, the Mortgagee may (but need not): (i) declare the entire principal indebtedness and interest thereon due and payable and pursue all other remedies by this Mortgage conferred upon Mortgagee or conferred upon Mortgagee by law as in the case of default; or (ii) complete the construction of said improvements and enter into the necessary - contracts therefor. All monies so expended shall be so much additional indebtedness secured by this Mortgage, and any monies expended in excess of the Notes shall be payable on demand with interest at the Default Interest Rate (as defined in Paragraph 33). Mortgagee may exercise either or both of the aforesaid remedies. The provisions, rights, powers and remedies contained in the Loan Agreement are in addition to, and not in substitution for, those contained herein.

6.   Payment of Taxes. Mortgagor shall pay before any penalty attaches, all general taxes and all special taxes, special assessments, water, drainage and sewer charges and all other charges, of any kind whatsoever, ordinary or extraordinary, which may be levied, assessed, imposed or charged on or against the Mortgaged Premises or any part thereof and which, if unpaid, might by law become a lien or charge upon the Mortgaged Premises or any part thereof, and shall upon request from Mortgagee exhibit to Mortgagee official receipts evidencing such payments, except that, unless and until foreclosure, distant, sale or other similar proceedings shall have been commenced, no such charge or claim need be paid if being contested (except to the extent any full or partial payment shall be required by law), after notice to Mortgagee, by appropriate proceedings which shall operate to prevent the collection thereof or the sale or forfeiture of the Mortgaged Premises or any part thereof to satisfy the same, conducted in good faith and with due diligence and if Mortgagor shall have furnished such security, if any, as may be required in the proceedings or required by Mortgagee's title insurer to insure over the lien of such taxes.

7.   Payment of Taxes on Notes, Mortgage or Interest of Mortgagee. Mortgagor agrees that if any tax, assessment or imposition upon this Mortgage or the indebtedness hereby secured or the Notes or the interest of Mortgagee in the Mortgaged Premises or upon Mortgagee by reason of any of the foregoing (including, without limitation, corporate privilege, franchise and excise taxes, but excepting therefrom any income tax on interest payments on the principal portion of the indebtedness hereby secured imposed by the United States or any State) is levied, assessed or charged, then, unless all such taxes are paid by Mortgagor to, for or on behalf of Mortgagee as they become due and payable (which Mortgagor agrees to. do upon demand of Mortgagee, to the extent permitted by law), or Mortgagee is reimbursed for any such sum advanced by Mortgagee, all sums hereby secured shall become immediately due and payable, at the option of Mortgagee upon thirty (30) days' notice to Mortgagor, notwithstanding anything contained herein or in any law heretofore or hereafter enacted, including any provision thereof forbidding Mortgagor from making any such payment. Mortgagor agrees to exhibit to Mortgagee, upon request, official receipts showing payment of all taxes and charges, which Mortgagor is required to pay hereunder.

8.   Tax and Insurance Deposits. After an Event of Default or after Mortgagor has failed to make any payment stated in paragraph 7 of this Mortgage, upon Mortgagee's request, Mortgagor covenants and agrees to deposit with Mortgagee, commencing on the date of Mortgagee's request and on the first day of each month thereafter until the indebtedness secured. by this Mortgage is fully paid, a sum equal to (i) one-twelfth (1/12th) of the annual taxes and assessments (general

and special) on the Mortgaged Premises (unless said taxes are based upon assessments which exclude the improvements thereof now constructed or to be constructed, in which event the amount of such deposits shall be based upon Mortgagee's reasonable estimate as to the amount of taxes and assessments to be levied and assessed) and (ii) one twelfth (1/12th) of the annual premiums payable for the insurance required to be maintained in accordance with Paragraph 11 hereof. Immediately following an Event of Default (as hereinafter defined), Mortgagor shall deposit with Mortgagee an amount of money, when together with the aggregate of the monthly deposits to be made pursuant to (i) above as of the one month prior to the date on which the total annual taxes and assessments for the current calendar year become due, shall be sufficient to pay in full the total annual taxes and assessments estimated by Mortgagee to become due and payable with respect to the Mortgaged Premises for the current calendar year, and an amount of money, when together with the aggregate deposits to be made pursuant to' (ii) above as of one month prior to the date on which the next annual insurance premium becomes due, shall be sufficient to pay in full the total annual insurance premium estimated by Mortgagee to next become due and payable with respect to the Mortgaged Premises. Such deposits are to be held without any allowance of interest and are to be used for the payment of taxes and assessments (general and special) and insurance premiums, respectively, on the Mortgaged Premises next due and payable when they become due. Mortgagee may, at its option, itself pay such taxes, assessments and insurance premiums when the same become due and payable (upon submission of appropriate bills therefor from Mortgagor) or shall release sufficient funds to Mortgagor for payment of such taxes, assessments and insurance premiums. If the funds so deposited are insufficient to pay any such taxes, assessments (general or special) and premiums for any year when the same shall become due and payable, Mortgagor shall within ten (10) days after receipt of demand therefor, deposit additional funds as may be necessary to pay such taxes, assessments (general and special) and premiums in full. If the funds so deposited exceed the amount required to pay such taxes, assessments (general and special) and premiums for any year, the excess shall be applied on a subsequent deposit or deposits. said deposits need not be kept separate and apart from any other funds of Mortgagee. Anything in this Paragraph 8 to the contrary notwithstanding, if the funds so deposited are insufficient to pay any such taxes, assessments (general or special) or premiums or any installment thereof, Mortgagor will, not later than the thirtieth (30th) day prior to the last day on which the same may be paid without penalty or interest, deposit with Mortgagee the full amount of any such deficiency.

9.   Mortgagee's Interest In and Use of Deposits. Upon the occurrence of an Event of Default, the Mortgagee may at its option, without being required so to do, apply any monies at the time on deposit pursuant to Paragraph 8 hereof, on any of Mortgagor's obligations herein or in the Notes contained, in such order and manner as Mortgagee may elect. When the indebtedness secured hereby has been fully paid, any remaining deposits shall be paid to Mortgagor. Such deposits are hereby pledged as additional security for the indebtedness hereunder and shall be irrevocably applied by Mortgagee for the purposes for which made hereunder and shall not be subject to the direction or control of Mortgagor; provided, however, that Mortgagee shall not be liable for any failure to apply to the payment of taxes, assessments and insurance premiums any amount so deposited unless Mortgagor, while not in default hereunder, shall have requested Mortgagee in writing to make application of such funds to the payment of which they were deposited, accompanied by the bills for such taxes, assessments and insurance premiums.

Mortgagee shall not. be liable for any act or omission taken in good faith or pursuant to the instruction of any party.

10.   Recordation and Payment of Taxes and Expenses Incident Thereto. Mortgagor will cause this Mortgage, all mortgages supplemental hereto and any financing statement or other notices of a security interest required by Mortgagee at all times to be kept, recorded and filed at its own expense in such manner and in such places as may be required by law for the recording and filing or for the rerecording and refiling of a mortgage, security interest, assignment or other lien or charge upon the Mortgaged Premises, or any part thereof, in order fully to preserve and protect the rights of Mortgagee hereunder, and, without limiting the foregoing, Mortgagor will pay or reimburse Mortgagee for the payment of any and all taxes, fees or other charges incurred in connection with any such recordation or rerecordation, including any documentary stamp tax or tax imposed upon the privilege of having this instrument or any instrument issued pursuant hereto recorded.

11.   Insurance. Mortgagor will, at its expense, maintain insurance in accordance with the requirements of the Loan Agreement. The proceeds of such insurance shall be applied as provided in Section 12 hereof. In the event of foreclosure, Mortgagor authorizes and empowers Mortgagee to effect insurance upon the Mortgaged Premises in the amounts aforesaid, for a period covering the time of redemption from foreclosure sale provided by law, and if necessary therefor, to cancel any or all existing insurance policies.

12.   Damage to and Destruction of the Improvements.

(a)   Notice. In the case of any material damage to or destruction of any improvements which are constructed on the Mortgaged Premises or any part thereof, Mortgagor shall promptly give notice thereof to Mortgagee generally describing the nature and extent of such damage or destruction. Material damage shall mean damages in excess of $10,000.00.

(b)   Restoration. Upon the occurrence of any damage to or destruction of any improvements on the Mortgaged Premises, provided Mortgagee permits the proceeds of insurance to be used for repairs, Mortgagor shall cause same to be restored, replaced or rebuilt as nearly as possible to their value, condition and character immediately prior to such damage or destruction. Such restoration, replacement or rebuilding shall be effected promptly and Mortgagor shall notify the Mortgagee if it appears that such restoration, replacement or rebuilding may unduly delay completion of such improvements. Any amounts required for repairs in excess of insurance proceeds shall be paid by Mortgagor.

(c)   Application of Insurance Proceeds. Net insurance proceeds received by the Mortgagee under the provisions of this Mortgage or any instrument supplemental hereto or thereto or any policy or policies of insurance covering any improvements on the Mortgaged Premises or any part thereof shall be applied by the Mortgagee at its option as and for a prepayment on the Notes (whether or not the same is then due or otherwise adequately secured) or shall be disbursed for restoration of such improvements (in which event the Mortgagee shall not be obligated to supervise restoration work nor shall the amount so released or used be deemed a payment of the indebtedness evidenced by the Notes). If Mortgagee elects to permit the use of insurance proceeds to restore such improvements it may do all necessary acts to accomplish that purpose including using funds deposited by Mortgagor with it for any purpose and advancing additional funds, all such additional funds to constitute part of the indebtedness secured by the Mortgage. If Mortgagee elects to make the insurance proceeds available to Mortgagor for the purpose of effecting such a restoration, or, following an Event of Default, elects to restore such improvements, any excess of insurance proceeds above the amount necessary to complete such restoration shall be applied as and for a prepayment on the Notes. Notwithstanding the foregoing provisions Mortgagee agrees that net insurance proceeds shall be made available for the restoration of the portion of the Mortgaged Premises damaged or destroyed if written application for such use is made within thirty (30) days after receipt of such proceeds and the following conditions are satisfied: (i) no Event of Default (as hereinafter defined), or event which if uncured within any applicable cure period, would constitute an Event of Default, shall have occurred or be continuing (and if such an event shall occur during restoration Mortgagee may, at its election, apply any insurance proceeds then remaining in its hands to the reduction of the indebtedness evidenced by the Notes and the other indebtedness hereby secured), (ii) if the cost of repairs exceeds $5,000, Mortgagor shall have submitted to Mortgagee plans and specification for the restoration which shall be satisfactory to it in Mortgagee's reasonable judgment, (iii) Mortgagor shall have submitted to Mortgagee fixed price contracts with good and responsible contractors and materialmen covering all work and materials necessary to complete restoration and providing for a total completion price not in excess of the amount of insurance proceeds available for restoration, or, if a deficiency shall exist, Mortgagor shall have deposited the amount of such deficiency with Mortgagee and (iv) Mortgagor shall have obtained a waiver of the right of subrogation from any insurer under such policies of insurance who at that time claim that no liability exists as to Mortgagor or the assured under such policies, and (v), no leases of the Mortgaged Premises may be terminated as a result of such casualty or those tenants who are able to terminate have elected in writing not to so terminate. Any insurance proceeds to be released pursuant to the foregoing provisions may at the option of Mortgagee be disbursed from time to time as restoration progresses to pay for restoration work completed and in place and such disbursements shall be disbursed in such manner as Mortgagee may determine. Mortgagee may impose such further conditions upon the release of insurance proceeds (including the receipt of title insurance) as are customarily imposed by prudent construction lenders to insure the completion of the restoration work free and clear of all liens or claims for lien. All necessary and reasonable title insurance charges and other costs and expenses paid to or for the account of Mortgagee in connection with the release of such insurance proceeds shall constitute so much additional indebtedness secured by this Mortgage to be payable upon demand and if not paid upon demand shall bear interest at the Default Interest Rate. Mortgagee may deduct any such costs and expenses from insurance proceeds at any time standing in its hands.

13. Eminent Domain.

(a) Mortgagor acknowledges that the Condemnation Awards have been assigned to Mortgagee, which awards Mortgagee is hereby irrevocably authorized to collect and receive, and to give appropriate receipts and acquittance therefor, and at Mortgagee's option, to apply the same toward the payment of the amount owing - on account of the indebtedness hereby secured in such order as Mortgagee may elect and whether or not the same may then be due and payable or otherwise adequately secured, and Mortgagor covenants and agrees that Mortgagor will give Mortgagee immediate notice of the actual or threatened commencement of any proceedings under condemnation or eminent domain affecting all or any part of the Mortgaged Premises including any easement therein or appurtenance thereof or severance and consequential damage and change in grade of streets, and will deliver to Mortgagee copies of any and all papers served in connection with any such proceedings. Mortgagor further covenants and agrees to make, execute and deliver to Mortgagee, at any time or times upon request, free, clear and discharged of any encumbrances of any kind whatsoever, any and all further assignments and/or instruments deemed necessary by Mortgagee for the purpose of validly and sufficiently assigning all awards and other compensation heretofore and hereafter to be made to Mortgagor for any taking, either permanent or temporary, under any such proceeding.

(b) Assignment of Claim, Power of Attorney to Collect, Etc. Any and all awards heretofore or hereafter made or to be made to the present and all subsequent owners of the Mortgaged Premises by any governmental body for taking or affecting the whole or any part of said Mortgaged Premises, the improvements on the Mortgaged Premises or any easement therein or appurtenance thereto (including any award from the United States Government at any time after the allowance of the claim therefor, the ascertainment of the amount thereof and the issuance of the award for payment thereof) are hereby assigned by Mortgagor to Mortgagee to the extent of the existing principal balance and other outstanding charges owed by Mortgagor to Mortgagee and Mortgagor hereby irrevocably constitutes and appoints Mortgagee its true and lawful attorney in fact with full power of substitution for them and in their name, place and stead to collect and receive the proceeds of any such award granted by virtue of any such taking and to give proper receipts and acquittance therefor. Mortgagee shall not settle any condemnation award with the condemning party without the consent of the Mortgagor which will not be unreasonably withheld. Mortgagor shall have the right to participate in any proceedings which determine the award to be granted.

(c) Effect of Condemnation and Application of Awards. In the event that any proceedings are commenced by any governmental body or other person to take or otherwise affect the Mortgaged Premises, the improvements thereon or any easement therein or appurtenance thereto the effect of which would be to materially interfere with the ability of Mortgagor to utilize the Mortgaged Premises for its intended purpose, Mortgagee may at its option apply the proceeds of any award made in such proceedings as and for a prepayment on the indebtedness evidenced by the Notes, notwithstanding the fact that said indebtedness may not then be due and payable or is otherwise adequately secured. In all other cases, the proceeds of any such award shall be applied as in the case of insurance proceeds.

14.   Construction, Repair, Waste, Etc. Except for the improvements on the Mortgaged Premises to be constructed pursuant to the provisions of the Loan Agreement, Mortgagor agrees: that no building or other improvement on the Mortgaged Premises and constituting a part thereof shall be materially altered, removed or demolished nor shall any fixtures or appliances on, in or about said buildings or improvements be severed, removed, sold or mortgaged, without the consent of Mortgagee and in the event of the demolition or destruction in whole or in part of any of the fixtures, chattels or articles of personal property covered hereby, Mortgagee covenants that the same will be replaced promptly by similar fixtures, chattels and articles of personal property at least equal in quality and condition to those replaced, free from any security interest in or encumbrance thereon or reservation of title thereto; to permit, commit or suffer no waste, impairment or deterioration of the Mortgaged Premises or any part thereof; to keep and maintain said Mortgaged Premises and every part thereof in good and first class repair and condition (ordinary wear and tear excepted); to effect such repairs as Mortgagee may reasonably require and from time to time to make all needful and proper replacements and additions so that said buildings, fixtures, machinery and appurtenances will, at all times, be in good and first class condition, fit and proper for the respective purposes for which they were originally erected or installed; to comply with all statutes, orders, requirements or decrees relating to said Mortgaged Premises by any Federal, State or Municipal authority; to observe and comply with all conditions and requirements necessary to preserve and extend any and all rights, licenses, permits (including, but not limited to, zoning variances, special exceptions and nonconforming uses), privileges, franchises and concessions which are applicable to the Mortgaged Premises or which have been granted to or contracted for by Mortgagor in connection with any existing or presently contemplated use of the Mortgaged Premises or any part hereof and not to initiate or acquiesce in any changes to or terminations of any of the foregoing or of zoning classifications affecting the use to which the Mortgaged Premises or any part thereof may be put without the prior written consent of Mortgagee; and to make no alterations in or improvements or additions to the Mortgaged Premises except as contemplated by the Loan Agreement or required by governmental authority.

15.   Liens and Encumbrances. Mortgagor will not, without the prior written consent of Mortgagee, directly or indirectly, create or suffer to be created to remain and will discharge or promptly cause to be discharged any mortgage, lien, encumbrance or charge on, pledge or conditional sale or other title retention agreement with respect to the Mortgaged Premises or any part thereof, whether superior or subordinate to the lien hereof, except for this instrument and of the lien of all other documents given to secure the indebtedness hereby secured; provided, however, that Mortgagor may contest the validity of any mechanics lien, charge or encumbrance (other than the lien of this Mortgage or of any other document securing payment of the Notes) upon giving Mortgagee timely notice of its intention to contest the same and making and thereafter either maintaining with Mortgagee a deposit of cash or negotiable securities reasonably satisfactory to Mortgagee in an amount sufficient in the reasonable opinion of Mortgagee to pay and discharge or to assure compliance with the matter under contest in the event of a .final determination thereof adversely to Mortgagor or obtaining title insurance coverage over such lien

on Mortgagee's title insurance policy. Mortgagor agrees to prosecute and contest diligently and by appropriate legal proceedings which will prevent the enforcement of the matter under contest and will not impair the lien of this Mortgage or interfere with the normal conduct of business on the Mortgaged Premises. On final disposition of such contest, any cash or securities in Mortgagee's possession not required to pay or discharge or assure compliance with the matter contested shall be returned promptly to Mortgagor.

16.   Right of Mortgagee to Perform Mortgagor's Covenants, Etc. If Mortgagor shall fail to make any payment or perform any act required to be made or performed hereunder, Mortgagee, without waiving or releasing any obligation or default, may (but shall be under no obligation to) at any time thereafter upon prior written notice to Mortgagor and failure of Mortgagor to make such payment or perform such act within any applicable cure period provided herein make such payment or perform such act for the account and at the expense of Mortgagor, and may enter upon the Mortgaged Premises or any part thereof for such purpose and take all such action thereon as, in the opinion of Mortgagee, may be necessary or appropriate therefor. All sums so paid by Mortgagee and all costs and expenses (including without limitation reasonable attorneys' fees and expenses) so incurred, together with interest thereon from the date of payment or incurrence at the interest rate applicable to the Notes on such date, shall constitute so much additional indebtedness hereby secured and shall be paid by Mortgagor to Mortgagee on demand. Mortgagee in making any payment authorized under this Section relating to taxes or assessments may do so according to any bill, statement or estimate procured from the appropriate public office without inquiry into the accuracy of such bill, statement or estimate or into the validity of any tax assessment, sale, forfeiture, tax lien or title or claim thereof. The performance by Mortgagee of any act hereunder, shall be prima facie evidence that Mortgagor is required to perform same under the terms of this Mortgage.

17.   After-Acquired Property. Any and all property hereafter acquired which is of the kind or nature herein provided and, related to the premises described in Granting Clause i hereof, or intended to be and become subject -to the lien hereof, shall ipso facto, and without any further conveyance, assignment or act on the part of Mortgagor, become and be subject to the lien of this Mortgage as fully and completely as though specifically described herein; but nevertheless Mortgagor shall from time to time, if requested by Mortgagee, execute and deliver any and all such further assurances, conveyances and assignments as Mortgagee may reasonably require for the purpose of expressly and specifically subjecting to the lien of this Mortgage all such property.

18.   Inspection by Mortgagee. Mortgagee and its agents shall have the right to inspect the Mortgaged Premises at all reasonable times, and access thereto shall be permitted for that purpose.

19.   Subrogation. Mortgagor acknowledges and agrees that Mortgagee shall be subrogated to any lien discharged out of the proceeds of the loan evidenced by the Notes or out - of any advance by Mortgagee hereunder or under the Loan Agreement, irrespective of whether or not any such lien may have been released of record.

20.   Transfer of the Mortgaged Premises. Except as expressly permitted in the Loan Agreement, Mortgagor shall not permit or suffer to occur any sale, assignment, conveyance, mortgage, lease, pledge, encumbrance or other transfer of, or the granting of any option in, or any contract for any of the foregoing (on an installment basis or otherwise) pertaining to:

(a)   the Mortgaged Premises, any part thereof, or any interest therein; or

(b)   any stock in Beneficiary; or

(c)   the beneficial interest in Mortgagor, any part thereof, or any interest therein whether by operation of law or otherwise, without the prior written consent of Mortgagee having been obtained to such sale, written assignment, conveyance, mortgage, lease option, pledge, encumbrance -or other transfer. Mortgagor agrees that in the event the ownership of the Mortgaged Premises or the beneficial interest in Mortgagor, any interest therein or any part thereof becomes vested in a person other than Mortgagor, Mortgagee may, without notice to Mortgagor, deal in any way with such successor or successors in interest with reference to this Mortgage, the Notes, and any other document evidencing the indebtedness secured hereby, without in any way vitiating or discharging Mortgagor's liability hereunder or under any other document evidencing the indebtedness secured hereby. No sale of the Mortgaged Premises, forbearance to any person with respect to this Mortgage, or extension to any person of the time for payment of the Notes given by Mortgagee shall operate to release, discharge, modify, change or affect the liability of Mortgagor, either in whole or in part, except to the extent specifically agreed in writing by Mortgagee. Without limitation of the foregoing, in any event in which the written consent of Mortgagee's required in this Paragraph 20, Mortgagee may condition its consent upon any combination of (i) the payment of compensation to be determined by Mortgagee, (ii) the increase of the interest rate payable under the Notes, (iii) the shortening of maturity of the Notes, and (iv) other modifications of the terms of the Notes or the other instruments evidencing the indebtedness secured hereby.

21.   Events of Default.   Any one or more of the following shall constitute an Event of Default hereunder:

(a)   Default in making payment when due (whether by lapse of time, acceleration, or otherwise) of the principal of or interest on any of the Notes or of any other indebtedness hereby secured and failure to cure such default within five (5) days after notice thereof;

(b)   The sale, assignment, conveyance, transfer, mortgage, lease, pledge, lien or encumbrance of, or the granting of an option in the Mortgaged Premises, the beneficial interest in Mortgagor, any general partnership interest in the Beneficiary any stock in a general partner of the Beneficiary or any contract for any of the foregoing (on an installment basis or otherwise), in violation of Paragraph 20 hereof;

(c)   The Mortgaged Premises is abandoned;

(d)   Default in the observance or performance of any other covenant, condition, agreement or provisions hereof or of the Notes, any additional collateral document or the Loan Agreement which is not remedied within thirty (30) days after written notice thereof to Mortgagor by Mortgagee or, if such default is incapable of being cured within such thirty (30) day period, the Mortgagor shall have undertaken within such period, and shall be diligently carrying forward, all steps which are necessary or desirable to remedy such condition as are approved by the Mortgagee in its sole discretion and shall complete such cure within sixty (60) days;

(e)   Any representation or warranty made by the Mortgagor, Beneficiary or the guarantors of the Notes (collectively, the "Guarantor") herein or in the Notes, Loan Agreement or any additional collateral documents or in any statement or certificate furnished pursuant hereto or thereto proves untrue in any material respect as of the date of the issuance or making thereof;

(f)   Mortgagor, Beneficiary, any general partner of Beneficiary, or any Guarantor becomes insolvent or bankrupt or admits in writing its or their inability to pay its or their debts as they mature or makes an assignment for the benefit of creditors or applies for or consents to the appointment of a trustee, custodian or receiver for any of them or for the major part of the property of any of them;

(g)   Neither Mortgagor nor Beneficiary is able to satisfy any condition of their right to the receipt of any advances under the Loan Agreement for a period in excess of thirty (30) days other than as a result of matters beyond their control;

(h)   Bankruptcy, reorganization, arrangement, insolvency or liquidation proceedings or other proceedings for relief under any bankruptcy laws or laws for the relief of debtors are instituted by or against the Mortgagor, Beneficiary, any general partner of Beneficiary, or any Guarantor and if instituted are not dismissed within sixty (60) days after such institution;

(i)   Any judgment or judgments, writ or writs or warrant or warrants of attachment or any similar process or processes in an aggregate amount in excess of $25,000 shall be entered or filed against the Mortgagor, Beneficiary, any general partner of Beneficiary, or any Guarantor or against any of their respective property or assets and remains unsatisfied, unvacated, unbonded or unstayed for a period of sixty (60) days;

(j)   The title company refuses to issue the endorsement provided for in Section 5.1(d) of the Loan Agreement because of a change in the state of title or a survey exception and neither Mortgagor nor Beneficiary is able to correct the condition giving rise to the refusal and procure issuance of the notice within thirty (30) days of notice of any such refusal given to the Beneficiary by Mortgagee; or

(k)   Any of the Guarantors die, unless such Guarantor's estate assumes his obligations under his guaranty by an instrument satisfactory to Mortgagee within thirty (30) days of such

Guarantor's death; provided that with respect to subparagraphs (f), (h) and (i) of this paragraph 21, if any of the events described therein occur with respect to a Guarantor such event may be cured if within thirty (30) days following such event, a substitute guarantor reasonably acceptable to Mortgagee assumes the Guarantor's obligation.

22.   Remedies. When any Event of Default which is not cured within the applicable grace period, if any, has happened and is continuing (regardless of the pendency of any proceeding which has or might have the effect of preventing Mortgagor from complying with the terms of this instrument) and in addition to such other rights as may be available under applicable law, under the Loan Agreement, but subject at all times to any mandatory legal requirements:

(a)   Acceleration. Mortgagee may, by written notice to Mortgagor, declare the Notes and all unpaid indebtedness of Mortgagor hereby secured, including interest then accrued thereon, to be forthwith due and payable, whereupon the same shall become and be forthwith due and payable, without other notice or demand of any kind.

(b)   Uniform Commercial Code. Mortgagee shall, with respect to any part of the Mortgaged Premises constituting property of the type in respect of which realization on a lien or security interest granted therein is governed by the Uniform Commercial Code, have all the rights, options and remedies of a secured party under the Uniform Commercial Code of Illinois, including without limitation, the right to the possession of any such property or any part thereof, and the right to enter with legal process any premises where any such property may be found. Any requirement of said Code for reasonable notification shall be met by mailing written notice to Mortgagor at its address above set forth at least ten (10) days prior to the sale or other event for which such notice is required. The expenses or retaking, selling and otherwise disposing of said property, including reasonable attorneys' fees and legal expenses incurred in connection therewith, shall constitute so much additional indebtedness hereby secured and shall be payable upon demand with interest at the Default Interest Rate.

(c)   Foreclosure. Mortgagee may proceed to protect and enforce the rights of Mortgagee hereunder (i) by any action at law, suit in equity or other appropriate proceedings, whether for the specific performance of any agreement contained herein, or for an injunction against the violation of any of the terms hereof, or in aid of the exercise of any power granted hereby or by law, or (ii) by the foreclosure of this Mortgage. In any suit to foreclose the lien hereof, there shall be allowed and included as additional indebtedness hereby secured in the decree of sale, all expenditures and expenses authorized by the Illinois Mortgage Foreclosure Law, Chapter 110, Section 15-1101, et seq. Illinois Revised Statutes (1987), as from time to time amended (the "Act") and all other expenditures and expenses which may be paid or incurred by or on behalf of Mortgagee for reasonable attorney's fees, appraiser's fees, outlays for documentary and expert evidence, stenographer's charges, publication costs, and costs (which may be estimated as to items to be expended after entry of the decree) of procuring all such abstracts of title, title searches and examinations, title insurance policies, and similar data and assurance with respect to title as Mortgagee may deem reasonably necessary either to prosecute such suit or to evidence to bidders at sales which may be had pursuant to such decree the true conditions of the title to or the value of the Mortgaged Premises. All expenditures and expenses of the nature mentioned in this paragraph, and such other expenses and fees as may be incurred in the protection of the Mortgaged Premises and rents and income therefrom and the maintenance of the lien of this Mortgage, including the reasonable fees of any attorney employed by Mortgagee in any litigation or proceedings affecting this Mortgage, the Notes or the Mortgaged Premises, including bankruptcy proceedings, or in preparation of the commencement or defense of any proceedings or threatened suit or proceeding, or otherwise in dealing specifically therewith, shall be so much additional indebtedness hereby secured and shall be immediately due and payable by Mortgagor, with interest thereon at the Default Interest Rate until pa*id*.

(d)   Appointment of Receiver. Mortgagee shall, as a matter of right, upon notice and without giving bond to Mortgagor or anyone claiming by, under or through it, and without regard to the solvency or insolvency of Mortgagor or Beneficiary or the then value of the Mortgaged Premises, be entitled to have a receiver appointed pursuant to the Act of all or any part of the Mortgaged Premises and the rents, issues and profits thereof, with such power as the court making such appointment shall confer, and Mortgagor hereby consents to the appointment of such receiver and shall not oppose any such appointment. Any such receiver may, to the extent permitted under applicable law, without notice, enter upon and take possession of the Mortgaged Premises or any part thereof by force, summary proceedings, ejectment or otherwise, and may remove Mortgagor or other persons and any and all property therefrom, and may hold, operate and manage the same and receive all earnings, income, rents, issues and proceeds accruing with respect thereto or any part thereof, whether during the pendency of any foreclosure or until any right of redemption shall expire or otherwise.

(e)   Taking Possession, Collecting Rents, Etc. Upon demand by Mortgagee, Mortgagor shall surrender to mortgagee and Mortgagee may enter and take possession of the Mortgaged Premises or any part thereof personally, by its agent or attorneys or be placed in possession pursuant to court order as mortgagee in possession or receiver as provided in the Act, and Mortgagee, in its discretion, personally, by its agents or attorneys or pursuant to court order as mortgagee in possession or receiver as provided in the Act may enter upon and take and maintain possession of all or any part of the Mortgaged Premises, together with all documents, books, records, papers,, and accounts of Mortgagor relating thereto, and may exclude Mortgagor and any agents and servants thereof wholly therefrom and may, on behalf of Mortgagor, or in its own name as Mortgagee and under the powers herein granted:

(1)   hold, operate, manage and control all or any part of the Mortgaged Premises and conduct the business, if any, thereof, either personally or by its agents, with full power to use such measures, legal or equitable, as in its discretion may be deemed proper or necessary to enforce the payment or security of the rents, issues, deposits, profits, and avails of the Mortgaged Premises, including without limitation actions for recovery of

rent, actions in forcible detainer, and actions in distress for rent, all without notice to Mortgagor;

(2)   cancel or terminate any lease or sublease of all or any part of the Mortgaged Premises for any cause or on any ground that would entitle Mortgagor to cancel the same;

(3)   elect to disaffirm any lease or sublease of all or any part of the Mortgaged Premises made subsequent to this Mortgage without Mortgagee's prior written consent;

(4)   extend or modify any then existing leases and make new leases of all or any part of the Mortgaged Premises, which extensions, modifications, and new leases may provide for terms to expire, or for options to lessees to extend or renew terms to expire, beyond the maturity date of the loan evidenced by the Notes and the issuance of a deed or deeds to a purchaser or purchasers at a foreclosure sale, it being understood and agreed that any such leases, and the options or other such provisions to be contained therein, shall be binding upon Mortgagor, all persons whose interests in the Mortgaged Premises are subject to the lien hereof, and the purchaser or purchasers at any foreclosure sale, notwithstanding any redemption from sale, discharge of the indebtedness hereby secured, satisfaction of any foreclosure decree, or issuance of any certificate of sale or deed to any such purchaser;

(5)   make all necessary or proper repairs, decorations, renewals, replacements, alterations, additions, betterments, and improvements in connection with the Mortgaged Premises as may seem judicious to Mortgagee, to insure and reinsure the Mortgaged Premises and all risks incidental to Mortgagee's possession, operation and management thereof, and to receive all rents, issues, deposits, profits, and avails therefrom; and

(6)   apply the net income, after allowing a reasonable fee for the collection thereof and for the management of the Mortgaged Premises, to the payment of taxes, premiums and other charges applicable to the Mortgaged Premises, or in reduction of the indebtedness hereby secured in such order and manner as Mortgagee shall select.

Nothing herein contained shall be construed as constituting Mortgagee a mortgagee in possession in the absence of the actual taking of possession of the Mortgaged Premises. The right to enter and take possession of the Mortgaged Premises and use any personal property therein, to manage, operate, conserve and improve the same, and to collect the rents, issues and profits thereof, shall be in addition to all other rights or remedies of Mortgagee hereunder or afforded by law, and may be exercised concurrently therewith or independently thereof. The expenses (including any receiver's fees, reasonable counsel fees, costs and agent's compensation) incurred pursuant to the powers herein contained shall be secured hereby which expenses Mortgagor promises to pay upon demand together with interest at the rate applicable to the Notes at the time such expenses are incurred. Mortgagee shall not be liable to account to Mortgagor for any action taken pursuant hereto other than to account for any rents actually received by Mortgagee. Without taking possession of the Mortgaged Premises, Mortgagee may, in the event the Mortgaged Premises become vacant or are abandoned, take such steps as it deems appropriate to protect and secure the Mortgaged Premises (including hiring watchmen therefor) and all costs incurred in so doing shall constitute so much additional indebtedness hereby secured payable upon demand with interest thereon at the Default Interest Rate.

23. Compliance with Illinois Mortgage Foreclosure Law.

(a)   In the event that any provision in this Mortgage shall be inconsistent with any provision of the Act the provisions of the Act shall take precedence over the provisions of this Mortgage, but shall not invalidate or render unenforceable any other provision of this Mortgage that can be construed in a manner consistent with the Act.

(b)   If any provision of this Mortgage shall grant to Mortgagee any rights or remedies upon default of the Mortgagor which are more limited than the rights that would otherwise be vested in Mortgagee under the Act in the absence of said provision, Mortgagee shall be vested with the rights granted in the Act to the full extent permitted by law.

(c)   Without limiting the generality of the foregoing, all expenses incurred by Mortgagee to the extent reimbursable under Sections 15-1510 and 15-1512 of the Act, whether incurred before or after any decree or judgment of foreclosure, and whether enumerated in Sections 22(c) or 25 of this Mortgage, shall be added to the indebtedness secured by this Mortgage or by the judgment of foreclosure.

24. . Waiver of Right to Redeem - Waiver of Appraisement, Valuation, Etc. Mortgagor shall not and will not apply for or avail itself of any appraisement, valuation, stay, extension or exemption laws, or any so-called "Moratorium Laws," now existing or hereafter enacted in -order to prevent or hinder the enforcement or foreclosure of this Mortgage, but hereby waives the benefit of such laws. Mortgagor for itself and all who may claim through or under it waives any and all right to have the property and estates comprising the Mortgaged Premises marshaled upon any foreclosure of the lien hereof and agrees that any court having jurisdiction to foreclose such lien may order the Mortgaged Premises sold as an entirety. In the event of any sale made under or by virtue of this instrument, the whole of the Mortgaged Premises may be sold in one parcel as an entirety or in separate lots or parcels at the same or different times, all as the Mortgagee may determine. Mortgagee shall have the right to become the purchaser at any sale made under or by virtue of this instrument and Mortgagee so purchasing at any such sale shall have the right to be credited upon the amount of the bid made therefor by Mortgagee with the amount payable to Mortgagee out of the net proceeds of such sale. In the event of any such sale, the Notes and the other indebtedness hereby secured, if not previously due, shall be and become immediately due and payable without demand or notice of any kind. TO THE FULLEST EXTENT PERMITTED BY LAW, MORTGAGOR HEREBY VOLUNTARILY AND KNOWINGLY WAIVES ITS RIGHTS OF REINSTATEMENT AND REDEMPTION AS ALLOWED UNDER SECTION 15-1601(b) OF THE ACT, ON BEHALF OF MORTGAGOR, AND EACH AND EVERY PERSON ACQUIRING ANY INTEREST IN, OR TITLE TO THE MORTGAGED PREMISES DESCRIBED HEREIN SUBSEQUENT TO THE DATE OF THIS MORTGAGE, AND ON BEHALF OF ALL OTHER PERSONS TO THE EXTENT PERMITTED BY APPLICABLE LAW.

25.   Costs and Expenses of Foreclosure. In any suit to foreclose the lien hereof there shall be allowed and included as additional indebtedness in the decree for sale all expenditures and expenses which may be paid or incurred by or on behalf of Mortgagee for reasonable attorneys' fees, appraiser's fees, outlays for documentary and expert evidence, stenographic charges, publication costs and costs (which may be estimated as the items to be expended after the entry of the decree) of .procuring all such abstracts of title, title searches and examination, guarantee polices, Torrens certificates and similar data and assurances with respect to title as Mortgagee may deem to be reasonably necessary either to prosecute any foreclosure action or to evidence to the bidder at any sale pursuant thereto the true condition of the title to or the value of the Mortgaged Premises, and all of which expenditures shall become so much additional indebtedness hereby secured which Mortgagor agrees to pay and all of such shall be immediately due and payable with interest thereon from the date of expenditure until paid at the Default Interest Rate.

26.   Application of Proceeds. The proceeds of any foreclosure sale of the Mortgaged Premises or of any sale of property pursuant to Section 22(b) hereof shall be distributed in the following order of priority: First, on account of all costs and expenses incident to the foreclosure or other proceedings including all such items as are mentioned in Sections 22(b), 22(c) and 25 hereof; Second, to all other items which under the terms hereof constitute indebtedness hereby secured in addition to that evidenced by the Notes with interest thereon as herein provided; Third, to all interest on the Notes; Fourth, to all principal on the Notes with any overplus to whomsoever shall be lawfully entitled to same.

27.   Mortgagee's Remedies Cumulative - No Waiver. No remedy or right of Mortgagee shall be exclusive of but shall be cumulative and in addition to every other remedy or right now or hereafter existing at law or in equity or by statute or provided for in the Loan Agreement. No delay in the exercise or omission to exercise any remedy or right accruing on any default shall impair any such remedy or right or be construed to be a waiver of any such default or acquiescence therein, nor shall it affect any subsequent default of the same or different nature. Every such remedy or right may be exercised concurrently or independently, and when and as often as may be deemed expedient by Mortgagee.

28.   Mortgagee Party to Suits. If Mortgagee shall be made a party to or shall intervene in any action or proceeding affecting the Mortgaged Premises or the title thereto or the interest of Mortgagee under this Mortgage (including probate and bankruptcy proceedings), or if Mortgagee employs an attorney to collect any or all of the indebtedness hereby secured or to enforce any of the terms hereof or realize hereupon or to protect the lien hereof, or if Mortgagee shall incur any costs or expenses in preparation for the commencement of any foreclosure proceeding or for the defense of any threatened suit or proceeding which might affect the Mortgaged Premises or the security hereof, whether or not any such foreclosure or other suit or proceeding shall be actually commenced, then in any such case, Mortgagor agrees to pay to Mortgagee, immediately and without demand, all reasonable costs, charges, expenses and attorneys' fees incurred by Mortgagee in any such case, and the same shall constitute so much additional indebtedness hereby secured payable upon demand with interest at the Default Interest Rate.

29.   Modifications Not To Affect Lien. Mortgagee, without notice to anyone, and without regard to the consideration, if any, paid therefor, or the presence of other liens on the Mortgaged Premises, may in its discretion release any part of the Mortgaged Premises or any person liable for any of the indebtedness hereby secured, may extend the time of payment of any of the indebtedness hereby secured and may grant waivers or other indulgences with respect hereto and thereto, without in any way affecting or impairing the liability of any party liable upon any of the indebtedness hereby secured or the priority of the lien of this Mortgage upon all of the Mortgaged Premises not expressly released, and may agree with Mortgagor to modifications to the terms and conditions contained herein or otherwise applicable to any of the indebtedness hereby secured (including modifications in the rates of interest applicable thereto).

30.   Notices. All notices or other communications required or permitted hereunder shall be (a) in writing and shall be deemed to be given when either (i) delivered in person, (ii) received after deposit in a regularly maintained receptacle of the United States mail as registered or certified mail, postage prepaid, (iii) received if sent by private courier service, (iv) on the day on which the party to whom such notice is addressed refuses delivery by mail or by private courier service or (v) three (3) days have elapsed after mailing by certified or registered mail postage prepaid, return receipted requested, and (b) addressed as follows:

To Lender: c/o   First Mortgage Bank
                        423 N. Michigan Avenue
                        Chicago, Illinois

To Borrower: c/o   Regent Real Estate Development Group
                        524 W. South Avenue
                        Chicago, Illinois

31.   Partial Invalidity. All rights, powers and remedies provided herein are intended to be limited to the extent necessary so that they will not render this Mortgage invalid, unenforceable or not entitled to be recorded, registered or filed under any applicable law. If any term of this Mortgage shall be held to be invalid or unenforceable, the validity and enforceability of the other terms of this Mortgage shall in no way be affected thereby.

32.   Successors and Assigns. Whenever any of the parties hereto is referred to, such reference shall be deemed to include the successors and assigns of such party; and all the covenants, promises and agreements in this Mortgage contained by or on behalf of Mortgagor, or by or on behalf of Mortgagee, shall bind and insure to the benefit of the respective successors and assigns of such parties, whether so expressed or not.

33.   Default Interest Rate. For purposes of this Mortgage, "Default Interest Rate" shall mean the rate per annum determined by adding 4% to the Prime Rate of interest as defined in the Notes.

34.   Headings. The headings in this instrument are for convenience of reference only and shall not limit or otherwise affect the meaning of any provision hereof.

35.   Changes, Etc. This instrument and the provisions hereof may be changed, waived, discharged or terminated only by an instrument in writing signed by the party against which enforcement of the change, waiver, discharge or termination is sought.

36.   Exculpation. This Mortgage is executed by First Mortgage Bank, not personally but as Trustee as aforesaid in the exercise of the power and authority conferred upon and vested in it as such Trustee (and said Trustee hereby warrants that it possesses full power and authority to execute this instrument), and it is expressly understood and agreed that nothing herein or in said Notes contained shall be construed as creating any liability on said Trustee personally to pay the said Notes or any interest that may accrue thereon, or any indebtedness accruing hereunder, or to perform any covenant, either express or implied, herein contained, all such liability, if any, being expressly waived by Mortgagee and by every person now or hereafter claiming any right or security hereunder, and that so far as said Trustee personally is concerned, the legal holder or holders of said Notes and the owners or owners of any indebtedness accruing hereunder shall look solely to the premises hereby conveyed for the payment thereof, by the enforcement of the lien hereby created, in the manner herein and in said Notes provided or by action to enforce the personal liability of any guarantors of the indebtedness hereby secured or by proceeding against any other collateral security therefor.

IN WITNESS WHEREOF, the undersigned has caused these presents to be signed as of the day and year first above written.

ATTEST:

FIRST MORTGAGE BANK, as
Trustee as aforesaid

By: _____   By: _____
    Its: _VICE PRESIDENT_   Its: _Assistant Secretary_

FOX VALLEY AUTO CARE CENTER
LIMITED PARTNERSHIP

By: Regent Real Estate
Development Corp.,
General Partner

By: _____
     Its: _PRESIDENT_

THIS INSTRUMENT PREPARED BY:

Jack Halloman
228 N. LaSalle Street
Suite 900
Chicago, Illinois 60604

ASSIGNMENT OF LEASES AND RENTS

KNOW ALL MEN BY THESE PRESENTS, that FIRST MORTGAGE BANK, not personally but as Trustee under Trust Agreement dated as of April 11, 1989 and known as Trust Number 108049-04 (the `Trustee') whose address is 423 N. Michigan Avenue, Chicago, Illinois 60690, and FOX VALLEY AUTO CARE CENTER LIMITED PARTNERSHIP, an Illinois limited partnership, whose address is 524 W. South Avenue, Illinois, 60610 (`Beneficiary'), (Trustee and Beneficiary being hereinafter collectively referred to as ``Assignors''), in consideration of the sum of $2,300,000.00 and other good and valuable considerations, the receipt and sufficiency whereof are hereby acknowledged, do hereby assign, transfer and set over unto FIRST MORTGAGE BANK, of 423 N. Michigan Avenue, Chicago, Illinois 60690 (hereinafter referred to as the ``Mortgagee''), all right, title and interest of the Assignors in, under or pursuant to any and all present or future leases, whether written or oral, or any lettings of possession of, or any agreements for the use or occupancy of, the whole or any part of the real estate and premises hereinafter described which the Assignors or either of them may have heretofore made or agrees to or may hereafter make or agree to, or which may be made or agreed to by the Mortgagee under the powers hereinafter granted, including all amendments and supplements to and renewals thereof at any time made (hereinafter a ``Lease'', or, collectively, the ``Leases''), all relating to the certain real estate situated in the County of DuPage, State of Illinois, described in Exhibit ``A'' attached hereto and made a part hereof and the improvements now or hereafter erected thereon (the ``Premises''), including, without limiting the generality of the foregoing, all right, title and interest of Assignors or either of them in and to all the rents (whether fixed or contingent), earnings, renewal rents and all other sums due or which may

227

hereafter become due under or by virtue of the Leases and all rights under or against guarantors of the obligations of lessees under the Leases.

This Assignment is made and given as collateral security for, and shall secure (i) the payment in full of all principal of and interest on two Promissory Notes of the Trustee and Beneficiary bearing even date herewith, payable to the order of the Mortgagee in the aggregate face principal sum of $2,300,000 and any note issued in extension or renewal thereof or in substitution thereof (the ``Notes''), (ii) the performance of all obligations, covenants, promises and agreements contained herein or in that certain Mortgage and Security Agreement with Assignments of Rents being even date herewith, from the Trustee to the Mortgagee (the ``Mortgage'') conveying and mortgaging the premises as security for the Notes and any and all other indebtedness intended to be secured thereby, (iii) the performance of all obligations, covenants, promises and agreements of the Trustee or the Beneficiary under that certain Construction Loan Agreement bearing even date herewith, by and among the Trustee, the Beneficiary and the Mortgagee (the ``Loan Agreement''), and (iv) the payment of all expenses and charges, legal or otherwise, paid or incurred by the Mortgagee in realizing upon or protecting the indebtedness referred to in the foregoing clauses (i) and (ii) or any security therefore, including this Assignment.

The Assignors do hereby irrevocably constitute and appoint the Mortgagee the true and lawful attorney of the Assignors with full power of substitution for Assignors and in Assignor's name, place and stead after an uncured default hereunder to ask, demand, collect, receive, receipt for, sue for, compound and give acquittance for any and all sums due or to become due under any Lease, with full power to settle, adjust or compromise any claim thereunder as fully as the Assignors could do, and to endorse the name of the Assignors or either of them on all commercial paper given in payment or in part payment thereof, and in the Mortgagee's discretion to file any claim or take any other action or proceeding, either in the Mortgagee's name or in the name of the Assignors or either of them or otherwise, which the Mortgagee may deem necessary or appropriate to collect any and all sums due or to become due under any Lease, or which may be necessary or appropriate to protect and preserve the right, title and interest of the Mortgagee in and to such sums and the security intended to be afforded hereby.

The Beneficiary warrants to the Mortgagee that the Assignors have good right to make this Assignment and that the Assignors have not heretofore alienated, assigned, pledged or otherwise disposed of any of the rights, rents and other sums due or which may hereafter become due and which are intended to be assigned hereunder.

Notwithstanding the foregoing provisions making and establishing a present and absolute transfer and assignment of all rents, earnings, income, issues and profits as aforesaid, and so long as no event of default shall exist under any of the Notes or Mortgage and no event shall exist which if uncured with any applicable cure period, has or would become an event of default thereunder, the Assignors shall have the right and license to collect, use and enjoy all rents and other sums due or to become due under or by virtue of any Lease as they respectively become due, but not more than 30 days in advance.

The Assignors hereby irrevocably consent to and authorize and direct that the tenant under any Lease upon demand and notice from the Mortgagee of the Mortgagee's right to receive the rents hereunder, shall pay such rents to the Mortgagee without any obligation on the part of such tenant to determine the actual existence of any default or event claimed by the Mortgagee as the basis for the Mortgagee's right to receive such rents and notwithstanding any notice from or claim of the Assignors or either of them to the contrary. The Assignors hereby waive either right or claim against any tenant for any such rents paid by any tenant to the Mortgagee.

Without limiting any legal rights of the Mortgagee as the absolute assignee of the rents, issues and profits of the premises and in furtherance thereof, Assignors agree that upon the occurrence of an Event of Default under said Mortgage, whether before or after either of the Notes is declared due in the accordance with their terms or under the terms of said Mortgage, the Mortgagee may, at its option, take actual possession of the premises hereinabove described, or of any part thereof, personally or by agent or attorney, as for condition broken, and with or without force and with or without process of law, enter upon, take, and maintain possession of all or any part of said premises together with all documents, books, records, papers and accounts relating thereto, and exclude the Assignors, their agents or servants, therefrom and hold, operate, manage and control the premises, and at the expense of the Assignors, from time to time, cause to be made all necessary or proper repairs, renewals, replacements, useful alterations, additions, betterments and improvements to the premises as may seem judicious, and pay taxes, assessments and prior or proper charges on the premises, or any part thereof, and insure and reinsure the same, and lease the premises in such parcels and for such times and on such terms as my deem fit, including leases for terms expiring beyond the maturity of the indebtedness secured by said Mortgage, and cancel any lease or sub-lease for any cause or on any ground which would entitle the Assignors or either of them to cancel the same and in every such case have the right to manage and operate the said premises and to carry on the business thereof as the Mortgagee shall deem best.

After payment of all proper charges and expenses, including the just and reasonable compensation for the services of the Mortgagee, its attorneys, agents, clerks, servants and others employed by the Mortgagee in connection with the operation, management and control of the premises and the conduct of the business thereof, and such further sums as may be sufficient to indemnify the Mortgagee against any liability, loss or damage on

account of any matter or thing done in good faith in pursuance of the rights and powers of the Mortgagee hereunder, the Mortgagee may, at its option, credit the net amount of income which the Mortgagee may receive by virtue of this Assignment and from the premises to any and all amounts due or owing to the Mortgagee under the terms and provisions of the Note, the Mortgage and any loan or security agreement pertaining thereto, whether or not the same may then be due or be otherwise adequately secured. Mortgagee shall have the right, but not the duty to apply such net income to the discharge of any other lien or charge upon the premises or to completion of the improvements being financed out of the proceeds of the Notes. The manner of the application of such net income and the item, which shall be credited, shall be within the sole discretion of the Mortgagee. Mortgagee shall be subrogated to any lien or charge discharged out of the rents, income and profits of the premises.

The Assignors hereby further covenant that the Assignors will, upon request of the Mortgagee, execute and deliver such further instruments and do and perform such other acts and things as the Mortgagee may reasonably deem necessary or appropriate to more effectively vest in and secure to the Mortgagee the rights and rents which are intended to be assigned to the Mortgagee hereunder.

Assignors covenant and agree to observe and perform all of the obligations imposed on them under the Leases and not to do or permit to be done anything to impair the security thereof, not to further assign or encumber their rights under the Leases or their rights to the rents or other sums due or to become due thereunder and not suffer or permit any of the Leases to be subordinated to any other liens or encumbrances whatsoever, any such subordination to be null and void unless done with the written consent of Mortgagee which consent shall not be unreasonably withheld or delayed. Assignors further covenant and agree not to enter into any new Lease and not to amend, modify or terminate any of the Leases without the prior written consent of Mortgagee which consent shall not be unreasonably withheld or delayed. Assignors further covenant and agree that they will, at the request of Mortgagee, submit the executed originals of all Leases to Mortgagee.

The acceptance by the Mortgagee of this Assignment, with all of the rights, powers, privileges and authority so created, shall not, prior to entry upon and taking of actual physical possession of the premises by the Mortgagee, be deemed or construed to constitute the Mortgagee a mortgagee in possession nor thereafter impose any obligation whatsoever upon the Mortgagee, it being understood and agreed that the Mortgagee does not hereby undertake to perform or discharge any obligation, duty or liability of the landlord under any Leases of the premises or under or by reason of this Assignment. Mortgagee shall have no liability to Assignors or anyone for any action taken or omitted to be taken by it hereunder, except for its willful misconduct or gross negligence. Should the Mortgagee incur any liability, loss or damage under or by reason of this Assignment or for any action taken by the Mortgagee hereunder, except for Mortgagee's gross negligence or willful misconduct, or in defense against any claim or demand whatsoever which may be asserted against the Mortgagee arising out of any lease, the amount thereof, including costs, expenses and reasonable attorneys' fees, together with interest thereon at the Default Rate (as such term is defined in the Loan Agreement) shall be secured by this Assignment and by the Mortgage, and the Assignors shall reimburse the Mortgagee therefor immediately upon demand.

The rights and remedies of the Mortgagee hereunder are cumulative and are not in lieu of, but are in addition to, any rights or remedies which the Mortgagee shall have under the said Note, Mortgage or any other instrument or document or under applicable law and the exercise by Mortgagee of any rights and remedies herein contained shall not be deemed a waiver of any other rights or remedies of Mortgagee whether arising under the Mortgage or otherwise, each and all of which may be exercised whenever Mortgagee deems it in its interest to do so. The rights and remedies of the Mortgagee may be exercised from time to time and as often as such exercise is deemed expedient and the failure of the Mortgagee to enforce any of the terms, provisions and conditions of this Assignment for any period of time, at any time or times, shall not be construed or deemed to be a waiver of any rights under the terms hereof. The right of the Mortgagee to collect and receive the rents assigned hereunder-or to exercise any of the rights or powers herein granted to the Mortgagee shall, to the extent not prohibited by law, extend also to the period from and after the filing of any suit to foreclose the lien of the Mortgage, including any period allowed by law for the redemption of the premises after any foreclosure sale.

This Assignment shall be assignable by the Mortgagee and all of the terms and provisions hereof shall be binding upon and inure to the benefit of the respective executors, administrators, legal representatives, successors and assigns of each of the parties hereto.

This instrument is executed by First Mortgage Bank, not personally but as Trustee as aforesaid in the exercise of the power and authority conferred upon and vested in its as such Trustee (and said bank hereby warrants that it possesses full power and authority to execute this instrument), and it is expressly understood and agreed that nothing herein or in said Notes contained shall be construed as creating any liability on said bank personally to pay said Notes or any interest that may accrue thereon, or any indebtedness accruing hereunder, or to perform any covenant either express or implied herein contained, all such liability, if any, being expressly waived by Mortgagee and by every person now or hereafter claiming any right or security hereunder, and that so far as said bank personally is concerned, the legal holder or holders of said Notes and the owner or owners of any indebtedness accruing hereunder shall look solely to the premises described herein and by the Mortgage conveyed for the payment thereof, by the enforcement of the liens hereby and thereby created, in the manner herein and in said Mortgage provided or by action to enforce the personal liability of Beneficiary or of any guarantor of the indebtedness hereby secured or by realization on any other collateral for the indebtedness hereby secured.

DATED as of the 2nd day of August, 1989.

FIRST MORTGAGE BANK, not
personally but solely as
Trustee aforesaid

ATTEST:
By. _Daniel Peterson_
Its: _VICE PRESIDENT_

By: _Julie A. Arnold_
Its: _Assistant Secretary_

FOX VALLEY AUTO CARE CENTER
LIMITED PARTNERSHIP, an
Illinois limited partnership

By: Regent Real Estate
     Development Corp.,
     General Partner

By: _David Delaney_
Its: _PRESIDENT_

234

STATE OF ILLINOIS   )
)   SS.
COUNTY OF COOK   )

        I, _____, a Notary Public, in and for said
County, in the State aforesaid, do hereby certify that
_____, _____ President of FIRST MORTGAGE BANK
and _____, _____ Secretary of said Bank who
are personally known to me to be the same persons whose names are
subscribed to the foregoing instrument as such President and
_____ Secretary, respectively, appeared before me this day
in person and acknowledged that they signed and delivered the
said instrument as their own free and voluntary act and as the
free and voluntary act of said Bank, as Trustee as aforesaid, for
the uses and purposes therein set forth; and the said Assistant
Secretary then and there acknowledged that he, as custodian of
the corporate seal of said Bank, did affix the corporate seal of
said Bank to said instrument as his own free and voluntary act
and as the free and voluntary act of said Bank, as Trustee as
aforesaid, for the uses and purposes therein set forth.

        GIVEN under my hand and notarial seal this _____ day of
_____ , 1989.

                                _____
                                Notary Public

My Commission Expires:

_____

STATE OF ILLINOIS   )
) SS
COUNTY OF DUPAGE   )

        I, a Notary Public in and for said County, in the State
aforesaid, DO HEREBY CERTIFY THAT _____who is
personally known to me to be the _____ of REGENT REAL
ESTATE DEVELOPMENT CORP., a corporation of the State of Illinois,
which is the general partner of FOX VALLEY AUTO CARE CENTER
LIMITED PARTNERSHIP, an Illinois limited partnership, and the
same person whose name is subscribed to the foregoing instrument,
appeared before me this day in person, and acknowledged that
he/she signed and delivered the said instrument as _____
 of said corporation pursuant to the authority given by the Board
of Directors of said corporation, as his/her own free and
voluntary act and as the free and voluntary act of said
corporation and partnership, for the uses and purposes therein
set forth.

        GIVEN under my hand and Notarial seal this _____day of
August, 1989.

                                    _____
                                    Notary Public

My Commission Expires:

_____

PARCEL 3:

EASEMENT APPURTENANT TO PARCEL 1 OVER, ACROSS AND UPON THE ACCESS ROAD FOR ACCESS, INGRESS AND EGRESS FROM PARCEL 1 TO SOUTH ROAD ON THE NORTH AND WESTBROOK DRIVE EXTENSION TO THE SOUTH AS CREATED BY DECLARATION OF EASEMENT RECORDED _____ AS DOCUMENT _____ SAID ACCESS ROAD DESCRIBED AS FOLLOWS:

THAT PART OF THE SOUTHEAST QUARTER OF SECTION 21, TOWNSHIP 38 NORTH, RANGE 9 EAST OF THE THIRD PRINCIPAL MERIDIAN DESCRIBED AS FOLLOWS: COMMENCING AT THE MOST NORTHERLY CORNER OF FOX VALLEY EAST, REGION 1, UNIT NO. 2,AURORA, DUPAGE COUNTY, ILLINOIS; THENCE EASTERLY ALONG THE SOUTHERLY LINE OF SOUTH ROAD 425.40 FEET FOR A POINT OF BEGINNING; THENCE SOUTHERLY AT RIGHT ANGLES TO THE SOUTH LINE (AS MONUMENTED) OF A TRACT OF LAND CONVEYED TO LA VERNE W. JACKSON AND CLARA L. JACKSON BY DOCUMENT 747981 RECORDED MARCH 2, 1955, 361.54 FEET TO SAID SOUTH LINE; THENCE WESTERLY ALONG SAID SOUTH LINE AT RIGHT ANGLES TO THE LAST DESCRIBED COURSE 15.0 FEET; THENCE NORTHERLY PARALLEL WITH THE PENULTIMATE DESCRIBED COURSE 358.29 FEET TO THE SOUTHERLY LINE OF SAID SOUTH ROAD: THENCE EASTERLY ALONG SAID SOUTHERLY LINE 15.35 FEET TO THE POINT OF BEGINNING, IN THE CITY OF AURORA, DUPAGE COUNTY, ILLINOIS.

ALSO

THAT PART OF THE SOUTHEAST QUARTER OF SECTION 21, TOWNSHIP 38 NORTH, RANGE 9 EAST OF THE THIRD PRINCIPAL MERIDIAN DESCRIBED AS FOLLOWS: COMMENCING AT THE MOST NORTHERLY CORNER OF FOX VALLEY EAST, REGION 1, UNIT NO. 2,AURORA, DUPAGE COUNTY, ILLINOIS; THENCE EASTERLY ALONG THE SOUTHERLY LINE OF SOUTH ROAD 425.40 FEET FOR A POINT OF BEGINNING; THENCE SOUTHERLY AT EIGHT ANGLES TO THE SOUTH LINE (AS MONUMENTED) OF A TRACT OF LAND CONVEYED TO LA VERNE W. JACKSON AND CLARA L. JACKSON BY DOCUMENT 747981 RECORDED MARCH 2, 1955, 361.54 FEET TO SAID SOUTH LINE; THENCE EASTERLY ALONG SAID SOUTH LINE AT RIGHT ANGLES TO THE LAST DESCRIBED COURSE 15.0 FEET; THENCE NORTHERLY PARALLEL WITH THE PENULTIMATE DESCRIBED COURSE 364.75 FEET TO THE SOUTHERLY LINE OF SAID SOUTH ROAD; THENCE WESTERLY ALONG SAID SOUTHERLY LINE 15.34 FEET TO

THE POINT OF BEGINNING, IN THE CITY OF AURORA, DUPAGE COUNTY, ILLINOIS.***

PARCEL 4:

EASEMENT APPURTENANT TO PARCEL 1, OVER, ACROSS AND UPON THE EASEMENT PREMISES FOR INGRESS AND EGRESS AS CREATED BY EASEMENT GRANT RECORDED _____ AS DOCUMENT _____, THE EASEMENT PREMISES DESCRIBED AS FOLLOWS:

COMMON BOUNDARY EASEMENT BETWEEN LOTS I AND 2

That part of Lot I, Fox Valley East. Region I. Unit No. 20. Aurora, DuPage County. Illinois described as follows: Commencing at the southwest corner of said Lot; thence easterly along the south line of said Lot 15.0 feet for a point of beginning; thence northerly parallel with the west line of said Lot 15.0 feet; thence easterly to a point on the east line of said Lot that is 13.0 feet northerly of the southeast corner V said Lot; thence southerly along said east line 13.0 feet to said southeast corner; thence westerly along the south line of said Lot 474.24 feet to the point of beginning. in the City of Aurora, DuPage County, Illinois

and also;

That part of Lot 2. Fox Valley East, Region I. Unit No. 20. Aurora. DuPage County. Illinois described as follows: Commencing at the northwest corner of said Lot; thence easterly along the north line of said Lot 15.0 feet for a point of beginning; thence southerly parallel with the west line of said Lot 15.0 feet: thence easterly to a point on the east line of said Lot that is 16.0 feet southerly of the northeast corner of amid Lot: thence northerly along said east line 16.0 feet to said northeast corner; thence westerly along said north line 474.24 feet to the point of beginning. In the City of Aurora, DuPage County. Illinois.

STATE OF ILLINOIS

UNIFORM COMMERCIAL CODE—FINANCING STATEMENT—FORM UCC-1

INSTRUCTIONS:

1. PLEASE TYPE this form. Fold only along perforation for mailing.
2. Remove Secured Party and Debtor copies and send other 3 copies with interleaved carbon paper to the filing officer. Enclose filing fee.
3. If the space provided for any item(s) on the form is inadequate the item(s) should be continued on additional sheets, preferably 5" x 8" or 8" x 10". Only one copy of such additional sheets need be presented to the filing officer with a set of three copies of the financing statement. Long schedules of collateral, indentures, etc., may be on any size paper that is convenient for the secured party.

This STATEMENT is presented to a filing officer for filing pursuant to the Uniform Commercial Code.

Debtor(s) (Last Name First) and address(es)	Secured Party(ies) and address(es)	For Filing Officer (Date, Time, Number, and Filing Office)
Fox Valley Auto Care Center Limited Partnership 524 W. South Avenue Chicago, Illinois 60610	First Mortgage Bank 423 N, Michigan Avenue Chicago, Illinois 60690	

1. This financing statement covers the following types (or items) of property:

See Exhibit "A" attached hereto

2. [X] Products of Collateral are also covered.
_____ Additional sheets presented.
_____ Filed with Office of Secretary of State of Illinois.
_____ Debtor is a transmitting utility as defined in UCC§9-105.

ASSIGNEE OF SECURED PARTY

Fox Valley Auto Care Center Limited Partnership

By: _____
Signature of (Debtor)   (Secured Party)*

* Signature of Debtor Required in Most Cases:
Signature of Secured Party in Cases Covered by UCC §9-402 (2)

This form of financing statement is approved by the Illinois Secretary of State.

(1) FILING OFFICER COPY-ALPHABETICAL

STANDARD FORM   UNIFORM COMMERCIAL CODE   FORM UCC-1   REV 1975

303172-DJ

STATE OF ILLINOIS

UNIFORM COMMERCIAL CODE – FINANCING STATEMENT – FORM UCC-2

INSTRUCTIONS

1. PLEASE TYPE this form. Fold only along perforation for mailing.
2. Remove Secured Party and Debtor copies and send other 3 copies with interleaved carbon paper to the filing officer. Enclose filing fee.
3. If the space provided for any item(s) on the form is inadequate the item(s) should be continued on additional sheets, preferably 5" x 8" or 8" x 10". Only one copy of such additional sheets need be presented to the filing officer with a set of three copies of the financing statement. Long schedules of Collateral, indentures, etc., may be on any size paper that is convenient for the secured party.

Perfection Legal Forms & Printing Co., Rockford, Ill.

This STATEMENT is presented to a filing officer for filing pursuant to the Uniform Commercial Code:

1. Debtor(s) (Last Name First) and address(es)	2. Secured Party(ies) and address(es)	For Filing Officer (Date, Time, Number, and Filing Office)
Fox Valley Auto Care Center Limited Partnership 524 W. South Avenue Chicago, IL 60610	First Mortgage Bank 423 N. Michigan Avenue Chicago, IL 60690	

ASSIGNEE OF SECURED PARTY

1. This financing statement covers the following types (or items) of property:

See Exhibit "A" attached hereto

2. (If collateral is crops) XXXXXXXXXXXXXXXXXXXXXXXXXXXXXXXXXXXX: (Describe Real Estate)

3. (If applicable) The above goods are to become fixtures on XXXXXXXXXXXXXXXXXXXXXXXXXXXXXXXXXXXXXXXXXXXX(s) XXXXXXXXXXXXXXXXXXXXXXXXXXXXXXXXXXXXXXXXXX (strike what is inapplicable) (Describe Real Estate)

and this financing statement is to be filed in the real estate records. (If the debtor does not have an interest of record) The name of a record owner is

First Mortgage Bank as Trustee under trust agreement dated 4/11/89 known as # 108049-04

4. ☒ Products of Collateral are also covered.

X ——— Additional sheets presented
X ——— Filed with Recorder's Office of   DuPage   County, Illinois.

Fox Valley Auto Care Center Limited

By: Partnership   Signature of (Debtor)

By: Regent Real Estate Development Corp.

(Secured Party)*

*Signature of Debtor Required in Most Cases:
Signature of Secured Party in Cases Covered by UCC §9-402(2).

This form of financing statement is approved by the Secretary of State

Filing Officer Copy—Alphabetical
STANDARD FORM — UNIFORM COMMERCIAL CODE — FORM UCC-2 — REV. 7-74

240

GUARANTY OF PAYMENT AND PERFORMANCE

THIS GUARANTY ("Guaranty") is made as of August 2, 1989 by the undersigned, DAVID DELANEY, RICHARD FLAMM and STEVEN MATTHEWS, jointly and severally, (referred to herein jointly and individually as "Guarantors"), to and for the benefit of FIRST MORTGAGE BANK, and its successors and assigns and the holder or holders from time to time of the Promissory Notes hereinafter described (said Bank and its successors and assigns and the holder or holders from time to time of said notes are hereinafter called the "Mortgagee").

WITNESSETH:

WHEREAS, FIRST MORTGAGE BANK, as Trustee under Trust Agreement dated April 11, 1989 and known as Trust No. 108049-04 ("Trustee") and Fox Valley Auto Care Center Limited Partnership, an Illinois limited partnership ("Fox Valley" together with Trustee, "Borrower"), have executed and delivered to Mortgagee Promissory Notes of even date herewith-in the original principal amounts of $2,100,000.00 and $200,000.00 ("Notes"), which Notes are secured, inter alia, by a certain Construction Mortgage and Security Agreement with Assignment of Rents of even date herewith from Trustee in favor of Mortgagee (the "Mortgage") and certain other instruments (collectively with the Mortgage, the "Loan Documents");

WHEREAS, the Notes evidence an indebtedness of Borrower to the Mortgagee arising from a loan (the "Loan") in the original principal amount of $2,300,000.00 from Mortgagee to Borrower and are issued pursuant to the terms of a Construction Loan Agreement of even date herewith between Borrower and Mortgagee (the "Loan Agreement");

WHEREAS, Mortgagee is unwilling to make the Loan unless the Guarantors execute this Guaranty and the Guarantors desire to give this Guaranty to Mortgagee to induce Mortgagee to make the Loan; and

WHEREAS, the Guarantors will be benefited by the disbursement by Mortgagee of the proceeds of the Loan to Borrower.

NOW, THEREFORE, in consideration of the foregoing and for the purpose of inducing Mortgagee to disburse the proceeds of the Loan to or at the direction of Borrower, the parties agree as follows:

1.   Guaranty of Payment and Performance. The undersigned jointly and severally guarantee, absolutely and unconditionally:

(i)   The full and complete payment of all costs and expenses needed or incurred for the lien—free completion and equipping of the Improvements (as defined in the Loan Agreement) within the time and in the manner required by the Loan Agreement and in accordance with the plans and specifications therefore now or hereafter approved by Mortgagee and any tenant which may have rights to approve such plans and specifications, including without limitation, costs and fees of all architects, engineers and construction consultants retained by Borrower or Mortgagee in connection with construction of the Improvements, and the payment of all costs and expenses in connection therewith; and

(ii)   The full and complete payment of any and all fees, costs and expenses (including reasonable attorneys' fees incurred by Mortgagee at any time prior or subsequent to default, whether litigation is involved or not, and if involved, whether at the trial or appellate levels or in pre- or post—judgment bankruptcy proceedings), in enforcing or realizing upon the obligations of the Guarantors hereunder (the obligations of Guarantors under this Paragraph 1 and the succeeding Paragraph 2 hereof are collectively hereinafter referred to as the "Obligations").

2.   Performance of Obligations. In addition to, and without limiting the provisions of Paragraph 1, if for any reason or-under any contingency Borrower shall abandon construction of the Improvements or shall fail to complete and equip the Improvements or portions thereof, in the manner and in accordance with the terms specified in the Loan Agreement or, if Mortgagee takes possession of the Project or any part thereof prior to the completion of the Improvements by reason of an Event of Default under the Loan Agreement or under any of the Loan Documents or if the right of Borrower to receive any other or further disbursement or advance under the Loan Agreement shall be terminated or temporarily suspended due to an Event of Default under the Loan Agreement then, in any such event, Guarantors shall, at each of their sole cost and expense, cause the Improvements to be completed and equipped, lien-free within the time and in the manner required by the Loan Agreement and in accordance with the plans and specifications therefore now or hereafter approved by Mortgagee and any tenant which ma y have rights to approve such plans and specifications. Guarantor shall pay all costs and expenses incurred in connection with the performance of the Obligations within thirty (30) days after giving of written notice by Mortgagee demanding performance hereunder. If performance of the Obligations cannot, with due diligence, be made within such thirty (30) day period and the Guarantor fails to commence to perform within such thirty (30) day period or does not thereafter diligently pursue performance and, in any event, if performance is not made within sixty (60) days of such written notice from Mortgagee, Mortgagee, at the Mortgagee's option, shall have the right to complete the Improvements, either before or after or Simultaneously with any other remedy of Mortgagee against the Guarantor or Borrower, and to expend such sums as Mortgagee, in its discretion, deems proper in order to so complete the Improvements, and the Guarantor shall pay all such amounts to Mortgagee upon demand, with interest thereon at the Default Interest Rate set forth in the Notes.

3.   Rights of Mortgagee. Guarantors authorize Mortgagee at any time in its discretion to alter any of the terms of the Obligations, to take and hold any security for the Obligations and to accept additional or substituted security, to subordinate, compromise or release any security, to release Borrower of its for all or any part of the Obligations, to release, substitute or add any one or more guarantors or endorsers, and to assign this Guaranty in whole or in part. Mortgagee may take any of the foregoing actions upon any terms and conditions as Mortgagee may elect, without giving notice to Guarantor or obtaining the consent of Guarantor and without affecting the liability of Guarantors to Mortgagee.

4.   Continuing Guaranty. This Guaranty shall be a continuing Guaranty, and shall not be discharged, impaired or affected by: (a) the existence or continuance of any obligation on the part of Borrower with respect to the Notes, Mortgage, Loan Agreement or other Loan Documents; (b) any forbearance or extension of the time of payment of the Notes or Mortgage; (c) any and all changes in the terms, covenants or conditions of the Notes, Mortgage, Loan Agreement or other Loan Documents or of any document evidencing or securing repayment of the Loan hereafter made or granted; (d) the release or agreement not to sue without reservation of rights of anyone liable in any way for repayment of the Loan; (e) the power or authority or lack thereof of Borrower to issue the Notes, or to execute, acknowledge or deliver the Notes, Mortgage, Loan Agreement or other Loan Documents; (f) the validity or invalidity of the Notes, Mortgage, Loan Agreement or other Loan Documents; (g) any defenses whatsoever that Borrower or any other party thereto may have to the performance or observance of any term, covenant or condition contained in the Notes, Mortgage, Loan Agreement or other Loan Documents; (h) the existence or non—existence of Borrower as a legal entity; (i) any limitation or exculpation of liability of Borrower that may be expressed in the Notes, Mortgage, Loan Agreement or other Loan Documents;(j) the transfer by Borrower of all, or any part of any interest in all or any part of the real estate described in the Mortgage or any property or rights described in any other Loan Document; (k) any sale, pledge, surrender, indulgence, alteration, substitution, exchange, release, modification or other disposition of any of the indebtedness hereby guaranteed or any collateral securing the Loan, all of which Mortgagee is expressly authorized to make from time to time; (l) the acceptance by Mortgagee of part of the indebtedness evidenced by the Notes, or any failure, neglect or omission on the part of the Mortgagee to realize on or protect any of the indebtedness evidenced by the Notes or any real estate, personal property, or mortgage or lien security given as security therefore, or to exercise any lien upon, or right of

appropriation of, any monies, credits or property of Borrower toward liquidation of the indebtedness hereby guaranteed; (m) the failure by Mortgagee or anyone acting on behalf of Mortgagee to perfect or maintain perfection of any lien or security interest upon any collateral given at any time to secure the repayment of the Loan; (n) any right or claim whatsoever which Guarantor may have against Borrower or Mortgagee or the successors or assigns of any of them; or (o) any defense (other than the payment of the indebtedness hereby guaranteed in accordance with the terms hereof) that Guarantor may have as to his undertakings liabilities and obligations hereunder, including any defenses based upon any legal disability of the Borrower or any discharge or limitation of the liability of Borrower to Mortgagee, whether consensual or arising by operation of law or any bankruptcy insolvency or debtor—relief proceeding, or from any other cause, each and every such defense being hereby waived by the Guarantors.

5. <u>Waivers.</u> Guarantors waive diligence, presentment, protest, notice of dishonor, demand for payment, extension of time of payment, notice of acceptance of this guaranty, non-payment at maturity and indulgences and notices of every kind. It is the intention of this Guaranty that Guarantors shall remain jointly and severally liable as principle, notwithstanding any act, omission or thing, which might otherwise operate as a legal or equitable discharge of Guarantors, until all of the Obligations shall have been fully paid and performed.

6. <u>Impairment of Subrogation Rights</u>. Upon a default of the Borrower, Mortgagee may elect to nonjudicially (if permitted by applicable law) or judicially foreclose against any real or personal property security it holds for the Obligations or any part thereof, or exercise any other remedy against Borrower or any security. No such action by Mortgagee will release or limit the liability of Guarantors even if the effect of that action is to deprive Guarantors of the right to collect reimbursement from Borrower for any sums paid to Mortgagee.

7. <u>Independent Obligations</u>. Mortgagee may enforce this Guaranty without first resorting to or exhausting any other Loan security or collateral, or without first having recourse to the Notes or any of the property encumbered by the Mortgage through foreclosure proceedings or otherwise; provided, however, that nothing herein contained shall preclude Mortgagee from suing on the Notes or foreclosing the Mortgage or from exercising any other rights, remedies or power under any document at any time securing the Loan, and if such foreclosure or other rights, powers or remedies are availed of, only the net proceeds therefrom, after deduction of all charges and expenses of every kind and nature whatsoever, shall be applied in reduction of the amount due on the Notes and the Mortgage; and Mortgagee shall not be required to institute or prosecute proceedings to recover any deficiency as a condition of any payment hereunder or enforcement hereof. At any sale of any security or collateral for the Loan, whether by foreclosure or otherwise, Mortgagee may, at its direction, purchase all or any part of such security or collateral offered for sale for its own account, and may apply against the amount bid therefore the unpaid balance or any part thereof due it pursuant to the terms of the Notes and the Mortgage.

8. <u>Effect of Bankruptcy</u>. This Guaranty shall continue in full force and effect notwithstanding the institution by or against Borrower of bankruptcy, reorganization, readjustment, receivership or insolvency proceedings of any nature, or the disaffirmance of the Mortgage in any such proceedings, or otherwise. In the event any payment by or on behalf of Borrower to Mortgagee is held to constitute a preference under the bankruptcy laws, or if for any other reason Mortgagee is required to refund such payment or pay the amount thereof to any other party, such payment by or on behalf of Borrower to Mortgagee shall not constitute a release of the Guarantor from any liability, but the Guarantor agrees to pay such amount to-Mortgagee upon demand.

9. <u>Borrower's Financial Condition</u>. Guarantors assume full responsibility for keeping fully informed of the financial condition of Borrower and all other circumstances affecting Borrower's ability to perform its obligations to Mortgagee, and agree that Mortgagee will have no duty to report to Guarantors any information which Mortgagee receives about Borrower's financial condition or any circumstances bearing on its ability to perform.

10. <u>Expenses</u>. The undersigned agrees to pay and reimburse Mortgagee for all costs and

243

attorneys' fees, which Mortgagee may expend or incur in the enforcement of this Guaranty or any of Borrower's obligations under the Notes, Mortgage or any other Loan Document.

11.   Delay: Cumulative Remedies. No delay or failure by Mortgagee to exercise any right or remedy against the Borrower or Guarantor will be construed as a waiver of that right or remedy.   All remedies of Mortgagee against the Borrower and Guarantor are cumulative.

12.   Binding Effect. This Guaranty shall inure to the benefit of and may be enforced by Mortgagee, and shall be binding upon and enforceable against each Guarantor and each Guarantor's heirs, legal representatives, successors and assigns. In the event of the death of any Guarantor, the obligations of such deceased Guarantor shall continue in full force and effect against his estate, personal representatives, successors and assigns. Without limiting the generality of the foregoing, Mortgagee (or its successors and assigns) may from time to time and without notice to the undersigned, assign any and all of its rights under this Guaranty without in any way affecting or diminishing the obligations of the undersigned hereunder, who shall continue to remain bound by and obligated to perform under and with respect to this Guaranty as though there had been no such assignment.

13.   Warranties.   Each Guarantor makes to Mortgagee the following representations and warranties, which relate solely to him:

(a)   Authorization. Guarantors have full right, power and authority to enter into this Guaranty and carry out his obligations hereunder.

(b)   No Conflict. The execution, delivery and performance by Guarantor of this Guaranty will not violate or be in conflict with, result in a breach of, or constitute a default under, any indenture, agreement or any other instrument to which each Guarantor is a party or by which Guarantor or any of his assets or properties is bound, or any order, writ, injunction or decree of any court or governmental institution.

(c)   Litigation. There are no actions, suits or proceedings pending, or to the knowledge of each Guarantor threatened against or adversely affecting him at law or in equity or before or by a governmental agency or instrumentality which involve any of the transactions herein contemplated, or the possibility of any judgment or liability which may result in any material and adverse change in the financial condition of Guarantors. Guarantors are not in default with respect to any judgment, order, writ, injunction, decree, rule or regulation of any court.

(d)   Enforceability. This Guaranty is a legal, valid and binding obligation of Guarantors, enforceable in accordance with its terms, except as enforceability may be limited by applicable bankruptcy, insolvency or similar laws affecting the rights of creditors generally.

(e)   Financial Statements. The financial statements and other financial information furnished by Guarantors to Mortgagee are correct and complete in all material respects and have been prepared in conformity with generally accepted accounting principles applied on a consistent basis.

14.   Affirmative Covenants. Each Guarantor covenants and agrees that from the date hereof and so long as any of the Obligations remain outstanding and unperformed, he will furnish to Mortgagee as soon as available, but in any event not later than April 1st, of each year, annual financial statements of such Guarantor, accurately reflecting his financial condition and prepared in accordance with generally accepted accounting principles applied on a consistent basis. In addition, each Guarantor covenants and agrees that he shall furnish to Mortgagee not more than thirty (30) days following written request from Mortgagee such other reports, financial statements and other financial, information concerning Guarantor as Mortgagee may from time to time request.

15. Injunctive Relief. Guarantors recognize that in the event Guarantors fail to perform, observe or discharge any of Guarantors obligations hereunder, no remedy of law will provide adequate relief to Bank, and agrees that Bank shall be entitled to temporary and permanent injunctive relief in any such case without the necessity of proving actual damages.

16. Governing Law Severability. This Guaranty shall be construed in accordance with and governed by the laws of the State of Illinois. If all or any portion of any provision of this Guaranty is declared or found by a court of competent jurisdiction to be unenforceable or null and void, such provision or portion thereof shall be deemed stricken and severed from this Agreement and the remaining provisions and portions hereof shall continue in full force and effect.

17. Venues and Waiver of Jury Trial. TO INDUCE LENDER TO ACCEPT THIS GUARANTY, GUARANTORS IRREVOCABLY AGREE THAT, SUBJECT TO LENDER'S SOLE AND ABSOLUTE ELECTION, ALL ACTIONS OR PROCEEDINGS IN ANY WAY, MANNER OR RESPECT, ARISING OUT OF OR FROM OR RELATED TO THIS GUARANTY OR OTHER LOAN DOCUMENTS SHALL BE LITIGATED ONLY IN COURTS HAVING SITUS WITHIN THE CITY OF CHICAGO, OR COUNTY OF DUPAGE, STATE OF ILLINOIS. GUARANTORS HEREBY CONSENT AND SUBMIT TO THE JURISDICTION OF ANY LOCAL, STATE OR FEDERAL COURT LOCATED WITHIN SAID CITY, COUNTY AND STATE. GRANTORS HEREBY WAIVE ANY RIGHT THEY MAY HAVE TO TRANSFER OR CHANGE THE VENUE OF ANY LITIGATION BROUGHT IN ACCORDANCE WITH THIS PARAGRAPH. GUARANTORS AND LENDER HEREBY IRREVOCABLY WAIVE THE RIGHT TO TRIAL BY JURY WITH RESPECT TO ANY ACTION IN WHICH BORROWER AND LENDER ARE PARTIES.

18. Amendments. This Guaranty may be amended, modified, revised, revoked or terminated only by a written instrument executed by the Guarantor and Mortgagee.

19. Terms. Whenever the context requires, all terms used in the singular will be construed in the plural and vice versa, and each gender will include each other gender. The term Borrower" will mean both the named Borrower and any other person or entity at any time assuming or otherwise becoming primarily liable for performance of any of the Obligations.

20. Time is of the Essence. Time is of the essence of this Guaranty as to the performance of the undersigned and the Borrower.

21. Death of Guarantor. In the event of the death of any of the Guarantors, the Mortgagee shall have the right to accelerate the indebtedness evidenced by the Notes, subject to the terms of the Loan Agreement; provided, however, Mortgagee shall not have the right to accelerate such indebtedness if within thirty (30) days of such death, the deceased Guarantor's estate or a substitute guarantor reasonably acceptable to Mortgagee assumes the deceased Guarantor's obligations hereunder.

22. Joint and Several. All obligations of the Guarantors hereunder shall be joint and several.

IN WITNESS WHEREOF, the undersigned Guarantors have executed this instrument as of the day and year first above written.

DAVID DELANEY

RICHARD FLAMM

STEVEN MATTHEWS

ACKNOWLEDGMENT

STATE OF ILLINOIS   )

)

COUNTY OF DUPAGE)

I, the undersigned, a Notary Public in and for the County and State aforesaid, DO HEREBY CERTIFY that David Delaney, personally known to me to be the same person whose name is subscribed to the foregoing instrument, appeared before me this day in person and acknowledged that he signed and delivered the said instrument as his own free and voluntary act for the uses and purposes therein set forth.

GIVEN under my hand and Notarial Seal this ___ day of __   _____, 1989.

_____

Notary Public

My Commission Expires:

_____

246

PAYMENT GUARANTY

THIS GUARANTY ("Guaranty") is made as of August 2, 1989 by the undersigned, DAVID DELANEY, RICHARD FLAMM and STEVEN MATTHEWS, jointly and severally, (referred to herein jointly and individually as "Guarantors"), to and for the benefit of FIRST MORTGAGE BANK, and its successors and assigns and the holder or holders from time to time of the Promissory Notes hereinafter described (said Bank and its successors and assigns and the holder or holders from time to time of said notes are hereinafter called the "Mortgagee").

WITNESSETH:

WHEREAS, FIRST MORTGAGE BANK, as Trustee under Trust Agreement dated April 11, 1989 and known as Trust No. 108049-04 ("Trustee") and Fox Valley Auto Care Center Limited Partnership, an Illinois limited partnership ("Fox Valley" together with Trustee, "Borrower"), have executed and delivered to Mortgagee Promissory Notes of even date herewith in the original principal amounts of $2,100,000.00 and $200,000.00 ("Notes"), which Notes are secured, inter alia, by a certain Construction Mortgage and Security Agreement with Assignment of Rents of even date herewith from Trustee in favor of Mortgagee (the "Mortgage") and certain other instruments (collectively with the Mortgage, the "Loan Documents");

WHEREAS, the Notes evidence an indebtedness of Borrower to the Mortgagee arising from a loan (the "Loan") in the original principal amount of $2,300,000.00 from Mortgagee to Borrower and are issued pursuant to the terms of a Construction Loan Agreement of even date herewith between Borrower and Mortgagee (the "Loan Agreement");

WHEREAS, Mortgagee is unwilling to make the Loan unless the Guarantors execute this Guaranty and the Guarantors desire to give this Guaranty to Mortgagee to induce Mortgagee to make the Loan; and

WHEREAS, the Guarantors will be benefited by the disbursement by Mortgagee of the proceeds of the Loan to Borrower.

NOW, THEREFORE, in consideration of the foregoing and for the purpose of inducing Mortgagee to disburse the proceeds of the Loan to or at the direction of Borrower, the parties agree as follows:

1.   Guaranty of Payment. The undersigned jointly and severally guarantee, absolutely and unconditionally: (i) the full, complete and prompt payment when due, whether at maturity, by declaration, by demand or otherwise, of all indebtedness and other sums payable by Borrower under the Notes, the Mortgage and the other Loan Documents within time and the manner required therein; and (ii) the full, complete and prompt payment of any and all fees, costs and expenses (including reasonable attorneys' fees incurred by Mortgagee at any time prior or subsequent to default, whether litigation is involved or not, and if involved, whether at the trial or appellate levels or in prior post—judgment bankruptcy proceedings), in enforcing or realizing upon the obligations of the Guarantors hereunder (the obligations of Guarantors under this Paragraph 1 are collectively hereinafter referred to as the "Obligations").

2.   Rights of Mortgagee Guarantors authorize Mortgagee at any time in its discretion to alter any of the terms of the Obligations, to take and hold any security for the Obligations and to accept additional or substituted security, to subordinate, compromise or release any security, to release Borrower of its liability for all or any part of the Obligations, to release, substitute or add any one or more guarantors or endorsers, and to assign this Guaranty in whole or in part. Mortgagee may take any of the foregoing actions upon any terms and conditions as Mortgagee may elect, without giving notice to Guarantor or obtaining the consent of Guarantor and without affecting the liability of Guarantors to Mortgagee.

3.   Continuing Guaranty. This Guaranty shall be a continuing Guaranty, and shall not be discharged, impaired or affected by: (a) the existence or continuance of any obligation on the, part of Borrower with respect to the Notes, Mortgage, Loan Agreement or other Loan Documents; (b) any forbearance or extension of the time of payment of the Notes or Mortgage; (c) any and all changes in the terms, covenants or conditions of the Notes, Mortgage, Loan Agreement or other Loan Documents or of any document evidencing or securing repayment of the Loan hereafter made or granted; (d) the release or agreement not to sue without reservation of rights of anyone liable in any way for repayment of the Loan; (e) the power or authority or lack thereof of Borrower to issue the Notes, or to execute, acknowledge or deliver the Notes, Mortgage, Loan Agreement or other Loan Documents; (f) the validity or invalidity of the Notes, Mortgage, Loan Agreement or other Loan Documents; (g) any defenses whatsoever that Borrower or any other party thereto may have to the performance or observance of any term, covenant or condition contained in the Notes, Mortgage, Loan Agreement or other Loan Documents; (h) the existence or non-existence of Borrower as a legal entity; (i) any limitation or exculpation of liability of Borrower that may be expressed in the Notes, Mortgage, Loan Agreement or other Loan Documents; (j) the transfer by Borrower of all, or any part of any interest in all or any part of the real estate described in the Mortgage or any property or rights described in any other Loan Document; (k) any sale, pledge, surrender, indulgence, alteration, substitution, exchange, release, modification or other disposition of any of the indebtedness hereby guaranteed or any collateral securing the Loan, all of which Mortgagee is expressly authorized to make from time to time; (1) the acceptance by Mortgagee of part of the indebtedness evidenced by the Notes, or any failure, neglect or omission on the part of the Mortgagee to realize on or protect any of the indebtedness evidenced by the Notes or any real estate, personal property, or mortgage or lien security given as security therefor, or to exercise any lien upon, or right of appropriation of, any Moines, credits or property of Borrower toward liquidation of the indebtedness hereby guaranteed; (in) the failure by Mortgagee or anyone acting on behalf of Mortgagee to perfect or maintain perfection of any lien or security interest upon any collateral given at any time to secure the repayment of the Loan; (n) any right or claim whatsoever which Guarantor may have against Borrower or Mortgagee or the successors or assigns of any of them; or (o) any defense (other than the payment of the indebtedness hereby guaranteed in accordance with the terms hereof) that Guarantor may have as to his undertakings liabilities and obligations hereunder, including any defenses based upon any legal disability of the Borrower or any discharge or limitation of the liability of Borrower to Mortgagee, whether consensual or arising by operation of law or any bankruptcy insolvency or debtor—relief proceeding, or from any other cause, each and every such defense being hereby waived by the Guarantors.

4.   Waivers. Guarantors waive diligence, presentment, protest, notice of dishonor, demand for payment, extension of time of payment, notice of acceptance of this Guaranty, nonpayment at maturity and indulgences and notices of every kind. It is the intention of this Guaranty that Guarantors shall remain jointly and severally liable as principal, notwithstanding any act, omission or thing which might otherwise operate as a legal or equitable discharge of Guarantors, until all of the Obligations shall have been fully paid and performed.

5.   Impairment of Subrogation Rights. Upon a default of the Borrower, Mortgagee may elect to nonjudicially (if permitted by applicable law) or judicially foreclose against any real or personal property security it holds for the Obligations or any part thereof, or exercise any other remedy against Borrower or any security. No such action by Mortgagee will release or limit the liability of Guarantors even if the effect of that action is to deprive Guarantors of the right to collect reimbursement from Borrower for any sums paid to Mortgagee.

6.   Independent Obligations. Mortgagee may enforce this Guaranty without first resorting to or exhausting any other Loan security or collateral, or without first having recourse to the Notes or any of the property encumbered by the Mortgage through foreclosure proceedings or otherwise; provided, however, that nothing herein contained shall preclude Mortgagee from suing on the Notes or foreclosing the Mortgage or from exercising any other rights, remedies or power under any document at any time securing the Loan, and if such foreclosure or other rights, powers or remedies are availed of, only the net

proceeds therefrom, after deduction of all charges and expenses of every kind and nature whatsoever, shall be applied in reduction of the amount due on the Notes and the Mortgage; and Mortgagee shall not be required to institute or prosecute proceedings to recover any deficiency as a condition of any payment hereunder or enforcement hereof. At any sale of any security or collateral for the Loan, whether by foreclosure or otherwise, Mortgagee may, at its direction, purchase all or any part of such security or collateral offered for sale for its own account, and may apply against the amount bid therefor the unpaid balance or any part thereof due it pursuant to the terms of the Notes and the Mortgage.

7. Effect of Bankruptcy. This Guaranty shall continue in full force and effect notwithstanding the institution by or against Borrower of bankruptcy, reorganization, readjustment, receivership or insolvency proceedings of any nature, or the disaffirmance of the Mortgage in any such proceedings, or otherwise. In the event any payment by or on behalf of Borrower to Mortgagee is held to constitute a preference under the bankruptcy laws, or if for any other reason Mortgagee is required to refund such payment or pay the amount thereof to any other party, such payment by or on behalf of Borrower to Mortgagee shall not constitute a release of the Guarantor from any liability, but the Guarantor agrees to pay such amount 'to Mortgagee upon demand.

8. Borrower's Financial Condition. Guarantors assume full responsibility for keeping fully informed of the financial condition of Borrower and all other circumstances affecting Borrower's ability to perform its obligations to Mortgagee, and agree that Mortgagee will have no duty to report to Guarantors any information which Mortgagee receives about Borrower's financial condition or any circumstances bearing on its ability to perform.

9. Expenses. The undersigned agrees to pay and reimburse Mortgagee for all costs and attorneys' fees which Mortgagee may expend or incur in the enforcement of this Guaranty or any of Borrower's obligations under the Notes, Mortgage or any other Loan Document.

10. Delay: Cumulative Remedies. No delay or failure by Mortgagee to exercise any right or remedy against the Borrower or Guarantor will be construed as a waiver of that right or remedy. All remedies of Mortgagee against the Borrower and Guarantor are cumulative.

11. Binding Effect. This Guaranty shall inure to the benefit of and may be enforced by Mortgagee, and shall be binding upon and enforceable against each Guarantor and each Guarantor's heirs, legal representatives, successors and assigns. In the event of the death of any Guarantor, the obligations of such deceased Guarantor shall continue in full force and effect against his estate, personal representatives, successors and assigns. Without limiting the generality of the foregoing, Mortgagee (or its successors and assigns) may from time to time and without notice to the undersigned, assign any and all of its rights under this Guaranty without in any way affecting or diminishing the obligations of the undersigned hereunder, who shall continue to remain bound by and obligated to perform under and with respect to this Guaranty as though there had been no such assignment.

12. Warranties. Each Guarantor makes to Mortgagee the following representations and warranties, which relate solely to him:

(a) Authorization. Guarantors have full right, power and authority to enter into this Guaranty and carry out his obligations hereunder.

(b) No Conflict. The execution, delivery and performance by Guarantor of this Guaranty will not violate or be in conflict with, result in a breach of, or constitute a default under, any indenture, agreement or any other instrument to which each Guarantor is a party or by which Guarantor or any of his assets or properties is bound, or any order, writ, injunction or decree of any court or governmental institution.

(c)   Litigation. There are no actions, suits or proceedings pending, or to the knowledge of each Guarantor threatened against or adversely affecting him at law or in equity or before or by a governmental agency or instrumentality which involve any of the transactions herein contemplated, or the possibility of any judgment or liability which may result in any material and adverse change in the financial condition of Guarantors. Guarantors are not in default with respect to any judgment, order, writ, injunction, decree, rule or regulation of any court.

(d)   Enforceability. This Guaranty is a legal, valid and binding obligation of Guarantors, enforceable in accordance with its terms, except as enforceability may be limited by applicable bankruptcy, insolvency or similar laws affecting the rights of creditors generally.

(e)   Financial Statements. The financial statements and other financial information furnished by Guarantors to Mortgagee are correct and complete in all material respects and have been prepared in conformity with generally accepted accounting principles applied on a consistent basis.

13.   Affirmative Covenants. Each Guarantors covenants and agrees that from the date hereof and so long as any of the Obligations remain outstanding and unperformed, he will furnish to Mortgagee as soon as available, but in any event not later than April 1st, of each year, annual financial statements of such Guarantor, accurately reflecting his financial condition and prepared in accordance with generally accepted accounting principles applied on a consistent basis. In addition, each Guarantor covenants and agrees that he shall furnish to Mortgagee not more than thirty (30) days following written request from Mortgagee such other reports, financial statements and other financial information concerning Guarantor as Mortgagee may from time to time request.

14.   Governing Law; Severability. This Guaranty shall be construed in accordance with and governed by the laws of the State of Illinois. If all or any portion of any provision of this Guaranty is declared or found by a court of competent jurisdiction to be unenforceable or null and void, such provision or portion thereof shall be deemed stricken and severed from this Agreement and the remaining provisions and portions hereof shall continue in full force and effect.

15.   Venue and Waiver of Jury Trial. TO INDUCE MORTGAGEE TO ACCEPT THIS GUARANTY, GUARANTORS IRREVOCABLY AGREE THAT, SUBJECT TO MORTGAGEE'S SOLE AND ABSOLUTE ELECTION, ALL ACTIONS OR PROCEEDINGS IN ANY WAY, MANNER OR RESPECT, ARISING OUT OF OR FROM OR RELATED TO THIS GUARANTY OR OTHER LOAN DOCUMENTS SHALL BE LITIGATED ONLY IN COURTS HAVING SITUS WITHIN THE CITY OF CHICAGO, OR COUNTY OF DUPAGE, STATE OF ILLINOIS. GUARANTORS HEREBY CONSENT AND SUBMIT TO THE JURISDICTION OF ANY LOCAL, STATE OR FEDERAL COURT LOCATED WITHIN SAID CITY, COUNTY AND STATE. GUARANTORS HEREBY WAIVE ANY RIGHT THEY MAY HAVE TO TRANSFER OR CHANGE THE VENUE OF ANY LITIGATION BROUGHT IN ACCORDANCE WITH THIS PARAGRAPH. GUARANTORS AND MORTGAGEE HEREBY IRREVOCABLY WAIVE THE RIGHT TO TRIAL BY JURY WITH RESPECT TO ANY ACTION IN WHICH GUARANTOR AND MORTGAGEE ARE PARTIES.

16.   Amendments. This Guaranty may be amended, modified, revised, revoked or terminated only by a written instrument executed by the Guarantor and Mortgagee.

17.   Terms. Whenever the context requires, all terms used in the singular will be construed in the plural and vice versa, and each gender will include each other gender. The term "Borrower" will mean both the named Borrower and any other person or entity at any time assuming or otherwise becoming primarily liable for performance of any of the Obligations.

18.   Time is of the Essence. Time is of the essence of this Guaranty as to the performance of the undersigned and the Borrower.

19.   Death of Guarantor. In the event of the death of any of the Guarantors, the Mortgagee shall have the right to accelerate the indebtedness evidenced by the Notes, subject to the terms of the Loan Agreement; provided, however, Mortgagee shall not have the right to accelerate such indebtedness if within thirty (30) days of such death, the deceased Guarantor's estate or a substitute guarantor reasonably acceptable to Mortgagee assumes the deceased Guarantor's obligations hereunder.

20. Joint and Several. All obligations of the Guarantors hereunder shall be joint and several.

IN WITNESS WHEREOF, the undersigned Guarantors have executed this instrument as of the day and year first above written.

DAVID DELANEY

RICHARD FLAMM

STEVEN MATTHEWS

<u>ACKNOWLEDGEMENT</u>

STATE OF ILLINOIS)
　　　　　　　　　　)
COUNTY OF　　　　)

　　　　I, the undersigned, a Notary Public in and for the County and State aforesaid, DO HEREBY CERTIFY that David Delaney, personally known to me to be the same person whose name is subscribed to the foregoing instrument, appeared before me this day in person and acknowledged that he signed and delivered the said instrument as his own free and voluntary act for the uses and purposes therein set forth.

GIVEN under my hand and Notarial Seal this ____day of

_____1989.

　　　　　　　　　　　　　　　　　　　　　_____
　　　　　　　　　　　　　　　　　　　　　　　　　　Notary Public

　　　　　　　　　　　　　　　　　　　　 My Commission Expires:

　　　　　　　　　　　　　　　　　　　　　_____

EXHIBIT "F"

SUBORDINATION, ATTORNMENT AND
NON-DISTURBANCE AGREEMENT

THIS SUBORDINATION, ATTORNMENT AND NON-DISTURBANCE AGREEMENT (The "Agreement") is made and entered into as of this 26th day of June, 1989 by and between Sparks Tune-Up Centers, Inc. ("Tenant") and FIRST MORTGAGE BANK, a national banking association ("Mortgagee").

A.   Tenant entered into a Lease dated June 26, 1989, (the "Lease") with First Mortgage Bank, as Trustee under a Trust Agreement dated April 11, 1989, and known as Trust No. 108049-04 (the "Landlord") for the premises situated on real estate legally described in Exhibit F1 attached hereto and made a part hereof (the "Real Estate"), and commonly known as The Fox Valley Auto Center in Aurora, Illinois (the "Leased Premises"), at a First Year Annual base rental of Eighty-six Thousand Six Hundred Twenty-five and 00/100 Dollars ($86,625.00) and for an initial term of Ten (10) years commencing thirty (30) days after delivery of the Premises to Tenant, and expiring Ten (10) years after said commencement date.

B.   Mortgagee, as a condition to making a construction loan in the amount of $ 2,300,000.00 secured by a mortgage (the "Mortgage") encumbering the Leased Premises, has requested the execution of this Agreement.

NOW, THEREFORE, in consideration of the mutual covenants and agreements of the parties and to induce Mortgagee to make the Loan upon the Real Estate, the parties do hereby covenant and agree as follows:

1.   The Lease is and shall be subject and subordinate to the Mortgage, insofar as it affects the Real Estate of which the Leased Premises forms a part, and to all renewals, modifications, consolidations, replacements and extensions thereof, to the full extent of the principal sum secured thereby and interest thereon.

2.   In the event it should become necessary to foreclose the Mortgage, the Mortgagee shall not join the Tenant under the Lease in summary or foreclosure proceedings so long as the Tenant is not in default under any of the terms, covenants or conditions of the Lease.

3.   In the event that the Mortgagee shall, in accordance with the foregoing, succeed to the interest of the Landlord under the Lease, then subject to the provisions of paragraph 4 of this Agreement, the Mortgagee agrees to be bound to the Tenant under all of the terms, covenants and conditions of the lease, provided Tenant is not in default of the Lease, and the Tenant agrees, from and after such event, to attorn to the Mortgagee and/or purchaser at any foreclosure sale, of the Real Estate, all rights and obligations under the lease to continue as though the interest of Landlord had not terminated or such foreclosure proceedings had not been brought. Such attornment shall be effective and elf-operative without the execution of any further instrument on the part of either of the parties hereto. Tenant agrees, however, to execute and deliver at any time and from time to time, upon the request of Landlord or of any holder(s) of any of the indebtedness or other

obligations secured by the Mortgage or any such purchaser, any instrument or certificate which, in the sole judgment of Landlord or of such holder(s) of any of the indebtedness or other obligations secured by the Mortgage or any such purchaser, any instrument or certificate which, in the sole judgment of Landlord or of such holder(s) or such purchaser, may be necessary or appropriate in any such foreclosure proceeding or otherwise to evidence such attornment.

4.   If Mortgagee shall succeed to the interest of Landlord under the Lease in any manner, or if any purchaser acquires the Leased Premises upon any foreclosure of the Mortgage or any trustee's sale under the Mortgage, Mortgagee or such purchaser, as the case may be, in the event of attornment shall have the same remedies by entry, action or otherwise in the event of any default by Tenant in the payment of rent or additional rent or in the performance of any of the terms, covenants and conditions of the Lease on Tenant's part to be performed that Landlord had or would have had if Mortgagee or such purchaser had not succeeded to the interest of Landlord. The Tenant shall have the same remedies against the Mortgagee for the breach of an agreement contained in the Lease that the Tenant might have had against the Landlord if the Mortgagee had not succeeded to the interest of the Landlord; provided, however, that the Mortgagee shall not be:

(a)   Liable for the construction, or the completion of any construction, of any improvements on the Real Estate; or

(b)   Liable for any act or omission of any prior landlord (including the Landlord); or

(c)   Subject to any offsets or defenses which the Tenant might have against any prior landlord (including the Landlord); or

(d)   Bound by any rent or additional rent which the Tenant might have paid for more than the current month to any prior landlord (including the Landlord); or

(e)   Bound by any amendment or modification of the Lease made without its consent.

5.   In the event of any act or omission of Landlord which would given Tenant the right, immediately or after lapse of a period of time, to cancel or terminate the Lease, or to claim a partial or total eviction, Tenant shall not exercise such right (a) until it has given written notice of such act or omission to the Mortgagee; and (b) unless such act or omission shall be one which is not capable of being remedied by Landlord or the Mortgagee within a reasonable period of time, until a reasonable period for remedying such act or omission shall have elapsed following the giving of such notice and following the time when the Mortgagee shall have become entitled under the Mortgage to remedy the same (which reasonable period shall in no event be less than the period to which Landlord would be entitled under the Lease or otherwise, after similar notice, to effect such remedy), provided the Mortgagee or Landlord shall with due diligence give Tenant written notice of intention to, and commence and continue to remedy such act or omission.

6.   The undersigned also agrees that in the event of any conflict or inconsistency between the provisions of the Mortgage and the provisions of the lease, the provisions of the Mortgage shall govern.

7.   Nothing herein contained is intended, nor shall it be construed, to abridge or adversely affect any right or remedy of Landlord under the Lease in the event of any default by Tenant in the payment of rent or additional rent or in the performance of any of the terms, covenants or conditions of the Lease on Tenant's part to be performed nor any rights of Landlord to terminate which are independent of Tenant's default.

8.   Tenant shall send to Mortgagee copies of all notices given to Landlord under the Lease, at the same time such notice is given to Landlord.

9.   Any notices which any party may be required, or may desire, to give hereunder shall be deemed to have been given if delivered personally, or if mailed by United States Registered or Certified Mail, postage prepaid, return receipt requested, or if delivered to a reputable overnight express courier, freight prepaid, addressed:

In the case of Landlord, to:

Regent Real Estate Corporation
524 W. South Avenue
Chicago, Illinois 60610

with a copy to :

Kaplan & Miller
Attn: Donna Smith, Esq.
450 Wacker Drive
Chicago, Illinois 60606

With a copy to:

First Mortgage Bank
Attn: Gerald Peterson
423 N. Michigan Avenue
Chicago, Illinois 60690

with a copy to:

Jack Halloman, Esq.
228 N. LaSalle Street
Suite 900
Chicago, Illinois 60604

or such other address (es) or addressee(s) as the party to be served with notice may have furnished to the other party in the manner herein provided for the service of notice. Notice by mail shall be deemed received three (3) days after the date of such mailing. Notice by reputable overnight express courier shall be deemed received the day after delivery to such courier.

10.   This Agreement may not be modified orally or in any manner other than by an agreement in writing signed by the parties hereto or their respective successors in interest. This Agreement shall inure to the benefit of, and be binding upon, the parties hereto, their successors and assigns, and any purchaser or purchasers at a foreclosure sale with respect to the Real Estate, and their respective heirs, personal representatives, successors and assigns.

        IN WITNESS WHEREOF,   the parties hereto have executed these presents the day and year first above written.

                                        TENANT:

                                        Sparks Tune-Up Centers, Inc.

                                        By: _____

                                        Its *Vice President*

                                        MORTGAGEE:

                                        First Mortgage Bank

                                        By: _____

                                        Its *VICE PRESIDENT*

State of Illinois)
) ss
County of Kane)

    This is to certify to Commonwealth Land Title Insurance Company, Title Services, Inc., Regent Real Estate Development Corporation, and First Mortgage Bank, as Trustee under Trust Agreement dated April 11, 1989 and known as Trust No. 108049-4, that I, John A. Thornhill, Jr., an Illinois Registered Land Surveyor of Donahue and Thornhill, Inc., have surveyed and located the improvements on that part of the Southeast Quarter of Section 21, Township 38 North, Range 9 East of the Third Principal Meridian described as follows: Commencing at the most northerly corner of Fox Valley East, Region 1, Unit No. 2 Aurora, DuPage County, Illinois: thence easterly along the southerly line of South Road 425.40 feet for a point of beginning: thence southerly at right angles to the north line (as monumented) of a tract of land conveyed to Alan W. Johnson and Barbara L. Johnson by Document 747981 recorded March 2, 1955. 171.37 feet: thence easterly at right angles to the last described course 439.24 feet to a point on the westerly line of a tract of land described in Parcel 3 of Document R75-34466 that is 44.0 feet northerly of the southwest corner of said Parcel 3: thence northerly along a westerly line of said Parcel 3 forming an angle of 88° 47'35" with the last described course (measured clockwise therefrom) 221.15 feet to an angle in the westerly line of said parcel 3; thence northwesterly along a southwesterly line of said Parcel 3 forming an angle of 210° 53'06" with the last described course (measured counter-clockwise therefrom) 25.94 feet to an angle in said southwesterly line of said Parcel 3, being also the southerly line of said South road; thence westerly along said southerly line 427.0 feet to the point of beginning, in the City of Aurora, DuPage County, Illinois and containing 2,220 acres in accordance with the official records and in strict compliance with the minimum standard detail requirements for Class A, ALTA/ACSM Land Title Surveys, tot he satisfaction of said Commonwealth Land Title Insurance Company, as adopted by the American Land Title Association and American Congress on Surveying and Mapping in 1988 except for underground farm drain tiles and utilities not visible by surface inspection, all as shown by the plat hereon drawn which is a correct representation of said survey and location. I further certify that no above-ground encroachment over any boundary line was found to exist except where shown. All distances are given in feet and decimal parts thereof.

Dated at Geneva, Illinois, June 8, 1989
Illinois Registered Land Surveyor No. 1740

D O N A H U E and T H O R N H I L L, I N C.
GENEVA   ILLINOIS
(312) 232-7418

CERTIFICATE OF INSURANCE DOCUMENTATION

Form XXXX

```
-----------------------------------------------------------------
DEDUCTIBLES-Section I  | IN CASE OF LOSS        |
$      500 BASIC       | UNDER THIS POLICY,     |
                       | THE DEDUCTIBLE WILL    |
                       | BE APPLIED TO EACH     |----------------------
                       | OCCURRENCE AND WILL    |
                       | BE DEDUCTED FROM       |
                       | THE AMOUNT OF THE      |
OTHER DEDUCTIBLES      | LOSS                   |
MAY APPLY - REFER TO   |                        |
POLICY                 |                        |
-----------------------------------------------------------------
FORMS, OPTIONS AND ENDORSEMENTS                 |
FP-6101            BUILDERS' RISK               | POLICY PREMIUM
FE-6213            IL AMENDATORY ENDORSEMENT     | $  1,704.00
                                                |
                                                |
                                                |----------------
                                                |
                                                |
                                                |
-----------------------------------------------------------------
```

MORTGAGEE:

FIRST MORTGAGE BANK
423 N. MICHIGAN AVENUE
CHICAGO, ILLINOIS   60690

Countersigned _____19____

PREPARED
08/01/89   *Your policy consists of this page, any endorsements*
FP-8030C   *and the policy form. Keep these together.*

By:_____
                                              Agent

PREMIUM NOTICE	POLICY NUMBER 93-21-3385-2	BILLING From: 08/01/89	PERIOD To: 08/01/90	Agent Code: 1971/59

STATE FARM INSURANCE COMPANIES

BUSINESS POLICY - BUILDERS' RISK

Location (if other   RT 59 SOUTH ROAD
than Named insured's   AURORA, IL 60505
Mailing Address)

INSURED   This is the only notice   PREMIUM $1,704.00
  REGENT REAL ESTATE   you will receive. Please
  DEVELOPMENT. CORP.   make check payable to STATE   AMOUNT DUE $1,704.00
  415 WEST NORTH AVENUE FARM and return it with this
  CHICAGO, IL 60610   notice to the address shown   DATE DUE   09/04/89
                         below. Your canceled check
                         is your receipt. Thanks for
                         letting us serve you.

                         ILLINOIS OFFICE
                         2309 East Oakland Avenue
                         Bloomington, Illinois   60709-0001

We will provide the insurance described in this policy in return for the premium and compliance with an applicable provision of this policy.

POLICY NO. 93-21-3385-2

BUSINESS POLICY - BUILDERS' RISK

Coverage afforded by the policy is provided by

STATE FARM FIRE AND CASUALTY COMPANY
2309 E. OAKLAND AV., BLOOMINGTON IL
61709-000

a Stock Company with Home Offices in Bloomington, Illinois

Named Insured and Mailing Address

REGENT REAL ESTATE DEV. CORP.
DBA FOX VALLEY CAR CENTER
524 W. SOUTH AVENUE
CHICAGO, ILLINOIS   60610
NAMED INSURED: PARTNERSHIP

THE POLICY PERIOD
BEGINS AND ENDS AT 12:01 AM
STANDARD TIME AT THE PREMISES LOCATIONS
08/01/89   :EFFECTIVE DATE
12 MONTHS :POLICY PERIOD
08/01/90   :EXPIRATION OF POLICY PERIOD

Automatic Renewal -- If the Policy Period is shown as 12 months, this policy will be renewed automatically subject to the premiums, rules and form in effect for each succeeding policy period. If the policy is terminated, we will give you and the Mortgagee/Lienholder written notice in compliance with the policy provisions or as required by law.

COVERAGES & PROPERTY	LIMITS OF LIABILITY	
SECTION I		**FOR SECTION I COVERAGE AND LOCATION INFORMATION, SEE THE ATTACHED SUPPLEMENTAL DECLARATIONS.
A BUILDINGS (BLANKET)	$ 900,000	
B BUSINESS PERSONAL PROPERTY	EXCLUDED	
C LOSS OF INCOME	$ACTUAL LOSS	
SECTION II		
L BUSINESS LIABILITY	$1,000,000	
M MEDICAL PAYMENTS	5,000	
PRODUCTS-COMPLETED OPERATIONS (POO) AGGREGATE	$2,000,000	
GENERAL AGGREGATE (OTHER THAN POO)	$2,000,000	

DEDUCTIBLES --
SECTION 1
$500 BASIC

OTHER DEDUCTIBLES
MAY APPLY - REFER
TO POLICY

IN CASE OF LOSS
UNDER THIS POLICY,
THE DEDUCTIBLE
WILL BE APPLIED
TO EACH OCCUR-
RENCE AND WILL
BE DEDUCTED FROM
THE AMOUNT OF
THE LOSS.

FORMS, OPTIONS AND ENDORSEMENTS
FP-6101   BUILDERS' RISK
FE-6213   IL AMENDATORY ENDORSEMENT

POLICY PREMIUM
$1,740.00

260

We will provide the insurance described in this policy in return for the premium and compliance with an applicable provision of this policy.

POLICY NO. 93-21-3385-2

BUSINESS POLICY - BUILDERS' RISK

Coverage afforded by the policy is provided by

STATE FARM FIRE AND CASUALTY COMPANY
2309 E. OAKLAND AV., BLOOMINGTON IL
61709-000

a Stock Company with Home Offices in Bloomington, Illinois

Named Insured and Mailing Address

REGENT REAL ESTATE DEV. CORP.
DBA FOX VALLEY CAR CENTER
415 WEST NORTH AVENUE
CHICAGO, ILLINOIS   60610

SUPPLEMENTAL DECLARATIONS
08/01/89
PAGE 01

THE LOCATION OF PREMISES IS EXTENDED TO INCLUDE THE FOLLOWING. INSURANCE IS PROVIDED SUBJECT TO ALL THE TERMS OF THIS POLICY INCLUDE FORMS, OPTIONS AND ENDORSEMENTS MADE A PART HEREOF:

Automatic Renewal – If the Policy Period is shown as 12 months, this policy will be renewed automatically subject to the premiums, rules and form in effect for each succeeding policy period. If the policy is terminated, we will give you and the Mortgagee/Lienholder written notice in compliance with the policy provisions or as required by law.

LOCATION OF PREMISES

LOCATION NO.

01)   RT 59 SOUTH ROAD (BLDG 01)
       AURORA IL 60505

02)   RT 59 SOUTH ROAD (BLDG 02)
       AURORA IL 60505

Countersigned _____, 19____

PREPARED
08/01/89

Your policy consists of this page and endorsements and the policy form. Keep these together.

By _____
                              Agent

261

AIA DOCUMENT | B141-1997

Standard Form of Agreement Between Owner and Architect with Standard Form of Architect's Services

AGREEMENT made as of the   day of
in the year
(In words, indicate day, month and year)

BETWEEN the Architect's client identified as the Owner:
(Name, address and other information)

and the Architect:
(Name, address and other information)

For the following Project:
(Include detailed description of Project)

The Owner and Architect agree as follows.

This document has important
legal consequences.
Consultation with an
attorney is encouraged
with respect to its
completion or modification.

TABLE OF ARTICLES

1.1 INITIAL INFORMATION

1.2 RESPONSIBILITIES OF THE

      PARTIES

1.3 TERMS AND CONDITIONS

1.4 SCOPE OF SERVICES AND

      OTHER SPECIAL TERMS

      AND CONDITIONS

1.5 COMPENSATION

© 1997 AIA®
AIA DOCUMENT B141-1997
STANDARD FORM
AGREEMENT

The American Institute
of Architects
1735 New York Avenue, N.W.
Washington, D.C. 20006-5292

1-1

ARTICLE 1.1 INITIAL INFORMATION

1.1.1 This Agreement is based on the following information and assumptions.

(Note the disposition for the following items by inserting the requested information or a statement such as "not applicable," "unknown at time of execution" or "to be determined later by mutual agreement.")

1.1.2 PROJECT PARAMETERS

1.1.2.1 The objective or use is:

(Identify or describe, if appropriate, proposed use or goals.)

1.1.2.2 The physical parameters are:

(Identify or describe, if appropriate, size, location, dimensions, or other pertinent information, such as geotechnical reports about the site.)

1.1.2.3 The Owner's Program is:

(Identify documentation or state the manner in which the program will be developed.)

1.1.2.4 The legal parameters are:

(Identify pertinent legal information, including, if appropriate, land surveys and legal descriptions and restrictions of the site.)

1.1.2.5 The financial parameters are as follows.

.1 Amount of the Owner's overall budget for the Project, including the Architect's compensation, is:

.2 Amount of the Owner's budget for the Cost of the Work, excluding the Architect's compensation, is:

1.1.2.6 The time parameters are:

(Identify, if appropriate, milestone dates, durations or fast track scheduling.)

1.1.2.7 The proposed procurement or delivery method for the Project is:

(Identify method such as competitive bid, negotiated contract, or construction management.)

1.1.2.8 Other parameters are:

(Identify special characteristics or needs of the Project such as energy, environmental or historic preservation requirements.)

© 1997 AIA®
AIA DOCUMENT B141-1997
STANDARD FORM
AGREEMENT

The American Institute
of Architects
1735 New York Avenue, N.W.
Washington, D.C. 20006-5292

1-2

264

1.1.3 PROJECT TEAM

1.1.3.1 The Owner's Designated Representative is:
(List name, address and other information.)

1.1.3.2 The persons or entities, in addition to the Owner's Designated Representative, who are required to review the Architect's submittals to the Owner are:
(List name, address and other information.)

1.1.3.3 The Owner's other consultants and contractors are:
(List discipline and, if known, identify them by name and address.)

1.1.3.4 The Architect's Designated Representative is:
(List name, address and other information.)

1.1.3.5 The consultants retained at the Architect's expense are:
(List discipline and, if known, identify them by name and address.)

1.1.4 Other important initial information is:

1.1.5 When the services under this Agreement include contract administration services, the General Conditions of the Contract for Construction shall be the edition of AIA Document A201 current as of the date of this Agreement, or as follows:

1.1.6 The information contained in this Article 1.1 may be reasonably relied upon by the Owner and Architect in determining the Architect's compensation. Both parties, however, recognize that such information may change and, in that event, the Owner and the Architect shall negotiate appropriate adjustments in schedule, compensation and Change in Services in accordance with Paragraph 1.3.3.

© 1997 AIA®
AIA DOCUMENT B141-1997
STANDARD FORM
AGREEMENT

The American Institute
of Architects
1735 New York Avenue, N.W.
Washington, D.C. 20006-5292

1-3

ARTICLE 1.2 RESPONSIBILITIES OF THE PARTIES

1.2.1 The Owner and the Architect shall cooperate with one another to fulfill their respective obligations under this Agreement. Both parties shall endeavor to maintain good working relationships among all members of the Project team.

1.2.2 OWNER

1.2.2.1 Unless otherwise provided under this Agreement, the Owner shall provide full information in a timely manner regarding requirements for and limitations on the Project. The Owner shall furnish to the Architect, within 15 days after receipt of a written request, information necessary and relevant for the Architect to evaluate, give notice of or enforce lien rights.

1.2.2.2 The Owner shall periodically update the budget for the Project, including that portion allocated for the Cost of the Work. The Owner shall not significantly increase or decrease the overall budget, the portion of the budget allocated for the Cost of the Work, or contingencies included in the overall budget or a portion of the budget, without the agreement of the Architect to a corresponding change in the Project scope and quality.

1.2.2.3 The Owner's Designated Representative identified in Paragraph 1.1.3 shall be authorized to act on the Owner's behalf with respect to the Project. The Owner or the Owner's Designated Representative shall render decisions in a timely manner pertaining to documents submitted by the Architect in order to avoid unreasonable delay in the orderly and sequential progress of the Architect's services.

1.2.2.4 The Owner shall furnish the services of consultants other than those designated in Paragraph 1.1.3 or authorize the Architect to furnish them as a Change in Services when such services are requested by the Architect and are reasonably required by the scope of the Project.

1.2.2.5 Unless otherwise provided in this Agreement, the Owner shall furnish tests, inspections and reports required by law or the Contract Documents, such as structural, mechanical, and chemical tests, tests for air and water pollution, and tests for hazardous materials.

1.2.2.6 The Owner shall furnish all legal, insurance and accounting services, including auditing services, that may be reasonably necessary at any time for the Project to meet the Owner's needs and interests.

1.2.2.7 The Owner shall provide prompt written notice to the Architect if the Owner becomes aware of any fault or defect in the Project, including any errors, omissions or inconsistencies in the Architect's Instruments of Service.

1.2.3 ARCHITECT

1.2.3.1 The services performed by the Architect, Architect's employees and Architect's consultants shall be as enumerated in Article 1.4.

1.2.3.2 The Architect's services shall be performed as expeditiously as is consistent with professional skill and care and the orderly progress of the Project. The Architect shall submit for the Owner's approval a schedule for the performance of the Architect's services which initially shall be consistent with the time periods established in Subparagraph 1.1.2.6 and which shall be adjusted, if necessary, as the Project proceeds. This schedule shall include allowances for periods of time required for the Owner's review, for the performance of the Owner's consultants, and for approval of submissions by authorities having jurisdiction over the Project. Time limits established by this schedule approved by the Owner shall not, except for reasonable cause, be exceeded by the Architect or Owner.

© 1997 AIA®
AIA DOCUMENT B141-1997
STANDARD FORM
AGREEMENT

The American Institute
of Architects
1735 New York Avenue, N.W.
Washington, D.C. 20006-5292

1-4

1.2.3.3 The Architect's Designated Representative identified in Paragraph 1.1.3 shall be authorized to act on the Architect's behalf with respect to the Project.

1.2.3.4 The Architect shall maintain the confidentiality of information specifically designated as confidential by the Owner, unless withholding such information would violate the law, create the risk of significant harm to the public or prevent the Architect from establishing a claim or defense in an adjudicatory proceeding. The Architect shall require of the Architect's consultants similar agreements to maintain the confidentiality of information specifically designated as confidential by the Owner.

1.2.3.5 Except with the Owner's knowledge and consent, the Architect shall not engage in any activity, or accept any employment, interest or contribution that would reasonably appear to compromise the Architect's professional judgment with respect to this Project.

1.2.3.6 The Architect shall review laws, codes, and regulations applicable to the Architect's services. The Architect shall respond in the design of the Project to requirements imposed by governmental authorities having jurisdiction over the Project.

1.2.3.7 The Architect shall be entitled to rely on the accuracy and completeness of services and information furnished by the Owner. The Architect shall provide prompt written notice to the Owner if the Architect becomes aware of any errors, omissions or inconsistencies in such services or information.

ARTICLE 1.3 TERMS AND CONDITIONS
1.3.1 COST OF THE WORK
1.3.1.1 The Cost of the Work shall be the total cost or, to the extent the Project is not completed, the estimated cost to the Owner of all elements of the Project designed or specified by the Architect.

1.3.1.2 The Cost of the Work shall include the cost at current market rates of labor and materials furnished by the Owner and equipment designed, specified, selected or specially provided for by the Architect, including the costs of management or supervision of construction or installation provided by a separate construction manager or contractor, plus a reasonable allowance for their overhead and profit. In addition, a reasonable allowance for contingencies shall be included for market conditions at the time of bidding and for changes in the Work.

1.3.1.3 The Cost of the Work does not include the compensation of the Architect and the Architect's consultants, the costs of the land, rights-of-way and financing or other costs that are the responsibility of the Owner.

1.3.2 INSTRUMENTS OF SERVICE
1.3.2.1 Drawings, specifications and other documents, including those in electronic form, prepared by the Architect and the Architect's consultants are Instruments of Service for use solely with respect to this Project. The Architect and the Architect's consultants shall be deemed the authors and owners of their respective Instruments of Service and shall retain all common law, statutory and other reserved rights, including copyrights.

1.3.2.2 Upon execution of this Agreement, the Architect grants to the Owner a nonexclusive license to reproduce the Architect's Instruments of Service solely for purposes of constructing, using and maintaining the Project, provided that the Owner shall comply with all obligations, including prompt payment of all sums when due, under this Agreement. The Architect shall

© 1997 A I A®
**AIA DOCUMENT B141-1997
STANDARD FORM
AGREEMENT**

The American Institute
of Architects
1735 New York Avenue, N.W.
Washington, D.C. 20006-5292

1-5

267

obtain similar nonexclusive licenses from the Architect's consultants consistent with this Agreement. Any termination of this Agreement prior to completion of the Project shall terminate this license. Upon such termination, the Owner shall refrain from making further reproductions of Instruments of Service and shall return to the Architect within seven days of termination all originals and reproductions in the Owner's possession or control. If and upon the date the Architect is adjudged in default of this Agreement, the foregoing license shall be deemed terminated and replaced by a second, nonexclusive license permitting the Owner to authorize other similarly credentialed design professionals to reproduce and, where permitted by law, to make changes, corrections or additions to the Instruments of Service solely for purposes of completing, using and maintaining the Project.

1.3.2.3 Except for the licenses granted in Subparagraph 1.3.2.2, no other license or right shall be deemed granted or implied under this Agreement. The Owner shall not assign, delegate, sublicense, pledge or otherwise transfer any license granted herein to another party without the prior written agreement of the Architect. However, the Owner shall be permitted to authorize the Contractor, Subcontractors, Sub-subcontractors and material or equipment suppliers to reproduce applicable portions of the Instruments of Service appropriate to and for use in their execution of the Work by license granted in Subparagraph 1.3.2.2. Submission or distribution of Instruments of Service to meet official regulatory requirements or for similar purposes in connection with the Project is not to be construed as publication in derogation of the reserved rights of the Architect and the Architect's consultants. The Owner shall not use the Instruments of Service for future additions or alterations to this Project or for other projects, unless the Owner obtains the prior written agreement of the Architect and the Architect's consultants. Any unauthorized use of the Instruments of Service shall be at the Owner's sole risk and without liability to the Architect and the Architect's consultants.

1.3.2.4 Prior to the Architect providing to the Owner any Instruments of Service in electronic form or the Owner providing to the Architect any electronic data for incorporation into the Instruments of Service, the Owner and the Architect shall by separate written agreement set forth the specific conditions governing the format of such Instruments of Service or electronic data, including any special limitations or licenses not otherwise provided in this Agreement.

1.3.3 CHANGE IN SERVICES
1.3.3.1 Change in Services of the Architect, including services required of the Architect's consultants, may be accomplished after execution of this Agreement, without invalidating the Agreement, if mutually agreed in writing, if required by circumstances beyond the Architect's control, or if the Architect's services are affected as described in Subparagraph 1.3.3.2. In the absence of mutual agreement in writing, the Architect shall notify the Owner prior to providing such services. If the Owner deems that all or a part of such Change in Services is not required, the Owner shall give prompt written notice to the Architect, and the Architect shall have no obligation to provide those services. Except for a change due to the fault of the Architect, Change in Services of the Architect shall entitle the Architect to an adjustment in compensation pursuant to Paragraph 1.5.2, and to any Reimbursable Expenses described in Subparagraph 1.3.9.2 and Paragraph 1.5.5.

1.3.3.2 If any of the following circumstances affect the Architect's services for the Project, the Architect shall be entitled to an appropriate adjustment in the Architect's schedule and compensation:
  .1 change in the instructions or approvals given by the Owner that necessitate revisions in Instruments of Service;
  .2 enactment or revision of codes, laws or regulations or official interpretations which necessitate changes to previously prepared Instruments of Service;

© 1997 AIA®
AIA DOCUMENT B141-1997
STANDARD FORM
AGREEMENT

The American Institute
of Architects
1735 New York Avenue, N.W.
Washington, D.C. 20006-5292

1-6

.3 decisions of the Owner not rendered in a timely manner;

.4 significant change in the Project including, but not limited to, size, quality, complexity, the Owner's schedule or budget, or procurement method;

.5 failure of performance on the part of the Owner or the Owner's consultants or contractors;

.6 preparation for and attendance at a public hearing, a dispute resolution proceeding or a legal proceeding except where the Architect is party thereto;

.7 change in the information contained in Article 1.1.

1.3.4 MEDIATION

1.3.4.1 Any claim, dispute or other matter in question arising out of or related to this Agreement shall be subject to mediation as a condition precedent to arbitration or the institution of legal or equitable proceedings by either party. If such matter relates to or is the subject of a lien arising out of the Architect's services, the Architect may proceed in accordance with applicable law to comply with the lien notice or filing deadlines prior to resolution of the matter by mediation or by arbitration.

1.3.4.2 The Owner and Architect shall endeavor to resolve claims, disputes and other matters in question between them by mediation which, unless the parties mutually agree otherwise, shall be in accordance with the Construction Industry Mediation Rules of the American Arbitration Association currently in effect. Request for mediation shall be filed in writing with the other party to this Agreement and with the American Arbitration Association. The request may be made concurrently with the filing of a demand for arbitration but, in such event, mediation shall proceed in advance of arbitration or legal or equitable proceedings, which shall be stayed pending mediation for a period of 60 days from the date of filing, unless stayed for a longer period by agreement of the parties or court order.

1.3.4.3 The parties shall share the mediator's fee and any filing fees equally. The mediation shall be held in the place where the Project is located, unless another location is mutually agreed upon. Agreements reached in mediation shall be enforceable as settlement agreements in any court having jurisdiction thereof.

1.3.5 ARBITRATION

1.3.5.1 Any claim, dispute or other matter in question arising out of or related to this Agreement shall be subject to arbitration. Prior to arbitration, the parties shall endeavor to resolve disputes by mediation in accordance with Paragraph 1.3.4.

1.3.5.2 Claims, disputes and other matters in question between the parties that are not resolved by mediation shall be decided by arbitration which, unless the parties mutually agree otherwise, shall be in accordance with the Construction Industry Arbitration Rules of the American Arbitration Association currently in effect. The demand for arbitration shall be filed in writing with the other party to this Agreement and with the American Arbitration Association.

1.3.5.3 A demand for arbitration shall be made within a reasonable time after the claim, dispute or other matter in question has arisen. In no event shall the demand for arbitration be made after the date when institution of legal or equitable proceedings based on such claim, dispute or other matter in question would be barred by the applicable statute of limitations.

1.3.5.4 No arbitration arising out of or relating to this Agreement shall include, by consolidation or joinder or in any other manner, an additional person or entity not a party to this Agreement, except by written consent containing a specific reference to this Agreement and signed by the Owner, Architect, and any other person or entity sought to be joined. Consent to arbitration involving an additional person or entity shall not constitute consent to arbitration of any claim,

© 1997 AIA®
AIA DOCUMENT B141-1997
STANDARD FORM
AGREEMENT

The American Institute
of Architects
1735 New York Avenue, N.W.
Washington, D.C. 20006-5292

1-7

dispute or other matter in question not described in the written consent or with a person or entity not named or described therein. The foregoing agreement to arbitrate and other agreements to arbitrate with an additional person or entity duly consented to by parties to this Agreement shall be specifically enforceable in accordance with applicable law in any court having jurisdiction thereof.

1.3.5.5 The award rendered by the arbitrator or arbitrators shall be final, and judgment may be entered upon it in accordance with applicable law in any court having jurisdiction thereof.

1.3.6   CLAIMS FOR CONSEQUENTIAL DAMAGES
The Architect and the Owner waive consequential damages for claims, disputes or other matters in question arising out of or relating to this Agreement. This mutual waiver is applicable, without limitation, to all consequential damages due to either party's termination in accordance with Paragraph 1.3.8.

1.3.7   MISCELLANEOUS PROVISIONS
1.3.7.1 This Agreement shall be governed by the law of the principal place of business of the Architect, unless otherwise provided in Paragraph 1.4.2.

1.3.7.2 Terms in this Agreement shall have the same meaning as those in the edition of AIA Document A201, General Conditions of the Contract for Construction, current as of the date of this Agreement.

1.3.7.3 Causes of action between the parties to this Agreement pertaining to acts or failures to act shall be deemed to have accrued and the applicable statutes of limitations shall commence to run not later than either the date of Substantial Completion for acts or failures to act occurring prior to Substantial Completion or the date of issuance of the final Certificate for Payment for acts or failures to act occurring after Substantial Completion. In no event shall such statutes of limitations commence to run any later than the date when the Architect's services are substantially completed.

1.3.7.4 To the extent damages are covered by property insurance during construction, the Owner and the Architect waive all rights against each other and against the contractors, consultants, agents and employees of the other for damages, except such rights as they may have to the proceeds of such insurance as set forth in the edition of AIA Document A201, General Conditions of the Contract for Construction, current as of the date of this Agreement. The Owner or the Architect, as appropriate, shall require of the contractors, consultants, agents and employees of any of them similar waivers in favor of the other parties enumerated herein.

1.3.7.5 Nothing contained in this Agreement shall create a contractual relationship with or a cause of action in favor of a third party against either the Owner or Architect.

1.3.7.6 Unless otherwise provided in this Agreement, the Architect and Architect's consultants shall have no responsibility for the discovery, presence, handling, removal or disposal of or exposure of persons to hazardous materials or toxic substances in any form at the Project site.

1.3.7.7 The Architect shall have the right to include photographic or artistic representations of the design of the Project among the Architect's promotional and professional materials. The Architect shall be given reasonable access to the completed Project to make such representations. However, the Architect's materials shall not include the Owner's confidential or proprietary information if the Owner has previously advised the Architect in writing of the specific information considered by the Owner to be confidential or proprietary. The Owner shall provide professional credit for the Architect in the Owner's promotional materials for the Project.

© 1997 AIA®
AIA DOCUMENT B141-1997
STANDARD FORM
AGREEMENT

The American Institute
of Architects
1735 New York Avenue, N.W.
Washington, D.C. 20006-5292

1-8

1.3.7.8 If the Owner requests the Architect to execute certificates, the proposed language of such certificates shall be submitted to the Architect for review at least 14 days prior to the requested dates of execution. The Architect shall not be required to execute certificates that would require knowledge, services or responsibilities beyond the scope of this Agreement.

1.3.7.9 The Owner and Architect, respectively, bind themselves, their partners, successors, assigns and legal representatives to the other party to this Agreement and to the partners, successors, assigns and legal representatives of such other party with respect to all covenants of this Agreement. Neither the Owner nor the Architect shall assign this Agreement without the written consent of the other, except that the Owner may assign this Agreement to an institutional lender providing financing for the Project. In such event, the lender shall assume the Owner's rights and obligations under this Agreement. The Architect shall execute all consents reasonably required to facilitate such assignment.

1.3.8   TERMINATION OR SUSPENSION

1.3.8.1 If the Owner fails to make payments to the Architect in accordance with this Agreement, such failure shall be considered substantial nonperformance and cause for termination or, at the Architect's option, cause for suspension of performance of services under this Agreement. If the Architect elects to suspend services, prior to suspension of services, the Architect shall give seven days' written notice to the Owner. In the event of a suspension of services, the Architect shall have no liability to the Owner for delay or damage caused the Owner because of such suspension of services. Before resuming services, the Architect shall be paid all sums due prior to suspension and any expenses incurred in the interruption and resumption of the Architect's services. The Architect's fees for the remaining services and the time schedules shall be equitably adjusted.

1.3.8.2 If the Project is suspended by the Owner for more than 30 consecutive days, the Architect shall be compensated for services performed prior to notice of such suspension. When the Project is resumed, the Architect shall be compensated for expenses incurred in the interruption and resumption of the Architect's services. The Architect's fees for the remaining services and the time schedules shall be equitably adjusted.

1.3.8.3 If the Project is suspended or the Architect's services are suspended for more than 90 consecutive days, the Architect may terminate this Agreement by giving not less than seven days' written notice.

1.3.8.4 This Agreement may be terminated by either party upon not less than seven days' written notice should the other party fail substantially to perform in accordance with the terms of this Agreement through no fault of the party initiating the termination.

1.3.8.5 This Agreement may be terminated by the Owner upon not less than seven days' written notice to the Architect for the Owner's convenience and without cause.

1.3.8.6 In the event of termination not the fault of the Architect, the Architect shall be compensated for services performed prior to termination, together with Reimbursable Expenses then due and all Termination Expenses as defined in Subparagraph 1.3.8.7.

1.3.8.7 Termination Expenses are in addition to compensation for the services of the Agreement and include expenses directly attributable to termination for which the Architect is not otherwise compensated, plus an amount for the Architect's anticipated profit on the value of the services not performed by the Architect.

1-9

271

1.3.9 PAYMENTS TO THE ARCHITECT

1.3.9.1 Payments on account of services rendered and for Reimbursable Expenses incurred shall be made monthly upon presentation of the Architect's statement of services. No deductions shall be made from the Architect's compensation on account of penalty, liquidated damages or other sums withheld from payments to contractors, or on account of the cost of changes in the Work other than those for which the Architect has been adjudged to be liable.

1.3.9.2 Reimbursable Expenses are in addition to compensation for the Architect's services and include expenses incurred by the Architect and Architect's employees and consultants directly related to the Project, as identified in the following Clauses:

    .1 transportation in connection with the Project, authorized out-of-town travel and subsistence, and electronic communications;

    .2 fees paid for securing approval of authorities having jurisdiction over the Project;

    .3 reproductions, plots, standard form documents, postage, handling and delivery of Instruments of Service;

    .4 expense of overtime work requiring higher than regular rates if authorized in advance by the Owner;

    .5 renderings, models and mock-ups requested by the Owner;

    .6 expense of professional liability insurance dedicated exclusively to this Project or the expense of additional insurance coverage or limits requested by the Owner in excess of that normally carried by the Architect and the Architect's consultants;

    .7 reimbursable expenses as designated in Paragraph 1.5.5;

    .8 other similar direct Project-related expenditures.

1.3.9.3 Records of Reimbursable Expenses, of expenses pertaining to a Change in Services, and of services performed on the basis of hourly rates or a multiple of Direct Personnel Expense shall be available to the Owner or the Owner's authorized representative at mutually convenient times.

1.3.9.4 Direct Personnel Expense is defined as the direct salaries of the Architect's personnel engaged on the Project and the portion of the cost of their mandatory and customary contributions and benefits related thereto, such as employment taxes and other statutory employee benefits, insurance, sick leave, holidays, vacations, employee retirement plans and similar contributions.

ARTICLE 1.4 SCOPE OF SERVICES AND OTHER SPECIAL TERMS AND CONDITIONS

1.4.1 Enumeration of Parts of the Agreement. This Agreement represents the entire and integrated agreement between the Owner and the Architect and supersedes all prior negotiations, representations or agreements, either written or oral. This Agreement may be amended only by written instrument signed by both Owner and Architect. This Agreement comprises the documents listed below.

1.4.1.1 Standard Form of Agreement Between Owner and Architect, AIA Document B141-1997.

1.4.1.2 Standard Form of Architect's Services: Design and Contract Administration, AIA Document B141-1997, or as follows:
(List other documents, if any, delineating Architect's scope of services.)

1.4.1.3 Other documents as follows:
(List other documents, if any, forming part of the Agreement.)

© 1997 AIA®
AIA DOCUMENT B141-1997
STANDARD FORM
AGREEMENT

The American Institute
of Architects
1735 New York Avenue, N.W.
Washington, D.C. 20006-5292

1-10

1.4.2 Special Terms and Conditions. Special terms and conditions that modify this Agreement are as follows:

ARTICLE 1.5 COMPENSATION

1.5.1 For the Architect's services as described under Article 1.4, compensation shall be computed as follows:

1.5.2 If the services of the Architect are changed as described in Subparagraph 1.3.3.1, the Architect's compensation shall be adjusted. Such adjustment shall be calculated as described below or, if no method of adjustment is indicated in this Paragraph 1.5.2, in an equitable manner.
(Insert basis of compensation, including rates and multiples of Direct Personnel Expense for Principals and employees, and identify Principals and classify employees, if required. Identify specific services to which particular methods of compensation apply.)

1.5.3 For a Change in Services of the Architect's consultants, compensation shall be computed as a multiple of   (   ) times the amounts billed to the Architect for such services.

1.5.4 For Reimbursable Expenses as described in Subparagraph 1.3.9.2, and any other items included in Paragraph 1.5.5 as Reimbursable Expenses, the compensation shall be computed as a multiple of   (   ) times the expenses incurred by the Architect, and the Architect's employees and consultants.

1.5.5 Other Reimbursable Expenses, if any, are as follows:

© 1997 A I A ®
AIA DOCUMENT B141-1997
STANDARD FORM
AGREEMENT

The American Institute
of Architects
1735 New York Avenue, N.W.
Washington, D.C. 20006-5292

1-11

1.5.6 The rates and multiples for services of the Architect and the Architect's consultants as set forth in this Agreement shall be adjusted in accordance with their normal salary review practices.

1.5.7 An initial payment of _____ Dollars
($ _____) shall be made upon execution of this Agreement and is the minimum payment under this Agreement. It shall be credited to the Owner's account at final payment. Subsequent payments for services shall be made monthly, and where applicable, shall be in proportion to services performed on the basis set forth in this Agreement.

1.5.8 Payments are due and payable (_____) days from the date of the Architect's invoice. Amounts unpaid (_____) days after the invoice date shall bear interest at the rate entered below, or in the absence thereof at the legal rate prevailing from time to time at the principal place of business of the Architect.
(Insert rate of interest agreed upon.)

(Usury laws and requirements under the Federal Truth in Lending Act, similar state and local consumer credit laws and other regulations at the Owner's and Architect's principal places of business, the location of the Project and elsewhere may affect the validity of this provision. Specific legal advice should be obtained with respect to deletions or modifications, and also regarding requirements such as written disclosures or waivers.)

1.5.9 If the services covered by this Agreement have not been completed within (_____) months of the date hereof, through no fault of the Architect, extension of the Architect's services beyond that time shall be compensated as provided in Paragraph 1.5.2.

This Agreement entered into as of the day and year first written above.

_____   _____
OWNER *(Signature)*   **ARCHITECT** *(Signature)*

_____   _____
(Printed name and title)   *(Printed name and title)*

© 1997 AIA®
AIA DOCUMENT B141-1997
STANDARD FORM
AGREEMENT

The American Institute
of Architects
1735 New York Avenue, N.W.
Washington, D.C. 20006-5292

1-12

274

1997 EDITION

AIA DOCUMENT | B141-1997

Standard Form of Architect's Services: Design and Contract Administration

This document has important legal consequences. Consultation with an attorney is encouraged with respect to its completion or modification.

TABLE OF ARTICLES

© 1997 AIA®
AIA DOCUMENT B141-1997
STANDARD FORM
SERVICES

The American Institute
of Architects
1735 New York Avenue, N.W.
Washington, D.C. 20006-5292

2-1

ARTICLE 2.1 PROJECT ADMINISTRATION SERVICES

2.1.1 The Architect shall manage the Architect's services and administer the Project. The Architect shall consult with the Owner, research applicable design criteria, attend Project meetings, communicate with members of the Project team and issue progress reports. The Architect shall coordinate the services provided by the Architect and the Architect's consultants with those services provided by the Owner and the Owner's consultants.

2.1.2 When Project requirements have been sufficiently identified, the Architect shall prepare, and periodically update, a Project schedule that shall identify milestone dates for decisions required of the Owner, design services furnished by the Architect, completion of documentation provided by the Architect, commencement of construction and Substantial Completion of the Work.

2.1.3 The Architect shall consider the value of alternative materials, building systems and equipment, together with other considerations based on program, budget and aesthetics in developing the design for the Project.

2.1.4 Upon request of the Owner, the Architect shall make a presentation to explain the design of the Project to representatives of the Owner.

2.1.5 The Architect shall submit design documents to the Owner at intervals appropriate to the design process for purposes of evaluation and approval by the Owner. The Architect shall be entitled to rely on approvals received from the Owner in the further development of the design.

2.1.6 The Architect shall assist the Owner in connection with the Owner's responsibility for filing documents required for the approval of governmental authorities having jurisdiction over the Project.

2.1.7 EVALUATION OF BUDGET AND COST OF THE WORK

2.1.7.1 When the Project requirements have been sufficiently identified, the Architect shall prepare a preliminary estimate of the Cost of the Work. This estimate may be based on current area, volume or similar conceptual estimating techniques. As the design process progresses through the end of the preparation of the Construction Documents, the Architect shall update and refine the preliminary estimate of the Cost of the Work. The Architect shall advise the Owner of any adjustments to previous estimates of the Cost of the Work indicated by changes in Project requirements or general market conditions. If at any time the Architect's estimate of the Cost of the Work exceeds the Owner's budget, the Architect shall make appropriate recommendations to the Owner to adjust the Project's size, quality or budget, and the Owner shall cooperate with the Architect in making such adjustments.

2.1.7.2 Evaluations of the Owner's budget for the Project, the preliminary estimate of the Cost of the Work and updated estimates of the Cost of the Work prepared by the Architect represent the Architect's judgment as a design professional familiar with the construction industry. It is recognized, however, that neither the Architect nor the Owner has control over the cost of labor, materials or equipment, over the Contractor's methods of determining bid prices, or over competitive bidding, market or negotiating conditions. Accordingly, the Architect cannot and does not warrant or represent that bids or negotiated prices will not vary from the Owner's budget for the Project or from any estimate of the Cost of the Work or evaluation prepared or agreed to by the Architect.

2.1.7.3 In preparing estimates of the Cost of the Work, the Architect shall be permitted to include contingencies for design, bidding and price escalation; to determine what materials, equipment, component systems and types of construction are to be included in the Contract Documents; to make reasonable adjustments in the scope of the Project and to include in the Contract Documents alternate bids as may be necessary to adjust the estimated Cost of the Work to meet the Owner's budget for the Cost of the Work. If an increase in the Contract Sum occurring after execution of the Contract between the Owner and the Contractor causes the budget for the Cost of the Work to be exceeded, that budget shall be increased accordingly.

2.1.7.4 If bidding or negotiation has not commenced within 90 days after the Architect submits the Construction Documents to the Owner, the budget for the Cost of the Work shall be adjusted to reflect changes in the general level of prices in the construction industry.

2.1.7.5 If the budget for the Cost of the Work is exceeded by the lowest bona fide bid or negotiated proposal, the Owner shall:
    .1 give written approval of an increase in the budget for the Cost of the Work;
    .2 authorize rebidding or renegotiating of the Project within a reasonable time;
    .3 terminate in accordance with Subparagraph 1.3.8.5; or
    .4 cooperate in revising the Project scope and quality as required to reduce the Cost of the Work.

2.1.7.6 If the Owner chooses to proceed under Clause 2.1.7.5.4, the Architect, without additional compensation, shall modify the documents for which the Architect is responsible under this Agreement as necessary to comply with the budget for the Cost of the Work. The modification of such documents shall be the limit of the Architect's responsibility under this Paragraph 2.1.7. The Architect shall be entitled to compensation in accordance with this Agreement for all services performed whether or not construction is commenced.

ARTICLE 2.2 SUPPORTING SERVICES

2.2.1 Unless specifically designated in Paragraph 2.8.3, the services in this Article 2.2 shall be provided by the Owner or the Owner's consultants and contractors.

2.2.1.1 The Owner shall furnish a program setting forth the Owner's objectives, schedule, constraints and criteria, including space requirements and relationships, special equipment, systems and site requirements.

2.2.1.2 The Owner shall furnish surveys to describe physical characteristics, legal limitations and utility locations for the site of the Project, and a written legal description of the site. The surveys and legal information shall include, as applicable, grades and lines of streets, alleys, pavements and adjoining property and structures; adjacent drainage; rights-of-way, restrictions, easements, encroachments, zoning, deed restrictions, boundaries and contours of the site; locations, dimensions and necessary data with respect to existing buildings, other improvements and trees; and information concerning available utility services and lines, both public and private, above and below grade, including inverts and depths. All the information on the survey shall be referenced to a Project benchmark.

2.2.1.3 The Owner shall furnish services of geotechnical engineers which may include but are not limited to test borings, test pits, determinations of soil bearing values, percolation tests, evaluations of hazardous materials, ground corrosion tests and resistivity tests, including necessary operations for anticipating subsoil conditions, with reports and appropriate recommendations.

© 1997 AIA®
AIA DOCUMENT B141-1997
STANDARD FORM
SERVICES

The American Institute
of Architects
1735 New York Avenue, N.W.
Washington, D.C. 20006-5292

2-3

ARTICLE 2.3 EVALUATION AND PLANNING SERVICES

2.3.1 The Architect shall provide a preliminary evaluation of the information furnished by the Owner under this Agreement, including the Owner's program and schedule requirements and budget for the Cost of the Work, each in terms of the other. The Architect shall review such information to ascertain that it is consistent with the requirements of the Project and shall notify the Owner of any other information or consultant services that may be reasonably needed for the Project.

2.3.2 The Architect shall provide a preliminary evaluation of the Owner's site for the Project based on the information provided by the Owner of site conditions, and the Owner's program, schedule and budget for the Cost of the Work.

2.3.3 The Architect shall review the Owner's proposed method of contracting for construction services and shall notify the Owner of anticipated impacts that such method may have on the Owner's program, financial and time requirements, and the scope of the Project.

ARTICLE 2.4 DESIGN SERVICES

2.4.1 The Architect's design services shall include normal structural, mechanical and electrical engineering services.

2.4.2 SCHEMATIC DESIGN DOCUMENTS

2.4.2.1 The Architect shall provide Schematic Design Documents based on the mutually agreed-upon program, schedule, and budget for the Cost of the Work. The documents shall establish the conceptual design of the Project illustrating the scale and relationship of the Project components. The Schematic Design Documents shall include a conceptual site plan, if appropriate, and preliminary building plans, sections and elevations. At the Architect's option, the Schematic Design Documents may include study models, perspective sketches, electronic modeling or combinations of these media. Preliminary selections of major building systems and construction materials shall be noted on the drawings or described in writing.

2.4.3 DESIGN DEVELOPMENT DOCUMENTS

2.4.3.1 The Architect shall provide Design Development Documents based on the approved Schematic Design Documents and updated budget for the Cost of the Work. The Design Development Documents shall illustrate and describe the refinement of the design of the Project, establishing the scope, relationships, forms, size and appearance of the Project by means of plans, sections and elevations, typical construction details, and equipment layouts. The Design Development Documents shall include specifications that identify major materials and systems and establish in general their quality levels.

2.4.4 CONSTRUCTION DOCUMENTS

2.4.4.1 The Architect shall provide Construction Documents based on the approved Design Development Documents and updated budget for the Cost of the Work. The Construction Documents shall set forth in detail the requirements for construction of the Project. The Construction Documents shall include Drawings and Specifications that establish in detail the quality levels of materials and systems required for the Project.

2.4.4.2 During the development of the Construction Documents, the Architect shall assist the Owner in the development and preparation of: (1) bidding and procurement information which describes the time, place and conditions of bidding; bidding or proposal forms; and the form of agreement between the Owner and the Contractor; and (2) the Conditions of the Contract for Construction (General, Supplementary and other Conditions). The Architect also shall compile the Project Manual that includes the Conditions of the Contract for Construction and Specifications and may include bidding requirements and sample forms.

©1997 AIA®
AIA DOCUMENT B141-1997
STANDARD FORM
SERVICES

The American Institute
of Architects
1735 New York Avenue, N.W.
Washington, D.C. 20006-5292

2-4

ARTICLE 2.5 CONSTRUCTION PROCUREMENT SERVICES

2.5.1 The Architect shall assist the Owner in obtaining either competitive bids or negotiated proposals and shall assist the Owner in awarding and preparing contracts for construction.

2.5.2 The Architect shall assist the Owner in establishing a list of prospective bidders or contractors.

2.5.3 The Architect shall assist the Owner in bid validation or proposal evaluation and determination of the successful bid or proposal, if any. If requested by the Owner, the Architect shall notify all prospective bidders or contractors of the bid or proposal results.

2.5.4 COMPETITIVE BIDDING

2.5.4.1 Bidding Documents shall consist of bidding requirements, proposed contract forms, General Conditions and Supplementary Conditions, Specifications and Drawings.

2.5.4.2 If requested by the Owner, the Architect shall arrange for procuring the reproduction of Bidding Documents for distribution to prospective bidders. The Owner shall pay directly for the cost of reproduction or shall reimburse the Architect for such expenses.

2.5.4.3 If requested by the Owner, the Architect shall distribute the Bidding Documents to prospective bidders and request their return upon completion of the bidding process. The Architect shall maintain a log of distribution and retrieval, and the amounts of deposits, if any, received from and returned to prospective bidders.

2.5.4.4 The Architect shall consider requests for substitutions, if permitted by the Bidding Documents, and shall prepare and distribute addenda identifying approved substitutions to all prospective bidders.

2.5.4.5 The Architect shall participate in or, at the Owner's direction, shall organize and conduct a pre-bid conference for prospective bidders.

2.5.4.6 The Architect shall prepare responses to questions from prospective bidders and provide clarifications and interpretations of the Bidding Documents to all prospective bidders in the form of addenda.

2.5.4.7 The Architect shall participate in or, at the Owner's direction, shall organize and conduct the opening of the bids. The Architect shall subsequently document and distribute the bidding results, as directed by the Owner.

2.5.5 NEGOTIATED PROPOSALS

2.5.5.1 Proposal Documents shall consist of proposal requirements, proposed contract forms, General Conditions and Supplementary Conditions, Specifications and Drawings.

2.5.5.2 If requested by the Owner, the Architect shall arrange for procuring the reproduction of Proposal Documents for distribution to prospective contractors. The Owner shall pay directly for the cost of reproduction or shall reimburse the Architect for such expenses.

2.5.5.3 If requested by the Owner, the Architect shall organize and participate in selection interviews with prospective contractors.

2.5.5.4 The Architect shall consider requests for substitutions, if permitted by the Proposal Documents, and shall prepare and distribute addenda identifying approved substitutions to all prospective contractors.

© 1997 AIA®
AIA DOCUMENT B141-1997
STANDARD FORM
SERVICES

The American Institute
of Architects
1735 New York Avenue, N.W.
Washington, D.C. 20006-5292

2-5

2.5.5.5 If requested by the Owner, the Architect shall assist the Owner during negotiations with prospective contractors. The Architect shall subsequently prepare a summary report of the negotiation results, as directed by the Owner.

ARTICLE 2.6 CONTRACT ADMINISTRATION SERVICES
2.6.1 GENERAL ADMINISTRATION

2.6.1.1 The Architect shall provide administration of the Contract between the Owner and the Contractor as set forth below and in the edition of AIA Document A201, General Conditions of the Contract for Construction, current as of the date of this Agreement. Modifications made to the General Conditions, when adopted as part of the Contract Documents, shall be enforceable under this Agreement only to the extent that they are consistent with this Agreement or approved in writing by the Architect.

2.6.1.2 The Architect's responsibility to provide the Contract Administration Services under this Agreement commences with the award of the initial Contract for Construction and terminates at the issuance to the Owner of the final Certificate for Payment. However, the Architect shall be entitled to a Change in Services in accordance with Paragraph 2.8.2 when Contract Administration Services extend 60 days after the date of Substantial Completion of the Work.

2.6.1.3 The Architect shall be a representative of and shall advise and consult with the Owner during the provision of the Contract Administration Services. The Architect shall have authority to act on behalf of the Owner only to the extent provided in this Agreement unless otherwise modified by written amendment.

2.6.1.4 Duties, responsibilities and limitations of authority of the Architect under this Article 2.6 shall not be restricted, modified or extended without written agreement of the Owner and Architect with consent of the Contractor, which consent will not be unreasonably withheld.

2.6.1.5 The Architect shall review properly prepared, timely requests by the Contractor for additional information about the Contract Documents. A properly prepared request for additional information about the Contract Documents shall be in a form prepared or approved by the Architect and shall include a detailed written statement that indicates the specific Drawings or Specifications in need of clarification and the nature of the clarification requested.

2.6.1.6 If deemed appropriate by the Architect, the Architect shall on the Owner's behalf prepare, reproduce and distribute supplemental Drawings and Specifications in response to requests for information by the Contractor.

2.6.1.7 The Architect shall interpret and decide matters concerning performance of the Owner and Contractor under, and requirements of, the Contract Documents on written request of either the Owner or Contractor. The Architect's response to such requests shall be made in writing within any time limits agreed upon or otherwise with reasonable promptness.

2.6.1.8 Interpretations and decisions of the Architect shall be consistent with the intent of and reasonably inferable from the Contract Documents and shall be in writing or in the form of drawings. When making such interpretations and initial decisions, the Architect shall endeavor to secure faithful performance by both Owner and Contractor, shall not show partiality to either, and shall not be liable for the results of interpretations or decisions so rendered in good faith.

2.6.1.9 The Architect shall render initial decisions on claims, disputes or other matters in question between the Owner and Contractor as provided in the Contract Documents. However, the Architect's decisions on matters relating to aesthetic effect shall be final if consistent with the intent expressed in the Contract Documents.

© 1997 AIA®
AIA DOCUMENT B141-1997
STANDARD FORM
SERVICES

The American Institute
of Architects
1735 New York Avenue, N.W.
Washington, D.C. 20006-5292

2-6

2.6.2 EVALUATIONS OF THE WORK

2.6.2.1 The Architect, as a representative of the Owner, shall visit the site at intervals appropriate to the stage of the Contractor's operations, or as otherwise agreed by the Owner and the Architect in Article 2.8, (1) to become generally familiar with and to keep the Owner informed about the progress and quality of the portion of the Work completed, (2) to endeavor to guard the Owner against defects and deficiencies in the Work, and (3) to determine in general if the Work is being performed in a manner indicating that the Work, when fully completed, will be in accordance with the Contract Documents. However, the Architect shall not be required to make exhaustive or continuous on-site inspections to check the quality or quantity of the Work. The Architect shall neither have control over or charge of, nor be responsible for, the construction means, methods, techniques, sequences or procedures, or for safety precautions and programs in connection with the Work, since these are solely the Contractor's rights and responsibilities under the Contract Documents.

2.6.2.2 The Architect shall report to the Owner known deviations from the Contract Documents and from the most recent construction schedule submitted by the Contractor. However, the Architect shall not be responsible for the Contractor's failure to perform the Work in accordance with the requirements of the Contract Documents. The Architect shall be responsible for the Architect's negligent acts or omissions, but shall not have control over or charge of and shall not be responsible for acts or omissions of the Contractor, Subcontractors, or their agents or employees, or of any other persons or entities performing portions of the Work.

2.6.2.3 The Architect shall at all times have access to the Work wherever it is in preparation or progress.

2.6.2.4 Except as otherwise provided in this Agreement or when direct communications have been specially authorized, the Owner shall endeavor to communicate with the Contractor through the Architect about matters arising out of or relating to the Contract Documents. Communications by and with the Architect's consultants shall be through the Architect.

2.6.2.5 The Architect shall have authority to reject Work that does not conform to the Contract Documents. Whenever the Architect considers it necessary or advisable, the Architect will have authority to require inspection or testing of the Work in accordance with the provisions of the Contract Documents, whether or not such Work is fabricated, installed or completed. However, neither this authority of the Architect nor a decision made in good faith either to exercise or not to exercise such authority shall give rise to a duty or responsibility of the Architect to the Contractor, Subcontractors, material and equipment suppliers, their agents or employees or other persons or entities performing portions of the Work.

2.6.3 CERTIFICATION OF PAYMENTS TO CONTRACTOR

2.6.3.1 The Architect shall review and certify the amounts due the Contractor and shall issue Certificates for Payment in such amounts. The Architect's certification for payment shall constitute a representation to the Owner, based on the Architect's evaluation of the Work as provided in Paragraph 2.6.2 and on the data comprising the Contractor's Application for Payment, that the Work has progressed to the point indicated and that, to the best of the Architect's knowledge, information and belief, the quality of the Work is in accordance with the Contract Documents. The foregoing representations are subject (1) to an evaluation of the Work for conformance with the Contract Documents upon Substantial Completion, (2) to results of subsequent tests and inspections, (3) to correction of minor deviations from the Contract Documents prior to completion, and (4) to specific qualifications expressed by the Architect.

© 1997 A I A®
AIA DOCUMENT B141-1997
STANDARD FORM
SERVICES

The American Institute
of Architects
1735 New York Avenue, N.W.
Washington, D.C. 20006-5292

2-7

2.6.3.2 The issuance of a Certificate for Payment shall not be a representation that the Architect has (1) made exhaustive or continuous on-site inspections to check the quality or quantity of the Work, (2) reviewed construction means, methods, techniques, sequences or procedures, (3) reviewed copies of requisitions received from Subcontractors and material suppliers and other data requested by the Owner to substantiate the Contractor's right to payment, or (4) ascertained how or for what purpose the Contractor has used money previously paid on account of the Contract Sum.

2.6.3.3 The Architect shall maintain a record of the Contractor's Applications for Payment.

2.6.4 SUBMITTALS

2.6.4.1 The Architect shall review and approve or take other appropriate action upon the Contractor's submittals such as Shop Drawings, Product Data and Samples, but only for the limited purpose of checking for conformance with information given and the design concept expressed in the Contract Documents. The Architect's action shall be taken with such reasonable promptness as to cause no delay in the Work or in the activities of the Owner, Contractor or separate contractors, while allowing sufficient time in the Architect's professional judgment to permit adequate review. Review of such submittals is not conducted for the purpose of determining the accuracy and completeness of other details such as dimensions and quantities, or for substantiating instructions for installation or performance of equipment or systems, all of which remain the responsibility of the Contractor as required by the Contract Documents. The Architect's review shall not constitute approval of safety precautions or, unless otherwise specifically stated by the Architect, of any construction means, methods, techniques, sequences or procedures. The Architect's approval of a specific item shall not indicate approval of an assembly of which the item is a component.

2.6.4.2 The Architect shall maintain a record of submittals and copies of submittals supplied by the Contractor in accordance with the requirements of the Contract Documents.

2.6.4.3 If professional design services or certifications by a design professional related to systems, materials or equipment are specifically required of the Contractor by the Contract Documents, the Architect shall specify appropriate performance and design criteria that such services must satisfy. Shop Drawings and other submittals related to the Work designed or certified by the design professional retained by the Contractor shall bear such professional's written approval when submitted to the Architect. The Architect shall be entitled to rely upon the adequacy, accuracy and completeness of the services, certifications or approvals performed by such design professionals.

2.6.5 CHANGES IN THE WORK

2.6.5.1 The Architect shall prepare Change Orders and Construction Change Directives for the Owner's approval and execution in accordance with the Contract Documents. The Architect may authorize minor changes in the Work not involving an adjustment in Contract Sum or an extension of the Contract Time which are consistent with the intent of the Contract Documents. If necessary, the Architect shall prepare, reproduce and distribute Drawings and Specifications to describe Work to be added, deleted or modified, as provided in Paragraph 2.8.2.

2.6.5.2 The Architect shall review properly prepared, timely requests by the Owner or Contractor for changes in the Work, including adjustments to the Contract Sum or Contract Time. A properly prepared request for a change in the Work shall be accompanied by sufficient supporting data and information to permit the Architect to make a reasonable determination without extensive investigation or preparation of additional drawings or specifications. If the Architect

2-8

determines that requested changes in the Work are not materially different from the requirements of the Contract Documents, the Architect may issue an order for a minor change in the Work or recommend to the Owner that the requested change be denied.

2.6.5.3 If the Architect determines that implementation of the requested changes would result in a material change to the Contract that may cause an adjustment in the Contract Time or Contract Sum, the Architect shall make a recommendation to the Owner, who may authorize further investigation of such change. Upon such authorization, and based upon information furnished by the Contractor, if any, the Architect shall estimate the additional cost and time that might result from such change, including any additional costs attributable to a Change in Services of the Architect. With the Owner's approval, the Architect shall incorporate those estimates into a Change Order or other appropriate documentation for the Owner's execution or negotiation with the Contractor.

2.6.5.4 The Architect shall maintain records relative to changes in the Work.

2.6.6 PROJECT COMPLETION
2.6.6.1 The Architect shall conduct inspections to determine the date or dates of Substantial Completion and the date of final completion, shall receive from the Contractor and forward to the Owner, for the Owner's review and records, written warranties and related documents required by the Contract Documents and assembled by the Contractor, and shall issue a final Certificate for Payment based upon a final inspection indicating the Work complies with the requirements of the Contract Documents.

2.6.6.2 The Architect's inspection shall be conducted with the Owner's Designated Representative to check conformance of the Work with the requirements of the Contract Documents and to verify the accuracy and completeness of the list submitted by the Contractor of Work to be completed or corrected.

2.6.6.3 When the Work is found to be substantially complete, the Architect shall inform the Owner about the balance of the Contract Sum remaining to be paid the Contractor, including any amounts needed to pay for final completion or correction of the Work.

2.6.6.4 The Architect shall receive from the Contractor and forward to the Owner: (1) consent of surety or sureties, if any, to reduction in or partial release of retainage or the making of final payment and (2) affidavits, receipts, releases and waivers of liens or bonds indemnifying the Owner against liens.

ARTICLE 2.7 FACILITY OPERATION SERVICES
2.7.1 The Architect shall meet with the Owner or the Owner's Designated Representative promptly after Substantial Completion to review the need for facility operation services.

2.7.2 Upon request of the Owner, and prior to the expiration of one year from the date of Substantial Completion, the Architect shall conduct a meeting with the Owner and the Owner's Designated Representative to review the facility operations and performance and to make appropriate recommendations to the Owner.

© 1997 AIA®
AIA DOCUMENT B141-1997
STANDARD FORM
SERVICES

The American Institute
of Architects
1735 New York Avenue, N.W.
Washington, D.C. 20006-5292

2-9

ARTICLE 2.8 SCHEDULE OF SERVICES

2.8.1 Design and Contract Administration Services beyond the following limits shall be provided by the Architect as a Change in Services in accordance with Paragraph 1.3.3:

   .1 up to   (   ) reviews of each Shop Drawing, Product Data item, sample and similar submittal of the Contractor.

   .2 up to   (   ) visits to the site by the Architect over the duration of the Project during construction.

   .3 up to   (   ) inspections for any portion of the Work to determine whether such portion of the Work is substantially complete in accordance with the requirements of the Contract Documents.

   .4 up to   (   ) inspections for any portion of the Work to determine final completion.

2.8.2 The following Design and Contract Administration Services shall be provided by the Architect as a Change in Services in accordance with Paragraph 1.3.3:

   .1 review of a Contractor's submittal out of sequence from the submittal schedule agreed to by the Architect;

   .2 responses to the Contractor's requests for information where such information is available to the Contractor from a careful study and comparison of the Contract Documents, field conditions, other Owner-provided information, Contractor-prepared coordination drawings, or prior Project correspondence or documentation;

   .3 Change Orders and Construction Change Directives requiring evaluation of proposals, including the preparation or revision of Instruments of Service;

   .4 providing consultation concerning replacement of Work resulting from fire or other cause during construction;

   .5 evaluation of an extensive number of claims submitted by the Owner's consultants, the Contractor or others in connection with the Work;

   .6 evaluation of substitutions proposed by the Owner's consultants or contractors and making subsequent revisions to Instruments of Service resulting therefrom;

   .7 preparation of design and documentation for alternate bid or proposal requests proposed by the Owner; or

   .8 Contract Administration Services provided 60 days after the date of Substantial Completion of the Work.

© 1997 AIA®
AIA DOCUMENT B141-1997
STANDARD FORM
SERVICES

The American Institute
of Architects
1735 New York Avenue, N.W.
Washington, D.C. 20006-5292

2-10

2.8.3 The Architect shall furnish or provide the following services only if specifically designated:

Services	Responsibility (Architect, Owner or Not Provided)	Location of Service Description
.1 Programming		
.2 Land Survey Services		
.3 Geotechnical Services		
.4 Space Schematics/Flow Diagrams		
.5 Existing Facilities Surveys		
.6 Economic Feasibility Studies		
.7 Site Analysis and Selection		
.8 Environmental Studies and Reports		
.9 Owner-Supplied Data Coordination		
.10 Schedule Development and Monitoring		
.11 Civil Design		
.12 Landscape Design		
.13 Interior Design		
.14 Special Bidding or Negotiation		
.15 Value Analysis		
.16 Detailed Cost Estimating		
.17 On-Site Project Representation		
.18 Construction Management		
.19 Start-Up Assistance		
.20 Record Drawings		
.21 Post-Contract Evaluation		
.22 Tenant-Related Services		
.23		
.24		
.25		

Description of Services.
(Insert descriptions of the services designated.)

© 1997 AIA®
AIA DOCUMENT B141-1997
STANDARD FORM
SERVICES

The American Institute
of Architects
1735 New York Avenue, N.W.
Washington, D.C. 20006-5292

2-11

ARTICLE 2.9 MODIFICATIONS

2.9.1 Modifications to this Standard Form of Architect's Services: Design and Contract Administration, if any, are as follows:

By its execution, this Standard Form of Architect's Services: Design and Contract Administration and modifications hereto are incorporated into the Standard Form of Agreement Between the Owner and Architect, AIA Document B141-1997, that was entered into by the parties as of the date:

OWNER*(Signature)*   **ARCHITECT***(Signature)*

_____   _____
(Printed name and title)   *(Printed name and title)*

The American Institute
of Architects
1735 New York Avenue, N.W.
Washington, D.C. 20006-5292

2-12

286

AIA DOCUMENT | A101-1997

Standard Form of Agreement Between Owner and Contractor
where the basis of payment is a STIPULATED SUM

AGREEMENT made as of the   day of
in the year
(In words, indicate day, month and year)

BETWEEN the Owner:
(Name, address and other information)

and the Contractor:
(Name, address and other information)

The Project is:
(Name and location)

The Architect is:
(Name, address and other information)

The Owner and Contractor agree as follows.

This document has important legal consequences. Consultation with an attorney is encouraged with respect to its completion or modification.

AIA Document A201-1997, General Conditions of the Contract for Construction, is adopted in this document by reference. Do not use with other general conditions unless this document is modified.

This document has been approved and endorsed by The Associated General Contractors of America.

© 1997 AIA®
AIA DOCUMENT A101-1997
OWNER-CONTRACTOR
AGREEMENT

The American Institute
of Architects
1735 New York Avenue, N.W.
Washington, D.C. 20006-5292

1

ARTICLE 1 THE CONTRACT DOCUMENTS

The Contract Documents consist of this Agreement, Conditions of the Contract (General, Supplementary and other Conditions), Drawings, Specifications, Addenda issued prior to execution of this Agreement, other documents listed in this Agreement and Modifications issued after execution of this Agreement; these form the Contract, and are as fully a part of the Contract as if attached to this Agreement or repeated herein. The Contract represents the entire and integrated agreement between the parties hereto and supersedes prior negotiations, representations or agreements, either written or oral. An enumeration of the Contract Documents, other than Modifications, appears in Article 8.

ARTICLE 2 THE WORK OF THIS CONTRACT

The Contractor shall fully execute the Work described in the Contract Documents, except to the extent specifically indicated in the Contract Documents to be the responsibility of others.

ARTICLE 3 DATE OF COMMENCEMENT AND SUBSTANTIAL COMPLETION

3.1 The date of commencement of the Work shall be the date of this Agreement unless a different date is stated below or provision is made for the date to be fixed in a notice to proceed issued by the Owner.

(Insert the date of commencement if it differs from the date of this Agreement or, if applicable, state that the date will be fixed in a notice to proceed.)

If, prior to the commencement of the Work, the Owner requires time to file mortgages, mechanic's liens and other security interests, the Owner's time requirement shall be as follows:

3.2 The Contract Time shall be measured from the date of commencement.

3.3 The Contractor shall achieve Substantial Completion of the entire Work not later than
days from the date of commencement, or as follows:

(Insert number of calendar days. Alternatively, a calendar date may be used when coordinated with the date of commencement. Unless stated elsewhere in the Contract Documents, insert any requirements for earlier Substantial Completion of certain portions of the Work.)

, subject to adjustments of this Contract Time as provided in the Contract Documents.

(Insert provisions, if any, for liquidated damages relating to failure to complete on time or for bonus payments for early completion of the Work.)

© 1997 AIA®
AIA DOCUMENT A101-1997
OWNER-CONTRACTOR
AGREEMENT

The American Institute
of Architects
1735 New York Avenue, N.W.
Washington, D.C. 20006-5292

2

ARTICLE 4 CONTRACT SUM

4.1   The Owner shall pay the Contractor the Contract Sum in current funds for the Contractor's performance of the Contract. The Contract Sum shall be

Dollars ($),

subject to additions and deductions as provided in the Contract Documents.

4.2   The Contract Sum is based upon the following alternates, if any, which are described in the Contract Documents and are hereby accepted by the Owner:
(State the numbers or other identification of accepted alternates. If decisions on other alternates are to be made by the Owner subsequent to the execution of this Agreement, attach a schedule of such other alternates showing the amount for each and the date when that amount expires.)

4.3   Unit prices, if any, are as follows:

ARTICLE 5 PAYMENTS

5.1   PROGRESS PAYMENTS

5.1.1   Based upon Applications for Payment submitted to the Architect by the Contractor and Certificates for Payment issued by the Architect, the Owner shall make progress payments on account of the Contract Sum to the Contractor as provided below and elsewhere in the Contract Documents.

5.1.2   The period covered by each Application for Payment shall be one calendar month ending on the last day of the month, or as follows:

5.1.3   Provided that an Application for Payment is received by the Architect not later than the   day of a month, the Owner shall make payment to the Contractor not later than the   day of the   month. If an Application for Payment is received by the Architect after the application date fixed above, payment shall be made by the Owner not later than   days after the Architect receives the Application for Payment.

5.1.4   Each Application for Payment shall be based on the most recent schedule of values submitted by the Contractor in accordance with the Contract Documents. The schedule of values shall allocate the entire Contract Sum among the various portions of the Work. The schedule of values shall be prepared in such form and supported by such data to substantiate its accuracy as the Architect may require. This schedule, unless objected to by the Architect, shall be used as a basis for reviewing the Contractor's Applications for Payment.

© 1 9 9 7   A I A ®
AIA DOCUMENT A101-1997
OWNER-CONTRACTOR
AGREEMENT

The American Institute
of Architects
1735 New York Avenue, N.W.
Washington, D.C. 20006-5292

3

5.1.5 Applications for Payment shall indicate the percentage of completion of each portion of the Work as of the end of the period covered by the Application for Payment.

5.1.6 Subject to other provisions of the Contract Documents, the amount of each progress payment shall be computed as follows:

    .1 Take that portion of the Contract Sum properly allocable to completed Work as determined by multiplying the percentage completion of each portion of the Work by the share of the Contract Sum allocated to that portion of the Work in the schedule of values, less retainage of   percent (%). Pending final determination of cost to the Owner of changes in the Work, amounts not in dispute shall be included as provided in Subparagraph 7.3.8 of AIA Document A201-1997;

    .2 Add that portion of the Contract Sum properly allocable to materials and equipment delivered and suitably stored at the site for subsequent incorporation in the completed construction (or, if approved in advance by the Owner, suitably stored off the site at a location agreed upon in writing), less retainage of   percent (%);

    .3 Subtract the aggregate of previous payments made by the Owner; and

    .4 Subtract amounts, if any, for which the Architect has withheld or nullified a Certificate for Payment as provided in Paragraph 9.5 of AIA Document A201-1997.

5.1.7 The progress payment amount determined in accordance with Subparagraph 5.1.6 shall be further modified under the following circumstances:

    .1 Add, upon Substantial Completion of the Work, a sum sufficient to increase the total payments to the full amount of the Contract Sum, less such amounts as the Architect shall determine for incomplete Work, retainage applicable to such work and unsettled claims; and *(Subparagraph 9.8.5 of AIA Document A201-1997 requires release of applicable retainage upon Substantial Completion of Work with consent of surety, if any.)*

    .2 Add, if final completion of the Work is thereafter materially delayed through no fault of the Contractor, any additional amounts payable in accordance with Subparagraph 9.10.3 of AIA Document A201-1997.

5.1.8 Reduction or limitation of retainage, if any, shall be as follows:

(If it is intended, prior to Substantial Completion of the entire Work, to reduce or limit the retainage resulting from the percentages inserted in Clauses 5.1.6.1 and 5.1.6.2 above, and this is not explained elsewhere in the Contract Documents, insert here provisions for such reduction or limitation.)

5.1.9 Except with the Owner's prior approval, the Contractor shall not make advance payments to suppliers for materials or equipment which have not been delivered and stored at the site.

5.2 FINAL PAYMENT

5.2.1 Final payment, constituting the entire unpaid balance of the Contract Sum, shall be made by the Owner to the Contractor when:

    .1 the Contractor has fully performed the Contract except for the Contractor's responsibility to correct Work as provided in Subparagraph 12.2.2 of AIA Document A201-1997, and to satisfy other requirements, if any, which extend beyond final payment; and

    .2 a final Certificate for Payment has been issued by the Architect.

4

5.2.2 The Owner's final payment to the Contractor shall be made no later than 30 days after the issuance of the Architect's final Certificate for Payment, or as follows:

ARTICLE 6 TERMINATION OR SUSPENSION
6.1 The Contract may be terminated by the Owner or the Contractor as provided in Article 14 of AIA Document A201-1997.

6.2 The Work may be suspended by the Owner as provided in Article 14 of AIA Document A201-1997.

ARTICLE 7 MISCELLANEOUS PROVISIONS
7.1 Where reference is made in this Agreement to a provision of AIA Document A201-1997 or another Contract Document, the reference refers to that provision as amended or supplemented by other provisions of the Contract Documents.

7.2 Payments due and unpaid under the Contract shall bear interest from the date payment is due at the rate stated below, or in the absence thereof, at the legal rate prevailing from time to time at the place where the Project is located.
(Insert rate of interest agreed upon, if any.)

(Usury laws and requirements under the Federal Truth in Lending Act, similar state and local consumer credit laws and other regulations at the Owner's and Contractor's principal places of business, the location of the Project and elsewhere may affect the validity of this provision. Legal advice should be obtained with respect to deletions or modifications, and also regarding requirements such as written disclosures or waivers.)

7.3 The Owner's representative is:
(Name, address and other information)

7.4 The Contractor's representative is:
(Name, address and other information)

7.5 Neither the Owner's nor the Contractor's representative shall be changed without ten days' written notice to the other party.

7.6 Other provisions:

© 1997 AIA®
AIA DOCUMENT A101-1997
OWNER-CONTRACTOR
AGREEMENT

The American Institute
of Architects
1735 New York Avenue, N.W.
Washington, D.C. 20006-5292

5

ARTICLE 8 ENUMERATION OF CONTRACT DOCUMENTS

8.1 The Contract Documents, except for Modifications issued after execution of this Agreement, are enumerated as follows:

8.1.1 The Agreement is this executed 1997 edition of the Standard Form of Agreement Between Owner and Contractor, AIA Document A101-1997.

8.1.2 The General Conditions are the 1997 edition of the General Conditions of the Contract for Construction, AIA Document A201-1997.

8.1.3 The Supplementary and other Conditions of the Contract are those contained in the Project Manual dated   , and are as follows:

Document	Title	Pages

8.1.4 The Specifications are those contained in the Project Manual dated as in Subparagraph 8.1.3, and are as follows:
(Either list the Specifications here or refer to an exhibit attached to this Agreement.)

Section	Title	Pages

8.1.5 The Drawings are as follows, and are dated   unless a different date is shown below:
(Either list the Drawings here or refer to an exhibit attached to this Agreement.)

Number	Title	Date

8.1.6 The Addenda, if any, are as follows:

Number   Date   Pages

Portions of Addenda relating to bidding requirements are not part of the Contract Documents unless the bidding requirements are also enumerated in this Article 8.

8.1.7 Other documents, if any, forming part of the Contract Documents are as follows:
(List here any additional documents that are intended to form part of the Contract Documents. AIA Document A201-1997 provides that bidding requirements such as advertisement or invitation to bid, Instructions to Bidders, sample forms and the Contractor's bid are not part of the Contract Documents unless enumerated in this Agreement. They should be listed here only if intended to be part of the Contract Documents.)

This Agreement is entered into as of the day and year first written above and is executed in at least three original copies, of which one is to be delivered to the Contractor, one to the Architect for use in the administration of the Contract, and the remainder to the Owner.

_____   _____
OWNER *(Signature)*   **CONTRACTOR** *(Signature)*

_____   _____
(Printed name and title)   *(Printed name and title)*

CAUTION: *You should sign an original AIA document or a licensed reproduction. Originals contain the AIA logo printed in red; licensed reproductions are those produced in accordance with the Instructions to this document.*

1997 EDITION

AIA DOCUMENT | A201-1997

General Conditions of the Contract for Construction

This document has important legal consequences. Consultation with an attorney is encouraged with respect to its completion or modification.

This document has been approved and endorsed by The Associated General Contractors of America.

TABLE OF ARTICLES

© 1997 AIA®
AIA DOCUMENT A201-1997
GENERAL CONDITIONS
OF THE CONTRACT FOR
CONSTRUCTION

The American Institute
of Architects
1735 New York Avenue, N.W.
Washington, D.C. 20006-5292

CAUTION: You should use an original AIA document with the AIA logo printed in red. An original assures that
changes will not be obscured as may occur when documents are reproduced.

1

INDEX

2

4

5

6

300

© 1997 AIA®
AIA DOCUMENT A201-1997
GENERAL CONDITIONS
OF THE CONTRACT FOR
CONSTRUCTION

The American Institute
of Architects
1735 New York Avenue, N.W.
Washington, D.C. 20006-5292

7

© 1997 AIA®
AIA DOCUMENT A201-1997
GENERAL CONDITIONS
OF THE CONTRACT FOR
CONSTRUCTION

The American Institute
of Architects
1735 New York Avenue, N.W.
Washington, D.C. 20006-5292

8

302

ARTICLE 1 GENERAL PROVISIONS

1.1 BASIC DEFINITIONS

1.1.1 THE CONTRACT DOCUMENTS

The Contract Documents consist of the Agreement between Owner and Contractor (hereinafter the Agreement), Conditions of the Contract (General, Supplementary and other Conditions), Drawings, Specifications, Addenda issued prior to execution of the Contract, other documents listed in the Agreement and Modifications issued after execution of the Contract. A Modification is (1) a written amendment to the Contract signed by both parties, (2) a Change Order, (3) a Construction Change Directive or (4) a written order for a minor change in the Work issued by the Architect. Unless specifically enumerated in the Agreement, the Contract Documents do not include other documents such as bidding requirements (advertisement or invitation to bid, Instructions to Bidders, sample forms, the Contractor's bid or portions of Addenda relating to bidding requirements).

1.1.2 THE CONTRACT

The Contract Documents form the Contract for Construction. The Contract represents the entire and integrated agreement between the parties hereto and supersedes prior negotiations, representations or agreements, either written or oral. The Contract may be amended or modified only by a Modification. The Contract Documents shall not be construed to create a contractual relationship of any kind (1) between the Architect and Contractor, (2) between the Owner and a Subcontractor or Sub-subcontractor, (3) between the Owner and Architect or (4) between any persons or entities other than the Owner and Contractor. The Architect shall, however, be entitled to performance and enforcement of obligations under the Contract intended to facilitate performance of the Architect's duties.

1.1.3 THE WORK

The term "Work" means the construction and services required by the Contract Documents, whether completed or partially completed, and includes all other labor, materials, equipment and services provided or to be provided by the Contractor to fulfill the Contractor's obligations. The Work may constitute the whole or a part of the Project.

1.1.4 THE PROJECT

The Project is the total construction of which the Work performed under the Contract Documents may be the whole or a part and which may include construction by the Owner or by separate contractors.

1.1.5 THE DRAWINGS

The Drawings are the graphic and pictorial portions of the Contract Documents showing the design, location and dimensions of the Work, generally including plans, elevations, sections, details, schedules and diagrams.

1.1.6 THE SPECIFICATIONS

The Specifications are that portion of the Contract Documents consisting of the written requirements for materials, equipment, systems, standards and workmanship for the Work, and performance of related services.

1.1.7 THE PROJECT MANUAL

The Project Manual is a volume assembled for the Work which may include the bidding requirements, sample forms, Conditions of the Contract and Specifications.

1.2 CORRELATION AND INTENT OF THE CONTRACT DOCUMENTS

1.2.1   The intent of the Contract Documents is to include all items necessary for the proper execution and completion of the Work by the Contractor. The Contract Documents are

© 1997 AIA®
AIA DOCUMENT A201-1997
GENERAL CONDITIONS
OF THE CONTRACT FOR
CONSTRUCTION

The American Institute
of Architects
1735 New York Avenue, N.W.
Washington, D.C. 20006-5292

9

complementary, and what is required by one shall be as binding as if required by all; performance by the Contractor shall be required only to the extent consistent with the Contract Documents and reasonably inferable from them as being necessary to produce the indicated results.

1.2.2 Organization of the Specifications into divisions, sections and articles, and arrangement of Drawings shall not control the Contractor in dividing the Work among Subcontractors or in establishing the extent of Work to be performed by any trade.

1.2.3 Unless otherwise stated in the Contract Documents, words which have well-known technical or construction industry meanings are used in the Contract Documents in accordance with such recognized meanings.

1.3 CAPITALIZATION
1.3.1 Terms capitalized in these General Conditions include those which are (1) specifically defined, (2) the titles of numbered articles and identified references to Paragraphs, Subparagraphs and Clauses in the document or (3) the titles of other documents published by the American Institute of Architects.

1.4 INTERPRETATION
1.4.1 In the interest of brevity the Contract Documents frequently omit modifying words such as "all" and "any" and articles such as "the" and "an," but the fact that a modifier or an article is absent from one statement and appears in another is not intended to affect the interpretation of either statement.

1.5 EXECUTION OF CONTRACT DOCUMENTS
1.5.1 The Contract Documents shall be signed by the Owner and Contractor. If either the Owner or Contractor or both do not sign all the Contract Documents, the Architect shall identify such unsigned Documents upon request.

1.5.2 Execution of the Contract by the Contractor is a representation that the Contractor has visited the site, become generally familiar with local conditions under which the Work is to be performed and correlated personal observations with requirements of the Contract Documents.

1.6 OWNERSHIP AND USE OF DRAWINGS, SPECIFICATIONS AND OTHER INSTRUMENTS OF SERVICE
1.6.1 The Drawings, Specifications and other documents, including those in electronic form, prepared by the Architect and the Architect's consultants are Instruments of Service through which the Work to be executed by the Contractor is described. The Contractor may retain one record set. Neither the Contractor nor any Subcontractor, Sub-subcontractor or material or equipment supplier shall own or claim a copyright in the Drawings, Specifications and other documents prepared by the Architect or the Architect's consultants, and unless otherwise indicated the Architect and the Architect's consultants shall be deemed the authors of them and will retain all common law, statutory and other reserved rights, in addition to the copyrights. All copies of Instruments of Service, except the Contractor's record set, shall be returned or suitably accounted for to the Architect, on request, upon completion of the Work. The Drawings, Specifications and other documents prepared by the Architect and the Architect's consultants, and copies thereof furnished to the Contractor, are for use solely with respect to this Project. They are not to be used by the Contractor or any Subcontractor, Sub-subcontractor or material or equipment supplier on other projects or for additions to this Project outside the scope of the Work without the specific written consent of the Owner, Architect and the Architect's consultants. The Contractor, Subcontractors, Sub-subcontractors and material or equipment suppliers are authorized to use and reproduce applicable portions of the Drawings, Specifications and other documents prepared by the Architect and the Architect's consultants appropriate to and for use in

©1997 AIA®
AIA DOCUMENT A201-1997
GENERAL CONDITIONS
OF THE CONTRACT FOR
CONSTRUCTION

The American Institute
of Architects
1735 New York Avenue, N.W.
Washington, D.C. 20006-5292

10

the execution of their Work under the Contract Documents. All copies made under this authorization shall bear the statutory copyright notice, if any, shown on the Drawings, Specifications and other documents prepared by the Architect and the Architect's consultants. Submittal or distribution to meet official regulatory requirements or for other purposes in connection with this Project is not to be construed as publication in derogation of the Architect's or Architect's consultants' copyrights or other reserved rights.

ARTICLE 2 OWNER

2.1 GENERAL

2.1.1 The Owner is the person or entity identified as such in the Agreement and is referred to throughout the Contract Documents as if singular in number. The Owner shall designate in writing a representative who shall have express authority to bind the Owner with respect to all matters requiring the Owner's approval or authorization. Except as otherwise provided in Subparagraph 4.2.1, the Architect does not have such authority. The term "Owner" means the Owner or the Owner's authorized representative.

2.1.2 The Owner shall furnish to the Contractor within fifteen days after receipt of a written request, information necessary and relevant for the Contractor to evaluate, give notice of or enforce mechanic's lien rights. Such information shall include a correct statement of the record legal title to the property on which the Project is located, usually referred to as the site, and the Owner's interest therein.

2.2 INFORMATION AND SERVICES REQUIRED OF THE OWNER

2.2.1 The Owner shall, at the written request of the Contractor, prior to commencement of the Work and thereafter, furnish to the Contractor reasonable evidence that financial arrangements have been made to fulfill the Owner's obligations under the Contract. Furnishing of such evidence shall be a condition precedent to commencement or continuation of the Work. After such evidence has been furnished, the Owner shall not materially vary such financial arrangements without prior notice to the Contractor.

2.2.2 Except for permits and fees, including those required under Subparagraph 3.7.1, which are the responsibility of the Contractor under the Contract Documents, the Owner shall secure and pay for necessary approvals, easements, assessments and charges required for construction, use or occupancy of permanent structures or for permanent changes in existing facilities.

2.2.3 The Owner shall furnish surveys describing physical characteristics, legal limitations and utility locations for the site of the Project, and a legal description of the site. The Contractor shall be entitled to rely on the accuracy of information furnished by the Owner but shall exercise proper precautions relating to the safe performance of the Work.

2.2.4 Information or services required of the Owner by the Contract Documents shall be furnished by the Owner with reasonable promptness. Any other information or services relevant to the Contractor's performance of the Work under the Owner's control shall be furnished by the Owner after receipt from the Contractor of a written request for such information or services.

2.2.5 Unless otherwise provided in the Contract Documents, the Contractor will be furnished, free of charge, such copies of Drawings and Project Manuals as are reasonably necessary for execution of the Work.

2.3 OWNER'S RIGHT TO STOP THE WORK

2.3.1 If the Contractor fails to correct Work which is not in accordance with the requirements of the Contract Documents as required by Paragraph 12.2 or persistently fails to carry out Work in

11

accordance with the Contract Documents, the Owner may issue a written order to the Contractor to stop the Work, or any portion thereof, until the cause for such order has been eliminated; however, the right of the Owner to stop the Work shall not give rise to a duty on the part of the Owner to exercise this right for the benefit of the Contractor or any other person or entity, except to the extent required by Subparagraph 6.1.3.

2.4 OWNER'S RIGHT TO CARRY OUT THE WORK

2.4.1 If the Contractor defaults or neglects to carry out the Work in accordance with the Contract Documents and fails within a seven-day period after receipt of written notice from the Owner to commence and continue correction of such default or neglect with diligence and promptness, the Owner may after such seven-day period give the Contractor a second written notice to correct such deficiencies within a three-day period. If the Contractor within such three-day period after receipt of such second notice fails to commence and continue to correct any deficiencies, the Owner may, without prejudice to other remedies the Owner may have, correct such deficiencies. In such case an appropriate Change Order shall be issued deducting from payments then or thereafter due the Contractor the reasonable cost of correcting such deficiencies, including Owner's expenses and compensation for the Architect's additional services made necessary by such default, neglect or failure. Such action by the Owner and amounts charged to the Contractor are both subject to prior approval of the Architect. If payments then or thereafter due the Contractor are not sufficient to cover such amounts, the Contractor shall pay the difference to the Owner.

ARTICLE 3 CONTRACTOR

3.1 GENERAL

3.1.1 The Contractor is the person or entity identified as such in the Agreement and is referred to throughout the Contract Documents as if singular in number. The term "Contractor" means the Contractor or the Contractor's authorized representative.

3.1.2 The Contractor shall perform the Work in accordance with the Contract Documents.

3.1.3 The Contractor shall not be relieved of obligations to perform the Work in accordance with the Contract Documents either by activities or duties of the Architect in the Architect's administration of the Contract, or by tests, inspections or approvals required or performed by persons other than the Contractor.

3.2 REVIEW OF CONTRACT DOCUMENTS AND FIELD CONDITIONS BY CONTRACTOR

3.2.1 Since the Contract Documents are complementary, before starting each portion of the Work, the Contractor shall carefully study and compare the various Drawings and other Contract Documents relative to that portion of the Work, as well as the information furnished by the Owner pursuant to Subparagraph 2.2.3, shall take field measurements of any existing conditions related to that portion of the Work and shall observe any conditions at the site affecting it. These obligations are for the purpose of facilitating construction by the Contractor and are not for the purpose of discovering errors, omissions, or inconsistencies in the Contract Documents; however, any errors, inconsistencies or omissions discovered by the Contractor shall be reported promptly to the Architect as a request for information in such form as the Architect may require.

3.2.2 Any design errors or omissions noted by the Contractor during this review shall be reported promptly to the Architect, but it is recognized that the Contractor's review is made in the Contractor's capacity as a contractor and not as a licensed design professional unless otherwise specifically provided in the Contract Documents. The Contractor is not required to ascertain that the Contract Documents are in accordance with applicable laws, statutes, ordinances, building codes, and rules and regulations, but any nonconformity discovered by or made known to the Contractor shall be reported promptly to the Architect.

12

3.2.3 If the Contractor believes that additional cost or time is involved because of clarifications or instructions issued by the Architect in response to the Contractor's notices or requests for information pursuant to Subparagraphs 3.2.1 and 3.2.2, the Contractor shall make Claims as provided in Subparagraphs 4.3.6 and 4.3.7. If the Contractor fails to perform the obligations of Subparagraphs 3.2.1 and 3.2.2, the Contractor shall pay such costs and damages to the Owner as would have been avoided if the Contractor had performed such obligations. The Contractor shall not be liable to the Owner or Architect for damages resulting from errors, inconsistencies or omissions in the Contract Documents or for differences between field measurements or conditions and the Contract Documents unless the Contractor recognized such error, inconsistency, omission or difference and knowingly failed to report it to the Architect.

3.3 SUPERVISION AND CONSTRUCTION PROCEDURES

3.3.1 The Contractor shall supervise and direct the Work, using the Contractor's best skill and attention. The Contractor shall be solely responsible for and have control over construction means, methods, techniques, sequences and procedures and for coordinating all portions of the Work under the Contract, unless the Contract Documents give other specific instructions concerning these matters. If the Contract Documents give specific instructions concerning construction means, methods, techniques, sequences or procedures, the Contractor shall evaluate the jobsite safety thereof and, except as stated below, shall be fully and solely responsible for the jobsite safety of such means, methods, techniques, sequences or procedures. If the Contractor determines that such means, methods, techniques, sequences or procedures may not be safe, the Contractor shall give timely written notice to the Owner and Architect and shall not proceed with that portion of the Work without further written instructions from the Architect. If the Contractor is then instructed to proceed with the required means, methods, techniques, sequences or procedures without acceptance of changes proposed by the Contractor, the Owner shall be solely responsible for any resulting loss or damage.

3.3.2 The Contractor shall be responsible to the Owner for acts and omissions of the Contractor's employees, Subcontractors and their agents and employees, and other persons or entities performing portions of the Work for or on behalf of the Contractor or any of its Subcontractors.

3.3.3 The Contractor shall be responsible for inspection of portions of Work already performed to determine that such portions are in proper condition to receive subsequent Work.

3.4 LABOR AND MATERIALS

3.4.1 Unless otherwise provided in the Contract Documents, the Contractor shall provide and pay for labor, materials, equipment, tools, construction equipment and machinery, water, heat, utilities, transportation, and other facilities and services necessary for proper execution and completion of the Work, whether temporary or permanent and whether or not incorporated or to be incorporated in the Work.

3.4.2 The Contractor may make substitutions only with the consent of the Owner, after evaluation by the Architect and in accordance with a Change Order.

3.4.3 The Contractor shall enforce strict discipline and good order among the Contractor's employees and other persons carrying out the Contract. The Contractor shall not permit employment of unfit persons or persons not skilled in tasks assigned to them.

3.5 WARRANTY

3.5.1 The Contractor warrants to the Owner and Architect that materials and equipment furnished under the Contract will be of good quality and new unless otherwise required or permitted by the Contract Documents, that the Work will be free from defects not inherent in the quality required or permitted, and that the Work will conform to the requirements of the Contract

© 1997 AIA®
AIA DOCUMENT A201-1997
GENERAL CONDITIONS
OF THE CONTRACT FOR
CONSTRUCTION

The American Institute
of Architects
1735 New York Avenue, N.W.
Washington, D.C. 20006-5292

13

Documents. Work not conforming to these requirements, including substitutions not properly approved and authorized, may be considered defective. The Contractor's warranty excludes remedy for damage or defect caused by abuse, modifications not executed by the Contractor, improper or insufficient maintenance, improper operation, or normal wear and tear and normal usage. If required by the Architect, the Contractor shall furnish satisfactory evidence as to the kind and quality of materials and equipment.

3.6   TAXES

3.6.1   The Contractor shall pay sales, consumer, use and similar taxes for the Work provided by the Contractor which are legally enacted when bids are received or negotiations concluded, whether or not yet effective or merely scheduled to go into effect.

3.7   PERMITS, FEES AND NOTICES

3.7.1   Unless otherwise provided in the Contract Documents, the Contractor shall secure and pay for the building permit and other permits and governmental fees, licenses and inspections necessary for proper execution and completion of the Work which are customarily secured after execution of the Contract and which are legally required when bids are received or negotiations concluded.

3.7.2   The Contractor shall comply with and give notices required by laws, ordinances, rules, regulations and lawful orders of public authorities applicable to performance of the Work.

3.7.3   It is not the Contractor's responsibility to ascertain that the Contract Documents are in accordance with applicable laws, statutes, ordinances, building codes, and rules and regulations. However, if the Contractor observes that portions of the Contract Documents are at variance therewith, the Contractor shall promptly notify the Architect and Owner in writing, and necessary changes shall be accomplished by appropriate Modification.

3.7.4   If the Contractor performs Work knowing it to be contrary to laws, statutes, ordinances, building codes, and rules and regulations without such notice to the Architect and Owner, the Contractor shall assume appropriate responsibility for such Work and shall bear the costs attributable to correction.

3.8   ALLOWANCES

3.8.1   The Contractor shall include in the Contract Sum all allowances stated in the Contract Documents. Items covered by allowances shall be supplied for such amounts and by such persons or entities as the Owner may direct, but the Contractor shall not be required to employ persons or entities to whom the Contractor has reasonable objection.

3.8.2   Unless otherwise provided in the Contract Documents:
> .1   allowances shall cover the cost to the Contractor of materials and equipment delivered at the site and all required taxes, less applicable trade discounts;
> .2   Contractor's costs for unloading and handling at the site, labor, installation costs, overhead, profit and other expenses contemplated for stated allowance amounts shall be included in the Contract Sum but not in the allowances;
> .3   whenever costs are more than or less than allowances, the Contract Sum shall be adjusted accordingly by Change Order. The amount of the Change Order shall reflect (1) the difference between actual costs and the allowances under Clause 3.8.2.1 and (2) changes in Contractor's costs under Clause 3.8.2.2.

3.8.3   Materials and equipment under an allowance shall be selected by the Owner in sufficient time to avoid delay in the Work.

3.9   SUPERINTENDENT

3.9.1   The Contractor shall employ a competent superintendent and necessary assistants who shall be in attendance at the Project site during performance of the Work. The superintendent shall represent the Contractor, and communications given to the superintendent shall be as binding as if given to the Contractor. Important communications shall be confirmed in writing. Other communications shall be similarly confirmed on written request in each case.

3.10   CONTRACTOR'S CONSTRUCTION SCHEDULES

3.10.1   The Contractor, promptly after being awarded the Contract, shall prepare and submit for the Owner's and Architect's information a Contractor's construction schedule for the Work. The schedule shall not exceed time limits current under the Contract Documents, shall be revised at appropriate intervals as required by the conditions of the Work and Project, shall be related to the entire Project to the extent required by the Contract Documents, and shall provide for expeditious and practicable execution of the Work.

3.10.2   The Contractor shall prepare and keep current, for the Architect's approval, a schedule of submittals which is coordinated with the Contractor's construction schedule and allows the Architect reasonable time to review submittals.

3.10.3   The Contractor shall perform the Work in general accordance with the most recent schedules submitted to the Owner and Architect.

3.11   DOCUMENTS AND SAMPLES AT THE SITE

3.11.1   The Contractor shall maintain at the site for the Owner one record copy of the Drawings, Specifications, Addenda, Change Orders and other Modifications, in good order and marked currently to record field changes and selections made during construction, and one record copy of approved Shop Drawings, Product Data, Samples and similar required submittals. These shall be available to the Architect and shall be delivered to the Architect for submittal to the Owner upon completion of the Work.

3.12   SHOP DRAWINGS, PRODUCT DATA AND SAMPLES

3.12.1   Shop Drawings are drawings, diagrams, schedules and other data specially prepared for the Work by the Contractor or a Subcontractor, Sub-subcontractor, manufacturer, supplier or distributor to illustrate some portion of the Work.

3.12.2   Product Data are illustrations, standard schedules, performance charts, instructions, brochures, diagrams and other information furnished by the Contractor to illustrate materials or equipment for some portion of the Work.

3.12.3   Samples are physical examples which illustrate materials, equipment or workmanship and establish standards by which the Work will be judged.

3.12.4   Shop Drawings, Product Data, Samples and similar submittals are not Contract Documents. The purpose of their submittal is to demonstrate for those portions of the Work for which submittals are required by the Contract Documents the way by which the Contractor proposes to conform to the information given and the design concept expressed in the Contract Documents. Review by the Architect is subject to the limitations of Subparagraph 4.2.7. Informational submittals upon which the Architect is not expected to take responsive action may be so identified in the Contract Documents. Submittals which are not required by the Contract Documents may be returned by the Architect without action.

3.12.5   The Contractor shall review for compliance with the Contract Documents, approve and submit to the Architect Shop Drawings, Product Data, Samples and similar submittals required by

15

the Contract Documents with reasonable promptness and in such sequence as to cause no delay in the Work or in the activities of the Owner or of separate contractors. Submittals which are not marked as reviewed for compliance with the Contract Documents and approved by the Contractor may be returned by the Architect without action.

3.12.6 By approving and submitting Shop Drawings, Product Data, Samples and similar submittals, the Contractor represents that the Contractor has determined and verified materials, field measurements and field construction criteria related thereto, or will do so, and has checked and coordinated the information contained within such submittals with the requirements of the Work and of the Contract Documents.

3.12.7 The Contractor shall perform no portion of the Work for which the Contract Documents require submittal and review of Shop Drawings, Product Data, Samples or similar submittals until the respective submittal has been approved by the Architect.

3.12.8 The Work shall be in accordance with approved submittals except that the Contractor shall not be relieved of responsibility for deviations from requirements of the Contract Documents by the Architect's approval of Shop Drawings, Product Data, Samples or similar submittals unless the Contractor has specifically informed the Architect in writing of such deviation at the time of submittal and (1) the Architect has given written approval to the specific deviation as a minor change in the Work, or (2) a Change Order or Construction Change Directive has been issued authorizing the deviation. The Contractor shall not be relieved of responsibility for errors or omissions in Shop Drawings, Product Data, Samples or similar submittals by the Architect's approval thereof.

3.12.9 The Contractor shall direct specific attention, in writing or on resubmitted Shop Drawings, Product Data, Samples or similar submittals, to revisions other than those requested by the Architect on previous submittals. In the absence of such written notice the Architect's approval of a resubmission shall not apply to such revisions.

3.12.10 The Contractor shall not be required to provide professional services which constitute the practice of architecture or engineering unless such services are specifically required by the Contract Documents for a portion of the Work or unless the Contractor needs to provide such services in order to carry out the Contractor's responsibilities for construction means, methods, techniques, sequences and procedures. The Contractor shall not be required to provide professional services in violation of applicable law. If professional design services or certifications by a design professional related to systems, materials or equipment are specifically required of the Contractor by the Contract Documents, the Owner and the Architect will specify all performance and design criteria that such services must satisfy. The Contractor shall cause such services or certifications to be provided by a properly licensed design professional, whose signature and seal shall appear on all drawings, calculations, specifications, certifications, Shop Drawings and other submittals prepared by such professional. Shop Drawings and other submittals related to the Work designed or certified by such professional, if prepared by others, shall bear such professional's written approval when submitted to the Architect. The Owner and the Architect shall be entitled to rely upon the adequacy, accuracy and completeness of the services, certifications or approvals performed by such design professionals, provided the Owner and Architect have specified to the Contractor all performance and design criteria that such services must satisfy. Pursuant to this Subparagraph 3.12.10, the Architect will review, approve or take other appropriate action on submittals only for the limited purpose of checking for conformance with information given and the design concept expressed in the Contract Documents. The Contractor shall not be responsible for the adequacy of the performance or design criteria required by the Contract Documents.

© 1997 AIA®
AIA DOCUMENT A201-1997
GENERAL CONDITIONS
OF THE CONTRACT FOR
CONSTRUCTION

The American Institute
of Architects
1735 New York Avenue, N.W.
Washington, D.C. 20006-5292

16

3.13   USE OF SITE

3.13.1 The Contractor shall confine operations at the site to areas permitted by law, ordinances, permits and the Contract Documents and shall not unreasonably encumber the site with materials or equipment.

3.14   CUTTING AND PATCHING

3.14.1 The Contractor shall be responsible for cutting, fitting or patching required to complete the Work or to make its parts fit together properly.

3.14.2 The Contractor shall not damage or endanger a portion of the Work or fully or partially completed construction of the Owner or separate contractors by cutting, patching or otherwise altering such construction, or by excavation. The Contractor shall not cut or otherwise alter such construction by the Owner or a separate contractor except with written consent of the Owner and of such separate contractor; such consent shall not be unreasonably withheld. The Contractor shall not unreasonably withhold from the Owner or a separate contractor the Contractor's consent to cutting or otherwise altering the Work.

3.15   CLEANING UP

3.15.1 The Contractor shall keep the premises and surrounding area free from accumulation of waste materials or rubbish caused by operations under the Contract. At completion of the Work, the Contractor shall remove from and about the Project waste materials, rubbish, the Contractor's tools, construction equipment, machinery and surplus materials.

3.15.2 If the Contractor fails to clean up as provided in the Contract Documents, the Owner may do so and the cost thereof shall be charged to the Contractor.

3.16   ACCESS TO WORK

3.16.1 The Contractor shall provide the Owner and Architect access to the Work in preparation and progress wherever located.

3.17   ROYALTIES, PATENTS AND COPYRIGHTS

3.17.1 The Contractor shall pay all royalties and license fees. The Contractor shall defend suits or claims for infringement of copyrights and patent rights and shall hold the Owner and Architect harmless from loss on account thereof, but shall not be responsible for such defense or loss when a particular design, process or product of a particular manufacturer or manufacturers is required by the Contract Documents or where the copyright violations are contained in Drawings, Specifications or other documents prepared by the Owner or Architect. However, if the Contractor has reason to believe that the required design, process or product is an infringement of a copyright or a patent, the Contractor shall be responsible for such loss unless such information is promptly furnished to the Architect.

3.18   INDEMNIFICATION

3.18.1 To the fullest extent permitted by law and to the extent claims, damages, losses or expenses are not covered by Project Management Protective Liability insurance purchased by the Contractor in accordance with Paragraph 11.3, the Contractor shall indemnify and hold harmless the Owner, Architect, Architect's consultants, and agents and employees of any of them from and against claims, damages, losses and expenses, including but not limited to attorneys' fees, arising out of or resulting from performance of the Work, provided that such claim, damage, loss or expense is attributable to bodily injury, sickness, disease or death, or to injury to or destruction of tangible property (other than the Work itself), but only to the extent caused by the negligent acts or omissions of the Contractor, a Subcontractor, anyone directly or indirectly employed by them or anyone for whose acts they may be liable, regardless of whether or not such claim, damage, loss or expense is caused in part by a party indemnified hereunder. Such obligation shall not be

© 1997   A I A ®
AIA DOCUMENT A201-1997
GENERAL CONDITIONS
OF THE CONTRACT FOR
CONSTRUCTION

The American Institute
of Architects
1735 New York Avenue, N.W.
Washington, D.C. 20006-5292

17

construed to negate, abridge, or reduce other rights or obligations of indemnity which would otherwise exist as to a party or person described in this Paragraph 3.18.

3.18.2 In claims against any person or entity indemnified under this Paragraph 3.18 by an employee of the Contractor, a Subcontractor, anyone directly or indirectly employed by them or anyone for whose acts they may be liable, the indemnification obligation under Subparagraph 3.18.1 shall not be limited by a limitation on amount or type of damages, compensation or benefits payable by or for the Contractor or a Subcontractor under workers' compensation acts, disability benefit acts or other employee benefit acts.

ARTICLE 4 ADMINISTRATION OF THE CONTRACT

4.1 ARCHITECT

4.1.1   The Architect is the person lawfully licensed to practice architecture or an entity lawfully practicing architecture identified as such in the Agreement and is referred to throughout the Contract Documents as if singular in number. The term "Architect" means the Architect or the Architect's authorized representative.

4.1.2   Duties, responsibilities and limitations of authority of the Architect as set forth in the Contract Documents shall not be restricted, modified or extended without written consent of the Owner, Contractor and Architect. Consent shall not be unreasonably withheld.

4.1.3   If the employment of the Architect is terminated, the Owner shall employ a new Architect against whom the Contractor has no reasonable objection and whose status under the Contract Documents shall be that of the former Architect.

4.2 ARCHITECT'S ADMINISTRATION OF THE CONTRACT

4.2.1   The Architect will provide administration of the Contract as described in the Contract Documents, and will be an Owner's representative (1) during construction, (2) until final payment is due and (3) with the Owner's concurrence, from time to time during the one-year period for correction of Work described in Paragraph 12.2. The Architect will have authority to act on behalf of the Owner only to the extent provided in the Contract Documents, unless otherwise modified in writing in accordance with other provisions of the Contract.

4.2.2   The Architect, as a representative of the Owner, will visit the site at intervals appropriate to the stage of the Contractor's operations (1) to become generally familiar with and to keep the Owner informed about the progress and quality of the portion of the Work completed, (2) to endeavor to guard the Owner against defects and deficiencies in the Work, and (3) to determine in general if the Work is being performed in a manner indicating that the Work, when fully completed, will be in accordance with the Contract Documents. However, the Architect will not be required to make exhaustive or continuous on-site inspections to check the quality or quantity of the Work. The Architect will neither have control over or charge of, nor be responsible for, the construction means, methods, techniques, sequences or procedures, or for the safety precautions and programs in connection with the Work, since these are solely the Contractor's rights and responsibilities under the Contract Documents, except as provided in Subparagraph 3.3.1.

4.2.3   The Architect will not be responsible for the Contractor's failure to perform the Work in accordance with the requirements of the Contract Documents. The Architect will not have control over or charge of and will not be responsible for acts or omissions of the Contractor, Subcontractors, or their agents or employees, or any other persons or entities performing portions of the Work.

© 1997 A I A ®
AIA DOCUMENT A201-1997
GENERAL CONDITIONS
OF THE CONTRACT FOR
CONSTRUCTION

The American Institute
of Architects
1735 New York Avenue, N.W.
Washington, D.C. 20006-5292

18

4.2.4 Communications Facilitating Contract Administration. Except as otherwise provided in the Contract Documents or when direct communications have been specially authorized, the Owner and Contractor shall endeavor to communicate with each other through the Architect about matters arising out of or relating to the Contract. Communications by and with the Architect's consultants shall be through the Architect. Communications by and with Subcontractors and material suppliers shall be through the Contractor. Communications by and with separate contractors shall be through the Owner.

4.2.5 Based on the Architect's evaluations of the Contractor's Applications for Payment, the Architect will review and certify the amounts due the Contractor and will issue Certificates for Payment in such amounts.

4.2.6 The Architect will have authority to reject Work that does not conform to the Contract Documents. Whenever the Architect considers it necessary or advisable, the Architect will have authority to require inspection or testing of the Work in accordance with Subparagraphs 13.5.2 and 13.5.3, whether or not such Work is fabricated, installed or completed. However, neither this authority of the Architect nor a decision made in good faith either to exercise or not to exercise such authority shall give rise to a duty or responsibility of the Architect to the Contractor, Subcontractors, material and equipment suppliers, their agents or employees, or other persons or entities performing portions of the Work.

4.2.7 The Architect will review and approve or take other appropriate action upon the Contractor's submittals such as Shop Drawings, Product Data and Samples, but only for the limited purpose of checking for conformance with information given and the design concept expressed in the Contract Documents. The Architect's action will be taken with such reasonable promptness as to cause no delay in the Work or in the activities of the Owner, Contractor or separate contractors, while allowing sufficient time in the Architect's professional judgment to permit adequate review. Review of such submittals is not conducted for the purpose of determining the accuracy and completeness of other details such as dimensions and quantities, or for substantiating instructions for installation or performance of equipment or systems, all of which remain the responsibility of the Contractor as required by the Contract Documents. The Architect's review of the Contractor's submittals shall not relieve the Contractor of the obligations under Paragraphs 3.3, 3.5 and 3.12. The Architect's review shall not constitute approval of safety precautions or, unless otherwise specifically stated by the Architect, of any construction means, methods, techniques, sequences or procedures. The Architect's approval of a specific item shall not indicate approval of an assembly of which the item is a component.

4.2.8 The Architect will prepare Change Orders and Construction Change Directives, and may authorize minor changes in the Work as provided in Paragraph 7.4.

4.2.9 The Architect will conduct inspections to determine the date or dates of Substantial Completion and the date of final completion, will receive and forward to the Owner, for the Owner's review and records, written warranties and related documents required by the Contract and assembled by the Contractor, and will issue a final Certificate for Payment upon compliance with the requirements of the Contract Documents.

4.2.10 If the Owner and Architect agree, the Architect will provide one or more project representatives to assist in carrying out the Architect's responsibilities at the site. The duties, responsibilities and limitations of authority of such project representatives shall be as set forth in an exhibit to be incorporated in the Contract Documents.

4.2.11 The Architect will interpret and decide matters concerning performance under, and requirements of, the Contract Documents on written request of either the Owner or Contractor.

© 1997 AIA®
AIA DOCUMENT A201-1997
GENERAL CONDITIONS
OF THE CONTRACT FOR
CONSTRUCTION

The American Institute
of Architects
1735 New York Avenue, N.W.
Washington, D.C. 20006-5292

19

The Architect's response to such requests will be made in writing within any time limits agreed upon or otherwise with reasonable promptness. If no agreement is made concerning the time within which interpretations required of the Architect shall be furnished in compliance with this Paragraph 4.2, then delay shall not be recognized on account of failure by the Architect to furnish such interpretations until 15 days after written request is made for them.

4.2.12 Interpretations and decisions of the Architect will be consistent with the intent of and reasonably inferable from the Contract Documents and will be in writing or in the form of drawings. When making such interpretations and initial decisions, the Architect will endeavor to secure faithful performance by both Owner and Contractor, will not show partiality to either and will not be liable for results of interpretations or decisions so rendered in good faith.

4.2.13 The Architect's decisions on matters relating to aesthetic effect will be final if consistent with the intent expressed in the Contract Documents.

4.3   CLAIMS AND DISPUTES

4.3.1   Definition. A Claim is a demand or assertion by one of the parties seeking, as a matter of right, adjustment or interpretation of Contract terms, payment of money, extension of time or other relief with respect to the terms of the Contract. The term "Claim" also includes other disputes and matters in question between the Owner and Contractor arising out of or relating to the Contract. Claims must be initiated by written notice. The responsibility to substantiate Claims shall rest with the party making the Claim.

4.3.2   Time Limits on Claims. Claims by either party must be initiated within 21 days after occurrence of the event giving rise to such Claim or within 21 days after the claimant first recognizes the condition giving rise to the Claim, whichever is later. Claims must be initiated by written notice to the Architect and the other party.

4.3.3   Continuing Contract Performance. Pending final resolution of a Claim except as otherwise agreed in writing or as provided in Subparagraph 9.7.1 and Article 14, the Contractor shall proceed diligently with performance of the Contract and the Owner shall continue to make payments in accordance with the Contract Documents.

4.3.4   Claims for Concealed or Unknown Conditions. If conditions are encountered at the site which are (1) subsurface or otherwise concealed physical conditions which differ materially from those indicated in the Contract Documents or (2) unknown physical conditions of an unusual nature, which differ materially from those ordinarily found to exist and generally recognized as inherent in construction activities of the character provided for in the Contract Documents, then notice by the observing party shall be given to the other party promptly before conditions are disturbed and in no event later than 21 days after first observance of the conditions. The Architect will promptly investigate such conditions and, if they differ materially and cause an increase or decrease in the Contractor's cost of, or time required for, performance of any part of the Work, will recommend an equitable adjustment in the Contract Sum or Contract Time, or both. If the Architect determines that the conditions at the site are not materially different from those indicated in the Contract Documents and that no change in the terms of the Contract is justified, the Architect shall so notify the Owner and Contractor in writing, stating the reasons. Claims by either party in opposition to such determination must be made within 21 days after the Architect has given notice of the decision. If the conditions encountered are materially different, the Contract Sum and Contract Time shall be equitably adjusted, but if the Owner and Contractor cannot agree on an adjustment in the Contract Sum or Contract Time, the adjustment shall be referred to the Architect for initial determination, subject to further proceedings pursuant to Paragraph 4.4.

20

314

4.3.5   Claims for Additional Cost. If the Contractor wishes to make Claim for an increase in the Contract Sum, written notice as provided herein shall be given before proceeding to execute the Work. Prior notice is not required for Claims relating to an emergency endangering life or property arising under Paragraph 10.6.

4.3.6 If the Contractor believes additional cost is involved for reasons including but not limited to (1) a written interpretation from the Architect, (2) an order by the Owner to stop the Work where the Contractor was not at fault, (3) a written order for a minor change in the Work issued by the Architect, (4) failure of payment by the Owner, (5) termination of the Contract by the Owner, (6) Owner's suspension or (7) other reasonable grounds, Claim shall be filed in accordance with this Paragraph 4.3.

4.3.7   CLAIMS FOR ADDITIONAL TIME
4.3.7.1 If the Contractor wishes to make Claim for an increase in the Contract Time, written notice as provided herein shall be given. The Contractor's Claim shall include an estimate of cost and of probable effect of delay on progress of the Work. In the case of a continuing delay only one Claim is necessary.

4.3.7.2 If adverse weather conditions are the basis for a Claim for additional time, such Claim shall be documented by data substantiating that weather conditions were abnormal for the period of time, could not have been reasonably anticipated and had an adverse effect on the scheduled construction.

4.3.8   Injury or Damage to Person or Property. If either party to the Contract suffers injury or damage to person or property because of an act or omission of the other party, or of others for whose acts such party is legally responsible, written notice of such injury or damage, whether or not insured, shall be given to the other party within a reasonable time not exceeding 21 days after discovery. The notice shall provide sufficient detail to enable the other party to investigate the matter.

4.3.9 If unit prices are stated in the Contract Documents or subsequently agreed upon, and if quantities originally contemplated are materially changed in a proposed Change Order or Construction Change Directive so that application of such unit prices to quantities of Work proposed will cause substantial inequity to the Owner or Contractor, the applicable unit prices shall be equitably adjusted.

4.3.10   Claims for Consequential Damages. The Contractor and Owner waive Claims against each other for consequential damages arising out of or relating to this Contract. This mutual waiver includes:

.1 damages incurred by the Owner for rental expenses, for losses of use, income, profit, financing, business and reputation, and for loss of management or employee productivity or of the services of such persons; and

.2 damages incurred by the Contractor for principal office expenses including the compensation of personnel stationed there, for losses of financing, business and reputation, and for loss of profit except anticipated profit arising directly from the Work.

This mutual waiver is applicable, without limitation, to all consequential damages due to either party's termination in accordance with Article 14. Nothing contained in this Subparagraph 4.3.10 shall be deemed to preclude an award of liquidated direct damages, when applicable, in accordance with the requirements of the Contract Documents.

4.4   RESOLUTION OF CLAIMS AND DISPUTES
4.4.1   Decision of Architect. Claims, including those alleging an error or omission by the Architect but excluding those arising under Paragraphs 10.3 through 10.5, shall be referred initially to the Architect for decision. An initial decision by the Architect shall be required as a

©1997 AIA®
AIA DOCUMENT A201-1997
GENERAL CONDITIONS
OF THE CONTRACT FOR
CONSTRUCTION

The American Institute
of Architects
1735 New York Avenue, N.W.
Washington, D.C. 20006-5292

21

condition precedent to mediation, arbitration or litigation of all Claims between the Contractor and Owner arising prior to the date final payment is due, unless 30 days have passed after the Claim has been referred to the Architect with no decision having been rendered by the Architect. The Architect will not decide disputes between the Contractor and persons or entities other than the Owner.

4.4.2 The Architect will review Claims and within ten days of the receipt of the Claim take one or more of the following actions: (1) request additional supporting data from the claimant or a response with supporting data from the other party, (2) reject the Claim in whole or in part, (3) approve the Claim, (4) suggest a compromise, or (5) advise the parties that the Architect is unable to resolve the Claim if the Architect lacks sufficient information to evaluate the merits of the Claim or if the Architect concludes that, in the Architect's sole discretion, it would be inappropriate for the Architect to resolve the Claim.

4.4.3 In evaluating Claims, the Architect may, but shall not be obligated to, consult with or seek information from either party or from persons with special knowledge or expertise who may assist the Architect in rendering a decision. The Architect may request the Owner to authorize retention of such persons at the Owner's expense.

4.4.4 If the Architect requests a party to provide a response to a Claim or to furnish additional supporting data, such party shall respond, within ten days after receipt of such request, and shall either provide a response on the requested supporting data, advise the Architect when the response or supporting data will be furnished or advise the Architect that no supporting data will be furnished. Upon receipt of the response or supporting data, if any, the Architect will either reject or approve the Claim in whole or in part.

4.4.5 The Architect will approve or reject Claims by written decision, which shall state the reasons therefor and which shall notify the parties of any change in the Contract Sum or Contract Time or both. The approval or rejection of a Claim by the Architect shall be final and binding on the parties but subject to mediation and arbitration.

4.4.6 When a written decision of the Architect states that (1) the decision is final but subject to mediation and arbitration and (2) a demand for arbitration of a Claim covered by such decision must be made within 30 days after the date on which the party making the demand receives the final written decision, then failure to demand arbitration within said 30 days' period shall result in the Architect's decision becoming final and binding upon the Owner and Contractor. If the Architect renders a decision after arbitration proceedings have been initiated, such decision may be entered as evidence, but shall not supersede arbitration proceedings unless the decision is acceptable to all parties concerned.

4.4.7 Upon receipt of a Claim against the Contractor or at any time thereafter, the Architect or the Owner may, but is not obligated to, notify the surety, if any, of the nature and amount of the Claim. If the Claim relates to a possibility of a Contractor's default, the Architect or the Owner may, but is not obligated to, notify the surety and request the surety's assistance in resolving the controversy.

4.4.8 If a Claim relates to or is the subject of a mechanic's lien, the party asserting such Claim may proceed in accordance with applicable law to comply with the lien notice or filing deadlines prior to resolution of the Claim by the Architect, by mediation or by arbitration.

4.5   MEDIATION

4.5.1 Any Claim arising out of or related to the Contract, except Claims relating to aesthetic effect and except those waived as provided for in Subparagraphs 4.3.10, 9.10.4 and 9.10.5 shall, after initial decision by the Architect or 30 days after submission of the Claim to the Architect, be

©1997 AIA®
AIA DOCUMENT A201-1997
GENERAL CONDITIONS
OF THE CONTRACT FOR
CONSTRUCTION

The American Institute
of Architects
1735 New York Avenue, N.W.
Washington, D.C. 20006-5292

22

subject to mediation as a condition precedent to arbitration or the institution of legal or equitable proceedings by either party.

4.5.2 The parties shall endeavor to resolve their Claims by mediation which, unless the parties mutually agree otherwise, shall be in accordance with the Construction Industry Mediation Rules of the American Arbitration Association currently in effect. Request for mediation shall be filed in writing with the other party to the Contract and with the American Arbitration Association. The request may be made concurrently with the filing of a demand for arbitration but, in such event, mediation shall proceed in advance of arbitration or legal or equitable proceedings, which shall be stayed pending mediation for a period of 60 days from the date of filing, unless stayed for a longer period by agreement of the parties or court order.

4.5.3 The parties shall share the mediator's fee and any filing fees equally. The mediation shall be held in the place where the Project is located, unless another location is mutually agreed upon. Agreements reached in mediation shall be enforceable as settlement agreements in any court having jurisdiction thereof.

4.6 ARBITRATION

4.6.1 Any Claim arising out of or related to the Contract, except Claims relating to aesthetic effect and except those waived as provided for in Subparagraphs 4.3.10, 9.10.4 and 9.10.5, shall, after decision by the Architect or 30 days after submission of the Claim to the Architect, be subject to arbitration. Prior to arbitration, the parties shall endeavor to resolve disputes by mediation in accordance with the provisions of Paragraph 4.5.

4.6.2 Claims not resolved by mediation shall be decided by arbitration which, unless the parties mutually agree otherwise, shall be in accordance with the Construction Industry Arbitration Rules of the American Arbitration Association currently in effect. The demand for arbitration shall be filed in writing with the other party to the Contract and with the American Arbitration Association, and a copy shall be filed with the Architect.

4.6.3 A demand for arbitration shall be made within the time limits specified in Subparagraphs 4.4.6 and 4.6.1 as applicable, and in other cases within a reasonable time after the Claim has arisen, and in no event shall it be made after the date when institution of legal or equitable proceedings based on such Claim would be barred by the applicable statute of limitations as determined pursuant to Paragraph 13.7.

4.6.4 Limitation on Consolidation or Joinder. No arbitration arising out of or relating to the Contract shall include, by consolidation or joinder or in any other manner, the Architect, the Architect's employees or consultants, except by written consent containing specific reference to the Agreement and signed by the Architect, Owner, Contractor and any other person or entity sought to be joined. No arbitration shall include, by consolidation or joinder or in any other manner, parties other than the Owner, Contractor, a separate contractor as described in Article 6 and other persons substantially involved in a common question of fact or law whose presence is required if complete relief is to be accorded in arbitration. No person or entity other than the Owner, Contractor or a separate contractor as described in Article 6 shall be included as an original third party or additional third party to an arbitration whose interest or responsibility is insubstantial. Consent to arbitration involving an additional person or entity shall not constitute consent to arbitration of a Claim not described therein or with a person or entity not named or described therein. The foregoing agreement to arbitrate and other agreements to arbitrate with an additional person or entity duly consented to by parties to the Agreement shall be specifically enforceable under applicable law in any court having jurisdiction thereof.

23

4.6.5 Claims and Timely Assertion of Claims. The party filing a notice of demand for arbitration must assert in the demand all Claims then known to that party on which arbitration is permitted to be demanded.

4.6.6 judgment on Final Award. The award rendered by the arbitrator or arbitrators shall be final, and judgment may be entered upon it in accordance with applicable law in any court having jurisdiction thereof.

ARTICLE 5 SUBCONTRACTORS

5.1 DEFINITIONS

5.1.1 A Subcontractor is a person or entity who has a direct contract with the Contractor to perform a portion of the Work at the site. The term "Subcontractor" is referred to throughout the Contract Documents as if singular in number and means a Subcontractor or an authorized representative of the Subcontractor. The term "Subcontractor" does not include a separate contractor or subcontractors of a separate contractor.

5.1.2 A Sub-subcontractor is a person or entity who has a direct or indirect contract with a Subcontractor to perform a portion of the Work at the site. The term "Sub-subcontractor" is referred to throughout the Contract Documents as if singular in number and means a Sub-subcontractor or an authorized representative of the Sub-subcontractor.

5.2 AWARD OF SUBCONTRACTS AND OTHER CONTRACTS FOR PORTIONS OF THE WORK

5.2.1 Unless otherwise stated in the Contract Documents or the bidding requirements, the Contractor, as soon as practicable after award of the Contract, shall furnish in writing to the Owner through the Architect the names of persons or entities (including those who are to furnish materials or equipment fabricated to a special design) proposed for each principal portion of the Work. The Architect will promptly reply to the Contractor in writing stating whether or not the Owner or the Architect, after due investigation, has reasonable objection to any such proposed person or entity. Failure of the Owner or Architect to reply promptly shall constitute notice of no reasonable objection.

5.2.2 The Contractor shall not contract with a proposed person or entity to whom the Owner or Architect has made reasonable and timely objection. The Contractor shall not be required to contract with anyone to whom the Contractor has made reasonable objection.

5.2.3 If the Owner or Architect has reasonable objection to a person or entity proposed by the Contractor, the Contractor shall propose another to whom the Owner or Architect has no reasonable objection. If the proposed but rejected Subcontractor was reasonably capable of performing the Work, the Contract Sum and Contract Time shall be increased or decreased by the difference, if any, occasioned by such change, and an appropriate Change Order shall be issued before commencement of the substitute Subcontractor's Work. However, no increase in the Contract Sum or Contract Time shall be allowed for such change unless the Contractor has acted promptly and responsively in submitting names as required.

5.2.4 The Contractor shall not change a Subcontractor, person or entity previously selected if the Owner or Architect makes reasonable objection to such substitute.

5.3 SUBCONTRACTUAL RELATIONS

5.3.1 By appropriate agreement, written where legally required for validity, the Contractor shall require each Subcontractor, to the extent of the Work to be performed by the Subcontractor, to be bound to the Contractor by terms of the Contract Documents, and to assume toward the Contractor all the obligations and responsibilities, including the responsibility for safety of the

24

Subcontractor's Work, which the Contractor, by these Documents, assumes toward the Owner and Architect. Each subcontract agreement shall preserve and protect the rights of the Owner and Architect under the Contract Documents with respect to the Work to be performed by the Subcontractor so that subcontracting thereof will not prejudice such rights, and shall allow to the Subcontractor, unless specifically provided otherwise in the subcontract agreement, the benefit of all rights, remedies and redress against the Contractor that the Contractor, by the Contract Documents, has against the Owner. Where appropriate, the Contractor shall require each Subcontractor to enter into similar agreements with Sub-subcontractors. The Contractor shall make available to each proposed Subcontractor, prior to the execution of the subcontract agreement, copies of the Contract Documents to which the Subcontractor will be bound, and, upon written request of the Subcontractor, identify to the Subcontractor terms and conditions of the proposed subcontract agreement which may be at variance with the Contract Documents. Subcontractors will similarly make copies of applicable portions of such documents available to their respective proposed Sub-subcontractors.

5.4   CONTINGENT ASSIGNMENT OF SUBCONTRACTS

5.4.1   Each subcontract agreement for a portion of the Work is assigned by the Contractor to the Owner provided that:

   .1   assignment is effective only after termination of the Contract by the Owner for cause pursuant to Paragraph 14.2 and only for those subcontract agreements which the Owner accepts by notifying the Subcontractor and Contractor in writing; and

   .2   assignment is subject to the prior rights of the surety, if any, obligated under bond relating to the Contract.

5.4.2   Upon such assignment, if the Work has been suspended for more than 30 days, the Subcontractor's compensation shall be equitably adjusted for increases in cost resulting from the suspension.

ARTICLE 6   CONSTRUCTION BY OWNER OR BY SEPARATE CONTRACTORS

6.1   OWNER'S RIGHT TO PERFORM CONSTRUCTION AND TO AWARD SEPARATE CONTRACTS

6.1.1   The Owner reserves the right to perform construction or operations related to the Project with the Owner's own forces, and to award separate contracts in connection with other portions of the Project or other construction or operations on the site under Conditions of the Contract identical or substantially similar to these including those portions related to insurance and waiver of subrogation. If the Contractor claims that delay or additional cost is involved because of such action by the Owner, the Contractor shall make such Claim as provided in Paragraph 4.3.

6.1.2   When separate contracts are awarded for different portions of the Project or other construction or operations on the site, the term "Contractor" in the Contract Documents in each case shall mean the Contractor who executes each separate Owner-Contractor Agreement.

6.1.3   The Owner shall provide for coordination of the activities of the Owner's own forces and of each separate contractor with the Work of the Contractor, who shall cooperate with them. The Contractor shall participate with other separate contractors and the Owner in reviewing their construction schedules when directed to do so. The Contractor shall make any revisions to the construction schedule deemed necessary after a joint review and mutual agreement. The construction schedules shall then constitute the schedules to be used by the Contractor, separate contractors and the Owner until subsequently revised.

6.1.4   Unless otherwise provided in the Contract Documents, when the Owner performs construction or operations related to the Project with the Owner's own forces, the Owner shall be deemed to be subject to the same obligations and to have the same rights which apply to the

© 1997 A I A ®
AIA DOCUMENT A201-1997
GENERAL CONDITIONS
OF THE CONTRACT FOR
CONSTRUCTION

The American Institute
of Architects
1735 New York Avenue, N.W.
Washington, D.C. 20006-5292

25

WARNING: Unlicensed photocopying violates U.S. copyright laws and will subject the violator to legal prosecution.

Contractor under the Conditions of the Contract, including, without excluding others, those stated in Article 3, this Article 6 and Articles 10, 11 and 12.

6.2 MUTUAL RESPONSIBILITY

6.2.1 The Contractor shall afford the Owner and separate contractors reasonable opportunity for introduction and storage of their materials and equipment and performance of their activities, and shall connect and coordinate the Contractor's construction and operations with theirs as required by the Contract Documents.

6.2.2 If part of the Contractor's Work depends for proper execution or results upon construction or operations by the Owner or a separate contractor, the Contractor shall, prior to proceeding with that portion of the Work, promptly report to the Architect apparent discrepancies or defects in such other construction that would render it unsuitable for such proper execution and results. Failure of the Contractor so to report shall constitute an acknowledgment that the Owner's or separate contractor's completed or partially completed construction is fit and proper to receive the Contractor's Work, except as to defects not then reasonably discoverable.

6.2.3 The Owner shall be reimbursed by the Contractor for costs incurred by the Owner which are payable to a separate contractor because of delays, improperly timed activities or defective construction of the Contractor. The Owner shall be responsible to the Contractor for costs incurred by the Contractor because of delays, improperly timed activities, damage to the Work or defective construction of a separate contractor.

6.2.4 The Contractor shall promptly remedy damage wrongfully caused by the Contractor to completed or partially completed construction or to property of the Owner or separate contractors as provided in Subparagraph 10.2.5.

6.2.5 The Owner and each separate contractor shall have the same responsibilities for cutting and patching as are described for the Contractor in Subparagraph 3.14.

6.3 OWNER'S RIGHT TO CLEAN UP

6.3.1 If a dispute arises among the Contractor, separate contractors and the Owner as to the responsibility under their respective contracts for maintaining the premises and surrounding area free from waste materials and rubbish, the Owner may clean up and the Architect will allocate the cost among those responsible.

ARTICLE 7 CHANGES IN THE WORK

7.1 GENERAL

7.1.1 Changes in the Work may be accomplished after execution of the Contract, and without invalidating the Contract, by Change Order, Construction Change Directive or order for a minor change in the Work, subject to the limitations stated in this Article 7 and elsewhere in the Contract Documents.

7.1.2 A Change Order shall be based upon agreement among the Owner, Contractor and Architect; a Construction Change Directive requires agreement by the Owner and Architect and may or may not be agreed to by the Contractor; an order for a minor change in the Work may be issued by the Architect alone.

7.1.3 Changes in the Work shall be performed under applicable provisions of the Contract Documents, and the Contractor shall proceed promptly, unless otherwise provided in the Change Order, Construction Change Directive or order for a minor change in the Work.

© 1997 AIA®
AIA DOCUMENT A201-1997
GENERAL CONDITIONS
OF THE CONTRACT FOR
CONSTRUCTION

The American Institute
of Architects
1735 New York Avenue, N.W.
Washington, D.C. 20006-5292

26

7.2 CHANGE ORDERS

7.2.1 A Change Order is a written instrument prepared by the Architect and signed by the Owner, Contractor and Architect, stating their agreement upon all of the following:

    .1 change in the Work;

    .2 the amount of the adjustment, if any, in the Contract Sum; and

    .3 the extent of the adjustment, if any, in the Contract Time.

7.2.2 Methods used in determining adjustments to the Contract Sum may include those listed in Subparagraph 7.3.3.

7.3 CONSTRUCTION CHANGE DIRECTIVES

7.3.1 A Construction Change Directive is a written order prepared by the Architect and signed by the Owner and Architect, directing a change in the Work prior to agreement on adjustment, if any, in the Contract Sum or Contract Time, or both. The Owner may by Construction Change Directive, without invalidating the Contract, order changes in the Work within the general scope of the Contract consisting of additions, deletions or other revisions, the Contract Sum and Contract Time being adjusted accordingly.

7.3.2 A Construction Change Directive shall be used in the absence of total agreement on the terms of a Change Order.

7.3.3 If the Construction Change Directive provides for an adjustment to the Contract Sum, the adjustment shall be based on one of the following methods:

    .1 mutual acceptance of a lump sum properly itemized and supported by sufficient substantiating data to permit evaluation;

    .2 unit prices stated in the Contract Documents or subsequently agreed upon;

    .3 cost to be determined in a manner agreed upon by the parties and a mutually acceptable fixed or percentage fee; or

    .4 as provided in Subparagraph 7.3.6.

7.3.4 Upon receipt of a Construction Change Directive, the Contractor shall promptly proceed with the change in the Work involved and advise the Architect of the Contractor's agreement or disagreement with the method, if any, provided in the Construction Change Directive for determining the proposed adjustment in the Contract Sum or Contract Time.

7.3.5 A Construction Change Directive signed by the Contractor indicates the agreement of the Contractor therewith, including adjustment in Contract Sum and Contract Time or the method for determining them. Such agreement shall be effective immediately and shall be recorded as a Change Order.

7.3.6 If the Contractor does not respond promptly or disagrees with the method for adjustment in the Contract Sum, the method and the adjustment shall be determined by the Architect on the basis of reasonable expenditures and savings of those performing the Work attributable to the change, including, in case of an increase in the Contract Sum, a reasonable allowance for overhead and profit. In such case, and also under Clause 7.3.3.3, the Contractor shall keep and present, in such form as the Architect may prescribe, an itemized accounting together with appropriate supporting data. Unless otherwise provided in the Contract Documents, costs for the purposes of this Subparagraph 7.3.6 shall be limited to the following:

    .1 costs of labor, including social security, old age and unemployment insurance, fringe benefits required by agreement or custom, and workers' compensation insurance;

    .2 costs of materials, supplies and equipment, including cost of transportation, whether incorporated or consumed;

    .3 rental costs of machinery and equipment, exclusive of hand tools, whether rented from the Contractor or others;

.4   costs of premiums for all bonds and insurance, permit fees, and sales, use or similar taxes related to the Work; and

.5   additional costs of supervision and field office personnel directly attributable to the change.

7.3.7.   The amount of credit to be allowed by the Contractor to the Owner for a deletion or change which results in a net decrease in the Contract Sum shall be actual net cost as confirmed by the Architect. When both additions and credits covering related Work or substitutions are involved in a change, the allowance for overhead and profit shall be figured on the basis of net increase, if any, with respect to that change.

7.3.8   Pending final determination of the total cost of a Construction Change Directive to the Owner, amounts not in dispute for such changes in the Work shall be included in Applications for Payment accompanied by a Change Order indicating the parties' agreement with part or all of such costs. For any portion of such cost that remains in dispute, the Architect will make an interim determination for purposes of monthly certification for payment for those costs. That determination of cost shall adjust the Contract Sum on the same basis as a Change Order, subject to the right of either party to disagree and assert a claim in accordance with Article 4.

7.3.9   When the Owner and Contractor agree with the determination made by the Architect concerning the adjustments in the Contract Sum and Contract Time, or otherwise reach agreement upon the adjustments, such agreement shall be effective immediately and shall be recorded by preparation and execution of an appropriate Change Order.

7.4   MINOR CHANGES IN THE WORK
7.4.1   The Architect will have authority to order minor changes in the Work not involving adjustment in the Contract Sum or extension of the Contract Time and not inconsistent with the intent of the Contract Documents. Such changes shall be effected by written order and shall be binding on the Owner and Contractor. The Contractor shall carry out such written orders promptly.

ARTICLE 8   TIME
8.1   DEFINITIONS
8.1.1   Unless otherwise provided, Contract Time is the period of time, including authorized adjustments, allotted in the Contract Documents for Substantial Completion of the Work.

8.1.2   The date of commencement of the Work is the date established in the Agreement.

8.1.3   The date of Substantial Completion is the date certified by the Architect in accordance with Paragraph 9.8.

8.1.4   The term "day" as used in the Contract Documents shall mean calendar day unless otherwise specifically defined.

8.2   PROGRESS AND COMPLETION
8.2.1   Time limits stated in the Contract Documents are of the essence of the Contract. By executing the Agreement the Contractor confirms that the Contract Time is a reasonable period for performing the Work.

8.2.2   The Contractor shall not knowingly, except by agreement or instruction of the Owner in writing, prematurely commence operations on the site or elsewhere prior to the effective date of insurance required by Article 11 to be furnished by the Contractor and Owner. The date of commencement of the Work shall not be changed by the effective date of such insurance. Unless the date of commencement is established by the Contract Documents or a notice to proceed given

© 1997   AIA®
AIA DOCUMENT A201-1997
GENERAL CONDITIONS
OF THE CONTRACT FOR
CONSTRUCTION

The American Institute
of Architects
1735 New York Avenue, N.W.
Washington, D.C. 20006-5292

28

by the Owner, the Contractor shall notify the Owner in writing not less than five days or other agreed period before commencing the Work to permit the timely filing of morgages, mechanic's liens and other security interests.

8.2.3 The Contractor shall proceed expeditiously with adequate forces and shall achieve Substantial Completion within the Contract Time.

8.3   DELAYS AND EXTENSIONS OF TIME
8.3.1 If the Contractor is delayed at any time in the commencement or progress of the Work by an act or neglect of the Owner or Architect, or of an employee of either, or of a separate contractor employed by the Owner, or by changes ordered in the Work, or by labor disputes, fire, unusual delay in deliveries, unavoidable casualties or other causes beyond the Contractor's control, or by delay authorized by the Owner pending mediation and arbitration, or by other causes which the Architect determines may justify delay, then the Contract Time shall be extended by Change Order for such reasonable time as the Architect may determine.

8.3.2 Claims relating to time shall be made in accordance with applicable provisions of Paragraph 4.3.

8.3.3 This Paragraph 8.3 does not preclude recovery of damages for delay by either party under other provisions of the Contract Documents.

ARTICLE 9   PAYMENTS AND COMPLETION
9.1   CONTRACT SUM
9.1.1 The Contract Sum is stated in the Agreement and, including authorized adjustments, is the total amount payable by the Owner to the Contractor for performance of the Work under the Contract Documents.

9.2   SCHEDULE OF VALUES
9.2.1 Before the first Application for Payment, the Contractor shall submit to the Architect a schedule of values allocated to various portions of the Work, prepared in such form and supported by such data to substantiate its accuracy as the Architect may require. This schedule, unless objected to by the Architect, shall be used as a basis for reviewing the Contractor's Applications for Payment.

9.3   APPLICATIONS FOR PAYMENT
9.3.1 At least ten days before the date established for each progress payment, the Contractor shall submit to the Architect an itemized Application for Payment for operations completed in accordance with the schedule of values. Such application shall be notarized, if required, and supported by such data substantiating the Contractor's right to payment as the Owner or Architect may require, such as copies of requisitions from Subcontractors and material suppliers, and reflecting retainage if provided for in the Contract Documents.

9.3.1.1 As provided in Subparagraph 7.3.8, such applications may include requests for payment on account of changes in the Work which have been properly authorized by Construction Change Directives, or by interim determinations of the Architect, but not yet included in Change Orders.

9.3.1.2 Such applications may not include requests for payment for portions of the Work for which the Contractor does not intend to pay to a Subcontractor or material supplier, unless such Work has been performed by others whom the Contractor intends to pay.

© 1997   A I A ®
AIA DOCUMENT A201-1997
GENERAL CONDITIONS
OF THE CONTRACT FOR
CONSTRUCTION

The American Institute
of Architects
1735 New York Avenue, N.W.
Washington, D.C. 20006-5292

29

9.3.2 Unless otherwise provided in the Contract Documents, payments shall be made on account of materials and equipment delivered and suitably stored at the site for subsequent incorporation in the Work. If approved in advance by the Owner, payment may similarly be made for materials and equipment suitably stored off the site at a location agreed upon in writing. Payment for materials and equipment stored on or off the site shall be conditioned upon compliance by the Contractor with procedures satisfactory to the Owner to establish the Owner's title to such materials and equipment or otherwise protect the Owner's interest, and shall include the costs of applicable insurance, storage and transportation to the site for such materials and equipment stored off the site.

9.3.3 The Contractor warrants that title to all Work covered by an Application for Payment will pass to the Owner no later than the time of payment. The Contractor further warrants that upon submittal of an Application for Payment all Work for which Certificates for Payment have been previously issued and payments received from the Owner shall, to the best of the Contractor's knowledge, information and belief, be free and clear of liens, claims, security interests or encumbrances in favor of the Contractor, Subcontractors, material suppliers, or other persons or entities making a claim by reason of having provided labor, materials and equipment relating to the Work.

9.4   CERTIFICATES FOR PAYMENT
9.4.1 The Architect will, within seven days after receipt of the Contractor's Application for Payment, either issue to the Owner a Certificate for Payment, with a copy to the Contractor, for such amount as the Architect determines is properly due, or notify the Contractor and Owner in writing of the Architect's reasons for withholding certification in whole or in part as provided in Subparagraph 9.5.1.

9.4.2 The issuance of a Certificate for Payment will constitute a representation by the Architect to the Owner, based on the Architect's evaluation of the Work and the data comprising the Application for Payment, that the Work has progressed to the point indicated and that, to the best of the Architect's knowledge, information and belief, the quality of the Work is in accordance with the Contract Documents. The foregoing representations are subject to an evaluation of the Work for conformance with the Contract Documents upon Substantial Completion, to results of subsequent tests and inspections, to correction of minor deviations from the Contract Documents prior to completion and to specific qualifications expressed by the Architect. The issuance of a Certificate for Payment will further constitute a representation that the Contractor is entitled to payment in the amount certified. However, the issuance of a Certificate for Payment will not be a representation that the Architect has (1) made exhaustive or continuous on-site inspections to check the quality or quantity of the Work, (2) reviewed construction means, methods, techniques, sequences or procedures, (3) reviewed copies of requisitions received from Subcontractors and material suppliers and other data requested by the Owner to substantiate the Contractor's right to payment, or (4) made examination to ascertain how or for what purpose the Contractor has used money previously paid on account of the Contract Sum.

9.5   DECISIONS TO WITHHOLD CERTIFICATION
9.5.1 The Architect may withhold a Certificate for Payment in whole or in part, to the extent reasonably necessary to protect the Owner, if in the Architect's opinion the representations to the Owner required by Subparagraph 9.4.2 cannot be made. If the Architect is unable to certify payment in the amount of the Application, the Architect will notify the Contractor and Owner as provided in Subparagraph 9.4.1. If the Contractor and Architect cannot agree on a revised amount, the Architect will promptly issue a Certificate for Payment for the amount for which the Architect is able to make such representations to the Owner. The Architect may also withhold a Certificate for Payment or, because of subsequently discovered evidence, may nullify the whole or a part of a Certificate for Payment previously issued, to such extent as may be necessary in the Architect's

30

opinion to protect the Owner from loss for which the Contractor is responsible, including loss resulting from acts and omissions described in Subparagraph 3.3.2, because of:

.1 defective Work not remedied;

.2 third party claims filed or reasonable evidence indicating probable filing of such claims unless security acceptable to the Owner is provided by the Contractor;

.3 failure of the Contractor to make payments properly to Subcontractors or for labor, materials or equipment;

.4 reasonable evidence that the Work cannot be completed for the unpaid balance of the Contract Sum;

.5 damage to the Owner or another contractor;

.6 reasonable evidence that the Work will not be completed within the Contract Time, and that the unpaid balance would not be adequate to cover actual or liquidated damages for the anticipated delay; or

.7 persistent failure to carry out the Work in accordance with the Contract Documents.

9.5.2 When the above reasons for withholding certification are removed, certification will be made for amounts previously withheld.

9.6   PROGRESS PAYMENTS

9.6.1   After the Architect has issued a Certificate for Payment, the Owner shall make payment in the manner and within the time provided in the Contract Documents, and shall so notify the Architect.

9.6.2   The Contractor shall promptly pay each Subcontractor, upon receipt of payment from the Owner, out of the amount paid to the Contractor on account of such Subcontractor's portion of the Work, the amount to which said Subcontractor is entitled, reflecting percentages actually retained from payments to the Contractor on account of such Subcontractor's portion of the Work. The Contractor shall, by appropriate agreement with each Subcontractor, require each Subcontractor to make payments to Sub-subcontractors in a similar manner.

9.6.3   The Architect will, on request, furnish to a Subcontractor, if practicable, information regarding percentages of completion or amounts applied for by the Contractor and action taken thereon by the Architect and Owner on account of portions of the Work done by such Subcontractor.

9.6.4   Neither the Owner nor Architect shall have an obligation to pay or to see to the payment of money to a Subcontractor except as may otherwise be required by law.

9.6.5   Payment to material suppliers shall be treated in a manner similar to that provided in Subparagraphs 9.6.2, 9.6.3 and 9.6.4.

9.6.6   A Certificate for Payment, a progress payment, or partial or entire use or occupancy of the Project by the Owner shall not constitute acceptance of Work not in accordance with the Contract Documents.

9.6.7   Unless the Contractor provides the Owner with a payment bond in the full penal sum of the Contract Sum, payments received by the Contractor for Work properly performed by Subcontractors and suppliers shall be held by the Contractor for those Subcontractors or suppliers who performed Work or furnished materials, or both, under contract with the Contractor for which payment was made by the Owner. Nothing contained herein shall require money to be placed in a separate account and not commingled with money of the Contractor, shall create any fiduciary liability or tort liability on the part of the Contractor for breach of trust or shall entitle any person or entity to an award of punitive damages against the Contractor for breach of the requirements of this provision.

© 1997   A I A ®
AIA DOCUMENT A201-1997
GENERAL CONDITIONS
OF THE CONTRACT FOR
CONSTRUCTION

The American Institute
of Architects
1735 New York Avenue, N.W.
Washington, D.C. 20006-5292

31

9.7 FAILURE OF PAYMENT

9.7.1 If the Architect does not issue a Certificate for Payment, through no fault of the Contractor, within seven days after receipt of the Contractor's Application for Payment, or if the Owner does not pay the Contractor within seven days after the date established in the Contract Documents the amount certified by the Architect or awarded by arbitration, then the Contractor may, upon seven additional days' written notice to the Owner and Architect, stop the Work until payment of the amount owing has been received. The Contract Time shall be extended appropriately and the Contract Sum shall be increased by the amount of the Contractor's reasonable costs of shut-down, delay and start-up, plus interest as provided for in the Contract Documents.

9.8 SUBSTANTIAL COMPLETION

9.8.1 Substantial Completion is the stage in the progress of the Work when the Work or designated portion thereof is sufficiently complete in accordance with the Contract Documents so that the Owner can occupy or utilize the Work for its intended use.

9.8.2 When the Contractor considers that the Work, or a portion thereof which the Owner agrees to accept separately, is substantially complete, the Contractor shall prepare and submit to the Architect a comprehensive list of items to be completed or corrected prior to final payment. Failure to include an item on such list does not alter the responsibility of the Contractor to complete all Work in accordance with the Contract Documents.

9.8.3 Upon receipt of the Contractor's list, the Architect will make an inspection to determine whether the Work or designated portion thereof is substantially complete. If the Architect's inspection discloses any item, whether or not included on the Contractor's list, which is not sufficiently complete in accordance with the Contract Documents so that the Owner can occupy or utilize the Work or designated portion thereof for its intended use, the Contractor shall, before issuance of the Certificate of Substantial Completion, complete or correct such item upon notification by the Architect. In such case, the Contractor shall then submit a request for another inspection by the Architect to determine Substantial Completion.

9.8.4 When the Work or designated portion thereof is substantially complete, the Architect will prepare a Certificate of Substantial Completion which shall establish the date of Substantial Completion, shall establish responsibilities of the Owner and Contractor for security, maintenance, heat, utilities, damage to the Work and insurance, and shall fix the time within which the Contractor shall finish all items on the list accompanying the Certificate. Warranties required by the Contract Documents shall commence on the date of Substantial Completion of the Work or designated portion thereof unless otherwise provided in the Certificate of Substantial Completion.

9.8.5 The Certificate of Substantial Completion shall be submitted to the Owner and Contractor for their written acceptance of responsibilities assigned to them in such Certificate. Upon such acceptance and consent of surety, if any, the Owner shall make payment of retainage applying to such Work or designated portion thereof. Such payment shall be adjusted for Work that is incomplete or not in accordance with the requirements of the Contract Documents.

9.9 PARTIAL OCCUPANCY OR USE

9.9.1 The Owner may occupy or use any completed or partially completed portion of the Work at any stage when such portion is designated by separate agreement with the Contractor, provided such occupancy or use is consented to by the insurer as required under Clause 11.4.1.5 and authorized by public authorities having jurisdiction over the Work. Such partial occupancy or use may commence whether or not the portion is substantially complete, provided the Owner and Contractor have accepted in writing the responsibilities assigned to each of them for payments, retainage, if any, security, maintenance, heat, utilities, damage to the Work and insurance, and

32

have agreed in writing concerning the period for correction of the Work and commencement of warranties required by the Contract Documents. When the Contractor considers a portion substantially complete, the Contractor shall prepare and submit a list to the Architect as provided under Subparagraph 9.8.2. Consent of the Contractor to partial occupancy or use shall not be unreasonably withheld. The stage of the progress of the Work shall be determined by written agreement between the Owner and Contractor or, if no agreement is reached, by decision of the Architect.

9.9.2 Immediately prior to such partial occupancy or use, the Owner, Contractor and Architect shall jointly inspect the area to be occupied or portion of the Work to be used in order to determine and record the condition of the Work.

9.9.3 Unless otherwise agreed upon, partial occupancy or use of a portion or portions of the Work shall not constitute acceptance of Work not complying with the requirements of the Contract Documents.

9.10 FINAL COMPLETION AND FINAL PAYMENT

9.10.1 Upon receipt of written notice that the Work is ready for final inspection and acceptance and upon receipt of a final Application for Payment, the Architect will promptly make such inspection and, when the Architect finds the Work acceptable under the Contract Documents and the Contract fully performed, the Architect will promptly issue a final Certificate for Payment stating that to the best of the Architect's knowledge, information and belief, and on the basis of the Architect's on-site visits and inspections, the Work has been completed in accordance with terms and conditions of the Contract Documents and that the entire balance found to be due the Contractor and noted in the final Certificate is due and payable. The Architect's final Certificate for Payment will constitute a further representation that conditions listed in Subparagraph 9.10.2 as precedent to the Contractor's being entitled to final payment have been fulfilled.

9.10.2 Neither final payment nor any remaining retained percentage shall become due until the Contractor submits to the Architect (1) an affidavit that payrolls, bills for materials and equipment, and other indebtedness connected with the Work for which the Owner or the Owner's property might be responsible or encumbered (less amounts withheld by Owner) have been paid or otherwise satisfied, (2) a certificate evidencing that insurance required by the Contract Documents to remain in force after final payment is currently in effect and will not be canceled or allowed to expire until at least 30 days' prior written notice has been given to the Owner, (3) a written statement that the Contractor knows of no substantial reason that the insurance will not be renewable to cover the period required by the Contract Documents, (4) consent of surety, if any, to final payment and (5), if required by the Owner, other data establishing payment or satisfaction of obligations, such as receipts, releases and waivers of liens, claims, security interests or encumbrances arising out of the Contract, to the extent and in such form as may be designated by the Owner. If a Subcontractor refuses to furnish a release or waiver required by the Owner, the Contractor may furnish a bond satisfactory to the Owner to indemnify the Owner against such lien. If such lien remains unsatisfied after payments are made, the Contractor shall refund to the Owner all money that the Owner may be compelled to pay in discharging such lien, including all costs and reasonable attorneys' fees.

9.10.3 If, after Substantial Completion of the Work, final completion thereof is materially delayed through no fault of the Contractor or by issuance of Change Orders affecting final completion, and the Architect so confirms, the Owner shall, upon application by the Contractor and certification by the Architect, and without terminating the Contract, make payment of the balance due for that portion of the Work fully completed and accepted. If the remaining balance for Work not fully completed or corrected is less than retainage stipulated in the Contract Documents, and if bonds have been furnished, the written consent of surety to payment of the balance due for that

© 1997 AIA®
AIA DOCUMENT A201-1997
GENERAL CONDITIONS
OF THE CONTRACT FOR
CONSTRUCTION

The American Institute
of Architects
1735 New York Avenue, N.W.
Washington, D.C. 20006-5292

33

portion of the Work fully completed and accepted shall be submitted by the Contractor to the Architect prior to certification of such payment. Such payment shall be made under terms and conditions governing final payment, except that it shall not constitute a waiver of claims.

9.10.4 The making of final payment shall constitute a waiver of Claims by the Owner except those arising from:

    .1 liens, Claims, security interests or encumbrances arising out of the Contract and unsettled;

    .2 failure of the Work to comply with the requirements of the Contract Documents; or

    .3 terms of special warranties required by the Contract Documents.

9.10.5 Acceptance of final payment by the Contractor, a Subcontractor or material supplier shall constitute a waiver of claims by that payee except those previously made in writing and identified by that payee as unsettled at the time of final Application for Payment.

ARTICLE 10 PROTECTION OF PERSONS AND PROPERTY

10.1 SAFETY PRECAUTIONS AND PROGRAMS

10.1.1 The Contractor shall be responsible for initiating, maintaining and supervising all safety precautions and programs in connection with the performance of the Contract.

10.2 SAFETY OF PERSONS AND PROPERTY

10.2.1 The Contractor shall take reasonable precautions for safety of, and shall provide reasonable protection to prevent damage, injury or loss to:

    .1 employees on the Work and other persons who may be affected thereby;

    .2 the Work and materials and equipment to be incorporated therein, whether in storage on or off the site, under care, custody or control of the Contractor or the Contractor's Subcontractors or Sub-subcontractors; and

    .3 other property at the site or adjacent thereto, such as trees, shrubs, lawns, walks, pavements, roadways, structures and utilities not designated for removal, relocation or replacement in the course of construction.

10.2.2 The Contractor shall give notices and comply with applicable laws, ordinances, rules, regulations and lawful orders of public authorities bearing on safety of persons or property or their protection from damage, injury or loss.

10.2.3 The Contractor shall erect and maintain, as required by existing conditions and performance of the Contract, reasonable safeguards for safety and protection, including posting danger signs and other warnings against hazards, promulgating safety regulations and notifying owners and users of adjacent sites and utilities.

10.2.4 When use or storage of explosives or other hazardous materials or equipment or unusual methods are necessary for execution of the Work, the Contractor shall exercise utmost care and carry on such activities under supervision of properly qualified personnel.

10.2.5 The Contractor shall promptly remedy damage and loss (other than damage or loss insured under property insurance required by the Contract Documents) to property referred to in Clauses 10.2.1.2 and 10.2.1.3 caused in whole or in part by the Contractor, a Subcontractor, a Sub-subcontractor, or anyone directly or indirectly employed by any of them, or by anyone for whose acts they may be liable and for which the Contractor is responsible under Clauses 10.2.1.2 and 10.2.1.3, except damage or loss attributable to acts or omissions of the Owner or Architect or anyone directly or indirectly employed by either of them, or by anyone for whose acts either of them may be liable, and not attributable to the fault or negligence of the Contractor. The foregoing obligations of the Contractor are in addition to the Contractor's obligations under Paragraph 3.18.

© 1997 AIA®
AIA DOCUMENT A201-1997
GENERAL CONDITIONS
OF THE CONTRACT FOR
CONSTRUCTION

The American Institute
of Architects
1735 New York Avenue, N.W.
Washington, D.C. 20006-5292

34

10.2.6 The Contractor shall designate a responsible member of the Contractor's organization at the site whose duty shall be the prevention of accidents. This person shall be the Contractor's superintendent unless otherwise designated by the Contractor in writing to the Owner and Architect.

10.2.7 The Contractor shall not load or permit any part of the construction or site to be loaded so as to endanger its safety.

10.3 HAZARDOUS MATERIALS

10.3.1 If reasonable precautions will be inadequate to prevent foreseeable bodily injury or death to persons resulting from a material or substance, including but not limited to asbestos or polychlorinated biphenyl (PCB), encountered on the site by the Contractor, the Contractor shall, upon recognizing the condition, immediately stop Work in the affected area and report the condition to the Owner and Architect in writing.

10.3.2 The Owner shall obtain the services of a licensed laboratory to verify the presence or absence of the material or substance reported by the Contractor and, in the event such material or substance is found to be present, to verify that it has been rendered harmless. Unless otherwise required by the Contract Documents, the Owner shall furnish in writing to the Contractor and Architect the names and qualifications of persons or entities who are to perform tests verifying the presence or absence of such material or substance or who are to perform the task of removal or safe containment of such material or substance. The Contractor and the Architect will promptly reply to the Owner in writing stating whether or not either has reasonable objection to the persons or entities proposed by the Owner. If either the Contractor or Architect has an objection to a person or entity proposed by the Owner, the Owner shall propose another to whom the Contractor and the Architect have no reasonable objection. When the material or substance has been rendered harmless, Work in the affected area shall resume upon written agreement of the Owner and Contractor. The Contract Time shall be extended appropriately and the Contract Sum shall be increased in the amount of the Contractor's reasonable additional costs of shut-down, delay and start-up, which adjustments shall be accomplished as provided in Article 7.

10.3.3 To the fullest extent permitted by law, the Owner shall indemnify and hold harmless the Contractor, Subcontractors, Architect, Architect's consultants and agents and employees of any of them from and against claims, damages, losses and expenses, including but not limited to attorneys' fees, arising out of or resulting from performance of the Work in the affected area if in fact the material or substance presents the risk of bodily injury or death as described in Subparagraph 10.3.1 and has not been rendered harmless, provided that such claim, damage, loss or expense is attributable to bodily injury, sickness, disease or death, or to injury to or destruction of tangible property (other than the Work itself) and provided that such damage, loss or expense is not due to the sole negligence of a party seeking indemnity.

10.4 The Owner shall not be responsible under Paragraph 10.3 for materials and substances brought to the site by the Contractor unless such materials or substances were required by the Contract Documents.

10.5 If, without negligence on the part of the Contractor, the Contractor is held liable for the cost of remediation of a hazardous material or substance solely by reason of performing Work as required by the Contract Documents, the Owner shall indemnify the Contractor for all cost and expense thereby incurred.

10.6 EMERGENCIES

10.6.1 In an emergency affecting safety of persons or property, the Contractor shall act, at the Contractor's discretion, to prevent threatened damage, injury or loss. Additional compensation or

© 1997 AIA®
AIA DOCUMENT A201-1997
GENERAL CONDITIONS OF THE CONTRACT FOR CONSTRUCTION

The American Institute of Architects
1735 New York Avenue, N.W.
Washington, D.C. 20006-5292

35

extension of time claimed by the Contractor on account of an emergency shall be determined as provided in Paragraph 4.3 and Article 7.

ARTICLE 11   INSURANCE AND BONDS

11.1   CONTRACTOR'S LIABILITY INSURANCE

11.1.1   The Contractor shall purchase from and maintain in a company or companies lawfully authorized to do business in the jurisdiction in which the Project is located such insurance as will protect the Contractor from claims set forth below which may arise out of or result from the Contractor's operations under the Contract and for which the Contractor may be legally liable, whether such operations be by the Contractor or by a Subcontractor or by anyone directly or indirectly employed by any of them, or by anyone for whose acts any of them may be liable:

.1   claims under workers' compensation, disability benefit and other similar employee benefit acts which are applicable to the Work to be performed;

.2   claims for damages because of bodily injury, occupational sickness or disease, or death of the Contractor's employees;

.3   claims for damages because of bodily injury, sickness or disease, or death of any person other than the Contractor's employees;

.4   claims for damages insured by usual personal injury liability coverage;

.5   claims for damages, other than to the Work itself, because of injury to or destruction of tangible property, including loss of use resulting therefrom;

.6   claims for damages because of bodily injury, death of a person or property damage arising out of ownership, maintenance or use of a motor vehicle;

.7   claims for bodily injury or property damage arising out of completed operations; and

.8   claims involving contractual liability insurance applicable to the Contractor's obligations under Paragraph 3.18.

11.1.2   The insurance required by Subparagraph 11.1.1 shall be written for not less than limits of liability specified in the Contract Documents or required by law, whichever coverage is greater. Coverages, whether written on an occurrence or claims-made basis, shall be maintained without interruption from date of commencement of the Work until date of final payment and termination of any coverage required to be maintained after final payment.

11.1.3   Certificates of insurance acceptable to the Owner shall be filed with the Owner prior to commencement of the Work. These certificates and the insurance policies required by this Paragraph 11.1 shall contain a provision that coverages afforded under the policies will not be canceled or allowed to expire until at least 30 days' prior written notice has been given to the Owner. If any of the foregoing insurance coverages are required to remain in force after final payment and are reasonably available, an additional certificate evidencing continuation of such coverage shall be submitted with the final Application for Payment as required by Subparagraph 9.10.2. Information concerning reduction of coverage on account of revised limits or claims paid under the General Aggregate, or both, shall be furnished by the Contractor with reasonable promptness in accordance with the Contractor's information and belief.

11.2   OWNER'S LIABILITY INSURANCE

11.2.1   The Owner shall be responsible for purchasing and maintaining the Owner's usual liability insurance.

11.3   PROJECT MANAGEMENT PROTECTIVE LIABILITY INSURANCE

11.3.1   Optionally, the Owner may require the Contractor to purchase and maintain Project Management Protective Liability insurance from the Contractor's usual sources as primary coverage for the Owner's, Contractor's and Architect's vicarious liability for construction operations under the Contract. Unless otherwise required by the Contract Documents, the Owner

© 1997   AIA®
AIA DOCUMENT A201-1997
GENERAL CONDITIONS
OF THE CONTRACT FOR
CONSTRUCTION

The American Institute
of Architects
1735 New York Avenue, N.W.
Washington, D.C. 20006-5292

36

330

shall reimburse the Contractor by increasing the Contract Sum to pay the cost of purchasing and maintaining such optional insurance coverage, and the Contractor shall not be responsible for purchasing any other liability insurance on behalf of the Owner. The minimum limits of liability purchased with such coverage shall be equal to the aggregate of the limits required for Contractor's Liability Insurance under Clauses 11.1.1.2 through 11.1.1.5.

11.3.2 To the extent damages are covered by Project Management Protective Liability insurance, the Owner, Contractor and Architect waive all rights against each other for damages, except such rights as they may have to the proceeds of such insurance. The policy shall provide for such waivers of subrogation by endorsement or otherwise.

11.3.3 The Owner shall not require the Contractor to include the Owner, Architect or other persons or entities as additional insureds on the Contractor's Liability Insurance coverage under Paragraph 11.1.

11.4   PROPERTY INSURANCE
11.4.1   Unless otherwise provided, the Owner shall purchase and maintain, in a company or companies lawfully authorized to do business in the jurisdiction in which the Project is located, property insurance written on a builder's risk "all-risk" or equivalent policy form in the amount of the initial Contract Sum, plus value of subsequent Contract modifications and cost of materials supplied or installed by others, comprising total value for the entire Project at the site on a replacement cost basis without optional deductibles. Such property insurance shall be maintained, unless otherwise provided in the Contract Documents or otherwise agreed in writing by all persons and entities who are beneficiaries of such insurance, until final payment has been made as provided in Paragraph 9.10 or until no person or entity other than the Owner has an insurable interest in the property required by this Paragraph 11.4 to be covered, whichever is later. This insurance shall include interests of the Owner, the Contractor, Subcontractors and Sub-subcontractors in the Project.

11.4.1.1 Property insurance shall be on an "all-risk" or equivalent policy form and shall include, without limitation, insurance against the perils of fire (with extended coverage) and physical loss or damage including, without duplication of coverage, theft, vandalism, malicious mischief, collapse, earthquake, flood, windstorm, falsework, testing and startup, temporary buildings and debris removal including demolition occasioned by enforcement of any applicable legal requirements, and shall cover reasonable compensation for Architect's and Contractor's services and expenses required as a result of such insured loss.

11.4.1.2   If the Owner does not intend to purchase such property insurance required by the Contract and with all of the coverages in the amount described above, the Owner shall so inform the Contractor in writing prior to commencement of the Work. The Contractor may then effect insurance which will protect the interests of the Contractor, Subcontractors and Sub-subcontractors in the Work, and by appropriate Change Order the cost thereof shall be charged to the Owner. If the Contractor is damaged by the failure or neglect of the Owner to purchase or maintain insurance as described above, without so notifying the Contractor in writing, then the Owner shall bear all reasonable costs properly attributable thereto.

11.4.1.3 If the property insurance requires deductibles, the Owner shall pay costs not covered because of such deductibles.

11.4.1.4 This property insurance shall cover portions of the Work stored off the site, and also portions of the Work in transit.

11.4.1.5 Partial occupancy or use in accordance with Paragraph 9.9 shall not commence until the insurance company or companies providing property insurance have consented to such partial

37

331

occupancy or use by endorsement or otherwise. The Owner and the Contractor shall take reasonable steps to obtain consent of the insurance company or companies and shall, without mutual written consent, take no action with respect to partial occupancy or use that would cause cancellation, lapse or reduction of insurance.

11.4.2 Boiler and Machinery Insurance. The Owner shall purchase and maintain boiler and machinery insurance required by the Contract Documents or by law, which shall specifically cover such insured objects during installation and until final acceptance by the Owner; this insurance shall include interests of the Owner, Contractor, Subcontractors and Sub-subcontractors in the Work, and the Owner and Contractor shall be named insureds.

11.4.3 Loss of Use Insurance. The Owner, at the Owner's option, may purchase and maintain such insurance as will insure the Owner against loss of use of the Owner's property due to fire or other hazards, however caused. The Owner waives all rights of action against the Contractor for loss of use of the Owner's property, including consequential losses due to fire or other hazards however caused.

11.4.4 If the Contractor requests in writing that insurance for risks other than those described herein or other special causes of loss be included in the property insurance policy, the Owner shall, if possible, include such insurance, and the cost thereof shall be charged to the Contractor by appropriate Change Order.

11.4.5 If during the Project construction period the Owner insures properties, real or personal or both, at or adjacent to the site by property insurance under policies separate from those insuring the Project, or if after final payment property insurance is to be provided on the completed Project through a policy or policies other than those insuring the Project during the construction period, the Owner shall waive all rights in accordance with the terms of Subparagraph 11.4.7 for damages caused by fire or other causes of loss covered by this separate property insurance. All separate policies shall provide this waiver of subrogation by endorsement or otherwise.

11.4.6 Before an exposure to loss may occur, the Owner shall file with the Contractor a copy of each policy that includes insurance coverages required by this Paragraph 11.4. Each policy shall contain all generally applicable conditions, definitions, exclusions and endorsements related to this Project. Each policy shall contain a provision that the policy will not be canceled or allowed to expire, and that its limits will not be reduced, until at least 30 days' prior written notice has been given to the Contractor.

11.4.7 Waivers of Subrogation. The Owner and Contractor waive all rights against (1) each other and any of their subcontractors, sub-subcontractors, agents and employees, each of the other, and (2) the Architect, Architect's consultants, separate contractors described in Article 6, if any, and any of their subcontractors, sub-subcontractors, agents and employees, for damages caused by fire or other causes of loss to the extent covered by property insurance obtained pursuant to this Paragraph 11.4 or other property insurance applicable to the Work, except such rights as they have to proceeds of such insurance held by the Owner as fiduciary. The Owner or Contractor, as appropriate, shall require of the Architect, Architect's consultants, separate contractors described in Article 6, if any, and the subcontractors, sub-subcontractors, agents and employees of any of them, by appropriate agreements, written where legally required for validity, similar waivers each in favor of other parties enumerated herein. The policies shall provide such waivers of subrogation by endorsement or otherwise. A waiver of subrogation shall be effective as to a person or entity even though that person or entity would otherwise have a duty of indemnification, contractual or otherwise, did not pay the insurance premium directly or indirectly, and whether or not the person or entity had an insurable interest in the property damaged.

© 1997 AIA ●
AIA DOCUMENT A201-1997
GENERAL CONDITIONS
OF THE CONTRACT FOR
CONSTRUCTION

The American Institute
of Architects
1735 New York Avenue, N.W.
Washington, D.C. 20006-5292

332

11.4.8 A loss insured under Owner's property insurance shall be adjusted by the Owner as fiduciary and made payable to the Owner as fiduciary for the insureds, as their interests may appear, subject to requirements of any applicable mortgagee clause and of Subparagraph 11.4.10. The Contractor shall pay Subcontractors their just shares of insurance proceeds received by the Contractor, and by appropriate agreements, written where legally required for validity, shall require Subcontractors to make payments to their Sub-subcontractors in similar manner.

11.4.9 If required in writing by a party in interest, the Owner as fiduciary shall, upon occurrence of an insured loss, give bond for proper performance of the Owner's duties. The cost of required bonds shall be charged against proceeds received as fiduciary. The Owner shall deposit in a separate account proceeds so received, which the Owner shall distribute in accordance with such agreement as the parties in interest may reach, or in accordance with an arbitration award in which case the procedure shall be as provided in Paragraph 4.6. If after such loss no other special agreement is made and unless the Owner terminates the Contract for convenience, replacement of damaged property shall be performed by the Contractor after notification of a Change in the Work in accordance with Article 7.

11.4.10 The Owner as fiduciary shall have power to adjust and settle a loss with insurers unless one of the parties in interest shall object in writing within five days after occurrence of loss to the Owner's exercise of this power; if such objection is made, the dispute shall be resolved as provided in Paragraphs 4.5 and 4.6. The Owner as fiduciary shall, in the case of arbitration, make settlement with insurers in accordance with directions of the arbitrators. If distribution of insurance proceeds by arbitration is required, the arbitrators will direct such distribution.

11.5 PERFORMANCE BOND AND PAYMENT BOND
11.5.1 The Owner shall have the right to require the Contractor to furnish bonds covering faithful performance of the Contract and payment of obligations arising thereunder as stipulated in bidding requirements or specifically required in the Contract Documents on the date of execution of the Contract.

11.5.2 Upon the request of any person or entity appearing to be a potential beneficiary of bonds covering payment of obligations arising under the Contract, the Contractor shall promptly furnish a copy of the bonds or shall permit a copy to be made.

ARTICLE 12 UNCOVERING AND CORRECTION OF WORK
12.1 UNCOVERING OF WORK
12.1.1 If a portion of the Work is covered contrary to the Architect's request or to requirements specifically expressed in the Contract Documents, it must, if required in writing by the Architect, be uncovered for the Architect's examination and be replaced at the Contractor's expense without change in the Contract Time.

12.1.2 If a portion of the Work has been covered which the Architect has not specifically requested to examine prior to its being covered, the Architect may request to see such Work and it shall be uncovered by the Contractor. If such Work is in accordance with the Contract Documents, costs of uncovering and replacement shall, by appropriate Change Order, be at the Owner's expense. If such Work is not in accordance with the Contract Documents, correction shall be at the Contractor's expense unless the condition was caused by the Owner or a separate contractor in which event the Owner shall be responsible for payment of such costs.

© 1997 AIA®
AIA DOCUMENT A201-1997
GENERAL CONDITIONS
OF THE CONTRACT FOR
CONSTRUCTION

The American Institute
of Architects
1735 New York Avenue, N.W.
Washington, D.C. 20006-5292

39

12.2 CORRECTION OF WORK

12.2.1 BEFORE OR AFTER SUBSTANTIAL COMPLETION

12.2.1.1 The Contractor shall promptly correct Work rejected by the Architect or failing to conform to the requirements of the Contract Documents, whether discovered before or after Substantial Completion and whether or not fabricated, installed or completed. Costs of correcting such rejected Work, including additional testing and inspections and compensation for the Architect's services and expenses made necessary thereby, shall be at the Contractor's expense.

12.2.2 AFTER SUBSTANTIAL COMPLETION

12.2.2.1 In addition to the Contractor's obligations under Paragraph 3.5, if, within one year after the date of Substantial Completion of the Work or designated portion thereof or after the date for commencement of warranties established under Subparagraph 9.9.1, or by terms of an applicable special warranty required by the Contract Documents, any of the Work is found to be not in accordance with the requirements of the Contract Documents, the Contractor shall correct it promptly after receipt of written notice from the Owner to do so unless the Owner has previously given the Contractor a written acceptance of such condition. The Owner shall give such notice promptly after discovery of the condition. During the one-year period for correction of Work, if the Owner fails to notify the Contractor and give the Contractor an opportunity to make the correction, the Owner waives the rights to require correction by the Contractor and to make a claim for breach of warranty. If the Contractor fails to correct nonconforming Work within a reasonable time during that period after receipt of notice from the Owner or Architect, the Owner may correct it in accordance with Paragraph 2.4.

12.2.2.2 The one-year period for correction of Work shall be extended with respect to portions of Work first performed after Substantial Completion by the period of time between Substantial Completion and the actual performance of the Work.

12.2.2.3 The one-year period for correction of Work shall not be extended by corrective Work performed by the Contractor pursuant to this Paragraph 12.2.

12.2.3 The Contractor shall remove from the site portions of the Work which are not in accordance with the requirements of the Contract Documents and are neither corrected by the Contractor nor accepted by the Owner.

12.2.4 The Contractor shall bear the cost of correcting destroyed or damaged construction, whether completed or partially completed, of the Owner or separate contractors caused by the Contractor's correction or removal of Work which is not in accordance with the requirements of the Contract Documents.

12.2.5 Nothing contained in this Paragraph 12.2 shall be construed to establish a period of limitation with respect to other obligations which the Contractor might have under the Contract Documents. Establishment of the one-year period for correction of Work as described in Subparagraph 12.2.2 relates only to the specific obligation of the Contractor to correct the Work, and has no relationship to the time within which the obligation to comply with the Contract Documents may be sought to be enforced, nor to the time within which proceedings may be commenced to establish the Contractor's liability with respect to the Contractor's obligations other than specifically to correct the Work.

12.3 ACCEPTANCE OF NONCONFORMING WORK

12.3.1 If the Owner prefers to accept Work which is not in accordance with the requirements of the Contract Documents, the Owner may do so instead of requiring its removal and correction, in which case the Contract Sum will be reduced as appropriate and equitable. Such adjustment shall be effected whether or not final payment has been made.

© 1997 AIA®
AIA DOCUMENT A201-1997
GENERAL CONDITIONS
OF THE CONTRACT FOR
CONSTRUCTION

The American Institute
of Architects
1735 New York Avenue, N.W.
Washington, D.C. 20006-5292

40

334

ARTICLE 13 MISCELLANEOUS PROVISIONS

13.1 GOVERNING LAW

13.1.1 The Contract shall be governed by the law of the place where the Project is located.

13.2 SUCCESSORS AND ASSIGNS

13.2.1 The Owner and Contractor respectively bind themselves, their partners, successors, assigns and legal representatives to the other party hereto and to partners, successors, assigns and legal representatives of such other party in respect to covenants, agreements and obligations contained in the Contract Documents. Except as provided in Subparagraph 13.2.2, neither party to the Contract shall assign the Contract as a whole without written consent of the other. If either party attempts to make such an assignment without such consent, that party shall nevertheless remain legally responsible for all obligations under the Contract.

13.2.2 The Owner may, without consent of the Contractor, assign the Contract to an institutional lender providing construction financing for the Project. In such event, the lender shall assume the Owner's rights and obligations under the Contract Documents. The Contractor shall execute all consents reasonably required to facilitate such assignment.

13.3 WRITTEN NOTICE

13.3.1 Written notice shall be deemed to have been duly served if delivered in person to the individual or a member of the firm or entity or to an officer of the corporation for which it was intended, or if delivered at or sent by registered or certified mail to the last business address known to the party giving notice.

13.4 RIGHTS AND REMEDIES

13.4.1 Duties and obligations imposed by the Contract Documents and rights and remedies available thereunder shall be in addition to and not a limitation of duties, obligations, rights and remedies otherwise imposed or available by law.

13.4.2 No action or failure to act by the Owner, Architect or Contractor shall constitute a waiver of a right or duty afforded them under the Contract, nor shall such action or failure to act constitute approval of or acquiescence in a breach thereunder, except as may be specifically agreed in writing.

13.5 TESTS AND INSPECTIONS

13.5.1 Tests, inspections and approvals of portions of the Work required by the Contract Documents or by laws, ordinances, rules, regulations or orders of public authorities having jurisdiction shall be made at an appropriate time. Unless otherwise provided, the Contractor shall make arrangements for such tests, inspections and approvals with an independent testing laboratory or entity acceptable to the Owner, or with the appropriate public authority, and shall bear all related costs of tests, inspections and approvals. The Contractor shall give the Architect timely notice of when and where tests and inspections are to be made so that the Architect may be present for such procedures. The Owner shall bear costs of tests, inspections or approvals which do not become requirements until after bids are received or negotiations concluded.

13.5.2 If the Architect, Owner or public authorities having jurisdiction determine that portions of the Work require additional testing, inspection or approval not included under Subparagraph 13.5.1, the Architect will, upon written authorization from the Owner, instruct the Contractor to make arrangements for such additional testing, inspection or approval by an entity acceptable to the Owner, and the Contractor shall give timely notice to the Architect of when and where tests and inspections are to be made so that the Architect may be present for such procedures. Such costs, except as provided in Subparagraph 13.5.3, shall be at the Owner's expense.

41

13.5.3 If such procedures for testing, inspection or approval under Subparagraphs 13.5.1 and 13.5.2 reveal failure of the portions of the Work to comply with requirements established by the Contract Documents, all costs made necessary by such failure including those of repeated procedures and compensation for the Architect's services and expenses shall be at the Contractor's expense.

13.5.4 Required certificates of testing, inspection or approval shall, unless otherwise required by the Contract Documents, be secured by the Contractor and promptly delivered to the Architect.

13.5.5 If the Architect is to observe tests, inspections or approvals required by the Contract Documents, the Architect will do so promptly and, where practicable, at the normal place of testing.

13.5.6 Tests or inspections conducted pursuant to the Contract Documents shall be made promptly to avoid unreasonable delay in the Work.

13.6   INTEREST
13.6.1 Payments due and unpaid under the Contract Documents shall bear interest from the date payment is due at such rate as the parties may agree upon in writing or, in the absence thereof, at the legal rate prevailing from time to time at the place where the Project is located.

13.7   COMMENCEMENT OF STATUTORY LIMITATION PERIOD
13.7.1 As between the Owner and Contractor:
> **.1** Before Substantial Completion. As to acts or failures to act occurring prior to the relevant date of Substantial Completion, any applicable statute of limitations shall commence to run and any alleged cause of action shall be deemed to have accrued in any and all events not later than such date of Substantial Completion;
> **.2** Between Substantial Completion and Final Certificate for Payment. As to acts or failures to act occurring subsequent to the relevant date of Substantial Completion and prior to issuance of the final Certificate for Payment, any applicable statute of limitations shall commence to run and any alleged cause of action shall be deemed to have accrued in any and all events not later than the date of issuance of the final Certificate for Payment; and
> **.3** After Final Certificate for Payment. As to acts or failures to act occurring after the relevant date of issuance of the final Certificate for Payment, any applicable statute of limitations shall commence to run and any alleged cause of action shall be deemed to have accrued in any and all events not later than the date of any act or failure to act by the Contractor pursuant to any Warranty provided under Paragraph 3.5, the date of any correction of the Work or failure to correct the Work by the Contractor under Paragraph 12.2, or the date of actual commission of any other act or failure to perform any duty or obligation by the Contractor or Owner, whichever occurs last.

ARTICLE 14 TERMINATION OR SUSPENSION OF THE CONTRACT
14.1   TERMINATION BY THE CONTRACTOR
14.1.1 The Contractor may terminate the Contract if the Work is stopped for a period of 30 consecutive days through no act or fault of the Contractor or a Subcontractor, Sub-subcontractor or their agents or employees or any other persons or entities performing portions of the Work under direct or indirect contract with the Contractor, for any of the following reasons:
> **.1** issuance of an order of a court or other public authority having jurisdiction which requires all Work to be stopped;
> **.2** an act of government, such as a declaration of national emergency which requires all Work to be stopped;

.3 because the Architect has not issued a Certificate for Payment and has not notified the Contractor of the reason for withholding certification as provided in Subparagraph 9.4.1, or because the Owner has not made payment on a Certificate for Payment within the time stated in the Contract Documents; or

.4 the Owner has failed to furnish to the Contractor promptly, upon the Contractor's request, reasonable evidence as required by Subparagraph 2.2.1.

14.1.2 The Contractor may terminate the Contract if, through no act or fault of the Contractor or a Subcontractor, Sub-subcontractor or their agents or employees or any other persons or entities performing portions of the Work under direct or indirect contract with the Contractor, repeated suspensions, delays or interruptions of the entire Work by the Owner as described in Paragraph 14.3 constitute in the aggregate more than 100 percent of the total number of days scheduled for completion, or 120 days in any 365-day period, whichever is less.

14.1.3 If one of the reasons described in Subparagraph 14.1.1 or 14.1.2 exists, the Contractor may, upon seven days' written notice to the Owner and Architect, terminate the Contract and recover from the Owner payment for Work executed and for proven loss with respect to materials, equipment, tools, and construction equipment and machinery, including reasonable overhead, profit and damages.

14.1.4 If the Work is stopped for a period of 60 consecutive days through no act or fault of the Contractor or a Subcontractor or their agents or employees or any other persons performing portions of the Work under contract with the Contractor because the Owner has persistently failed to fulfill the Owner's obligations under the Contract Documents with respect to matters important to the progress of the Work, the Contractor may, upon seven additional days' written notice to the Owner and the Architect, terminate the Contract and recover from the Owner as provided in Subparagraph 14.1.3.

14.2   TERMINATION BY THE OWNER FOR CAUSE

14.2.1 The Owner may terminate the Contract if the Contractor:

.1 persistently or repeatedly refuses or fails to supply enough properly skilled workers or proper materials;

.2 fails to make payment to subcontractors for materials or labor in accordance with the respective agreements between the Contractor and the Subcontractors;

.3 persistently disregards laws, ordinances, or rules, regulations or orders of a public authority having jurisdiction; or

.4 otherwise is guilty of substantial breach of a provision of the Contract Documents.

14.2.2 When any of the above reasons exist, the Owner, upon certification by the Architect that sufficient cause exists to justify such action, may without prejudice to any other rights or remedies of the Owner and after giving the Contractor and the Contractor's surety, if any, seven days' written notice, terminate employment of the Contractor and may, subject to any prior rights of the surety:

.1 take possession of the site and of all materials, equipment, tools, and construction equipment and machinery thereon owned by the Contractor;

.2 accept assignment of subcontracts pursuant to Paragraph 5.4; and

.3 finish the Work by whatever reasonable method the Owner may deem expedient. Upon request of the Contractor, the Owner shall furnish to the Contractor a detailed accounting of the costs incurred by the Owner in finishing the Work.

14.2.3 When the Owner terminates the Contract for one of the reasons stated in Subparagraph 14.2.1, the Contractor shall not be entitled to receive further payment until the Work is finished.

© 1997   AIA®
AIA DOCUMENT A201-1997
GENERAL CONDITIONS
OF THE CONTRACT FOR
CONSTRUCTION

The American Institute
of Architects
1735 New York Avenue, N.W.
Washington, D.C. 20006-5292

43

337

14.2.4 If the unpaid balance of the Contract Sum exceeds costs of finishing the Work, including compensation for the Architect's services and expenses made necessary thereby, and other damages incurred by the Owner and not expressly waived, such excess shall be paid to the Contractor. If such costs and damages exceed the unpaid balance, the Contractor shall pay the difference to the Owner. The amount to be paid to the Contractor or Owner, as the case may be, shall be certified by the Architect, upon application, and this obligation for payment shall survive termination of the Contract.

14.3 SUSPENSION BY THE OWNER FOR CONVENIENCE

14.3.1 The Owner may, without cause, order the Contractor in writing to suspend, delay or interrupt the Work in whole or in part for such period of time as the Owner may determine.

14.3.2 The Contract Sum and Contract Time shall be adjusted for increases in the cost and time caused by suspension, delay or interruption as described in Subparagraph 14.3.1. Adjustment of the Contract Sum shall include profit. No adjustment shall be made to the extent:

    .1 that performance is, was or would have been so suspended, delayed or interrupted by another cause for which the Contractor is responsible; or

    .2 that an equitable adjustment is made or denied under another provision of the Contract.

14.4 TERMINATION BY THE OWNER FOR CONVENIENCE

14.4.1 The Owner may, at any time, terminate the Contract for the Owner's convenience and without cause.

14.4.2 Upon receipt of written notice from the Owner of such termination for the Owner's convenience, the Contractor shall:

    .1 cease operations as directed by the Owner in the notice;

    .2 take actions necessary, or that the Owner may direct, for the protection and preservation of the Work; and

    .3 except for Work directed to be performed prior to the effective date of termination stated in the notice, terminate all existing subcontracts and purchase orders and enter into no further subcontracts and purchase orders.

14.4.3 In case of such termination for the Owner's convenience, the Contractor shall be entitled to receive payment for Work executed, and costs incurred by reason of such termination, along with reasonable overhead and profit on the Work not executed.

AIA DOCUMENT | A401-1997

Standard Form of Agreement Between Contractor and Subcontractor

AGREEMENT made as of the   day of
in the year
(In words, indicate day, month and year)

BETWEEN the Contractor:
(Name, address and other information)

and the Subcontractor:
(Name, address and other information)

The Contractor has made a contract for construction dated

With the Owner:
(Name, address and other information)

For the following Project:
(Include detailed description of Project, location and address)

which Contract is hereinafter referred to as the Prime Contract and which provides for the
furnishing of labor, materials, equipment and services in connection with the construction of
the Project. A copy of the Prime Contract, consisting of the Agreement Between Owner and
Contractor (from which compensation amounts may be deleted) and the other Contract
Documents enumerated therein has been made available to the Subcontractor.

The Architect for the Project is:
(Name, address and other information)

The Contractor and the Subcontractor agree as follows

This document has important legal consequences. Consultation with an attorney is encouraged with respect to its completion or modification.

This document has been approved and endorsed by the American Subcontractors Association and the Associated Specialty Contractors, Inc.

© 1997 AIA®
AIA DOCUMENT A401-1997
CONTRACTOR-
SUBCONTRACTOR
AGREEMENT

The American Institute
of Architects
1735 New York Avenue, N.W.
Washington, D.C. 20006-5292

1

ARTICLE 1 THE SUBCONTRACT DOCUMENTS

1.1   The Subcontract Documents consist of (1) this Agreement; (2) the Prime Contract, consisting of the Agreement between the Owner and Contractor and the other Contract Documents enumerated therein; (3) Modifications issued subsequent to the execution of the Agreement between the Owner and Contractor, whether before or after the execution of this Agreement; (4) other documents listed in Article 16 of this Agreement; and (5) Modifications to this Subcontract issued after execution of this Agreement. These form the Subcontract, and are as fully a part of the Subcontract as if attached to this Agreement or repeated herein. The Subcontract represents the entire and integrated agreement between the parties hereto and super-sedes prior negotiations, representations or agreements, either written or oral. An enumeration of the Subcontract Documents, other than Modifications issued subsequent to the execution of this Agreement, appears in Article 16.

1.2   Except to the extent of a conflict with a specific term or condition contained in the Subcontract Documents, the General Conditions governing this Subcontract shall be the edition of AIA Document A201, General Conditions of the Contract for Construction, current as of the date of this Agreement.

1.3   The Subcontract may be amended or modified only by a Modification. The Subcontract Documents shall not be construed to create a contractual relationship of any kind (1) between the Architect and the Subcontractor, (2) between the Owner and the Subcontractor, or (3) between any persons or entities other than the Contractor and Subcontractor.

1.4   The Subcontractor shall be furnished copies of the Subcontract Documents upon request, but the Contractor may charge the Subcontractor for the reasonable cost of reproduction.

ARTICLE 2 MUTUAL RIGHTS AND RESPONSIBILITIES

2.1   The Contractor and Subcontractor shall be mutually bound by the terms of this Agreement and, to the extent that the provisions of the edition of AIA Document A201 current as of the date of this Agreement apply to this Agreement pursuant to Paragraph 1.2 and provisions of the Prime Contract apply to the Work of the Subcontractor, the Contractor shall assume toward the Subcontractor all obligations and responsibilities that the Owner, under such documents, assumes toward the Contractor, and the Subcontractor shall assume toward the Contractor all obligations and responsibilities which the Contractor, under such documents, assumes toward the Owner and the Architect. The Contractor shall have the benefit of all rights, remedies and redress against the Subcontractor which the Owner, under such documents, has against the Contractor, and the Subcontractor shall have the benefit of all rights, remedies and redress against the Contractor which the Contractor, under such documents, has against the Owner, insofar as applic-able to this Subcontract. Where a provision of such documents is inconsistent with a provision of this Agreement, this Agreement shall govern.

2.2   The Contractor may require the Subcontractor to enter into agreements with Sub-subcontractors performing portions of the Work of this Subcontract by which the Subcontractor and the Sub-subcontractor are mutually bound, to the extent of the Work to be performed by the Sub-subcontractor, assuming toward each other all obligations and responsibil-ities which the Contractor and Subcontractor assume toward each other and having the benefit of all rights, remedies and redress each against the other which the Contractor and Subcontractor have by virtue of the provisions of this Agreement.

© 1997   A I A ®
AIA DOCUMENT A401-1997
CONTRACTOR-
SUBCONTRACTOR
AGREEMENT

The American Institute
of Architects
1735 New York Avenue, N.W.
Washington, D.C. 20006-5292

2

ARTICLE 3   CONTRACTOR

3.1   SERVICES PROVIDED BY THE CONTRACTOR

3.1.1   The Contractor shall cooperate with the Subcontractor in scheduling and performing the Contractor's Work to avoid conflicts or interference in the Subcontractor's Work and shall expedite written responses to submittals made by the Subcontractor in accordance with Paragraph 4.1 and Article 5. As soon as practicable after execution of this Agreement, the Contractor shall provide the Subcontractor copies of the Contractor's construction schedule and schedule of submittals, together with such additional scheduling details as will enable the Subcontractor to plan and perform the Subcontractor's Work properly. The Subcontractor shall be notified promptly of subsequent changes in the construction and submittal schedules and additional scheduling details.

3.1.2   The Contractor shall provide suitable areas for storage of the Subcontractor's materials and equipment during the course of the Work. Additional costs to the Subcontractor resulting from relocation of such facilities at the direction of the Contractor, except as previously agreed upon, shall be reimbursed by the Contractor.

3.1.3   Except as provided in Article 14, the Contractor's equipment will be available to the Subcontractor only at the Contractor's discretion and on mutually satisfactory terms.

3.2   COMMUNICATIONS

3.2.1   The Contractor shall promptly make available to the Subcontractor information, including information received from the Owner which affects this Subcontract and which becomes available to the Contractor subsequent to execution of this Subcontract.

3.2.2   The Contractor shall not give instructions or orders directly to the Subcontractor's employees or to the Subcontractor's Sub-subcontractors or material suppliers unless such persons are designated as authorized representatives of the Subcontractor.

3.2.3   The Contractor shall permit the Subcontractor to request directly from the Architect information regarding the percentages of completion and the amount certified on account of Work done by the Subcontractor.

3.2.4   If hazardous substances of a type of which an employer is required by law to notify its employees are being used on the site by the Contractor, a subcontractor or anyone directly or indirectly employed by them (other than the Subcontractor), the Contractor shall, prior to harmful exposure of the Subcontractor's employees to such substance, give written notice of the chemical composition thereof to the Subcontractor in sufficient detail and time to permit the Subcontractor's compliance with such laws.

3.2.5   The Contractor shall furnish to the Subcontractor within 30 days after receipt of a written request, or earlier if so required by law, information necessary and relevant for the Subcontractor to evaluate, give notice of or enforce mechanic's lien rights. Such information shall include a correct statement of the record legal title to the property, usually referred to as the site, on which the Project is located and the Owner's interest therein.

3.2.6   If the Contractor asserts or defends a claim against the Owner which relates to the Work of the Subcontractor, the Contractor shall make available to the Subcontractor information relating to that portion of the claim which relates to the Work of the Subcontractor.

3.3   CLAIMS BY THE CONTRACTOR

3.3.1   Liquidated damages for delay, if provided for in Paragraph 9.3 of this Agreement, shall be assessed against the Subcontractor only to the extent caused by the Subcontractor or any person or entity for whose acts the Subcontractor may be liable, and in no case for delays or causes arising outside the scope of this Subcontract.

© 1997   AIA®
AIA DOCUMENT A401-1997
CONTRACTOR-
SUBCONTRACTOR
AGREEMENT

The American Institute
of Architects
1735 New York Avenue, N.W.
Washington, D.C. 20006-5292

3

3.3.2 The Contractor's claims for services or materials provided the Subcontractor shall require:

    .1 seven days' prior written notice except in an emergency;

    .2 written compilations to the Subcontractor of services and materials provided and charges for such services and materials no later than the fifteenth day of the following month.

3.4 CONTRACTOR'S REMEDIES

3.4.1 If the Subcontractor defaults or neglects to carry out the Work in accordance with this Agreement and fails within three working days after receipt of written notice from the Contractor to commence and continue correction of such default or neglect with diligence and promptness, the Contractor may, after three days following receipt by the Subcontractor of an additional written notice, and without prejudice to any other remedy the Contractor may have, make good such deficiencies and may deduct the reasonable cost thereof from the payments then or thereafter due the Subcontractor.

ARTICLE 4 SUBCONTRACTOR

4.1 EXECUTION AND PROGRESS OF THE WORK

4.1.1 The Subcontractor shall supervise and direct the Subcontractor's Work, and shall cooperate with the Contractor in scheduling and performing the Subcontractor's Work to avoid conflict, delay in or interference with the Work of the Contractor, other subcontractors or Owner's own forces.

4.1.2 The Subcontractor shall promptly submit Shop Drawings, Product Data, Samples and similar submittals required by the Subcontract Documents with reasonable promptness and in such sequence as to cause no delay in the Work or in the activities of the Contractor or other subcontractors.

4.1.3 The Subcontractor shall submit to the Contractor a schedule of values allocated to the various parts of the Work of this Subcontract, aggregating the Subcontract Sum, made out in such detail as the Contractor and Subcontractor may agree upon or as required by the Owner, and supported by such evidence as the Contractor may require. In applying for payment, the Subcontractor shall submit statements based upon this schedule.

4.1.4 The Subcontractor shall furnish to the Contractor periodic progress reports on the Work of this Subcontract as mutually agreed, including information on the status of materials and equipment which may be in the course of preparation, manufacture or transit.

4.1.5 The Subcontractor agrees that the Contractor and the Architect will each have the authority to reject Work of the Subcontractor which does not conform to the Prime Contract. The Architect's decisions on matters relating to aesthetic effect shall be final and binding on the Subcontractor if consistent with the intent expressed in the Prime Contract.

4.1.6 The Subcontractor shall pay for all materials, equipment and labor used in connection with the performance of this Subcontract through the period covered by previous payments received from the Contractor, and shall furnish satisfactory evidence, when requested by the Contractor, to verify compliance with the above requirements.

4.1.7 The Subcontractor shall take necessary precautions to protect properly the Work of other subcontractors from damage caused by operations under this Subcontract.

4.1.8 The Subcontractor shall cooperate with the Contractor, other subcontractors and the Owner's own forces whose Work might interfere with the Subcontractor's Work. The

© 1997 AIA®
AIA DOCUMENT A401-1997
CONTRACTOR-
SUBCONTRACTOR
AGREEMENT

The American Institute
of Architects
1735 New York Avenue, N.W.
Washington, D.C. 20006-5292

4

Subcontractor shall participate in the preparation of coordinated drawings in areas of congestion, if required by the Prime Contract, specifically noting and advising the Contractor of potential conflicts between the Work of the Subcontractor and that of the Contractor, other subcontractors or the Owner's own forces.

4.2 LAWS, PERMITS, FEES AND NOTICES
4.2.1 The Subcontractor shall give notices and comply with laws, ordinances, rules, regulations and orders of public authorities bearing on performance of the Work of this Subcontract. The Subcontractor shall secure and pay for permits and governmental fees, licenses and inspections necessary for proper execution and completion of the Subcontractor's Work, the furnishing of which is required of the Contractor by the Prime Contract.

4.2.2 The Subcontractor shall comply with Federal, state and local tax laws, social security acts, unemployment compensation acts and workers' compensation acts insofar as applicable to the performance of this Subcontract.

4.3 SAFETY PRECAUTIONS AND PROCEDURES
4.3.1 The Subcontractor shall take reasonable safety precautions with respect to performance of this Subcontract, shall comply with safety measures initiated by the Contractor and with applicable laws, ordinances, rules, regulations and orders of public authorities for the safety of persons and property in accordance with the requirements of the Prime Contract. The Subcontractor shall report to the Contractor within three days an injury to an employee or agent of the Subcontractor which occurred at the site.

4.3.2 If hazardous substances of a type of which an employer is required by law to notify its employees are being used on the site by the Subcontractor, the Subcontractor's Sub-subcontractors or anyone directly or indirectly employed by them, the Subcontractor shall, prior to harmful exposure of any employees on the site to such substance, give written notice of the chemical composition thereof to the Contractor in sufficient detail and time to permit compliance with such laws by the Contractor, other subcontractors and other employers on the site.

4.3.3 If reasonable precautions will be inadequate to prevent foreseeable bodily injury or death to persons resulting from a material or substance, including but not limited to asbestos or polychlorinated biphenyl (PCB), encountered on the site by the Subcontractor, the Subcontractor shall, upon recognizing the condition, immediately stop Work in the affected area and report the condition to the Contractor in writing. When the material or substance has been rendered harmless, the Subcontractor's Work in the affected area shall resume upon written agreement of the Contractor and Subcontractor. The Subcontract Time shall be extended appropriately and the Subcontract Sum shall be increased in the amount of the Subcontractor's reasonable additional costs of demobilization, delay and remobilization, which adjustments shall be accomplished as provided in Article 5 of this Agreement.

© 1997 A I A ®
AIA DOCUMENT A401-1997
CONTRACTOR-
SUBCONTRACTOR
AGREEMENT

The American Institute
of Architects
1735 New York Avenue, N.W.
Washington, D.C. 20006-5292

4.3.4 To the fullest extent permitted by law, the Contractor shall indemnify and hold harmless the Subcontractor, the Subcontractor's Sub-subcontractors, and agents and employees of any of them from and against claims, damages, losses and expenses, including but not limited to attorneys' fees, arising out of or resulting from performance of the Work in the affected area if in fact the material or substance presents the risk of bodily injury or death as described in Subparagraph 4.3.3 and has not been rendered harmless, provided that such claim, damage, loss or expense is attributable to bodily injury, sickness, disease or death, or to injury to or destruction of tangible property (other than the Work itself) including loss of use resulting therefrom and provided that such damage, loss or expense is not due to the sole negligence of a party seeking indemnity.

5

4.4   CLEANING UP

4.4.1   The Subcontractor shall keep the premises and surrounding area free from accumulation of waste materials or rubbish caused by operations performed under this Subcontract. The Subcontractor shall not be held responsible for unclean conditions caused by other contractors or subcontractors.

4.4.2   As provided under Subparagraph 3.3.2, if the Subcontractor fails to clean up as provided in the Subcontract Documents, the Contractor may charge the Subcontractor for the Subcontractor's appropriate share of cleanup costs.

4.5   WARRANTY

4.5.1   The Subcontractor warrants to the Owner, Architect and Contractor that materials and equipment furnished under this Subcontract will be of good quality and new unless otherwise required or permitted by the Subcontract Documents, that the Work of this Subcontract will be free from defects not inherent in the quality required or permitted, and that the Work will conform to the requirements of the Subcontract Documents. Work not conforming to these requirements, including substitutions not properly approved and authorized, may be considered defective. The Subcontractor's warranty excludes remedy for damage or defect caused by abuse, modifications not executed by the Subcontractor, improper or insufficient maintenance, improper operation, or normal wear and tear under normal usage. This warranty shall be in addition to and not in limitation of any other warranty or remedy required by law or by the Subcontract Documents.

4.6   INDEMNIFICATION

4.6.1   To the fullest extent permitted by law, the Subcontractor shall indemnify and hold harmless the Owner, Contractor, Architect, Architect's consultants, and agents and employees of any of them from and against claims, damages, losses and expenses, including but not limited to attorney's fees, arising out of or resulting from performance of the Subcontractor's Work under this Subcontract, provided that any such claim, damage, loss or expense is attributable to bodily injury, sickness, disease or death, or to injury to or destruction of tangible property (other than the Work itself), but only to the extent caused by the negligent acts or omissions of the Subcontractor, the Subcontractor's Sub-subcontractors, anyone directly or indirectly employed by them or anyone for whose acts they may be liable, regardless of whether or not such claim, damage, loss or expense is caused in part by a party indemnified hereunder. Such obligation shall not be construed to negate, abridge, or otherwise reduce other rights or obligations of indemnity which would otherwise exist as to a party or person described in this Paragraph 4.6.

4.6.2   In claims against any person or entity indemnified under this Paragraph 4.6 by an employee of the Subcontractor, the Subcontractor's Sub-subcontractors, anyone directly or indirectly employed by them or anyone for whose acts they may be liable, the indemnification obligation under Subparagraph 4.6.1 shall not be limited by a limitation on the amount or type of damages, compensation or benefits payable by or for the Subcontractor or the Subcontractor's Sub-subcontractors under workers' compensation acts, disability benefit acts or other employee benefit acts.

4.7   REMEDIES FOR NONPAYMENT

4.7.1   If the Contractor does not pay the Subcontractor through no fault of the Subcontractor, within seven days from the time payment should be made as provided in this Agreement, the Subcontractor may, without prejudice to any other available remedies, upon seven additional days' written notice to the Contractor, stop the Work of this Subcontract until payment of the amount owing has been received. The Subcontract Sum shall, by appropriate adjustment, be increased by the amount of the Subcontractor's reasonable costs of demobilization, delay and remobilization.

ARTICLE 5 CHANGES IN THE WORK

5.1   The Owner may make changes in the Work by issuing Modifications to the Prime Contract. Upon receipt of such a Modification issued subsequent to the execution of the Subcontract Agreement, the Contractor shall promptly notify the Subcontractor of the Modification. Unless otherwise directed by the Contractor, the Subcontractor shall not thereafter order materials or perform Work which would be inconsistent with the changes made by the Modifications to the Prime Contract.

5.2   The Subcontractor may be ordered in writing by the Contractor, without invalidating this Subcontract, to make changes in the Work within the general scope of this Subcontract consisting of additions, deletions or other revisions, including those required by Modifications to the Prime Contract issued subsequent to the execution of this Agreement, the Subcontract Sum and the Subcontract Time being adjusted accordingly. The Subcontractor, prior to the commencement of such changed or revised Work, shall submit promptly to the Contractor written copies of a claim for adjustment to the Subcontract Sum and Subcontract Time for such revised Work in a manner consistent with requirements of the Subcontract Documents.

5.3   The Subcontractor shall make all claims promptly to the Contractor for additional cost, extensions of time and damages for delays or other causes in accordance with the Subcontract Documents. A claim which will affect or become part of a claim which the Contractor is required to make under the Prime Contract within a specified time period or in a specified manner shall be made in sufficient time to permit the Contractor to satisfy the requirements of the Prime Contract. Such claims shall be received by the Contractor not less than two working days preceding the time by which the Contractor's claim must be made. Failure of the Subcontractor to make such a timely claim shall bind the Subcontractor to the same consequences as those to which the Contractor is bound.

ARTICLE 6 MEDIATION AND ARBITRATION

6.1   MEDIATION

6.1.1   Any claim arising out of or related to this Subcontract, except claims as otherwise provided in Subparagraph 4.1.5 and except those waived in this Subcontract, shall be subject to mediation as a condition precedent to arbitration or the institution of legal or equitable proceedings by either party.

6.1.2   The parties shall endeavor to resolve their claims by mediation which, unless the parties mutually agree otherwise, shall be in accordance with the Construction Industry Mediation Rules of the American Arbitration Association currently in effect. Request for mediation shall be filed in writing with the other party to this Subcontract and the American Arbitration Association. The request may be made concurrently with the filing of a demand for arbitration but, in such event, mediation shall proceed in advance of arbitration or legal or equitable proceedings, which shall be stayed pending mediation for a period of 60 days from the date of filing, unless stayed for a longer period by agreement of the parties or court order.

6.1.3   The parties shall share the mediator's fee and any filing fees equally. The mediation shall be held in the place where the Project is located, unless another location is mutually agreed upon. Agreements reached in mediation shall be enforceable as settlement agreements in any court having jurisdiction thereof.

6.2   ARBITRATION

6.2.1   Any claim arising out of or related to this Subcontract, except claims as otherwise provided in Subparagraph 4.1.5 and except those waived in this Subcontract, shall be subject to arbitration. Prior to arbitration, the parties shall endeavor to resolve disputes by mediation in accordance with the provisions of Paragraph 6.1.

© 1997 AIA®
AIA DOCUMENT A401-1997
CONTRACTOR-
SUBCONTRACTOR
AGREEMENT

The American Institute
of Architects
1735 New York Avenue, N.W.
Washington, D.C. 20006-5292

7

6.2.2 Claims not resolved by mediation shall be decided by arbitration which, unless the parties mutually agree otherwise, shall be in accordance with the Construction Industry Arbitration Rules of the American Arbitration Association currently in effect. Demand for arbitration shall be filed in writing with the other party to this Subcontract and with the American Arbitration Association, and a copy shall be filed with the Architect.

6.2.3 A demand for arbitration shall be made within the time limits specified in the conditions of the Prime Contract as applicable, and in other cases within a reasonable time after the claim has arisen, and in no event shall it be made after the date when institution of legal or equitable proceedings based on such claim would be barred by the applicable statute of limitations.

6.2.4 Limitation on Consolidation or Joinder. Except by written consent of the person or entity sought to be joined, no arbitration arising out of or relating to the Subcontract shall include, by consolidation or joinder or in any other manner, any person or entity not a party to the Subcontract under which such arbitration arises, unless it is shown at the time the demand for arbitration is filed that (1) such person or entity is substantially involved in a common question of fact or law, (2) the presence of such person or entity is required if complete relief is to be accorded in the arbitration, (3) the interest or responsibility of such person or entity in the matter is not insubstantial, and (4) such person or entity is not the Architect, the Architect's employee, the Architect's consultant, or an employee or agent of any of them. This agreement to arbitrate and any other written agreement to arbitrate with an additional person or persons referred to herein shall be specifically enforceable under applicable law in any court having jurisdiction thereof.

6.2.5 Claims and Timely Assertion of Claims. The party filing a notice of demand for arbitration must assert in the demand all claims then known to that party on which arbitration is permitted to be demanded.

6.2.6 Judgment on Final Award. The award rendered by the arbitrator or arbitrators shall be final, and judgment may be entered upon it in accordance with applicable law in any court having jurisdiction thereof.

ARTICLE 7 TERMINATION, SUSPENSION OR ASSIGNMENT OF THE SUBCONTRACT
7.1 TERMINATION BY THE SUBCONTRACTOR

7.1.1 The Subcontractor may terminate the Subcontract for the same reasons and under the same circumstances and procedures with respect to the Contractor as the Contractor may terminate with respect to the Owner under the Prime Contract, or for nonpayment of amounts due under this Subcontract for 60 days or longer. In the event of such termination by the Subcontractor for any reason which is not the fault of the Subcontractor, Sub-subcontractors or their agents or employees or other persons performing portions of the Work under contract with the Subcontractor, the Subcontractor shall be entitled to recover from the Contractor payment for Work executed and for proven loss with respect to materials, equipment, tools, and construction equipment and machinery, including reasonable overhead, profit and damages.

7.2 TERMINATION BY THE CONTRACTOR

7.2.1 If the Subcontractor persistently or repeatedly fails or neglects to carry out the Work in accordance with the Subcontract Documents or otherwise to perform in accordance with this Subcontract and fails within seven days after receipt of written notice to commence and continue correction of such default or neglect with diligence and promptness, the Contractor may, after seven days following receipt by the Subcontractor of an additional written notice and without prejudice to any other remedy the Contractor may have, terminate the Subcontract and finish the Subcontractor's Work by whatever method the Contractor may deem expedient. If the

© 1997 AIA®
AIA DOCUMENT A401-1997
CONTRACTOR-
SUBCONTRACTOR
AGREEMENT

The American Institute
of Architects
1735 New York Avenue, N.W.
Washington, D.C. 20006-5292

8

unpaid balance of the Subcontract Sum exceeds the expense of finishing the Subcontractor's Work and other damages incurred by the Contractor and not expressly waived, such excess shall be paid to the Subcontractor. If such expense and damages exceed such unpaid balance, the Subcontractor shall pay the difference to the Contractor.

7.2.2   If the Owner terminates the Contract for the Owner's convenience, the Contractor shall deliver written notice to the Subcontractor.

7.2.3   Upon receipt of written notice of termination, the Subcontractor shall:
.1   cease operations as directed by the Contractor in the notice;
.2   take actions necessary, or that the Contractor may direct, for the protection and preservation of the Work; and
.3   except for Work directed to be performed prior to the effective date of termination stated in the notice, terminate all existing Sub-subcontracts and purchase orders and enter into no further Sub-subcontracts and purchase orders.

7.2.4   In case of such termination for the Owner's convenience, the Subcontractor shall be entitled to receive payment for Work executed, and costs incurred by reason of such termination, along with reasonable overhead and profit on the Work not executed.

7.3   SUSPENSION BY THE CONTRACTOR FOR CONVENIENCE
7.3.1   The Contractor may, without cause, order the Subcontractor in writing to suspend, delay or interrupt the Work of this Subcontract in whole or in part for such period of time as the Contractor may determine. In the event of suspension ordered by the Contractor, the Subcontractor shall be entitled to an equitable adjustment of the Subcontract Time and Subcontract Sum.

7.3.2   An adjustment shall be made for increases in the Subcontract Time and Subcontract Sum, including profit on the increased cost of performance, caused by suspension, delay or interruption. No adjustment shall be made to the extent:
.1   that performance is, was or would have been so suspended, delayed or interrupted by another cause for which the Subcontractor is responsible;
.2   that an equitable adjustment is made or denied under another provision of this Subcontract.

7.4   ASSIGNMENT OF THE SUBCONTRACT
7.4.1   In the event of termination of the Prime Contract by the Owner, the Contractor may assign this Subcontract to the Owner, with the Owner's agreement, subject to the provisions of the Prime Contract and to the prior rights of the surety, if any, obligated under bonds relating to the Prime Contract. In such event, the Owner shall assume the Contractor's rights and obligations under the Subcontract Documents. If the Work of the Prime Contract has been suspended for more than 30 days, the Subcontractor's compensation shall be equitably adjusted.

7.4.2   The Subcontractor shall not assign the Work of this Subcontract without the written consent of the Contractor, nor subcontract the whole of this Subcontract without the written consent of the Contractor, nor further subcontract portions of this Subcontract without written notification to the Contractor when such notification is requested by the Contractor.

9

ARTICLE 8 THE WORK OF THIS SUBCONTRACT

8.1   The Subcontractor shall execute the following portion of the Work described in the Subcontract Documents, including all labor, materials, equipment, services and other items required to complete such portion of the Work, except to the extent specifically indicated in the Subcontract Documents to be the responsibility of others.

(Insert a precise description of the Work of this Subcontract, referring where appropriate to numbers of Drawings, sections of Specifications and pages of Addenda, Modifications and accepted Alternates.)

ARTICLE 9 DATE OF COMMENCEMENT AND SUBSTANTIAL COMPLETION

9.1   The Subcontractor's date of commencement is the date from which the Contract Time of Paragraph 9.3 is measured; it shall be the date of this Agreement, as first written above, unless a different date is stated below or provision is made for the date to be fixed in a notice to proceed issued by the Contractor.

(Insert the date of commencement, if it differs from the date of this Agreement or, if applicable, state that the date will be fixed in a notice to proceed.)

9.2   Unless the date of commencement is established by a notice to proceed issued by the Contractor, or the Contractor has commenced visible Work at the site under the Prime Contract, the Subcontractor shall notify the Contractor in writing not less than five days before commencing the Subcontractor's Work to permit the timely filing of mortgages, mechanic's liens and other security interests.

9.3   The Work of this Subcontract shall be substantially completed not later than
(Insert the calendar date or number of calendar days after the Subcontractor's date of commencement. Also insert any requirements for earlier Substantial Completion of certain portions of the Subcontractor's Work, if not stated elsewhere in the Subcontract Documents.)

, subject to adjustments of this Subcontract Time as provided in the Subcontract Documents.
(Insert provisions, if any, for liquidated damages relating to failure to complete on time.)

9.4   With respect to the obligations of both the Contractor and the Subcontractor, time is of the essence of this Subcontract.

9.5   No extension of time will be valid without the Contractor's written consent after claim made by the Subcontractor in accordance with Paragraph 5.3.

10

ARTICLE 10 SUBCONTRACT SUM

10.1   The Contractor shall pay the Subcontractor in current funds for performance of the Subcontract the Subcontract Sum of

Dollars (**s**   ), subject to additions and deductions as provided in the Subcontract Documents.

10.2   The Subcontract Sum is based upon the following alternates, if any, which are described in the Subcontract Documents and have been accepted by the Owner and the Contractor:
(Insert the numbers or other identification of accepted alternates.)

10.3   Unit prices, if any, are as follows:

ARTICLE 11 PROGRESS PAYMENTS

11.1   Based upon applications for payment submitted to the Contractor by the Subcontractor, corresponding to applications for payment submitted by the Contractor to the Architect, and certificates for payment issued by the Architect, the Contractor shall make progress payments on account of the Subcontract Sum to the Subcontractor as provided below and elsewhere in the Subcontract Documents. Unless the Contractor provides the Owner with a payment bond in the full penal sum of the Contract Sum, payments received by the Contractor and Subcontractor for Work properly performed by their contractors and suppliers shall be held by the Contractor and Subcontractor for those contractors or suppliers who performed Work or furnished materials, or both, under contract with the Contractor or Subcontractor for which payment was made to the Contractor by the Owner or to the Subcontractor by the Contractor, as applicable. Nothing contained herein shall require money to be placed in a separate account and not commingled with money of the Contractor or Subcontractor, shall create any fiduciary liability or tort liability on the part of the Contractor or Subcontractor for breach of trust or shall entitle any person or entity to an award of punitive damages against the Contractor or Subcontractor for breach of the requirements of this provision.

11.2   The period covered by each application for payment shall be one calendar month ending on the last day of the month, or as follows:

11.3   Provided an application for payment is received by the Contractor not later than the   day of a month, the Contractor shall include the Subcontractor's Work covered by that application in the next application for payment which the Contractor is entitled to submit to the Architect. The Contractor shall pay the Subcontractor each progress payment within three working days after the Contractor receives payment from the Owner. If the Architect does not issue a certificate for payment or the Contractor does not receive payment for any cause which is not the fault of the Subcontractor, the Contractor shall pay the Subcontractor, on demand, a progress payment computed as provided in Paragraphs 11.7, 11.8 and 11.9.

© 1997   A I A ®
AIA DOCUMENT A401-1997
CONTRACTOR-
SUBCONTRACTOR
AGREEMENT

The American Institute
of Architects
1735 New York Avenue, N.W.
Washington, D.C. 20006-5292

11

11.4 If an application for payment is received by the Contractor after the application date fixed above, the Subcontractor's Work covered by it shall be included by the Contractor in the next application for payment submitted to the Architect.

11.5 Each application for payment shall be based upon the most recent schedule of values submitted by the Subcontractor in accordance with the Subcontract Documents. The schedule of values shall allocate the entire Subcontract Sum among the various portions of the Subcontractor's Work and be prepared in such form and supported by such data to substantiate its accuracy as the Contractor may require. This schedule, unless objected to by the Contractor, shall be used as a basis for reviewing the Subcontractor's applications for payment.

11.6 Applications for payment submitted by the Subcontractor shall indicate the percentage of completion of each portion of the Subcontractor's Work as of the end of the period covered by the application for payment.

11.7 Subject to the provisions of the Subcontract Documents, the amount of each progress payment shall be computed as follows:

11.7.1 Take that portion of the Subcontract Sum properly allocable to completed Work as determined by multiplying the percentage completion of each portion of the Subcontractor's Work by the share of the total Subcontract Sum allocated to that portion of the Subcontractor's Work in the schedule of values, less that percentage actually retained, if any, from payments to the Contractor on account of the Work of the Subcontractor. Pending final determination of cost to the Contractor of changes in the Work which have been properly authorized by the Contractor, amounts not in dispute shall be included to the same extent provided in the Prime Contract, even though the Subcontract Sum has not yet been adjusted.

11.7.2 Add that portion of the Subcontract Sum properly allocable to materials and equipment delivered and suitably stored at the site by the Subcontractor for subsequent incorporation in the Subcontractor's Work or, if approved by the Contractor, suitably stored off the site at a location agreed upon in writing, less the same percentage retainage required by the Prime Contract to be applied to such materials and equipment in the Contractor's application for payment;

11.7.3 Subtract the aggregate of previous payments made by the Contractor; and

11.7.4 Subtract amounts, if any, calculated under Subparagraph 11.7.1 or 11.7.2 which are related to Work of the Subcontractor for which the Architect has withheld or nullified, in whole or in part, a certificate of payment for a cause which is the fault of the Subcontractor.

11.8 Upon the partial or entire disapproval by the Contractor of the Subcontractor's application for payment, the Contractor shall provide written notice to the Subcontractor. When the basis for the disapproval has been remedied, the Subcontractor shall be paid the amounts withheld.

11.9 SUBSTANTIAL COMPLETION

11.9.1 When the Subcontractor's Work or a designated portion thereof is substantially complete and in accordance with the requirements of the Prime Contract, the Contractor shall, upon application by the Subcontractor, make prompt application for payment for such Work. Within 30 days following issuance by the Architect of the certificate for payment covering such substantially completed Work, the Contractor shall, to the full extent allowed in the Prime Contract, make payment to the Subcontractor, deducting any portion of the funds for the Subcontractor's Work withheld in accordance with the certificate to cover costs of items to be completed or corrected by the Subcontractor. Such payment to the Subcontractor shall be the entire unpaid balance of the Subcontract Sum if a full release of retainage is allowed under the

© 1997 AIA®
AIA DOCUMENT A401-1997
CONTRACTOR-
SUBCONTRACTOR
AGREEMENT

The American Institute
of Architects
1735 New York Avenue, N.W.
Washington, D.C. 20006-5292

12

Prime Contract for the Subcontractor's Work prior to the completion of the entire Project. If the Prime Contract does not allow for a full release of retainage, then such payment shall be an amount which, when added to previous payments to the Subcontractor, will reduce the retainage on the Subcontractor's substantially completed Work to the same percentage of retainage as that on the Contractor's Work covered by the certificate.

ARTICLE 12 FINAL PAYMENT

12.1 Final payment, constituting the entire unpaid balance of the Subcontract Sum, shall be made by the Contractor to the Subcontractor when the Subcontractor's Work is fully performed in accordance with the requirements of the Subcontract Documents, the Architect has issued a certificate for payment covering the Subcontractor's completed Work and the Contractor has received payment from the Owner. If, for any cause which is not the fault of the Subcontractor, a certificate for payment is not issued or the Contractor does not receive timely payment or does not pay the Subcontractor within three working days after receipt of payment from the Owner, final payment to the Subcontractor shall be made upon demand.
(Insert provisions for earlier final payment to the Subcontractor, if applicable.)

12.2 Before issuance of the final payment, the Subcontractor, if required, shall submit evidence satisfactory to the Contractor that all payrolls, bills for materials and equipment, and all known indebtedness connected with the Subcontractor's Work have been satisfied.

ARTICLE 13 INSURANCE AND BONDS

13.1 The Subcontractor shall purchase and maintain insurance of the following types of coverage and limits of liability:

13.2 Coverages, whether written on an occurrence or claims-made basis, shall be maintained without interruption from date of commencement of the Subcontractor's Work until date of final payment and termination of any coverage required to be maintained after final payment to the Subcontractor.

13.3 Certificates of insurance acceptable to the Contractor shall be filed with the Contractor prior to commencement of the Subcontractor's Work. These certificates and the insurance policies required by this Article 13 shall contain a provision that coverages afforded under the policies will not be canceled or allowed to expire until at least 30 days' prior written notice has been given to the Contractor. If any of the foregoing insurance coverages are required to remain in force after final payment and are reasonably available, an additional certificate evidencing continuation of such coverage shall be submitted with the final application for payment as required in Article 12. If any information concerning reduction of coverage is not furnished by the insurer, it shall be furnished by the Subcontractor with reasonable promptness according to the Subcontractor's information and belief.

© 1997 AIA®
AIA DOCUMENT A401-1997
CONTRACTOR-
SUBCONTRACTOR
AGREEMENT

The American Institute
of Architects
1735 New York Avenue, N.W.
Washington, D.C. 20006-5292

13

13.4   The Contractor shall furnish to the Subcontractor satisfactory evidence of insurance required of the Contractor under the Prime Contract.

13.5   The Contractor shall promptly, upon request of the Subcontractor, furnish a copy or permit a copy to be made of any bond covering payment of obligations arising under the Subcontract.

13.6   Performance Bond and Payment Bond:
(If the Subcontractor is to furnish bonds, insert the specific requirements here.)

13.7   PROPERTY INSURANCE
13.7.1   When requested in writing, the Contractor shall provide the Subcontractor with copies of the property and equipment policies in effect for the Project. The Contractor shall notify the Subcontractor if the required property insurance policies are not in effect.

13.7.2   If the required property insurance is not in effect for the full value of the Subcontractor's Work, then the Subcontractor shall purchase insurance for the value of the Subcontractor's Work, and the Subcontractor shall be reimbursed for the cost of the insurance by an adjustment in the Subcontract Sum.

13.7.3   Property insurance for the Subcontractor's materials and equipment required for the Subcontractor's Work, stored off site or in transit and not covered by the Project property insurance, shall be paid for through the application for payment process.

13.8   WAIVERS OF SUBROGATION
13.8.1   The Contractor and Subcontractor waive all rights against (1) each other and any of their subcontractors, sub-subcontractors, agents and employees each of the other, and (2) the Owner, the Architect, the Architect's consultants, separate contractors, and any of their subcontractors, sub-subcontractors, agents and employees for damages caused by fire or other causes of loss to the extent covered by property insurance provided under the Prime Contract or other property insurance applicable to the Work, except such rights as they may have to proceeds of such insurance held by the Owner as a fiduciary. The Subcontractor shall require of the Subcontractor's Sub-subcontractors, agents and employees, by appropriate agreements, written where legally required for validity, similar waivers in favor of the parties enumerated herein. The policies shall provide such waivers of subrogation by endorsement or otherwise. A waiver of subrogation shall be effective as to a person or entity even though that person or entity would otherwise have a duty of indemnification, contractual or otherwise, did not pay the insurance premium directly or indirectly, and whether or not the person or entity had an insurable interest in the property damaged.

ARTICLE 14 TEMPORARY FACILITIES AND WORKING CONDITIONS
14.1   The Contractor shall furnish and make available to the Subcontractor the following temporary facilities, equipment and services; these shall be furnished at no cost to the Subcontractor unless otherwise indicated below:

© 1997 AIA®
AIA DOCUMENT A401-1997
CONTRACTOR-
SUBCONTRACTOR
AGREEMENT

The American Institute
of Architects
1735 New York Avenue, N.W.
Washington, D.C. 20006-5292

14

14.2   Specific working conditions:
(Insert any applicable arrangements concerning working conditions and labor matters for the Project.)

ARTICLE 15 MISCELLANEOUS PROVISIONS

15.1   Where reference is made in this Subcontract to a provision of another Subcontract Document, the reference refers to that provision as amended or supplemented by other provisions of the Subcontract Documents.

15.2   Payments due and unpaid under this Subcontract shall bear interest from the date payment is due at such rate as the parties may agree upon in writing or, in the absence thereof, at the legal rate prevailing from time to time at the place where the Project is located.
(Insert rate of interest agreed upon, if any.)

(Usury laws and requirements under the Federal Truth in Lending Act, similar state and local consumer credit laws and other regulations at the Owner's, Contractor's and Subcontractor's principal places of business, the location of the Project and elsewhere may affect the validity of this provision. Legal advice should be obtained with respect to deletions or modifications, and also regarding requirements such as written disclosures or waivers.)

15.3   Retainage and any reduction thereto is as follows:

15.4   The Contractor and Subcontractor waive claims against each other for consequential damages arising out of or relating to this Subcontract, including without limitation, any consequential damages due to either party's termination in accordance with Article 7.

ARTICLE 16 ENUMERATION OF SUBCONTRACT DOCUMENTS

16.1   The Subcontract Documents, except for Modifications issued after execution of this Subcontract, are enumerated as follows:

16.1.1   This executed 1997 edition of the Standard Form of Agreement Between Contractor and Subcontractor, AIA Document A401-1997;

16.1.2   The Prime Contract, consisting of the Agreement between the Owner and Contractor dated as first entered above and the other Contract Documents enumerated in the Owner-Contractor Agreement;

© 1997   AIA®
AIA DOCUMENT A401-1997
CONTRACTOR-
SUBCONTRACTOR
AGREEMENT

The American Institute
of Architects
1735 New York Avenue, N.W.
Washington, D.C. 20006-5292

15

16.1.3 The following Modifications to the Prime Contract, if any, issued subsequent to the execution of the Owner-Contractor Agreement but prior to the execution of this Agreement:

Modification   Date

16.1.4 Other Documents, if any, forming part of the Subcontract Documents are as follows:
(List any additional documents that are intended to form part of the Subcontract Documents. Requests for proposal and the Subcontractor's bid or proposal should be listed here only if intended to be part of the Subcontract Documents.)

This Agreement entered into as of the day and year first written above.

CONTRACTOR*(Signature)*   **SUBCONTRACTOR***(Signature)*

(Printed name and title)   *(Printed name and title)*

© 1 9 9 7 A I A ®
AIA DOCUMENT A401-1997
CONTRACTOR-
SUBCONTRACTOR
AGREEMENT

The American Institute
of Architects
1735 New York Avenue, N.W.
Washington, D.C. 20006-5292

16

APPLICATION AND CERTIFICATE FOR PAYMENT AIA DOCUMENT G702 (Instructions on reverse side) PAGE ONE OF PAGES

TO OWNER:

PROJECT:

APPLICATION NO.:

PERIOD TO:

PROJECT NOS.:

Distribution to:
☐ OWNER
☐ ARCHITECT
☐ CONTRACTOR
☐

FROM CONTRACTOR:

VIA ARCHITECT:

CONTRACT DATE:

CONTRACT FOR:

CONTRACTOR'S APPLICATION FOR PAYMENT

Application is made for payment, as shown below, in connection with the Contract.
Continuation Sheet, AIA Document G703, is attached.

1. ORIGINAL CONTRACT SUM.................... $
2. Net change by Change Orders .... $
3. CONTRACT SUM TO DATE (Line 1 ± 2)..... $
4. TOTAL COMPLETED & STORED TO DATE.... $
   (Column G on G703)
5. RETAINAGE:
   a. ____ % of Completed Work $
      (Columns D + E on G703)
   b. ____ % of Stored Material $
      (Column F on G703)
   Total Retainage (Line 5a + 5b or
   Total in Column I of G703)............. $
6. TOTAL EARNED LESS RETAINAGE............. $
   (Line 4 less Line 5 Total)
7. LESS PREVIOUS CERTIFICATES FOR PAYMENT
   (Line 6 from prior Certificate).............. $
8. CURRENT PAYMENT DUE .... $
9. BALANCE TO FINISH, INCLUDING RETAINAGE
   (Line 3 less Line 6) $

CHANGE ORDER SUMMARY	ADDITIONS	DEDUCTIONS
Total changes approved in previous months by Owner		
Total approved this Month		
TOTALS		
NET CHANGES by Change Order		

The undersigned Contractor certifies that to the best of the Contractor's knowledge, information and belief the Work covered by this Application for Payment has been completed in accordance with the Contract Documents, that all amounts have been paid by the Contractor for Work for which previous Certificates for Payment were issued and payments received from the Owner, and that current payment shown herein is now due.

CONTRACTOR:

By: _____ Date: _____

State of:
County of:
Subscribed and sworn to before
me this ____ day of ____

Notary Public:
My Commission expires:

ARCHITECT'S CERTIFICATE FOR PAYMENT

In accordance with the Contract Documents, based on on-site observations and the data comprising this application, the Architect certifies to the Owner that to the best of the Architect's knowledge, information and belief the Work has progressed as indicated, the quality of the Work is in accordance with the Contract Documents, and the Contractor is entitled to payment of the AMOUNT CERTIFIED.

AMOUNT CERTIFIED.............................. $

(Attach explanation if amount certified differs from the amount applied for. Initial all figures on this Application and on the Continuation Sheet that are changed to conform to the amount certified.)

ARCHITECT:

By: _____ Date: _____

This Certificate is not negotiable. The AMOUNT CERTIFIED is payable only to the Contractor named herein. Issuance, payment and acceptance of payment are without prejudice to any rights of the Owner or Contractor under this Contract.

CONTINUATION SHEET

AIA Document G703   (Instructions on reverse side)   PAGE   OF   PAGES

AIA Document G702, APPLICATION AND CERTIFICATE FOR PAYMENT, containing
Contractor's signed Certification is attached.

In tabulations below, amounts are stated to the nearest dollar.

Use Column I on Contracts where variable retainage for line items may apply.

APPLICATION NUMBER:
APPLICATION DATE:
PERIOD TO:
ARCHITECT'S PROJECT NO:

A	B	C	D	E	F	G		H	I
			WORK COMPLETED						
ITEM NO.	DESCRIPTION OF WORK	SCHEDULED VALUE	FROM PREVIOUS APPLICATION (D + E)	THIS PERIOD	MATERIALS PRESENTLY STORED (NOT IN D OR E)	TOTAL COMPLETED AND STORED TO DATE (D + E + F)	% (G ÷ C)	BALANCE TO FINISH (C − G)	RETAINAGE

G703-1983

CERTIFICATE OF
SUBSTANTIAL COMPLETION

AIA DOCUMENT G704

(Instructions on reverse side)

OWNER ☐
ARCHITECT ☐
CONTRACTOR ☐
FIELD ☐
OTHER ☐

PROJECT:
(Name and address)

PROJECT NO.:

CONTRACT FOR:
CONTRACT DATE:

TO OWNER:
(Name and address)

TO CONTRACTOR:
(Name and address)

DATE OF ISSUANCE:
PROJECT OR DESIGNATED PORTION SHALL INCLUDE:

The Work performed under this Contract has been reviewed and found, to the Architect's best knowledge, information and belief, to be substantially complete. Substantial Completion is the stage in the progress of the Work when the Work or designated portion thereof is sufficiently complete in accordance with the Contract Documents so the Owner can occupy or utilize the Work for its intended use. The date of Substantial Completion of the Project or portion thereof designated above is hereby established as

which is also the date of commencement of applicable warranties required by the Contract Documents, except as stated below:

_____

A list of items to be completed or corrected is attached hereto. The failure to include any items on such list does not alter the responsibility of the Contractor to complete all Work in accordance with the Contract Documents.

_____   BY _____   DATE _____
ARCHITECT

The Contractor will complete or correct the Work on the list of items attached hereto within _____ days from the above date of Substantial Completion.

_____   BY _____   DATE _____
CONTRACTOR

The Owner accepts the Work or designated portion thereof as substantially complete and will assume full possession thereof at _____ (time) on _____ (date).

_____   BY _____   DATE _____
OWNER

The responsibilities of the Owner and the Contractor for security, maintenance, heat, utilities, damage to the Work and insurance shall be as follows:
(Note—Owner's and Contractor's legal and insurance counsel should determine and review insurance requirements and coverage.)

 CAUTION: You should use an original AIA document which has this caution printed in red. An original assures that changes will not be obscured as may occur when documents are reproduced.

ARTICLE 1

BASIC LEASE PROVISIONS
ENUMERATION OF EXHIBITS

Section 1.01 Basic Lease Provisions

(A)	DATE :	December 4, 1989
(B)	LANDLORD:	First Mortgage Bank as Trustee (Trust No. 108049-04, date April 11, 1989)
(C)	LANDLORD'S MANAGING AGENT:	Regent Real Estate Corporation
(D)	ADDRESS OF LANDLORD:	c/o The Regent Group 524 W. South Avenue Chicago, Illinois 60610
(E)	TENANT:	Cellular Communications
(F)	ADDRESS OF TENANT:	622 W. Fifth Avenue Naperville, IL 60540-2902

PERMITTED USES (Section 3.02): PRINCIPAL USE: Sale and service of cellular telephones, alarm systems, radar detectors and automotive electronic accessories ("Principal Uses") and SECONDARY USE: Sale and service of miscellaneous automotive accessories ("Secondary Uses") (the Principal Use and Secondary Use are collectively referred to as the "Permitted Use").

TENANT'S TRADE NAME (Section 3.02): Cellular Communications or such other name as Tenant may elect ("Trade Name")

AUTO SERVICE CENTER (Section 2.01): The land and improvements located at SWC of Route 59 and South Road ("Auto Service Center"), situated in City of Aurora, County of DuPage, State of Illinois.

PREMISES (Section 2.01): That portion of the Auto Service Center outlined in red on Exhibit A with the following approximate dimensions and area: Width: 25 ft. Depth: 55 ft. Area: 1,375 sq. ft. ("Premises")

LEASE YEAR: The term lease year ("lease year") as used herein shall mean a period of twelve (12) consecutive full calendar months. The first lease year ("First Lease Year") shall begin on the Rental Commencement Date of the term hereof if the date of commencement shall occur on the first day of the calendar month; if not, then the first lease year shall commence upon the first day of the calendar month next following the date of Rental Commencement. Each succeeding lease year shall commence upon the anniversary date of the first lease year.

INITIAL TERM AND RENTAL COMMENCEMENT DATE (Section 2.05)(if applicable): Ten (10) Lease Years ("Initial Term") to commence thirty (30) days after notice by Landlord that the Premises are available to Tenant ready for Tenant's Work ("Rental Commencement Date").

OPTION PERIOD(S) (Section 2.05): Two (2) consecutive periods consisting of five (5) Lease Years each, with the first option period commencing at the end of the Initial Term ("Option Period(s)"). The Initial Term plus any Option Period(s) are referred to herein as the "Lease Term".

FIXED MINIMUM RENT (Section 3.01):

	Initial Term		Option #1		Option #2
Year	1 - $ 20,625		11 - $ 30,530	16-	$ 37,144
	2 - 21,450		12 - 31,751	17 -	38,630
	3 - 22,308		13 - 33,021	18 -	40,175
	4 - 23,200		14 - 34,342	19 -	41,782
	5 - 24,128		15 - 35,716	20 -	45,454
	6 - 25,093				
	7 - 26,097				
	8 - 27,141				
	9 - 28,227				
	10 - 29,356				

359

COMMON AREA MAINTENANCE PAYMENT (Section 4.01): Proportionate Share

REAL ESTATE TAX EXPENSE (Section 4.01): Proportionate Share

ADVERTISING AND PROMOTION (Section 5.01): Tenant Costs

PREPAID RENT: $1,718.75 paid upon execution of this Lease to be applied to the first installment(s) of Fixed Minimum Rent due hereunder.

SECURITY DEPOSIT (Section 3.07): One Thousand Seven Hundred Eighteen and 75/100 Dollars ($1,718.75) ("Security Deposit").

PAYMENT OF SUMS DUE: All sums due hereunder form Tenant to Landlord shall be made payable to Regent Real Estate Corporation ("landlord's Managing Agent) or to such other payee which Landlord may designate by written notice to Tenant.

SECTION 1.02 Significance of a Basic Lease Provision

Each reference in the "Lease" to any of the Basic Lease Provisions contained in Section 1.01 of this Article shall be deemed and construed to incorporate all of the terms thereof. The Basic Lease Provisions shall be construed in connection with and limited by any such reference.

SECTION 1.03 Enumeration of Exhibits.

The exhibits enumerated in this Section and attached to this Lease are incorporated in this Lease by this reference and are to be construed as a part of this Lease.

Exhibit A:	Site Plan of Auto Service Center
Exhibit B:	Landlord's Work
Exhibit C:	Tenant's Work
Exhibit D;	Sign Criteria
Exhibit E:	Environmental Compliance (if applicable)
Exhibit F:	Subordination, Attornment and Non-disturbance Agreement

Article II

DEMISE OF PREMISES AND QUIET ENJOYMENT

SECTION 2.01   Description and General Obligations

Landlord owns the land shown on Exhibit A, together with the certain proposed buildings and improvements thereon depicted, all of which constitute the Auto Service center. In consideration of the rents, covenants and agreements reserved and contained in this Lease, Landlord hereby leases and demises the Premises to Tenant and Tenant rents same, in order that Tenant shall continuously operate its retail business operation thereon in accordance with its Permitted Use, subject only to the terms and conditions herein contained and all easements, restrictions, zoning laws, and governmental or other regulations affecting the Auto Service Center. The approximate location of the Premises is outlined in red on the Site Plan attached hereto as Exhibit A.

The Premises shall include only the appurtenances specifically granted in this Lease with Landlord specifically excepting and reserving fro itself, the roof, the air space above the roof, the space below the floor, the exterior portions of the Premises (other than the storefront), and the right to install, maintain, use, repair and replace pipes, ductwork, conduits, utility lines, and wires in the Premises. Landlord agrees that where possible all work in the Premises shall be performed n a manner which shall not unreasonably interfere with the normal business operations of Tenant. No rights are conferred on Tenant and Landlord specifically excepts and reserves unto itself, unless otherwise specifically provided, all rights to the land and improvements below the floor level of the Premises and to the air rights above the Premises, and to the land and improvements located on and within the Common Areas.

SECTION 2.02   Use of Additional Area.

The uses and occupation by the Tenant of the Leased Premises shall include a revocable license to use in common with the others entitled thereto, the Common Areas, as may be designated from time to time by the Landlord, subject however to the terms and conditions of this Lease and to rules and regulations for the use thereof as prescribed from time to time by the Landlord. The purpose of this Site Plan is solely to show the approximate location of the Premises. Landlord reserves the right at anytime to relocate the automobile parking areas and other Common Areas; to change the number of buildings, buildings' dimensions, the number of floors in any of the buildings, sort dimensions, Common Areas, the identity and type of others stores and tenancies, and the right to construct other buildings or improvements in the Auto Service Center form time to time and to construct double-deck or elevated parking facilities, provided only that the size of the Premises, reasonable access to the Premises and the parking facilities shall not be materially impaired, nor shall such changes cause the existing ratio of parking spaces to gross leasable area of the Auto Service Center as shown on Exhibit A to diminish. Landlord shall have the right to redesign and/or otherwise change or alter the storefront of the Premises in connection with a general change in substantially all of the storefronts in the Center. The term "Common Areas" as uses in this Lease shall mean all facilities furnished in the Auto Service Center and designate by Landlord for the general use, in common, of occupants of the Auto Service Center, including Tenant hereunder, its officers, agents, employees and customers, which facilities may include, but are not limited to, the parking areas, streets, passenger vehicle roadways, sidewalks, walkways, service areas, roadways, loading platforms, drainage and plumbing systems, roof, canopies, ramps, landscaped areas and other similar facilities available for common use which may from time to time exist. Landlord shall have no obligation to permit any of the Common Areas to be operated beyond the hour designate by Landlord. All Common Areas not within the Premises, which Tenant may be permitted to use and occupy, are to be used and occupied under a revocable license, and if the amount of the Common Areas be diminished. Landlord shall not be subject to any liability nor shall Tenant be entitled to any compensation or diminution of abatement of rent, except as otherwise provided elsewhere herein, nor shall such diminution of Common Areas be deemed constructive or actual eviction.

SECTION 2.03   Constructive/Possession.

Landlord and Tenant hereby agree that Tenant's taking possession of the Premises shall be deemed conclusive evidence of Tenant's acceptance of the Premises in satisfactory condition and in full compliance with all covenants and obligations of Landlord in connection therewith, except for punchlist items and latent defects of which Landlord is notified in writing within sixty (60) days after Tenant takes possession and pertaining only to Landlord improvements as described in Exhibit B attached hereto.

Prior to the Rental Commencement Date, Landlord will make all of the Landlord's improvements in and to the Premises in accordance with Exhibit B attached hereto, all of which shall be completed at Landlord's expense. Any finished work required beyond the scope of Landlord's work as described in Exhibit B shall be done by Landlord at Tenant's expense or, at Landlord's option, by Tenant at Tenant's expense. Landlord agrees to substantially complete its work in and to the Premises in accordance with Exhibit B on or before June 1, 1990. In the event such work is not substantially complete on or before June 1, 1990, Tenant shall have the option of terminating this Lease provided notice of Tenant's election is given to Landlord on or before June 15, 1990.

Annexed hereto as Exhibit C is a description of "Tenant's Work" (including the installation of trade fixtures)_ which shall be done by Tenant at Tenant's expense. Within thirty (30) days after written notice from Landlord, Tenant shall, at its sole cost and expense, commence and complete all of Tenant's work. For the purpose of completing such work and installing its fixtures and other equipment, Tenant may enter the Premises prior to the Rental Commencement Date, provide that prior to such entry by Tenant, Landlord has substantially completed Landlord's work and Tenant and Landlord have agreed upon a punchlist for such work (Tenant shall inspect Landlord's Work and agree upon a punchlist regarding same within three (3) days after Landlord notifies Tenant that Landlord's Work is substantially completed) on condition that (1) all such works shall be conducted in such a manner as will not interfere with Landlord's construction activities, and in compliance with all of the terms and conditions enumerated in Exhibit C, (2) Tenant shall, at its won expense remove from the Premises and the

Common Areas, all trash which may accumulate in connection with Tenant's activities and keep the Common Areas free of building material and equipment used in connection with Tenant's Work, and (3) Tenant shall perform all duties and obligations imposed by the Lease, including but not limited to those provisions relating to utilities, insurance and indemnification, saving and excepting only the obligation to pay Fixed Minimum Rent which obligation shall commence on the Rental Commencement Date.

Notwithstanding anything to the contrary contained in this Lease, Landlord shall not be responsible or liable to Tenant, its agents, servants, employees, licensees, or contractors, for any loss or damage to the property of such parties occurring prior to or after the commencement of the Lease Term.

The Tenant shall not suffer any mechanics' lien to be filed against the Premises or the Auto Service Center by reason of work, labor, services or materials performed or furnished to the Tenant or to anyone holding the Premise through or under the Tenant. If any such mechanics' lien shall at any time be filed, the Tenant shall forthwith cause the same to be discharged of record by payment, bond, order of a court of competent jurisdiction or otherwise, but the Tenant shall have the right to contest any and all such liens, provide the same are bonded. If the Tenant shall fail to cause such lien to be discharged or bonded with ten (10) days after being notified of the filing thereof and before judgment or seal thereunder, then, in addition to any other right or remedy of the Landlord, the Landlord may, but shall not be obligated to, discharge the same by paying the amount claimed to be due or by bonding or other proceeding deemed appropriate by the Landlord, and the amount so paid by the Landlord and all costs and expenses, including attorneys' fees, incurred by the Landlord, in procuring the discharge of such lien, shall be deemed to be Additional Rent for the Premises and shall be due and payable by the Tenant to the Landlord on demand. Nothing in this Lease contained shall be construed as a consent on the part of the Landlord to any lien or liability under the Mechanics' Lien Law or other law of Illinois, and nay action of the Tenant in violation of this covenant shall be default under the Lease and Landlord shall be entitled to all remedies against Tenant provided for hereunder in the event of default.

Tenant shall perform all Tenant work in the Premises in accordance with Exhibit C attached hereto and shall thereafter install such stock, fixtures and equipment and perform such other work as shall be necessary or appropriate in order to prepare the Premises for the opening and continuous operation of its business thereon. Tenant shall observe and perform all of its obligations under the Lease except for the payment of Fixed Minimum Rent (which obligation does no commence until the Rental Commencement Date), and shall pay charges for temporary water, heating, cooling and lighting from the date upon which the Premises are made available to Tenant for its work (or from the date when Tenant commences to perform its said work, if earlier) until the Rental Commencement Date.

SECTION 2.04   Quiet Enjoyment.

Landlord covenant that Tenant, upon paying all sums due from Tenant to Landlord hereunder and performing and observing all of Tenant's obligation under the Lease, shall peacefully and quietly have, hold and enjoy the Premises and the appurtenances through the Lease Term without interference by the Landlord, subject, nevertheless, to the other terms and provisions of this Lease.

SECTION 2.05   Statement of Lease Term.

Within five (5) days after the Rental Commencement Date, Landlord and Tenant shall execute and deliver written statement in recordable form specifying therein the Rental Commencement Dave and termination date of the Lease Term, and Tenant shall acknowledge there that the Premises (including the building or building of which the Premises is a part and the parking, facilities and other Common Areas and facilities of the Auto Service Center) are completed in accordance with the terms of the Lease and certify that the Lease is in full force and effect.

Provided that Tenant is not in default hereunder at the time of the commencement of each applicable Option Period, and provide further that Tenant has not assigned or sublet all or any part of the Premises, this Lease shall automatically be extended for each Option Period, upon the same terms and conditions as provided for herein, except that the Fixed Minimum Rent shall be the amount specified for same for said Option Period(s) in Section 1.01 hereof. Tenant may terminate this Lease at the end of the Initial Term or any subsequent Option Period if Tenant shall give written notice to Landlord at least one hundred twelve (12) days (which may be reduced to ninety (90) days provided Tenant sends a written request for such reduction to Landlord one hundred twenty (120) days prior to then end of the Initial Term or the current Option Period) prior to the end of the Initial Term or the current Option Period that it does not desire to extend this Lease.

Landlord agrees to grant Tenant, at any time throughout the term of this Lease, the right of first refusal to lease adjacent space which may be vacant and available to lease. Said right of first refusal shall be granted provided that in the event Tenant leases only a portion of such adjacent space, the remaining space not lease by Tenant shall have a minimum storefront width of twenty-five (25) feet.

This Lease and the tenancy herby created shall cease and terminate at the end of the original term hereof (if no option to renew is granted hereunder)_, or at the end of any Option Period(s) (if an option to renew is granted hereunder), without the necessity of any notice from either the Landlord or Tenant to terminate the same, and Tenant, upon notification from Landlord, shall vacate the Premises and agrees that the Landlord shall be entitled to the benefit of all provisions of laws respecting the summary recovery of possession of the Premises from a Tenant holding over to the same extend as if statutory notice had been given.

SECTION 2.06   Failure of Tenant to Open.

Tenant shall open the Premises for business fully fixtured, stocked and staffed within sixty (60) days after the Rental Commencement Date. In the event the Tenant fails to open the Premises fro business fully fixtured, stocked and staffed on the Rental Commencement Date or by such late date as permitted in the succeeding sentence, then Landlord shall have in addition to any and all remedies herein provide the right at its option to collect not only the Fixed Minimum Rent but additional rent at the rate of 1/360th per day of the annual Fixed Minimum Rent. Notwithstanding anything to the contrary contained in the foregoing sentence or anywhere else in this Lease, Tenant shall not be in default hereunder if Tenant fails to open the Premises on or before the Rental Commencement Date due to delays due to any strike, lockout, civil commotion, warlike operation, invasion, rebellion, hostilities, military or usurped power, sabotage, governmental regulations or controls, inability to obtain any material, serve or financing through Act of God, severe weather conditions or other causes beyond the control of Tenant, but the date by which Tenant must open the Premises for business shall be extended only for the period of the delay caused by any of such events and in the event Tenant is delayed din opening the Premises for business for a period in excess of the period of delay caused by such events, Tenant shall be in default hereunder.

SECTION 2.07   Excuse of Landlord's Performance.

Anything in this Lease to the contrary notwithstanding, providing such cause is not due to the willful act or neglect of the Landlord, the Landlord shall not be deemed in default with respect to the performance of any of the terms, covenants and conditions of the Lease if same shall be due to any strike, lockout, civil commotion, warlike operation, invasion, rebellion, hostilities, military or usurped power, sabotage, governmental regulations or controls, inability to obtain any material, service or financing, through Act of God, severe weather conditions or other cause beyond the control of the Landlord.

SECTION 2.08   Landlord's Purchase of Auto Service Center (Deleted)

ARTICLE III

RENT

SECTION 3.01   Fixed Minimum Rent.

During the entire Lease Term, Tenant covenants and agrees to pay to Landlord, in lawful money of the United States, without any prior demand and without any deduction or setoff whatsoever, the Fixed Minimum Rent as provided in Section 1.01. The payment of Fixed Minimum Rent by Tenant to Landlord shall be made in advance on the first day of each calendar month during the Lease Term, except that the first monthly installment shall be paid prior to the Rental Commencement Date. Fixed Minimum Rent for any partial calendar month during the Lease Term shall be prorated on a per diem basis.

SECTION 3.02   Permitted Uses

Tenant hereby covenants and agrees: (i) to operate in the Premises only under the Trade Name set forth in Section 1.01, (ii) to continuously and diligently use, occupy and operate the whole of the Premises for the retail sale of its goods or services in accordance with it Permitted Use during such days of the week and such hours as are from time to time designated by local ordinance or the Fox Valley Planned Development District, and for no other purpose whatsoever, and (iii) not to own, operate or be financially interested in, either directly or indirectly (by itself or with others), a business like or similar to the business permitted to be conducted hereunder, or which employs the same or similar Trade Name, with a radius of one (1) mile of the perimeter of the Auto Service Center, except for those which Tenant has in operation as of the date hereof. Without limiting Landlord's other available remedies, in the event Tenant should violate the covenant (iii) above, Landlord may, at its option, terminate this Lease upon thirty (30) days written notice to Tenant.

Tenant covenants and agrees that the Premises shall be used and occupied by Tenant only in accordance with its Permitted Use and for no other purpose or purposes. Tenant also covenants and agrees that Tenant shall not increase its Secondary Use of the Premises to the extent that any of said uses shall become a Principal Use. FO the purposes of this Lease, any use which generates more than twenty-five (25%) of the total gross receipts for a particular lease year for the premises shall be deemed a Principal Use of the Premises. Landlord acknowledges that by reason of its character as a full service Auto Service Center, activities of some Tenants may be similar to those of other Tenants, however, Landlord represents that it shall not lease space in the Auto Service Center to any other tenant whose Principal Use as reflected in such tenant's lease is the same as that of the Tenant's as reflected in this Lease and that all of said leases shall prohibit each tenant thereunder from engaging as its Principal Use in the same Principal Use as that of the Tenant as recited above. Landlord agrees to prohibit other tenants in the Auto Service Center from engaging, as a Principal Use or Secondary Use, in the sale or service of cellular telephones or cellular telephone service.

SECTION 3.03   Gross Receipts Defined (Deleted)

SECTION 3.04   Tenant's Records (Deleted)

SECTION 3.05   Reports by Tenant (Deleted)

SECTION 3.06   Termination by Landlord for Insufficient Percentage Rent (if applicable) (Deleted)

SECTION 3.07   Security Deposit

Tenant has concurrently with the execution of this Lease deposited with Landlord the Security Deposit as security for the full performance of every provision of this Lease by Tenant. Landlord may apply all or any par t of the Security Deposit to cure any default by Tenant hereunder, and Tenant shall promptly restore to the Security Deposit all amounts so applied upon invoice. If Tenant shall fully perform each provision of the Lease, any portion of the Security Deposit which ash not been appropriated by Landlord in accordance with the provisions hereof shall be returned to Tenant without interest within thirty (30) days after the expiration of the Lease Term. Landlord may deliver the funds deposited hereunder by Tenant to the purchaser or transferee of Landlord's interest in the Premises in the even that such interest be sold or transferred and Landlord shall be discharged from any further liability with respect to such deposit.

SECTION 3.08   Additional Charges.

In addition to Fixed Minimum Rent, all other payments, including but not limited to Operating Costs (hereinafter defined) to be made by Tenant to Landlord, shall be deemed to be and shall become "Additional Rent" hereunder whether or not the same be designate as such, and shall be due and payable on demand together with any interest thereon; an landlord shall have the same remedies for failure to pay same as for a non-payment of Fixed Minimum Rent. (Fixed Minimum Rent and Additional Rent are hereinafter sometimes collectively referred to as "Rent".) If Tenant shall fail to make any payment of Rent when due as required under the applicable provisions of this Lease, Tenant shall pay a late charge in accordance with Section 3.09 hereof.

SECTION 3.09   Past Due Rent and Additional Rent.

If Tenant shall fail to pay, when the same is due and payable, any Rent or any Additional Rent, or amounts or charge of the character described in Section 3.08 hereof, such unpaid amounts shall bear interest at the rate which is the lesser of eighteen percent (18%) per annum or the maximum interest rate permitted by law. Tenant shall in addition, pay as Additional Rent a fee of Fifty Dollars ($50.00) for processing of late payments. Tenants obligation to pay interest and processing fee for late payments shall commence five (5) days after notice from Landlord for such unpaid amounts. Interest on such unpaid amounts shall accrue until the date of payment.

ARTICLE IV

COMMON AREAS AND OPERATING COSTS

SECTION 4.01   Operating Costs.

Commencing upon occupancy of the Premises by Tenant and during each month of the Lease Term, Tenant shall pay without demand, deduction or setoff, as Additional Rent to Landlord, Tenant's proportionate share of all costs incurred by Landlord in maintaining, repairing, operating and insuring the portions of the Auto Service Center which are the responsibility of Landlord hereunder (herein sometimes referred to as the "Operating Costs"). Beginning on the Rent Commencement Date as set forth in Section 1.01 hereof, said payment of Tenant's proportionate share of operating costs shall be paid along with its monthly installment of Fixed Minimum Rent. Such operations costs shall include without limitation, the total costs of operating, repairing, lighting, cleaning, maintaining (including maintenance service agreements, maintaining the HVAC with the Premises and maintenance reserve charge, which such maintenance reserve charge shall not increase by more than five percent (5%) per annum [the funds for the maintenance reserve charge shall be placed in an escrow account and disbursed and replenished for maintenance costs as Landlord deems necessary or appropriate]). Landscaping, painting, securing, managing and insuring (including liability insurance for personal injury, wrongful arrest or detainer, death and property damage; insurance and extended coverage against fire, theft, flood or other casualty; Workman's Compensation insurance; fidelity bonds for personnel; plate glass insurance and any other insurance which Landlord shall deem necessary or desirable0 the Auto Service Center and paying all taxes, public charges and assessments or whatsoever nature directly or indirectly assessed or imposed upon the land, buildings, equipment and improvements constituting the Auto Service Center and rents therefrom, including, but not limited to, all real property taxes, rates, duties and assessments, local improvement taxes, import charges or levies, whether general or special, that are levied, charged or assessed against the Auto Service Center by any lawful taxing authority whether federal, state, county, municipal, school or otherwise (other than income, inheritance and franchise taxes thereon) which are payable during each Lease year of the Lease Term, plus an administrative cost equal to fifteen percent (15%) of the foregoing costs. Landlord's expenditures for attorneys' fees, appraisers' fees, experts' fees and other costs incurred in any Lease Year, without regard to the tax year involved, in any efforts by Landlord to minimize real estate taxes an assessments shall be included in the definition of taxes to be paid pursuant to the terms of this Section. If, at any time during the Lease Term, the methods of taxation or assessment shall be altered so that in lieu of, as substitute for, or in addition to the whole or any part of the taxes now levied, assessed or imposed on real estate as such or personal property, there shall be levied, assessed or imposed a tax, assessment, levy, charge, fee or the like, including, without limitation (i) a tax on the rents received from such real estate, or (ii) a charge, fee or tax imposed upon Landlord which is otherwise measured by or based in whole or in part upon the Auto Service Center or any portion thereof, then the same shall be include in the computation of taxes hereunder, computed as if the amount of such tax or fee so payable were that due as if the Auto Service Center were the only property of Landlord subject thereto.

Tenant's proportionate share of Operating Costs shall be computed by multiplying Operating Costs by a fraction, the numerator of which shall be the number of square fee of floor area of the Premises and the denominator of which shall be the number of square feet of gross leasable area of the Auto Service Center. Tenant's proportionate share of all Operating Costs during the Lease Term shall be paid in monthly installments on or before the first day of each calendar month during the Lease Term, in advance, in an amount estimated in writing by Landlord. Upon receipt of all bills attributable to any calendar year during the Lease Term, Landlord shall furnish Tenant with a written statement of the actual amount of Tenant's proportionate share of the Operating Costs for such year. If the total amount paid by Tenant under this Article for any calendar year during the lease Term shall be less than the actual amount due from Tenant for such year as shown on such statement, Tenant shall pay to Landlord the difference between the amount paid by Tenant and the actual amount due, such deficiency to be paid with ten (10) days after demand therefore by Landlord; and if the total amount due from Tenant for such calendar year, such excess shall be credited against payments hereunder next due, or, if no payments are next due, refunded by Landlord. All amounts due hereunder shall be payable in the manner and at such place as the rent payments provided for herein. Landlord's and Tenant's obligations under this Article shall survive expiration of the Lease Term.

ARTICLE V

ADVERTISING AND PROMOTION

SECTION 5.01   Tenant Costs (Deleted)

ARTICLE VI

UTILITIES

SECTION 6.01   Tenant Responsibilities

Tenant shall make application for, obtain, pay for, and be solely responsible for all utilities required, used or consumed in the Premises, including, but not limited to, gas, water (including water for domestic uses and for fire protection), telephone, electricity, sewer service or any similar service (herein sometimes collectively referred to as the "Utility Services"). In the event that any charge for any utility supplied to the Premises is not paid by Tenant to the utility supplier when due, then Landlord may, but shall not be required to, pay such charge for and on behalf of Tenant, with any such amount paid by Landlord being repaid by Tenant to Landlord, as Additional Rent, promptly upon demand. Landlord and Tenant hereby agree that Landlord shall not be liable for any interruptions or curtailment in utility services. In the event that any utility is provided to the Premises in common with other tenant's premises, Tenant shall pay Landlord for such utility based upon Landlord's reasonable allocation thereof.

ARTICLE VII

INSTALLATION, MAINTENANCE, OPERATION AND REPAIR AND ENVIRONMENTAL MATTERS

SECTION 7.01   Tenant Installation.

Tenant, shall, at Tenant's sole expense, install al trade fixtures and equipment required to operate it business (all of which shall be of first-class quality and workmanship). All trade fixtures, signs, or other personal property installed in the Premises by Tenant shall remain the property of Tenant and may be removed at any time provided that Tenant is not in default hereunder and provided the removal thereof does not cause, contribute to, or result in Tenant's default hereunder; and further provide that Tenant shall at Tenant's sole expense promptly repair any damage to the Premises resulting from the removal of personal property. The term "Trade Fixtures" as used herein shall not including carpeting, floor coverings, attached shelving, lighting fixtures other than free-standing lamps, wall coverings, or similar Tenant improvements which shall become the property of Landlord on surrender of the Premises by Tenant for whatever reason. Tenant shall not attach any fixtures or articles to any portion of the Premises, nor make any alterations, additions, improvements, or changes or perform any other work whatsoever in and to the Premises, other than minor interior, cosmetic and decorative changes which do not exceed Five Thousand and No/100 Dollars ($5,000.00) in the aggregate per Lease Year, without in each instance obtaining the prior written approval of Landlord. Any alterations, additions, improvements, changes to the Premises or other work permitted herein shall be made by Tenant at Tenant's sole cost and expense in the manner set forth in Exhibit C.

SECTION 7.02   Maintenance by Tenant.

Except as provided in Section 7.01 hereof, Tenant shall, at Tenant's expense, at all times keep the Premises (interior and exterior) and appurtenances thereto in good order, condition, and repair, clean, sanitary, and safe, including garbage removal, the replacement of equipment and fixtures and shall, in a manner satisfactory to

366

Landlord, decorate and paint the Premises when necessary to maintain at all times a clean and sightly appearance. In the even Tenant fails to perform any of its obligations as required hereunder, Landlord may, but shall not be required to, perform and satisfy same with Tenant hereby agreeing to reimburse Landlord, as Additional Rent, for the cost thereof promptly upon demand. Tenant shall make any and all additions, improvements, alterations, and repairs to or on the Premises (including, without limitation, all modifications to any fire sprinkler system located within the Premises which Tenant has installed), other than those required for the structural repair and maintenance of the roof, foundation, or exterior walls, which may at any time during the Lease Term be required or recommended by any lawful authorities, insurance underwriters, Inspection Rating Bureaus, or insurance inspectors designated by Landlord. Landlord may, but shall not be obligated to, deal directly with any authorities respecting their requirements for additions, improvement alterations, or repairs. All such work shall be performed in a good and workmanlike manner in accordance with the requirements set forth in Exhibit C. All Tenant's Work (as set forth in Exhibit C) and all such additions, improvements, and alterations thereto shall become the property of the Landlord upon the expiration or earlier termination of this Lease. Notwithstanding anything to the contrary contained herein, Tenant shall not make any additions, improvements, alterations or repairs to the Premises without first notifying Landlord thereof and obtaining Landlord's written consent thereto. Tenant shall deliver to Landlord any and all documents relative to said work which Landlord requests and deems are necessary or desirable, including, without limitation, performance and payment bonds, upon written notification from Landlord provided said notification is prior to the commencement of Tenant's work, covering all contractors performing said work and building plans detailing said work, and shall comply with any additional restrictions or impositions reasonably imposed by Landlord in connection therewith.

SECTION 7.03   Signs, Awnings and Canopies.

Tenant will not place or suffer to be placed or maintained on any exterior door, wall or window of the Leased Premises any sign, awning or canopy, or advertising matter or other thing of any kind, and will not place or maintain any exterior lighting, plumbing fixture or protruding object or any decoration, lettering or advertising matter on the glass of any window or door of the Premises without first obtaining Landlord's written approval and consent. Tenant further agrees to maintain such sign, awning, canopy, decorating, lettering, advertising matter or other thing as may be approved in good condition and repair at all times. Any such signs will conform to all governmental sign restrictions and/or deed restrictions and Exhibit D attaché hereto. Tenant shall install any exterior signs for the benefit of Tenant for his specific location, as Landlord requires in accordance with all of the terms of the Lease. In any event, if Landlord deems it necessary to install a freestanding sign for the benefit of all tenants, the Tenant will reimburse Landlord in full for his pro rata share of the common sign(s).

Landlord agrees to allow Tenant to place signage on all exterior walls of the Premises and neon signage in the windows of the Premises, provide all such signage conforms to all governmental sign ordinances and Exhibit D attached hereto.

SECTION 7.04   Tenant Shall Discharge All Liens.

Tenant will not create or permit to be created or to remain, and will discharge, any lien (including, but not limited to, the liens of mechanics, laborers or materialmen for work or materials alleged to be done or furnished in connection with the Premises), encumbrance or other charge upon the Premises or nay part thereof, upon Tenant's leasehold interest therein, provided, that Tenant shall not be required to discharge any such liens, encumbrances or charges as may be placed upon the Premises by the act of Landlord.

Tenant shall have the right to contest, in good faith and by appropriate legal proceedings, the validity or amount of any mechanics', laborers' or materialmen's liens or claimed lien. In the event of such contest and only during such time as Landlord is contemplating the possible sale of the Auto Service Center, Tenant shall give to Landlord reasonable security as may be required by Landlord to insure payment thereof and to prevent any sale, foreclosure or forfeiture of the lease Premises or any part thereof by reason of such non-payment. In the event Landlord is not contemplating the sale of the Auto Service Center at such time as any lien, encumbrance or other charge is place upon the Premises, Tenant shall be required to notify Landlord in writing within ten (10) days of such time as the claim for lien is filed and shall diligently pursue the release or satisfaction of the same. On final determination of such lien or such claim for lien, Tenant will immediately pay any judgment rendered, with all proper costs and charges, and shall have such lien released or judgment satisfied at Tenant's expense, and upon such payment and release of satisfaction, Landlord will promptly return to Tenant such security as Landlord shall have received in connection with such contest. Landlord reserves the right to enter the Premises to post and keep posted notices of non-responsibility for any such lien. Tenant will pay, protect and indemnify Landlord within ten (10) days after demand therefore, from and against all liabilities, losses, claims, damages, costs and expenses, including reasonable attorney's fees, incurred by Landlord by reason of the filing of any lien and/or removal of the same.

SECTION 7.05   Surrender of Leased Premises.

At the termination of this Lease, Tenant shall surrender the Premises in the same condition (subject to the removals hereinafter required) as the Premises were on the date the Tenant opened the Premises for business to the public, reasonable wear and tear and loss due to insured casualty excepted, and shall surrender all keys for the Premises to Landlord at the place then fixed for the payment of rent, and shall inform Landlord of all combinations on locks, safes and vaults, if any, in the Premises. Tenant during the last thirty (30) days of such term shall remove all of its trade fixtures, and, to the extent required by Landlord by written notice, any other installation, alterations or improvements (except interior partitions and floocoverings) before surrendering the Premises as aforesaid and shall repair any damage to the Premises caused thereby. Tenant's obligation to observe or perform this covenant shall survive the expiration or other termination of the Lease Term.

SECTION 7.06   Maintenance by Landlord.

Landlord shall keep the exterior supporting walls, the foundations and the roof of the Premises and the Common Areas in reasonable repair, provided the Tenant shall promptly give Landlord written notice of the necessity for such repairs, and provided that the damage thereto shall not have been caused by negligence of Tenant, its concessionaries, officers, agents, employees, licensees, or invitees; in which enfve Tenant shall be responsible for the payment of the costs for such repairs (it being understood and agreed that only Landlord may perform any of said repairs and that in no event whatsoever shall Tenant perform any of said repairs). Landlord shall have no obligation to repair, maintain, alter, or perform any other acts with reference to the Premises or any part thereof, or any plumbing, heating, ventilating, electrical, air conditioning, or other mechanical installations therein, except for the structural repairs and maintenance referred to in Section 7.02 above. Notwithstanding anything to the contrary contained in the forgoing sentence, Landlord shall perform and pay for the maintenance and repair of HVAC with respect to the Premises.

SECTION 7.07   Environmental Matters.

Tenant agrees and covenants that it will not generate, transport, treat, store nor dispose, nor, in any matter, arrange for the disposal or treatment [within the meaning of the Resource Conservation and Recovery Act, 42 U.S.C. 6901, et seq. ("RCRA"), the Comprehensive Environmental Response, Compensation and Liability Act, 42 U.S.C. 9601, et seq. ("CERCLA"), or any applicable federal, sate, or local law, regulation, ordinance or requirement, as amended or hereinafter amended (collectively hereinafter referred to as "Environmental Law")] of any hazardous substances as defined below, except as provided in Exhibit E. For the substances specifically identified in Exhibit E, Tenants aggress and covenants that it will comply with all Environmental Laws pertaining to the generation, transportation, storage, treatment or disposal or for, in any manner, arranging for disposal or treatment.

Hazardous Substances. "Hazardous Substances", for the purposes of this Agreement, means hazardous substances or hazardous wastes, as those terms are defined by the Environmental Laws. "Hazardous Substances" shall also include, but not be limited to, petroleum, including but not limited to, crude oil or any fraction thereof which is liquid at standard conditions of temperature and pressure (60 degrees Fahrenheit and 14.7 pounds per square inch absolute) and any radioactive material, including but not limited to, any source, special nuclear or by-product material as defined at 42 U.S.C. 2011, et seq., as amended or hereafter amended and asbestos in any form or condition.

Tenant agrees and covenants that it will comply with all Environmental Laws. At the election of Landlord (which election shall be exercised by Landlord giving Tenant notice thereof within thirty (30) days before the expiration of the Lease Term), Tenant shall, on or before the expiration of the Lease Term, restore the Premises to the condition of the Premises upon the execution of this Lease, including, without limitation, removing, in compliance with all Environmental Laws, any and all underground storage tanks or above ground storage tanks installed by

368

Tenant. Tenant represents and warrants to Landlord that there are no pending, or threatening actions or proceedings (or notice of potential actions or proceedings) against Tenant from any governmental agency or any other entity regarding any matter relating to the Environmental Laws or to requirements relating to health, safety and protection of the environment, except as noted in Exhibit E.

Tenant agrees and covenants that it will not engage in any conduct, events or actions which could interfere with or prevent Tenant's compliance with the Environmental Laws or with requirements relating to health, safety and protection of the environment, or which may give rise to any legal liability or otherwise forms the basis of any claim, action, proceeding, hearing or investigation based on any condition or violation or alleged violation of the Environmental Laws or requirements relating to health, safety and protection of the environment.

Tenant's Indemnity. Tenant agrees to indemnify, defined and hold Landlord forever harmless from and against any and all conditions, liabilities, demands, claims, actions or causes of action, assessments, losses, costs, damages or expenses, whether asserted or unasserted, direct or indirect, existing or inchoated, know or unknown, having arise or to arise in the future (whether by existing or subsequently adopted federal, state, or local statutes, ordinances, regulations or other requirements), including reasonable attorneys' fees, sustained or incurred resulting from or arising out of, relating to, or by virtue of any condition of the Premises, the Auto Service Center or any other property created by or contributed to by Tenant (without limiting the generality of the foregoing, by means of arranging for the disposal or treatment of Hazardous Substances), or Tenant's violation of the Environmental Laws existing or subsequently enacted, or requirements relating to health, safety and protection of the environment, including but not limited to, those relating to the release or threatened release of Hazardous Substances or by reason of the imposition of any lien for the recovery of any costs related to the release or threatened release of Hazardous Substances (or allegations of the release or threatened release of Hazardous Substances) expended; and Tenant, its successors and assigns, hereby waive, release and agree not to make any claim or bring any cost recovery action from or against Landlord under the Environmental Laws.

Landlord and Tenant further agree that Landlord will indemnify Tenant for any cost, liability or expense imposed upon Tenant under local, state or federal environmental law or judicial or administrative order by virtue of contamination of the Premises or by virtue of contamination of ground water or surrounding lands resulting from said contamination of the Premises. This indemnification is expressly limited to any claims for ground water pollution, nuisance or site clean up for chemicals or materials and to claims for the clean up of ground water or surface soil of hazardous substances which were on the Premises prior to possession of said Premises by Tenant. Landlord further agrees that Tenant shall not be responsible or in any way contribute to the cost of remediating any form of environmental contamination not caused by Tenant whether such contamination was pre-existing, caused during Tenant's Lease Term or after Tenant's Lease Term has expired.

ARTICLE VIII

OPERATING RULES AND REGULATIONS

SECTION 8.01   Rules and Regulations

Tenant agrees to comply with and observer the following rules and regulations:

1.   All loading and unloading of goods by Tenant, its agents, employees and customers, shall not at any time impede the flow of traffic into and out of the Auto Service Center or any portion thereof, including the demised area of other tenants, and shall be done only at such times, in the areas, and through the entrances as may be required by the City of Aurora or such other regulating entity.

2.   The delivery or shipping of merchandise, supplies and fixtures to and from the Premises shall be subject to such rules and regulations as in the reasonable judgment of Landlord are necessary to ensure the quiet enjoyment and continued operation for all tenants.

3.   All garbage and refuse shall be kept in the kind of container specified by Landlord, and shall be placed in those areas designated by Landlord for collection in the manner and at the time and places specified by Landlord. Outside storage of any and all materials shall be strictly prohibited including, but not limited to tires, batteries, transmissions and engine parts.

4. No radio or television or other similar device shall be installed without first obtaining in each instance Landlord's consent in writing. No aerial shall be erected on the roof or exterior walls of the Lease Premises or on the grounds. Any aerial so installed without written consent shall be subject to removal without notice at any time. Landlord acknowledges that Tenant desires to erect an aerial on the roof above the Premises and consents to such erection provided the installer is approved by the roof manufacturer so as not to void the roof warranty.

5. No loud speakers, televisions, phonographs, radios, or other devices shall be used in a manner so as to be heard or seen outside the Premises.

6. If the Premises are equipped with heating facilities separate from those in the remainder of the Auto Service Center, Tenant shall keep the Premises at a temperature sufficiently high to prevent freezing of water in pipes and fixtures.

7. Tenant and Tenant's employees shall park their cars only in those parking areas designated for that purpose by Landlord and only during the hours which Tenant is required hereunder to operate in the Premises. Parking by Tenant may not exceed the proportion of the floor area of the Premises to the floor area of the lease space of the entire Auto Service Center. Except where forbidden by Law, vehicles parked overnight must be maintained within the area of the Premises. Vehicles shall be strictly prohibited from parking overnight in the common areas including driveways, fire lanes and parking areas. Tenant, its agents, employees and customers may not park any unlicensed or junk cars within the Auto Service Center or a portion thereof at any time.

8. The plumbing facilities shall not be sued for any other purposes than that for which they are constructed, and no foreign substances of any kind shall be thrown therein, and the expense of any breakage, stoppage, or damage resulting from a violation of this provision shall be borne by Tenant who shall, or whose employees, agents or invitees shall, have caused it.

9. Tenant shall use at Tenant's cost such pest extermination contractor as may be necessary to keep the Premises free of infestation.

10. Tenant shall not burn any trash or garbage of any kind in or about the Premises, the Auto Service Center, or within one mile of the outside property lines of the Auto Service Center.

11. Tenant shall not make noises, cause disturbances, or create odors which may be offensive to other tenants of the Auto Service Center or their officers, employees, agents, servants, customers, or invitees.

12. Tenant shall not commit or suffer to be committed any waste upon the Premises or any nuisance or other act or thing which may disturb the quiet enjoyment of nay other tenant in the building in which the Premises may be located, or in the Auto Service Center, or which may disturb the quiet enjoyment of any person within three hundred feet of the boundaries of the Auto Service Center.

13. Tenant shall, at Tenant's sole cost and expense, comply with all of the requirements of all county, municipal, state, federal and other applicable governmental authorities, now in force, or which may hereafter be in force, pertaining to the Premises, and shall faithfully observe in the use of the Premises all municipal and county ordinances and state and federal statutes now in force or which may hereafter be in force, and all regulations, orders and other requirements issued or made pursuant to any such ordinances and statutes.

14. Tenant shall keep the Premises and any other areas used by Tenant, its agent, employees and customers in a clean and sanitary condition.

15. Tenant shall restrict the subject matter of its advertising and promotional activities which occur at the Auto Service Center, or any part thereof, solely to its Principal Use. Notwithstanding anything to contrary contained herein, Tenant may advertise and promote its secondary uses provided such uses are not a Principal Use of any other tenant with the Auto Service Center. Tenant shall not install any signs on any of the windows of the Premises and shall only install signs where expressly permitted by Landlord. This regulation shall be uniformly imposed upon all tenants of the Auto Service Center.

16. All business conducted by the Tenant including, but no t limited to, merchandise sales, vehicle inspections, repair or service of any kind or nature shall be performed with the area of the Premises. Such business shall be strictly prohibited, without limitation, from the common areas including walkways, driveways, fire lanes, landscaped areas and parking areas.

17. The hours of operation shall be restricted as follows:

    a. Normal business hours (Sunday through Saturday) shall not extend beyond 9:00 p.m.

Tenant agrees to comply with and observe the rules and regulations set forth above. Tenant's failure to keep and observe said rules and regulations shall constitute a breach of the terms of this Lease in the manner as if the smear were contained herein as covenants. Landlord reserves the right from time to time to amend or supplement said rules and regulations, and to adopt and promulgate additional rules and regulations applicable to the Leased Premises and the Auto Service Center and Tenant agrees to comply with and observe said amended, supplemented or additional rules and regulations.

ARTICLE IX

INSURANCE

SECTION 9.01   Tenant's Coverage.

Tenant shall maintain at its sole expense during the term hereof, public liability insurance covering the Premises in an amount of $1,000,000.00 for injury and/or death and third party property damage per occurrence and in an amount of $2,000,000.00for injury and/or death and third party property damage in the aggregate and property damage insurance in an amount of $1,000,000.00 in companies satisfactory to Landlord in the joint names of Landlord and Tenant. Landlord may, from time to time, in the exercise of reasonable business judgment, increase the amounts of coverage required hereunder. Tenant shall also keep in force business interruption insurance as well as fire and extended coverage insurance of an "all risk" nature, to include vandalism and malicious mischief, loss of earnings coverage, coverage of all improvements to the Premises made by Tenant, including, but not limited to, inventory, trade fixtures, furnishings, signs and any personal property for the full replacement value of said improvements. Tenant will cause such insurance policies to name Landlord, Landlord's beneficiary (if applicable) and Landlord's Managing Agent as an additional insured and to be written so as to provide that the insurer waives all right of recovery by way of subrogation against Landlord, Landlord's beneficiary (if applicable) and Landlord's Managing Agent in connection with any loss or damage covered by the policy. In addition, Tenant shall keep in force workmen's compensation or similar insurance to the extent required by law. Tenant shall deliver said policies or certificates thereof to Landlord at least five (5) days prior to the commencement of the Lease Term. Should Tenant fail to effect the insurance called for herein, Landlord may, at its sole option, procure said insurance and pay the requisite premiums, in which event, Tenant shall pay all sums so expended to Landlord, as Additional Rent following invoice. Each insurer under the polices required hereunder shall agree by endorsement on the policy issued by it or by independent instrument furnished to Landlord that it will give Landlord thirty (30) days prior written notice before the policy or policies in question shall be altered or cancelled.

SECTION 9.02   Increase in Fire Insurance Premium.

Tenant shall not keep, use, sell or offer for sale in on upon the Premises any article which may be prohibited by the standard form of fire insurance policy. Tenant agrees to pay any increase in premiums for fire and extended coverage insurance that may be charged during the Lease Term on the amount of such insurance which may be carried by Landlord on the Premises or the Auto Service Center, resulting from the type of merchandise sold by Tenant in the Premises, whether or not Landlord has consented to the same. In determining whether increased premiums are the result of Tenant's use of the Premises, a schedule, issued by the organization making the insurance rate on the Premises, showing the various components of such rate, shall be conclusive evidence of the several items and charges which make up the fire insurance rate on the Premises.

In the event Tenant's occupancy causes any increase of premium for the fire, and/or casualty rates on the Premises, Tenant shall pay the additional premium on the fire and/or casualty insurance policies by reason thereof. The Tenant also shall pay, in such event, any additional premium on the rent insurance policy that may be carried by the Landlord for its protection against rent loss through fire. Bill for such additional premiums shall be rendered by Landlord to Tenant at such times as Landlord may elect, and shall be due from, and payable by, Tenant when rendered, and the amount thereof shall be deemed to be, and be paid as, Additional Rent.

SECTION 9.03   Indemnification.

Tenant hereby agrees to indemnify and hold forever Landlord harmless from any and all claims, damages, liabilities or expenses arising out of (a) Tenant's use of the Premises or the Auto Service Center, (b) any and all claims arising from any breach or default in the performance of any obligation of Tenant, (c) any act, omission or negligence of Tenant, its agents or employees. Tenant further releases Landlord from liability for any damages sustained by Tenant or any other person claiming by, through or under Tenant due to the Premises, the Auto Service Center, or any part thereof or any appurtenances thereto becoming out of repair, or due to the happening of any accident, including, but not limited to, any damage caused by water, snow, windstorm, tornado, gas, steam, electrical wiring, sprinkler system, plumbing, heating and air conditioning apparatus and from any acts or omission of co-tenants other occupants of the Auto Service Center. Landlord shall not be liable for any damage to or loss of Tenant's personal property, inventory, fixtures or improvements, from any cause whatsoever, except the affirmative acts of proven gross negligence of Landlord, and then only to the extent not covered by insurance to be obtained by Tenant in accordance with Section 9.01 hereof.

SECTION 9.04   Host Liquor Liability Insurance.

Tenant is hereby expressly prohibited from (i) storing, selling, using, bartering, trading or giving any intoxicating liquors in, on or from the Premises at any time, or (ii) permitting any other person or entity from doing any of same. Notwithstanding the foregoing, Tenant agrees to provide, in addition to the other insurance required under this Article IX, a policy or policies of insurance known as "Host Liquor Liability Insurance" protecting Landlord and Landlord's beneficiaries (if applicable) and Landlord's Managing Agent, their agents and employees, Tenant and the Premises of, from and against any and all damages, judgment, claims, liens, costs and expenses, including court costs and reasonable attorneys' fees, arising out of or in any manner connected with such matters as are typically covered by said insurance, such policy or policies of insurance to be reasonably satisfactory to Landlord and with companies reasonably satisfactory to Landlord and in the following minimum limits (or such other amounts as Landlord, may, from time to time, require) by virtue of either basic coverage or basic combined with umbrella coverage:

(a)   Bodily injury in an amount of $1,000,000.00; and
(b)   Damage to property of $1,000,000.00.

Tenant shall provide Landlord with certificates evidencing the above insurance coverages and showing that such insurance provides for at least thirty (30) days prior notice to the Landlord by the insurance company or companies prior to cancellation or termination of such insurance or alteration of the terms thereof. Such certificates shall be delivered to Landlord on or before the Rental Commencement Date and renewals shall be delivered to Landlord before the expiration of prior certificates.

ARTICLE X

CONDEMNATION

SECTION 10.01   Fire, Explosion or Other Casualty

In the event the Premises are damaged by fire, explosion or any other casualty to an extent which is less than fifty percent (50%) of the cost of replacement of the Premises, the damage, except as provided in Section 10.02, shall promptly be repaired by Landlord at Landlord's expense, provided that Landlord shall not be obligated to expend for such repair an amount in excess of the insurance proceeds recovered or recoverable as a result of such damage, and that in no event shall Landlord be required to repair or replace Tenant's stock in trade fixtures, furniture, furnishings, floor coverings and equipment. In the event of any such damage and (a) Landlord is not required to repair as hereinabove provided, or (b) the Premises shall be damaged to the extent of fifty percent (50%) or more of the cost of replacement, or (c) the building of which the Premises are a part is damaged to the extent of twenty-five percent (25%) or more of the cost of replacement, or (d) the buildings (taken in the aggregate) in the Auto Service Center shall be damaged to the extent of more than twenty-five percent (25%) or more of the cost of replacement, Landlord may elect either to repair or rebuild the Premises or the building or buildings, or to terminate this Lease upon giving notice of such election in writing to Tenant within ninety (90) days after the occurrence of the event causing the damage. In the event of a casualty with renders the Premises untenantable, in whole or in part, Tenant shall be allowed an abatement of Rent in the same proportion as the casualty renders the Premises untenantable and for such period of time until the Premises are restored to its original condition. During such repairing or rebuilding, Landlord agrees to allow Tenant the use of some portion of the Common Areas in order to maintain a temporary base of operations provided, however, that such temporary facility shall not disrupt or disturb Landlord's efforts in repairing or rebuilding or the efficient operation of other tenants in the Auto Service Center.

In the event of a casualty which renders the Premises wholly untenantable and provided such repairs are not completed with six (6) months after the occurrence of the even causing the damage, then Tenant may have the option of terminating the Lease.

SECTION 10.02 Landlord's and Tenant's Work

The provisions of this Article X with respect to repair by Landlord shall be limited to such repair as is necessary to place the Premises in the same condition as when possession was delivered by Landlord. Promptly following such casualty, Tenant shall, at Tenant's expense, perform any work required to place the Premises in the condition pursuant to Exhibit C and Tenant shall restore, repair or replace its stock in trade fixtures, furniture, furnishings, floor coverings, and equipment, and if Tenant has closed, Tenant shall promptly reopen for business.

SECTION 10.03 Condemnation.

If the whole of the Premises, or so much thereof as to render the balance unusable by Tenant, shall betaken under power of eminent domain, or otherwise transferred in lieu thereof, or if any part of the Auto Service Center is taken and its continued operation is not, in Landlord's sole opinion, economical, this Lease shall automatically terminate as of the date possession is taken by the condemning authority. No award for any total or partial taking shall be apportioned, and Tenant hereby unconditionally assigns to Landlord any award which may be made in such taking or condemnation. In the event of a partial taking which does not result in the termination of this Lease, Fixed Minimum Rent shall be apportioned according to the part of the Premises remaining unusable by Tenant. Nothing contained herein shall limit Tenant's right to file a claim with the condemning authorities.

SECTION 10.04 Condemnation Award.

All compensation awarded or paid for any taking or acquiring under the power of threat of eminent domain, whether for the whole or a part of the Premises or Auto Service Center, shall be the property of Landlord, whether such damages shall be awarded as compensation for diminution in the value of the leasehold or to the fee of the Premises or otherwise, and Tenant hereby assigns to landlord all of the Tenant's right, title and interest in and to any and all such compensation; provided, however, that Landlord shall not be entitled to any award specifically made to Tenant.

ARTICLE XI

DEFAULT AND REMEDIES

SECTION 11.01 Definitions.

In the event that Tenant (a) fails to pay all or any portion of any sum due from Tenant hereunder or pursuant to any exhibit hereto within five (5) days following written notice; (b) fails to cease all conduct prohibited hereby immediately upon receipt of written notice from Landlord; (c) fails to take action in accordance with the provisions of written notice from Landlord to remedy Tenant's failure to perform any of the terms, covenants and conditions hereof; (d) fails to conduct business in the Premises as herein required; (e) commits an act in violation of the Lease which Landlord has previously notified Tenant to cease more than once in any year; (f) becomes bankrupt, insolvent or files any debtor proceeding, takes or has take against Tenant any petition of bankruptcy; takes action or has taken action against Tenant for the appointment of a receive for all or a portion of Tenant's assets; files a petition for a corporate reorganization; makes as assignment for the benefit of creditors, or if in any other manner Tenant's interest hereunder shall pass to another by operation of law (any or all of the occurrences in this said Section 11.01; (f)shall be deemed a default on account of bankruptcy for the purposes hereof san such default on account of bankruptcy shall apply to and include an Guarantor of this Lease); (g) commits waster to the Premises; or (h) is otherwise in breach of Tenant's obligations hereunder and shall not have cured same within that period of time as set forth in Section 11.02 hereof, following written notice from

Landlord; then Tenant shall be in default hereunder and Landlord may, at its option and without further notice to Tenant, terminate Tenant's right to possession of the Premises and without terminating this Lease re-enter and resume possession of the Premises and/or declare this Lease terminated, and may thereupon in either event remove all persons and property from the Premises, with or without resort to process of any court, either by force or otherwise. Notwithstanding such re-entry by Landlord, Tenant hereby indemnifies and holds Landlord harmless from any and all loss or damage with Tenant may incur by reason of this termination of this Lease and/or Tenant's right to possession hereunder. In no event shall Landlord's termination of this Lease and/or Tenant's right to possession of the Premises abrogate Tenant's agreement to pay rent and additional charges due hereunder for the full term hereof. Following re-entry of the Premises by Landlord, Tenant shall continue to pay all such rent and additional charges as same become due under the terms of this Lease, (unless Landlord has declared the entire Rent for the balance of the Lease Term due and terminated this Lease, in which case Tenant shall pay at once to Landlord a sum of money equal to the Rent provided to be paid by Tenant to Landlord for the balance of the Lease Term, less the fair rental value of the Premises for said period plus any other sum of money and damages due or to become due to Landlord from Tenant) together with all other expenses incurred by Landlord in regaining possession until such time, if any, as Landlord relets same and the Premises are occupied by such successor. Upon reletting, sums received from such new lessee by Landlord shall be applied first to payment of costs incident to reletting; any excess shall then be applied to any indebtedness to Landlord from Tenant other than for Fixed Minimum Rent and any excess shall then be applied to the payment of Minimum Rent due and unpaid. The balance, if any, shall be applied against the deficiency between all amounts receive hereunder and sums to be receive by Landlord on reletting, which deficiency Tenant shall pay to Landlord in full within five days of notice of same from Landlord. Tenant shall have no right to any proceeds of reletting that remain following application of same in the manner set forth herein.

Notwithstanding anything contained herein to the contrary, in the event Landlord forcibly re-enters or takes possession of the Premises when the Tenant is current with his rent payments and is not disturbing the use and quiet enjoyment of the premise by other Tenants, then the Tenant's obligation to pay rent shall terminate as of the day the Landlord takes possession. In the event the Tenant vacates the premises the Landlord shall have all rights of re-entry and possession provided for in the lease or by operation of law. In the even the Tenant's leasehold interests are terminated by a court of law, the court shall determine the rent due the Landlord.

SECTION 11.02 Rights and Remedies.

The various rights and remedies herein granted to Landlord shall be cumulative and in addition to any others Landlord may be entitled to by law or in equity, and the exercise of one or more rights or remedies shall not impair Landlord's right to exercise any other right or remedy. In all events, Landlord shall have the right upon notice to Tenant to cure any breach by Tenant at Tenant's sole cost and expense, and Tenant shall reimburse Landlord for such expense upon demand. In all vents, Tenant shall have the right, upon written notice from the Landlord, to cure any breach or alleged breach before Landlord takes any further action or attempts to terminate Tenant's right to possession or leasehold interests or rights, with cure periods as follows:

    (i)   Five (5) days for monthly rent;
    (ii)   Ten (10) days for other financial matters;
    (iii)   Thirty (30 days for all non-financial matters

SECTION 11.03 Bankruptcy

If Landlord shall not be permitted to terminate this Lease as hereinabove provided because of the provisions of Title 11 of the United States Code relating to Bankruptcy, as amended ("Bankruptcy Code"), the Tenant as a debtor-in –possession or any trustee for Tenant agrees promptly, within no more than thirty (30) days upon request by Landlord to the Bankruptcy Court, to assume or reject this Lease and Tenant on behalf of itself, an any trustee agrees not to seek or request any extension or adjournment of any application to assume or reject this Lease by Landlord with such Court. In such event, Tenant or any trustee for Tenant may only assume this Lease if (a) it cures or provides adequate assurances that the trustees will promptly cure any default hereunder, (b) compensates or provides adequate assurance that Tenet will promptly compensate Landlord for any actual pecuniary loss to Landlord resulting from Tenant's default, and (c) provides adequate assurance of performance during the fully state term hereof of all the terms, covenants, and provisions of this Lease to be performed by Tenant. N no event after the assumption of this Lease shall any then existing default remain uncured for a period in excess of the earlier of ten (10) days or the time period set forth herein. Adequate assurance of performance of this Lease, as set forth hereinabove, shall include, without limitation, adequate assurance (1) of the source of rent reserved hereunder, and (2) the assumption of this Lease will not breach any provision hereunder.

If Tenant assumes this Lease and proposes to assign the same pursuant to the provisions of the Bankruptcy Code to any person or entity who shall have made a bona fied offer to accept an assignment of this Lease on terms acceptable to Tenant, then notice of such proposed assignment, setting forth (i) the name and address of such person, (ii) all of the terms and conditions of such offer, and (iii) the adequate assurance to be provided Landlord to assume such persons' future performance under the Lease, including, without limitation, the assurance referred to in section 365(b)(3) of the Bankruptcy Code, shall be given to Landlord by the Tenant no later than twenty (20) days after receipt by the Tenant but in any event no later than ten (10) days prior to the date that the Tenant shall make application to a court of competent jurisdiction for authority and approval to enter into such assignment and assumption, and Landlord shall thereupon have the prior right and option, to be exercised by notice to the Tenant given at any time prior to the effective date of such proposed assignment, to accept an assignment of this Lease upon the same terms and conditions and for the same consideration, if any, as the bona fide offer made by such person, less any brokerage commission which may e payable out of the consideration to be paid by such person for the assignment of this Lease.

If this Lease is assigned to any person or entity pursuant to the provisions of the Bankruptcy Code any and all monies or other considerations payable or otherwise to be deliver to Landlord, shall be and remain the exclusive property of Landlord and shall not constitute property of Tenant or of the estate of the Tenant with the meaning of the Bankruptcy Code. Any and all monies or other considerations constituting the Landlord's property under the preceding sentence not paid or delivered to the Landlord shall be held in trust for the benefit of Landlord and shall be promptly paid to the Landlord.

Any person or entity to which this Lease is assigned pursuant to the provisions of the Bankruptcy Code shall be deemed without further act or deed to have assumed all of the obligations arising under this Lease on and after the ate of such assignment. Any such assignee shall upon demand execute and deliver to Landlord an instrument confirming such assumption. Nothing contained in this section shall, in any way, constitute a waiver of the provisions of Section 12.01 of this Lease relating to assignment. Tenant shall not, by virtue of this section, have any further rights relating to assignment other than those granted in the Bankruptcy Code. Notwithstanding anything in this Lease to the contrary, all amounts payable by Tenant to or on behalf of Landlord under this Lease, whiter or not expressly denominated as rent, shall constitute rent for the purpose of section 502(b)(6) of the Bankruptcy Code.

In the event of a filing of a petition under the Bankruptcy Code, Landlord shall have no obligation to provide Tenant with any serviced or utilities as herein required, unless Tenant shall have paid and be current in all payments of Operating Costs, utilities or other charges thereof.

ARTICLE XII

ASSIGNMENT AND SUBLETTING

SECTION 12.01 Assignment and Subletting.

Tenant acknowledges that Tenant's agreement to operate in the Premises for the Permitted Use set forth in Section 1.01 hereof for the fully stated term hereof was a primary inducement and precondition to Landlord's agreement to lease the Premises to Tenant. Accordingly, Tenant's interest in the Premises shall be limited to the use and occupancy thereof in accordance with the provisions hereof ands shall be nontransferable. Any attempts by Tenant to sublet the Premises in whole or in part or to sell, assign, lien, encumber or in any manner transfer this Lease or any interest therein shall constitute a default hereunder, as shall any attempt by Tenant to assign or delegate the management or to permit the use or occupancy of the Premises or any pert hereof by anyone other than Tenant. Notwithstanding anything contained herein to the contrary, Landlord shall consent to such assignment or sublease of the Premises provided (i) the principal sue of the assignee or subtenant does not conflict with the Principal Use of any other existing tenant in the Auto Service Center, and (ii) the tangible net worth of the assignee or subtenant is equal to or greater than the tangible net worth of Tenant immediately prior to such assignment or sublease. Landlord and Tenant acknowledge and agree that the foregoing provisions have been freely negotiated by the parties hereto and that Landlord would not have entered into this Lease without Tenant's consent to the terms of this Section 12.01. Any attempt by Tenant to sublet all or any portion of the Premises, to encumber same. Or to in any manner transfer, convey, assign Tenant's interest therein, allow the use of management thereof, shall be void ab initio (from the beginning). If this Lease be assigned or the Premises or any part thereof be sublet or occupied by anybody other than the Tenant, the Landlord may collect rent from the assignee, undertenant or occupant and apply the net amount colleted to the rent herein reserved, but no such assignment, underletting, occupancy of collection shall be deemed a waiver of this covenant, or the acceptance of the assignee, undertenant or occupancy as Tenant or a release of the Tenant from the further performance by Tenant of the covenants on the part of the Tenant herein contained. Notwithstanding any assignment or sublease, the Tenant shall remain fully liable on this Lease and shall not be released from performing the terms, covenants and conditions of this Lease.

SECTION 12.02 Change of Control.

In furtherance of the provisions of Section 12.01 hereof, if Tenant is a corporation and if the persons or persons who own a majority of its voting shares at the time of the execution hereof cease to own a majority of such shares at any time hereafter, except as a result of transfers by gift, bequest, or inheritance by or among immediate family members, Tenant shall so notify Landlord. In the event of such change of ownership, whether or not Tenant has notified Landlord thereof, Landlord may terminate this Lease by notice to Tenant effective sixty (60) days from the date of such notice from Tenant or the date on which Landlord first has knowledge of such transfer, whichever shall first occur. This Section 12.02 shall not apply as long as Tenant is a corporation, the outstanding voting stock of which is listed on a recognized security exchange. If tenant is a partnership and if any partner or partners withdraw from the partnership, or if the partnership is otherwise dissolved, Tenant shall so notify Landlord. In the event of such withdrawal or dissolution, Landlord may terminate this Lease by notice to Tenant effective sixty (60) days from the date of notification from Tenant or the date on which Landlord first has knowledge of such withdrawal or dissolution, whichever shall first occur. If Tenant is a sole proprietorship, in the event of his incapacity or death, Landlord shall have the option to terminate this Lease upon sixty (60) days prior written notice to Tenant or his legal representative.

Notwithstanding provisions to the contrary contained in the lease, the Tenant and its shareholders shall have the unrestricted right to buy and sell its stock or to transfer the same by operation of law, gifts or by will. In the even the entire business is sold to an unrelated third party, the Landlord shall be notified in writing prior to the sale and the credit worthiness of the purchase shall be subject to verification and approval by the Landlord. In the event the same type of business is continuing and the buyer is financially stable in Landlord's reasonable judgment, the Landlord shall not object to the sale or transfer of the stock or business and assumption of the lease and shall acknowledge in writing his willingness to deal directly with the new owner. The original Tenant shall remain liable for the remaining lease term unless release from the lease by the Landlord in writing.

SECTION 12.03 Dissolution of Partnership (Deleted)

ARTICLE XIII

RIGHT OF ENTRY

SECTION 13.01 Right of Entry

Landlord or Landlord's agents shall have the right to enter the Premises at the times provided for herein to examine the same, and to show them to prospective purchasers or tenants of the building or Auto Service Center, and to make such repairs, alterations, improvements or additions as Landlord may deem necessary or desirable, and to determine if Tenant is complying with the terms and provisions of this Lease, including, without limitation, complying with the Rule and Regulations set forth herein, and Landlord shall be allowed to take all material into and upon the Premises that may be required therefore without the same constituting an eviction of Tenant in whole or in part, and the rent reserved shall in no way abate while said repairs, alterations, improvements, or additions are being made, by reason of loss or interruption of business of Tenant, or otherwise. During the six months prior to the expiration of the Lease Term or any renewal term, Landlord may exhibit the Premises to prospective tenants or purchasers, and place upon the Premises the usual notices "To Let" or "For Sale" which notices Tenant shall permit to remain thereon without molestation. If Tenant shall not be personally present to open and permit entry into the Premises, at any time when for any reason entry therein shall be necessary or permissible, Landlord or Landlord's agents may enter the same without in any manner affecting the obligations and covenants of this Lease. Nothing herein contained, however, shall be deemed or construed to impose upon Landlord, any obligation, responsibility or liability whatsoever, for the care, maintenance or repair of the Auto Service Center or any part thereof, except as otherwise herein specifically provided.

Notwithstanding provisions in the lease to the contrary, the Landlord shall have limited rights to enter the Tenant's premises in non-emergency situations as follows: (i) during normal business hours after advising Tenant so a time may be agreed upon to minimize the disruption of Tenant's business; (ii) for repaired purposes after normal business hours as arranged with the Tenant; or (iii) for emergency purposes at any time. In the event the premises are vacant, the Landlord may enter at any time.

ARTICLE XIV

TENANT'S PROPERTY

SECTION 14.01 Taxes.

Tenant shall be responsible for and shall pay before delinquency all municipal, county or state taxes, levies and fees of every kind and nature, including, but not limited to, general or special assessments assessed during the Lease Term against any personal property of any kind, owned by or placed in, upon or about the Premises by the Tenant and taxes assessed on the basis of Tenant's occupancy thereof, including, but not limited to, taxes measured by Rents due from Tenant hereunder.

SECTION 14.02 Notices by Tenant.

Tenant shall give immediate telephone or telegraphic notice to Landlord I case of fire, casualty, or accidents in the Premises or in the building of which the Premises are a part or of defects therein or in any fixtures or equipment and shall promptly thereafter confirm such notice in writing.

ARTICLE XV

SUCCESSION TO LANDLORD'S INTEREST

SECTION 15.01 Attornment.

Tenant shall attorn (agree to become the tenant of) and be bound to any of Landlord's successors under all the terms, covenants and conditions of this Lease for the balance of the remaining term.

SECTION 15.02 Subordination.

This Lease shall be subordinate to the lien of any mortgage or security deed or the lien resulting from any other method of financing or refinancing now or hereafter in force against the Auto Service Center, any portion thereof, or upon any buildings hereafter placed upon land of which the Premises are a part, and to any and all advances to be made under such mortgages, and all renewals, modifications, extensions, consolidations and replacements thereof, provided, however, that if the mortgagee trustee or holder of any such mortgage or deed of trust elect to have Tenant's interest in this Lease superior to any such instrument, then by notice to Tenant from such mortgagee, trustee or holder of such election, this Lease shall be deemed superior to such lien, whether his Lease was executed before of after said mortgage or deed of trust. The aforesaid provisions shall be self-operative and no further instrument of subordinations shall be required to evidence such subordinations. Tenant covenants and agrees to execute and deliver, upon demand, such further instrument or instruments subordinating the Lease on the foregoing basis to the lien of any such mortgage or mortgages as shall be desired by Landlord and any mortgages or proposed mortgages and hereby irrevocably appoints Landlord the attorney-in-fact of Tenant to execute and deliver such instrument or instrument within ten (10) days after written notice to do so.

377

SECTION 15.03 Mortgagee's Approval.

The Tenant hereby agrees to modify non-essential or inconsequential terms of the lease if so requested by the Landlord's mortgagee during a refinance or sale of the Auto Service Center. Any revisions of major importance which may impact upon the Tenant's business or his rights of occupancy shall be renegotiated by the Landlord and the Tenant.

SECTION 15.04 Estoppel Certificate.

Within ten (10) days after request thereof by Landlord, or in the event that upon any sale, assignment or hypothecation of the Premises and/or the land thereunder by Landlord an estoppel certificate shall be required from Tenant, Tenant agrees to deliver in recordable form, a certificate to any proposed mortgagee or purchaser, or to Landlord, certifying that this Lease is unmodified and in full force and effect (or, if there have been modifications, that the same is in full force and effect as modified, and stating the modifications), that there are no defenses or offsets thereto (or stating those claimed by Tenant) and the dates to which Fixed Minimum Rent and other charges have been paid any other information reasonably requested by said mortgagee or purchaser, it being intended that any such statements may be relied upon by any proposed mortgagee or purchaser or by Landlord.

SECTION 15.05 Financing.

Landlord reserves the right to add to or sever the ownership of or title to the various sections of the Auto Service Center and/or to place separate mortgages on said sections, in which case the right of Tenant and other tenants in the Auto Service Center will be reserved by a written declaration or agreement, to be executed by Landlord and duly recorded, creating mutual, reciprocal and interdependent rights to use the parking and other Common Areas and the utilities and facilities needed for the full use and enjoyment of the Premises by the Tenant and other tenants in the Auto Service Center under this Lease. Tenant covenants to execute from time to time such instruments reasonable required by Landlord and its mortgage to effectuate the provisions of this Section. Landlord covenants not to alter or change any existing Lease provisions except as provided for in Section 15.03 hereof, by its actions in severing ownership or title or by refinancing or place separate mortgages on the Auto Service Center or sections thereof.

ARTICLE XVI

SURRENDER OF PREMISES

SECTION 16.01 Condition of Surrender.

At the expiration of earlier termination of this Lease, Tenant shall surrender the Premises to Landlord broom clean and in the same condition as when tendered by Landlord, reasonable wear and tear and insured casualty excepted. Tenant shall promptly repair any damage to the Premises caused by the removal of any furniture, trade fixtures or other personal property placed in the Premises.

SECTION 16.02 Holding Over.

Should Tenant, with Landlord's written consent, hold over at the end of the term, Tenant shall become a Tenant at will and any such holding over shall not constitute an extension of this Lease. During such holding over, Tenant shall pay rent (including Fixed Minimum Rent and Additional Rent) and other charges at the highest monthly rate provided for herein. If Tenant holds over at the end of the term without Landlord's written consent, Tenant shall pay Landlord as liquidated damages, a sum equal to twice the rent most recently paid (including Fixed Minimum Rent and additional Rent) to be paid by Tenant to Landlord for all the time Tenant shall so retain possession of the Premises; provided that the exercise of Landlord's rights under this clause shall not be interpreted as a grant of permission to Tenant to continue in possession nor shall Landlord relinquish its right to pursue further remedies against Tenant.

MISCELLANEOUS

SECTION 17.01 Waiver.

The waiver by Landlord of any breach of any term, covenant or condition herein contained shall not be deemed to be a waiver of such term, covenant or condition of any subsequent breach of the same or any other term, covenant or condition herein contained. The subsequent acceptance of rent hereunder by Landlord shall not be deemed to be a waiver of any preceding breach by Tenant of any term, covenant or condition of this Lease, other than the failure of Tenant to pay the particular rental so accepted, regardless of Landlord's knowledge of such preceding breach at the time of acceptance of such rent. No covenant, term or condition of this Lease shall be deemed to have been waived by Landlord, unless such waiver by in writing and sent by Landlord to Tenant within ninety (90) days of such breach.

SECTION 17.02 Accord and Satisfaction.

No payment by Tenant or receipt by Landlord of a lesser amount than the monthly rent herein stipulated shall be deemed to be other than on account of the earliest stipulated rent, nor shall any endorsement or statement on any check or any letter companying any check or payment as rent be deemed an accord and satisfaction, and Landlord may accept such check or payment without prejudice to Landlord's right to recover the balance of such rent or pursue any other remedy in this Lease provided.

SECTION 17.03 Entire Agreement.

This Lease and the Exhibits and Rider, if any, attached hereto and forming a part hereof, set forth all the covenants, promises, agreements, conditions and understandings between Landlord and Tenant concerning the Premises and there are no covenants, promises, agreements, conditions or understandings, either oral or written, between them other than as were herein set forth. Except as herein otherwise provided, no subsequent alteration, amendments, change or addition to this Lease shall be binding upon Landlord or Tenant unless reduced to writing and signed by them.

SECTION 17.04 No Partnership.

Landlord does not, in any way or for any purpose, become a partner of Tenant in the conduct of its business, or otherwise, or joint venture or a member of a joint enterprise with Tenant.

SECTION 17.05 Force Majeure.

In the event that Landlord shall be delayed or hindered in or prevented from doing or performing any act or thing required hereunder by reason of strikes, lockouts, casualties, Acts of God, labor troubles, inability to procure materials, failure of power, governmental laws or regulations, riots, insurrections, war, severe weather conditions or other causes beyond the reasonable control of Landlord, then Landlord shall not be liable or responsible for any such delays and the doing or performing of such act or thing shall be excused for the period of the delay and the period for the performance of any such act shall be extended for a period equivalent to the period of such delay.

SECTION 17.05 Notices.

Any notice, demand, request or other instruments which may be or required to be given under this Lease shall be delivered personally or sent by either United States certified mail postage prepaid, Federal Express or expedited mail service and shall be addressed (a) if to Landlord at the address provided in Section 1.01 for Landlord or at such other address as Landlord may designate by written notice and (b) if to Tenant at the address provided in Section 1.01 for Tenant or as such other address as Tenant shall designate by written notice. Notices shall be effective upon delivery unless delivery is refused or cannot be made in which event notice shall be effective on mailing.

SECTION 17.07 Captions and Section Numbers.

The captions, section numbers, article numbers, and index appearing in this Lease are inserted only as a matter of convenience and in no way define, limit, construe, or describe the scope or intent of such section or articles of this Lease nor in any way affect this Lease.

SECTION 17.08 Tenant Defined, Use of Pronoun.

The word "Tenant" shall be deemed and taken to mean each and every person or party mentioned an Tenant herein, be the same one or more; and if there shall be more then one Tenant, any notice required or permitted by the terms of this Lease may be given by or to any one thereof, and shall have the same force and effect as if given by or to all thereof. The sue for the neuter singular pronoun to refer to Landlord or Tenant shall be deemed a proper reference even though Landlord or Tenant may be an individual, a corporation, a group of two or more individuals or corporations. The necessary grammatical changes required to make the provisions of this Lease apply in the plural sense where there is more than one Landlord or Tenant and to either corporations, associations, partnerships, or individuals, males or females, shall in all instances be assumed as though in each case fully expressed.

SECTION 17.09 Broker's Commission.

Tenant warrants that it has had no dealings with any broker or agent in connection with this Lease, except as designated in Section 1.01, and covenants to pay, hold harmless and indemnify Landlord from and against any and all cost, expense or liability for any compensation, commissions, and charges claimed by any broker or agent with respect to this Lease or the negotiation thereof on behalf of Tenant.

SECTION 17.10 Partial Invalidity.

If any term, covenant or conditions of this Lease or the application thereof to any person or circumstance shall, to any extent, be invalid or unenforceable, the remainder of this Lease, or the application of such term, covenant or condition to persons or circumstances other than those as to which it is held invalid or unenforceable, shall not be affected thereby and each term, covenant or condition of this Lease shall be valid and be enforced to the fullest extent permitted by law.

SECTION 17.11 Execution of Lease.

The submission of this Lease for examination does not constitute a reservation of or option for the Premises and this Lease becomes effective as a Lease only upon execution and delivery thereof by Landlord and Tenant on or before December 15, 1989. If Tenant is a corporation or Partnership, Tenant shall furnish Landlord with such evidence as Landlord reasonably requires to evidence the binding effect on Tenant of the execution and delivery of this Lease.
SECTION 17.12 Recording.

Tenant agrees not to record this Lease. However, Tenant and Landlord, upon request of either, agree to execute and deliver a memorandum or so-called "short form" of this Lease in recordable form the purposes of recordation at the expense of the requesting party. Said memorandum or short form of this Lease shall describe the parties, the Premises and the Lease Term and shall incorporate this Lease by reference.

SECTION 17.13 Applicable Law.

The Laws of the State of Illinois shall govern the validity, performance and enforcement of this Lease.

SECTION 17.14 Rider (if applicable) (Deleted)

SECTION 17.15 Time is of the Essence.

Time is of the essence of this Agreement.

SECTION 17.16 Successors and Assigns.

Except as otherwise provided herein, this Lease shall be binding upon and inure to the benefit of the parties hereto and their respective heirs, personal representatives, executors, successors and assigns.

SECTION 17.17 Survival of Obligations.

The provisions of this Lease with respect to any obligation of Landlord or Tenant to pay any sum owing in order to perform any act after the expiration or other termination of this Lease shall survive the expiration or other termination of this Lease.

SECTION 17.18 Representations.

Tenant acknowledges that neither Landlord nor Landlord's agents, employees or contractors have made any representatives or promises with respect to the Premises, the Auto Service Center or this Lease except as expressly set forth herein.

SECTION 17.19 Loan Provision.

Notwithstanding anything herein to the contrary, in the event the holder of any indebtedness secured by a mortgage or deed of trust covering the Premises requires, after a casualty or condemnation, that the insurance proceeds or award, as the case may be, be applied to such indebtedness, then Landlord shall have the right to terminate this Lease be delivering written notice of termination to Tenant within fifteen (15) days after such requirement is made by any such holder, whereupon all rights and obligations hereunder shall cease and terminate.

SECTION 17.20 Franchise (Deleted)

SECTION 17.21 Exculpation.

It is expressly understood and agreed that this Lease is executed by First Mortgage Bank, not personally but as Trustee as aforesaid, in the exercise of the power and authority conferred upon and invested in it as such Trustee, and under the direction of the beneficiaries of that certain Trust Agreement described aforesaid. It is further expressly understood and agreed that First Mortgage Bank, as Trustee as aforesaid, has no right or power whatsoever to manage, control or operate said real estate in any way or to any extent and is not entitled at any time to collect or receive for any purpose, directly or indirectly, the rents, issues, profiles or proceeds of said real estate or any lease or sale or any mortgage or any disposition thereof. Nothing in this Lease contained shall be construed as creating any personal liability or personal responsibility of the Trustee or any of the beneficiaries of the Trust and, in particular, without limiting the generality of the foregoing, there shall be no personal liability to pay any indebtedness accruing hereunder or to perform any covenant, either expressly or impliedly herein contained, or to keep, preserve or sequester any property of said Trust or for said Trustee to continue as said Trustee, and that so far as the parties herein are concerned the owner of any indebtedness or liability accruing hereunder shall look solely to the trust estate from time to time subject to the provisions of said Trust Agreement for payment thereof, Tenant hereby expressly waiving and releasing said personal liability and personal responsibility on behalf of itself and all persons claims by, through or under Tenant.

IN WITNESS WHEREOF, the parties hereto have executed this Lease this day and year first above written.

Landlord

_____

_____
Witness

Tenant

_____

_____
Witness

EXHIBIT B

LANDLORD'S WORK

This Exhibit B is hereby attached to Lease dated December 4, 1989. All work other than that which is specifically provided for hereunder to be performed by Landlord and as per Landlord's plans and specifications, is to be performed by Tenant, at Tenant's expense.

The following work shall be performed by Landlord:

1. DEMISING WALL: The demising walls will be constructed of metal studs and 5/8"drywall or concrete block, as determined by Landlord or as required by local building code, and will run from the floor to the underside of permanent construction above.

2. INTERIOR PARTITIONS: Interior partitiions shall be provided for the washrooms and, when necessary, as a dividing wall between the service are and the office/showroom/customer waiting are pre Landlord's plans and specifications.

3. STOREFRONT CONSTRUCTION: The storefront construction will consist of tubular aluminum frames glazed with clear tempered glass of thickness required by building codes. A glass entrance door will be provided for the Premises. The storefront shall include a customer entrance and a display window as designed per Landlord's plans and specifications.

4. OVERHEAD DOORS: One (1) 10' x 12' glass panel door with an exhaust port shall be provided in the rear of the Premises per Landlord's plans and specifications.

5. DELIVERY DOOR: A delivery door shall be provided in the rear wall of the Premises as required by building codes to meet exit requirements. The unit shall consist of one 3' x 7' hollow metal door, frame and standard hardware; any special hardware shall be provided by Tenant.

6. FLOORING: A concrete floor will be installed throughout the entire Premises.

7. ELECTRIC: Electrical system shall include an electrical distribution panel, wiring and circuit breakers, as required by code. A 200-amp service panel will be mounted on the rear wall of the Premises. Service shall be 120/208, 3 phase, 4 wire, or 100-amp single phase, as may be required or as Landlord's plans and specifications indicate.

8. HEATING, VENTILATION: HVAC shall be supplied, but not ducted, per the following specifications:

    Heating installation within the office, washrooms, showroom and customer waiting area will be such as to provide interior conditions of 70 degrees inside when the outside conditions are minus 10 degrees F. Additional heat required fro specialized Tenant exhaust shall be provided by the Tenant, including any necessary increase in electrical service. Service areas shall be equipped with unit heater per Landlord's plans and specifications.

    Air conditioning will be installed on the basis of 1-ton of air conditioning for every four hundred (400) square feet of office, washroom, showroom and customer waiting area.

9. UTILITIES: Utilities (i.e. water, sewer, and gas) shall be stubbed into the Premises by the Landlord.

10. WASHROOMS: Each washroom (one employee, one customer) will have a water closet, lavatory, combination exhaust fanlight and 6-gallon electric water heater.

11. DRAINAGE: Drainage systems shall be installed per Landlord's plans and specifications.

12. PAINTING AND DECORATING: The interior walls will be taped, sanded, and ready for paint. Painting shall be done by Tenant at Tenant's sole cost and expense.

13. WATER SERVICE: Sufficient water supply will be provided for the operation of the ordinary loads imposed by the toilet room fixtures as described under item 8 above. Any additional plumbing shall be provided by Tenant at Tenant's sole cost and expense.

14. CEILING: An acoustical ceiling will be installed in order to provide an approximate ceiling height of 10' and will consist of 2' x4' painted metal grid system with lay-in acoustical tile, and the ceiling will be installed in the office, washroom, showroom and customer waiting area per Landlord's plans and specifications.

15. LIGHTING: One (1) 2' x 4' four-lamp recessed fluorescent fixture shall be supplied on the basis of one (1) fixture for every seventy-five (75) square feet of the area within the office, showroom and customer service waiting area. One (1) 2-lampflourescent utility fixture shall be supplied on the basis on one (1) fixture for every one hundred fifty (150) square feet of area within the service area.

EXHIBIT C

TENANT'S WORK

This Exhibit C is hereby attached to Lease dated December 4, 1989. Tenant shall submit its building plans which are stamped by a certified architect (and any other information relative to the Tenant's Work which Landlord deems necessary or desirable) to Landlord within thirty (30) days after the execution of the Lease for approval by Landlord. Tenant shall at its own cost and expense equip the Premises and perform the following work (the equipping of the Premises and the work listed below are referred to in the Lease as "Tenant's Work"), which work shall conform to all applicable governing codes:

1. FLOORING: All floor coverings including materials and installation.

2. WALLS: All interior partitions (except washroom partitions and service area dividing wall). No exposed studs shall be permitted in areas accessible to the public. NO concrete block will be permitted in customer waiting rooms. No combustible material shall be permitted above ceiling.

3. COLUMNS: Centerline of Tenant divider walls may or may not be on the centerline of columns. Any special treatment, furring or finishes of these columns occurring in the Tenant divider walls shall be by the Lessee, in accordance with applicable building and fire codes.

4. CEILINGS: All special coves, drops and ceilings. Ceilings to be constructed of Underwriters approved noon-combustible material permitted above ceiling.

5. SIGNS: Shall be in accordance with Landlord's sign requirements (See Exhibit D for Sign Criteria)

6. FIXTURES: All store fixtures, cases, paneling cornices, etc. All of the aforesaid shall be new and of first quality, including installation.

7. SPECIAL EQUIPMENT: Alarm systems or other protective devices, p.a. systems, fire extinguishers, conveyers, elevators, escalators, dub waiter, time-clocks, delivery door, buzzers, storm and screen doors, storm enclosures, dry chemical fire protection system, all lighting and electrical not covered in items 5 and 15 of Landlord's Work, and all additional plumbing and/or water services not covered in items 10 and 13 of Landlord's Work.

8. SPECIAL VENTILATIONS: All ventilation and related equipment.

9. TELEPHONE EQUIPMENT: All conduits for telephone wires. Lessee shall make all necessary arrangements with telephone company for service.

10. PLUMBING: Any drinking fountains, water coolers, or other plumbing fixtures beyond the washroom fixtures to be installed at Tenant's expense. This provision shall also include any additional plumbing/sewage lines and/or drains.

11. UTILITIY CONNECTIONS: All connections to the following utilities: gas, water, sewer and electrical, including, without limitation meters, equipment and hookup.

In connection with the aforedescribed work, Tenant aggress to the following additional terms provisions and conditions:

1. All utility lines may pass through the Premises to service other tenants and building area.

2. Tenant will obtain and pay for all permits and comply with all building codes, ordinances, regulations and requirements of Fire Insurance Rating Bureau. Landlord's approval of plans does not release Tenant from this obligation. Landlord's approval is limited to general compliance with Landlords' plans, specifications and intended uses. Tenant is responsible in total for their own plans.

3. Tenant will require it contractors and/or subcontractors to furnish Landlord with evidence of adequate insurance coverage prior to Tenant's contractor performing any work in the Premises, and any claims, actions or damages resulting from acts or neglects of Tenant, its agents, employees, contractors or subcontractors in the performance of Tenant's work.

4. Tenant and/or it contractors and/or subcontractors are limited to performing their work including any office or storage for construction purposes with the Premises only. Tenant and/or its contractors and/or subcontractors shall each be responsible for daily removal from the project of all trash, rubbish and surplus material resulting from construction fixturing and merchandising of the Premises.

5. Tenant and/or its contractors and/or subcontractors are responsible for temporary utility connections for their work including payment of utility charges.

6. Upon approval by Landlord of Tenant's working plans, and subject to the other terms and conditions of the Lease, Tenant shall cause construction to promptly commence and shall promptly repair any damage incurred (if any) to the Auto Service Center or Common Areas.

7. Tenant and/or its contractor must present to the Landlord's project manage at the project, one (1) complete set of working drawings and specifications approved by the Landlord and applicable governing authorities before permission will be given to start construction on the Premises and Tenant shall submit one set to Landlord c/o The Regent Group, Leasing Department, 524 W. South Avenue, Chicago, Illinois 60610.

8. Tenant shall obtain all necessary permits for Tenant's Work.

9. Tenant and/or its subcontractor must carry the following insurance requirements and delivery copies to the Landlord prior to the start of construction:

   A.   Workman's Compensation
   B. $1,000,000.00 Public Liability
   C. $1,000,000.00 Property Damage

10. Any equipment and/or fixtures suspended from the ceiling shall be attached to a structural member only, and not from any ductwork, conduit, decking, etc. Tenant is responsible for any damage resulting from overloading the capacity of these structural members.

EXHIBIT D

SIGN CRITERIA

This Exhibit D is hereby attached to Lease dated December 4, 1989. Tenant agrees to observe and perform the following, terms, provisions and conditions regarding signage in connection with the Premises:

1. Sign content will be limited to the principal business name(s) of Tenant.
2. All building signs will be individually letter type, either block or script (and will be individually illuminated) and mounted to the area designated by Landlord.
3. All sign illumination must be constant diffused (flashing and bare light sources [i.e., darkness on any of the lettering or other parts of any signs] will not be allowed). All signs must remain illuminated from one-half (1/2) hour before suck until midnight, or until such other time as determined by lock city authorities.
4. All letter heights for building signage will not exceed 30" nor be smaller than 18" in height.
5. Sign width coverage equivalent will be limited to the maximum allowable percentage of the lease area frontage of the Premises and be centered on front facia.
6. If Tenant is a corner tenant, Tenant may mount signs on all exterior walls.
7. All signs mounted to facia must be of a non-corrosive and rust-proof material. Electrical penetration must be added with neoprene washers.
8. Under canopy signs will not be allowed.
9. Tenant will send two copies or blueprints of signs to The Regent Group, Leasing Department, 524 W. South Avenue, Chicago, Illinois 60610 for written approval.
10. All sides of letters to match framework of windows, or of a material or color approved by Landlord.
11. If provided, Tenant shall be allowed signage upon the freestanding center identification sign subject to Landlord's plans and specifications.
12. Final stamped approval by local city authorities must be obtained prior to installation of sign(s).
13. At termination of Lease, Tenant will engage sign contractor approved by Landlord to remove sign and Tenant must patch or repair all holes to bring front facia in front of Auto Service Center back to the original appearance.

EXHIBIT E

ENVIRONMENT COMPLIANCE
(If applicable)

388

EXHIBIT F

SUBORDINATION, ATTORNMENT AND NON-DISTURBANCE AGREEMENT

(Ed. Note. See elsewhere in Document Book)

I.B.2   BASIC LEASE PROVISIONS

The Auto Service Center will contain six lessees who are each involved with various aspects of servicing automobiles. The following pages outline the basic lease terms for each of the lessees in addition to Cellular Communications.

a.   Globe Glass & Mirror Company

b.   Master Werks Automotive, Inc.

c.   Chicago Muffler, Inc.

d.   K&P Automotive, Inc.

e.   Lube Pros

ARTICLE 1

BASIC LEASE PROVISIONS
ENUMERATION OF EXHIBITS

Section 1.01 Basic Lease Provisions

(A)	DATE :	August 24, 1990
(B)	LANDLORD:	First Mortgage Bank as Trustee
		(Trust No. 108049-04, date April 11, 1989)
(C)	LANDLORD'S MANAGING AGENT:	Regent Real Estate Corporation
(D)	ADDRESS OF LANDLORD:	c/o The Regent Group
		524 W. South Avenue
		Chicago, Illinois 60610
(E)	TENANT:	Globe Glass and Mirror Company
(F)	ADDRESS OF TENANT:	1880 West Fullerton Avenue
		Chicago, Illinois 60614

PERMITTED USES (Section 3.02): PRINCIPAL USE: Sale of services and products related to auto glass replacement and repair ("Principal Use") and SECONDARY USE: Sale of miscellaneous automotive services and products including glazing services ("Secondary Use")(the Principal Use and Secondary Use are collectively referred to herein as the "Permitted Use").

TENANT'S TRADE NAME (Section 3.02): Globe Glass and Mirror Company ("Trade Name")

AUTO SERVICE CENTER (Section 2.01): The land and improvements located at 7 south Route 59 ("Auto Service Center"), situated in City of Aurora, County of DuPage, State of Illinois.

PREMISES (Section 2.01): That portion of the Auto Service Center outlined in red on Exhibit A with the following approximate dimensions and area: Width: 62.5 ft. Depth: 55 ft. Area: 3,437.5 sq. ft. ("Premises")

LEASE YEAR: The term lease year ("lease year") as used herein shall mean a period of twelve (12) consecutive full calendar months. The first lease year ("First Lease Year") shall begin on the Rental Commencement Date of the term hereof if the date of commencement shall occur on the first day of the calendar month; if not, then the first lease year shall commence upon the first day of the calendar month next following the date of Rental Commencement. Each succeeding lease year shall commence upon the anniversary date of the first lease year.

INITIAL TERM AND RENTAL COMMENCEMENT DATE (Section 2.05)(if applicable): One (1) consecutive option period consisting of five (5) Lease Years, with the option period commencing at the end of the Initial Term ("Option Period"). The Initial Term plus any Option Period(s) are referred to herein as the "Lease Term".

FIXED MINIMUM RENT (Section 3.01):

	Initial Term		Option #1	
Year	1 -	$ 51,563	6 -	$ 59,775
	2 -	53,109	7 -	61,568
	3 -	54,703	8 -	63,415
	4 -	56,344	9 -	65,318
	5 -	58,034	10 -	67,277

ARTICLE 1

BASIC LEASE PROVISIONS
ENUMERATION OF EXHIBITS

Section 1.01 Basic Lease Provisions

(A)	DATE :	March 19, 1991
(B)	LANDLORD:	First Mortgage Bank as Trustee (Trust No. 108049-04, date April 11, 1989)
(C)	LANDLORD'S MANAGING AGENT:	Regent Real Estate Corporation
(D)	ADDRESS OF LANDLORD:	c/o The Regent Group 524 W. South Avenue Chicago, Illinois 60610
(E)	TENANT:	Master Werks Automotive, Inc. (an Illinois Corporation)
(F)	ADDRESS OF TENANT:	10046 Main Street Wheaton, IL 60187

PERMITTED USES (Section 3.02): PRINCIPAL USE: Sale of service and products related to auto collision, body repair and painting or any other related service.

TENANT'S TRADE NAME (Section 3.02): Master Werks ("Trade Name")

AUTO SERVICE CENTER (Section 2.01): The land and improvements located at 7 south Route 59 ("Auto Service Center"), situated in City of Aurora, County of DuPage, State of Illinois.

PREMISES (Section 2.01): That portion of the Auto Service Center outlined in red on Exhibit A with the following approximate dimensions and area: Width: 37.5 ft. Depth: 55 ft. Area: 2,063 sq. ft. ("Premises")

LEASE YEAR: The term lease year ("lease year") as used herein shall mean a period of twelve (12) consecutive full calendar months. The first lease year ("First Lease Year") shall begin on the Rental Commencement Date of the term hereof if the date of commencement shall occur on the first day of the calendar month; if not, then the first lease year shall commence upon the first day of the calendar month next following the date of Rental Commencement. Each succeeding lease year shall commence upon the anniversary date of the first lease year.

INITIAL TERM AND RENTAL COMMENCEMENT DATE (Section 2.05)(if applicable): Five(5) Lease Years ("Initial Term") to commence forty-five (45) days after notice by Landlord that the Premises are available to Tenant ready for Tenant's work, or the date Tenant opens for business, whichever is sooner ("Rental Commencement Date").

OPTION PERIOD(S) (Section 2.05)(if applicable): One (1) consecutive period consisting of Five (5) Lease Years commencing at the end of the Initial Term ("Option Period"). The Initial Term plus the Option Period are referred to herein as the "Lease Term".

FIXED MINIMUM RENT (Section 3.01):

Initial Term		Option #1	
Year 1			
0-3 month	0.00		
4-12 month	2,406.84	6 - $	33,453.75
2 -	28,882.00	7 -	34,457.36
3 -	29,748.00	8 -	35,491.08
4 -	30,640.92	9 -	36,555.82
5 -	31,560.15	10 -	37,652.49

ARTICLE 1

BASIC LEASE PROVISIONS
ENUMERATION OF EXHIBITS

Section 1.01 Basic Lease Provisions

(A)	DATE :	June 30, 1989
(B)	LANDLORD:	First Mortgage Bank as Trustee (Trust No. 108049-04, date April 11, 1989)
(C)	LANDLORD'S MANAGING AGENT:	Regent Real Estate Corporation
(D)	ADDRESS OF LANDLORD:	c/o The Regent Group 524 W. South Avenue Chicago, Illinois 60610
(E)	TENANT:	Chicago Muffler, Inc. dba Casey Muffler and Brake
(F)	ADDRESS OF TENANT:	164 Dundee Road East Dundee, Illinois 60118

PERMITTED USES (Section 3.02): PRINCIPAL USE: Sale of service of automotive exhaust system units and parts, brakes and brake parts, front-end alignments, shock absorbers and other related equipment, accessories and services ("Principal Uses") and SECONDARY USE: Miscellaneous sale of automotive products and services ("Secondary Uses") (the Principal Use and Secondary Use are collectively referred to herein as the "Permitted Use").

TENANT'S TRADE NAME (Section 3.02): Globe Glass and Mirror Company ("Trade Name")

AUTO SERVICE CENTER (Section 2.01): The land and improvements located at SWC of Route 59 and South Road ("Auto Service Center"), situated in City of Aurora, County of DuPage, State of Illinois.

PREMISES (Section 2.01): That portion of the Auto Service Center outlined in red on Exhibit A with the following approximate dimensions and area: Width: 50 ft. Depth: 55 ft. Area: 2,750 sq. ft. ("Premises")

LEASE YEAR: The term lease year ("lease year") as used herein shall mean a period of twelve (12) consecutive full calendar months. The first lease year ("First Lease Year") shall begin on the Rental Commencement Date of the term hereof if the date of commencement shall occur on the first day of the calendar month; if not, then the first lease year shall commence upon the first day of the calendar month next following the date of Rental Commencement. Each succeeding lease year shall commence upon the anniversary date of the first lease year.

INITIAL TERM AND RENTAL COMMENCEMENT DATE (Section 2.05)(if applicable): Ten (10) Lease Years ("Initial Term") to commence thirty (30) days after notice by Landlord that the Premises are available to Tenant ready for Tenant's Work, or the date Tenant opens for business, whichever is sooner ("Rental Commencement Date").

OPTION PERIOD(S) (Section 2.05): Two (2) consecutive periods consisting of five (5) Lease Years each, with the first option period commencing at the end of the Initial Term ("Option Period(s)"). The Initial Term plus any Option Period(s) are referred to herein as the "Lease Term".

FIXED MINIMUM RENT (Section 3.01):

Initial Term	Option #1	Option #2
Year 1 - $ 39,875	11 - $ 55,133	16- $ 67,078
2 - 39,879	12 - 57,338	17 - 69,761
3 - 41,071	13 - 59,632	18 - 72,551
4 - 42,303	14 - 62,017	19 - 75,453
5 - 43,572	15 - 64,498	20 - 78,472
6 - 45,315		
7 - 47,128		
8 - 49,013		
9 - 50,974		
10 - 53,013		

ARTICLE 1

BASIC LEASE PROVISIONS
ENUMERATION OF EXHIBITS

Section 1.01 Basic Lease Provisions

(A)	DATE :	January 1, 1992
(B)	LANDLORD:	First Mortgage Bank as Trustee
		(Trust No. 108049-04, date April 11, 1989)
(C)	LANDLORD'S MANAGING AGENT:	Regent Real Estate Corporation
(D)	ADDRESS OF LANDLORD:	c/o The Regent Group
		524 W. South Avenue
		Chicago, Illinois 60610
(E)	TENANT:	K & P Automotive
(F)	ADDRESS OF TENANT:	10724 Revere Road
		Mokena, IL 60448

PERMITTED USES (Section 3.02): The business of performing tune-ups and servicing automotive engines including: air conditioning, cooling, electrical, electronic fuel injection and automotive services in connection with which diagnostic equipment is uses as the primary use ("Principle Use") and SECONDARY USE: fluid and lubrication system, brakes, shocks, struts, related accessories and other automotive services ("Secondary Use"). Secondary Use will not exceed 25% of gross sales. (the Principal Use and Secondary Use are collectively referred to herein as the "Permitted Use").

TENANT'S TRADE NAME (Section 3.02): Globe Glass and Mirror Company ("Trade Name")

AUTO SERVICE CENTER (Section 2.01): The land and improvements located at SWC of Route 59 and South Road ("Auto Service Center"), situated in City of Aurora, County of DuPage, State of Illinois.

PREMISES (Section 2.01): That portion of the Auto Service Center outlined in red on Exhibit A with the following approximate dimensions and area: 2,547 sq. ft. ("Premises")

LEASE YEAR: The term lease year ("lease year") as used herein shall mean a period of twelve (12) consecutive full calendar months. The first lease year ("First Lease Year") shall begin on the Rental Commencement Date of the term hereof if the date of commencement shall occur on the first day of the calendar month; if not, then the first lease year shall commence upon the first day of the calendar month next following the date of Rental Commencement. Each succeeding lease year shall commence upon the anniversary date of the first lease year.

INITIAL TERM AND RENTAL COMMENCEMENT DATE (Section 2.05)(if applicable): Ten (10) Lease Years ("Initial Term") to commence January 1, 1992

OPTION PERIOD(S) (Section 2.05): Two (2) consecutive periods consisting of five (5) Lease Years each, with the first option period commencing at the end of the Initial Term ("Option Period(s)"). The Initial Term plus any Option Period(s) are referred to herein as the "Lease Term".

FIXED MINIMUM RENT (Section 3.01):

	Initial Term		Option #1		Option #2
Year	1 - $ 28,016		11 - $ 56,476		16- $ 65,471
	2 - 43,299		12 - 58,171		17 - 67,436
	3 - 44,573		13 - 59,916		18 - 69,459
	4 - 45,922		14 - 61,713		19 - 71,542
	5 - 47,298		15 - 63,565		20 - 73,689
	6 - 48,717				
	7 - 50,178				
	8 - 51,684				
	9 - 53,234				
	10 - 54,831				

394

ARTICLE 1

BASIC LEASE PROVISIONS
ENUMERATION OF EXHIBITS

Section 1.01 Basic Lease Provisions

(A)	DATE :	June 16, 1989
(B)	LANDLORD:	First Mortgage Bank as Trustee
		(Trust No. 108049-04, date April 11, 1989)
(C)	LANDLORD'S MANAGING AGENT:	Regent Real Estate Corporation
(D)	ADDRESS OF LANDLORD:	c/o The Regent Group
		524 W. South Avenue
		Chicago, Illinois 60610
(E)	TENANT:	PRT2 Ltd. dba Lube Pros
(F)	ADDRESS OF TENANT:	164 Dundee Road
		East Dundee, Illinois 60118

PERMITTED USES (Section 3.02): PRINCIPAL USE: Sale of preventative maintenance services and products related to automotive oil and lubrication systems including but not limited to oil and filter changes, other replacement filters, transmission and differential services ("Principal Uses") and SECONDARY USE: Sale of Miscellaneous of automotive products and services ("Secondary Uses") (the Principal Use and Secondary Use are collectively referred to herein as the "Permitted Use").

TENANT'S TRADE NAME (Section 3.02): Lube Pros ("Trade Name")

AUTO SERVICE CENTER (Section 2.01): The land and improvements located at SWC of Route 59 and South Road ("Auto Service Center"), situated in City of Aurora, County of DuPage, State of Illinois.

PREMISES (Section 2.01): That portion of the Auto Service Center outlined in red on Exhibit A with the following approximate dimensions and area: Width: 30 ft. Depth: 60 ft. Area: 1,800 sq. ft. ("Premises")

LEASE YEAR: The term lease year ("lease year") as used herein shall mean a period of twelve (12) consecutive full calendar months. The first lease year ("First Lease Year") shall begin on the Rental Commencement Date of the term hereof if the date of commencement shall occur on the first day of the calendar month; if not, then the first lease year shall commence upon the first day of the calendar month next following the date of Rental Commencement. Each succeeding lease year shall commence upon the anniversary date of the first lease year.

INITIAL TERM AND RENTAL COMMENCEMENT DATE (Section 2.05)(if applicable): Twenty (20) Lease Years ("Initial Term") to commence thirty (30) days after notice by Landlord that the Premises are available to Tenant ready for Tenant's Work, or the date Tenant opens for business, whichever is sooner ("Rental Commencement Date").

OPTION PERIOD(S) (Section 2.05): Two (2) consecutive periods consisting of five (5) Lease Years each, with the first option period commencing at the end of the Initial Term ("Option Period(s)"). The Initial Term plus any Option Period(s) are referred to herein as the "Lease Term".

FIXED MINIMUM RENT (Section 3.01):

Initial Term		Option #1	Option #2
Year 1 - $ 54,000	11 - $ 72,571	21 - $ 97,530	26 - $ 113,064
2 - 55,620	12 - 74,749	22 - 100,456	27 - 116,456
3 - 57,289	13 - 76,991	23 - 103,470	28 - 119,950
4 - 59,007	14 - 79,301	24 - 106,574	29 - 123,458
5 - 60,007	15 - 81,680	25 - 109,771	30 - 127,255
6 - 62,601	16 - 84,130		
7 - 64,479	17 - 86,654		
8 - 66,413	18 - 89,254		
9 - 68,406	19 - 91,931		
10 - 70,458	20 - 94,689		